Odyssey
A Guide to Better Writing

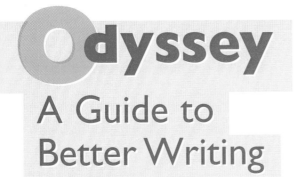

A Guide to
Better Writing

Second Edition

William J. Kelly
Bristol Community College

Deborah L. Lawton
Bristol Community College

Allyn and Bacon

Boston　London　Toronto　Sydney　Tokyo　Singapore

Vice President, Humanities: *Joseph Opiela*
Editorial Assistant: *Mary Beth Varney*
Executive Marketing Manager: *Lisa Kimball*
Editorial–Production Service: *Omegatype Typography, Inc.*
Composition and Prepress Buyer: *Linda Cox*
Manufacturing Buyer: *Suzanne Lareau*
Cover Administrator: *Linda Knowles*
Cover Designer: *Studio Nine*
Text Designer: *Glenna Collett*
Illustrations: *LMY Studio, Inc.*
Color Graphics: *Schneck–DePippo Graphics*
Electronic Composition: *Omegatype Typography, Inc.*

ISBN 0-205-31457-0

Text credits appear on page 569, which constitutes an extension of the copyright page.

Printed in the United States of America
10 9 8 7 6 5 4 3 2   WEB   04 03 02 01 00

Dedication

To Charles and Virginia Soucy—
Thank you for the wonderful beginning of all my
own journeys.

D. L. L.

To Michelle—
Thanks once again for all, which, without you,
would never be possible.

W. J. K.

Brief Contents

Preface *xxi*

About the Authors *xxix*

Part One   Starting Out   1

1 Ensuring Success in Writing   2

2 Generating Ideas through Prewriting   13

3 Composing: Creating a Draft   32

4 Refining and Polishing Your Draft   56

Part Two   Using the Patterns of Paragraph Development   83

5 Narration   84

6 Description   92

7 Example   100

8 Process   107

9 Definition   116

10 Comparison and Contrast   124

11 Cause and Effect   133

12 Division and Classification   141

13 Argument   150

Part Three   Moving On to the Essay   165

14 Developing an Essay   166

15 Examining Types of Essays   196

16 Answering Essay Questions   225

Part Four   Developing Sentence Sense   235

17 The Sentence   236

18 Fragments   246

19 Subordination and Coordination   261

20 Comma Splices and Run-On Sentences   274

Part Five   Understanding Subjects and Verbs   291

21 Subject–Verb Agreement   292

22 Basic Tenses for Regular Verbs   310

23 Irregular Verbs and Frequently
Confused Verbs   320

24 Passive Voice, Additional Tenses, and Maintaining
Consistency in Tense   336

Part Six   Keeping Your Writing Correct   349

25 Nouns and Pronouns   350

26 Adjectives, Adverbs, and Other Modifiers   367

27 Ensuring Pronoun–Antecedent Agreement   385

28 Maintaining Parallelism   404

29 Spelling   415

30 Commas   436

31 Other Punctuation and Capitalization   450

Part Seven   Connecting: Responding to Reading   471

Appendix A: Writing with a Computer   *515*

Appendix B: Tips for ESL Writers   *521*

Appendix C: Exploring the Dictionary   *541*

Rhetorical Index   *547*

Index   *555*

Contents

Preface *xxi*

About the Authors *xxix*

Part One   Starting Out   1

1   Ensuring Success in Writing   2

**Overview: Understanding the Importance of Good
   Writing Skills** *2*
Recognizing the Dynamics of Writing *3*
Understanding the Basic Components of Writing *6*
Focusing on the Reader *6*
Understanding the Purpose behind Your Writing *8*
Recap: Ensuring Success in Writing *12*

2   Generating Ideas through Prewriting   13

Overview: Seeing Prewriting as a Way to Explore Ideas *13*
Understanding Prewriting *14*
Freewriting *14*
Brainstorming *17*
Clustering *19*
Branching *22*
Idea Mapping *24*
Maintaining a Journal *27*
Recap: Generating Ideas through Prewriting *30*

3   Composing: Creating a Draft   32

Overview: Understanding Composing *32*
Recognizing the Structure of a Paragraph *33*

Focusing a Topic   *36*
Writing a Clear, Specific Topic Sentence   *39*
Providing the Best Support for the Topic Sentence   *42*
Deciding on the Most Effective Arrangement   *45*
Making Your Material Reader Centered   *47*
Using a Reader Evaluation Checklist   *49*
Developing a Complete Draft   *51*
Recap: Composing: Creating a Draft   *54*

4   **Refining and Polishing Your Draft**   56

Overview: Understanding the Revising Stage   *56*
Reassessing: Reseeing Your Work   *57*
   Maintaining Unity   *57*
   Providing Coherence   *59*
      Transitions   *59*   •   Organizing Sentences Effectively   *63*
   Choosing Effective Language   *69*
      Keeping Your Writing Specific   *70*   •   Keeping Your Writing Concise   *70*
   Getting Feedback from an Objective Reader   *74*
Redrafting   *76*
Editing   *78*
   Developing a Personal Proofreading System   *78*
   Using Computer Tools to Your Advantage   *79*
Recap: Refining and Polishing Your Draft   82

Part Two   Using the Patterns of Paragraph Development   83

5   **Narration**   84

Overview: Telling Your Story   *84*
Writing a Clear Topic Sentence That Establishes a Context   *85*
Relying on Chronological Order   *87*
Choosing the Most Effective Point of View   *88*
Recap: Narration   *91*

6   **Description**   92

Overview: Creating a Picture in Words   *92*
Previewing the Focus of Description through the
   Topic Sentence   *93*
Using Sensory Details   *94*
Relying on Objective and Subjective Description   *95*
Using Spatial Order   *96*
Recap: Description   *99*

7 Example 100

Overview: Learning to Illustrate Your Point *100*
Providing a Topic Sentence That States the Point
 You Will Illustrate *101*
Providing Specific Examples *103*
Ensuring That Your Examples Are Relevant *103*
Recap: Example *106*

8 Process 107

Overview: Explaining "How to" or "How It Happens" *107*
Including a Topic Sentence That Clearly States the Process *108*
Using the Imperative Mood: You *109*
Dividing the Process into Simple, Logical Steps *110*
Relying on Linear Order *111*
Recap: Process *114*

9 Definition 116

Overview: Making Meaning Crystal Clear *116*
Providing a Topic Sentence That Highlights the Term
 to Be Defined *117*
Understanding the Pattern of an Effective Definition *118*
Recognizing the Full Effect of the Term Defined *120*
Recap: Definition *123*

10 Comparison and Contrast 124

Overview: Expressing Similarities and Differences *124*
Providing a Topic Sentence That Specifies Both Subjects
 and Indicates the Focus *125*
Establishing Your Bases for Comparison *125*
Arranging Your Ideas Effectively *127*
Recap: Comparison and Contrast *131*

11 Cause and Effect 133

Overview: Explaining Reasons and Consequences *133*
Providing a Topic Sentence That Focuses on Cause or Effect *134*
Distinguishing between Direct and Related Causes
 and Effects *135*
Avoiding Oversimplification of Causes and Effects *137*
Recap: Cause and Effect *140*

12 Division and Classification   141

Overview: Analyzing the Whole in Terms of the Parts   *141*
Specifying Scope and Emphasis through a Topic Sentence   *142*
Establishing a Logical Method of Analysis   *143*
Maintaining a Consistent Presentation   *145*
Using Distinct and Complete Groupings   *146*
Recap: Division and Classification   *149*

13 Argument   150

Overview: Understanding Persuasion   *150*
Providing a Topic Sentence That Expresses a Clear Stance
    on the Issue   *151*
Developing Sufficient Support through Sound Reasons   *152*
Using a Reasonable, Convincing Tone   *156*
Using Sound Logic   *157*
Arranging Your Support in Emphatic Order   *159*
Recap: Argument   *162*

Part Three   Moving On to the Essay   165

14 Developing an Essay   166

Overview: Comparing the Paragraph and the Essay   *166*
Understanding the Structure of an Essay   *167*
    The Introduction   *167*
    The Body   *167*
    The Conclusion   *167*
Understanding the Role of the Thesis   *168*
Examining an Effective Essay   *171*
Examining the Process of Writing an Essay   *173*
    Prewriting: Generating Ideas and Developing a Thesis   *174*
    Composing: Creating the Draft   *176*
        Focusing on the Most Promising Material   *176*   •   Considering Introductions
        and Conclusions   *177*   •   Understanding the Relationship between Topic
        Sentences and the Thesis   *180*   •   Developing a Solid First Draft   *180*
    Revising: Turning Something Good into Something Better   *182*
        Revising for Unity   *183*   •   Revising for Coherence   *184*   •   Revising for
        Effective Language   *186*   •   Seeking Help from an Objective Reader   *188*   •
        Redrafting   *189*
    Editing: Eliminating Errors   *189*
Looking Again at the Final Draft   *190*
Recap: Developing an Essay   *194*

15 Examining Types of Essays   196

Overview: Understanding the Use of Modes in Essays   *196*
The Relationship between Your Purpose and the Modes   *197*
Using Narration to Develop an Essay   *197*
   Examining a Narrative Essay   *198*
Using Description to Develop an Essay   *200*
   Examining a Descriptive Essay   *200*
Using Example to Develop an Essay   *202*
   Examining an Example Essay   *203*
Using Process to Develop an Essay   *205*
   Examining a Process Essay   *205*
Using Definition to Develop an Essay   *208*
   Examining a Definition Essay   *208*
Using Comparison and Contrast to Develop an Essay   *211*
   Examining a Comparison and Contrast Essay   *211*
Using Cause and Effect to Develop an Essay   *215*
   Examining a Cause and Effect Essay   *215*
Using Division and Classification to Develop an Essay   *217*
   Examining a Division and Classification Essay   *218*
Writing an Argument Essay   *220*
   Examining an Argument Essay   *221*
Recap: Examining Types of Essays   *223*

16 Answering Essay Questions   225

Overview: Laying the Foundation for Answering Essay Questions   *225*
Approaching an Essay Question   *225*
   Preparation   *226*
     Active Reading   *226*   •   Effective Note-Taking   *227*
   Anticipation   *228*
   Rehearsal   *229*
     Drawing Up a Practice Question   *229*   •   Answering a
     Practice Question   *229*
Examining an Answer to a Practice Question   *230*
Recap: Answering Essay Questions   *233*

Part Four   Developing Sentence Sense   235

17 The Sentence   236

Overview: Understanding Sentence Basics   *236*
Understanding Verbs   *237*

Recognizing Subjects   *239*
Recap: The Sentence   244

18 Fragments   246

Overview: Recognizing and Writing Complete Sentences   *246*
Correcting Fragments with Missing Subjects or Verbs   *247*
Correcting Phrase Fragments   *250*
Correcting Subordinate Clause Fragments   *252*
Correcting Appositive Fragments   *255*
Recap: Fragments   259

19 Subordination and Coordination   261

Overview: Combining Clauses for Sentence Complexity   *261*
Using Subordination   *262*
Using Coordination   *265*
    Achieving Coordination by Using Coordinating Conjunctions   *265*
    Achieving Coordination by Using Semicolons   *267*
Recap: Subordination and Coordination   *271*

20 Comma Splices and Run-On Sentences   274

Overview: Understanding Sentence-Combining Errors   *274*
Identifying Comma Splices and Run-On Sentences   *275*
**Correcting Comma Splices and Run-Ons by Using
    Coordinating Conjunctions**   *277*
**Correcting Comma Splices and Run-Ons by Using
    Subordinating Conjunctions**   *279*
Correcting Comma Splices and Run-Ons by Using Semicolons   *281*
Correcting Comma Splices and Run-Ons by Using Periods   *285*
Recap: Comma Splices and Run-On Sentences   *289*

Part Five   Understanding Subjects and Verbs   291

21 Subject–Verb Agreement   292

Overview: Understanding Subject–Verb Agreement   *292*
Avoiding Agreement Errors When the Subject Follows the Verb   *293*
**Avoiding Agreement Errors When Words Come between
    the Subject and Verb**   *295*
Avoiding Agreement Errors with Indefinite Pronouns   *298*
Avoiding Agreement Errors from Other Causes   *301*
    When the Subject Is Compound   *301*
    When the Subject Is a Collective Noun   *302*

When the Subject Is a Singular Word Ending in -s, a Word Referring
    to an Amount, or a Word That Has the Same Singular
    and Plural Form   *302*
Recap: Subject–Verb Agreement   308

22 Basic Tenses for Regular Verbs   310

Overview: Understanding Tense   *310*
**Using the Simple Present, Simple Future, and Simple
    Past Tenses**   *311*
Using the Perfect Tenses   *314*
Recap: Basic Tenses for Regular Verbs   318

23 Irregular Verbs and Frequently Confused Verbs   320

**Overview: Understanding Irregular Verbs and Other
    Verb Problems**   *320*
Identifying Irregular Verbs   *321*
Working with Forms of *to Be*   *327*
**Choosing between *Can* and *Could* and between
    Will and *Would***   *330*
Recap: Irregular Verbs and Frequently Confused Verbs   334

24 Passive Voice, Additional Tenses, and Maintaining Consistency in Tense   336

Overview: Understanding Additional Elements of Verb Use   *336*
Forming the Passive and Active Voice   *337*
Using the Progressive and Perfect Progressive Tenses   *339*
    The Progressive Tenses   *339*
    The Perfect Progressive Tenses   *340*
Maintaining Consistency in Tense   *342*
**Recap: Passive Voice, Additional Tenses, and Maintaining
    Consistency in Tense   346**

Part Six   Keeping Your Writing Correct   349

25 Nouns and Pronouns   350

Overview: Understanding Words That Name   *350*
Making Singular Nouns Plural   *351*
Working with Collective Nouns and Cue Words   *353*
Understanding Pronoun Case   *356*
Using Personal Pronouns Correctly   *359*

Using Indefinite Pronouns *361*
Recap: Nouns and Pronouns *366*

26 Adjectives, Adverbs, and Other Modifiers 367

Overview: Understanding the Roles of Adjectives
  and Adverbs *367*
Understanding Adjectives and Adverbs *368*
Creating Comparative and Superlative Forms of Adjectives
  and Adverbs *369*
Working with Confusing Pairs of Adjectives and Adverbs *371*
Avoiding Dangling and Misplaced Modifiers *373*
Avoiding Double Negatives *378*
Recap: Adjectives, Adverbs, and Other Modifiers *383*

27 Ensuring Pronoun–Antecedent Agreement 385

Overview: Choosing the Correct Pronoun *385*
Maintaining Agreement in Number *386*
Maintaining Agreement with Indefinite Pronouns *388*
Maintaining Agreement with Demonstrative and Reflexive
  or Intensive Pronouns *390*
Keeping the Relationship between Pronoun and
  Antecedent Clear *393*
Maintaining Agreement with *That, Who,* and *Which* Clauses *396*
Avoiding Problems with Gender in
  Pronoun–Antecedent Agreement *397*
Recap: Ensuring Pronoun–Antecedent Agreement *402*

28 Maintaining Parallelism 404

Overview: Balancing Ideas in Your Writing *404*
Maintaining Parallelism with Words in a Series *405*
Maintaining Parallelism with Phrases *406*
Maintaining Parallelism When Using Correlative Conjunctions *409*
Recap: Maintaining Parallelism *413*

29 Spelling 415

Overview: Understanding the Importance of Correct Spelling *415*
Basic Rules for Forming Plurals *416*
Basic Rules for Prefixes and Suffixes *419*
The Basic Rule for *ie* or *ei* *422*
Basic Rules for *-sede, -ceed,* and *-cede,* and Other Endings
  That Sound Alike *423*

Dealing with Commonly Confused Words *425*
Learning the Most Commonly Misspelled Words *431*
Recap: Spelling *435*

30 Commas 436

Overview: Understanding Comma Usage *436*
Using a Comma between Clauses Connected by Conjunctions *437*
Using Commas to Separate Items in a Series *438*
Using a Comma to Set Off Introductory Material *440*
**Using Commas to Set Off Elements That Interrupt
    Sentence Flow** *441*
Using Commas to Set Off Direct Quotations *443*
Recognizing Other Situations in Which Commas Are Needed *444*
Recap: Commas *449*

31 Other Punctuation and Capitalization 450

**Overview: Using Punctuation and Capitalization
    to Clarify Meaning** *450*
Using Periods, Question Marks, and Exclamation Points *451*
Using Quotation Marks *452*
Using Apostrophes *454*
Using Other Marks of Punctuation *458*
    Colons *458*
    Semicolons *459*
    Parentheses and Dashes *460*
Understanding Capitalization *462*
Recap: Other Punctuation and Capitalization *469*

Part Seven   Connecting: Responding to Reading 471

Overview: Responding to Reading *472*
Taking Notes *472*
Active Reading Strategies *472*
Active Reading Illustrated *474*
Teaching as an Amusing Activity   Neil Postman   475
Fish Cheeks   Amy Tan   477
Intimacy and Independence   Deborah Tannen   479
Nightwatch   Paul Fletcher   481
Caesar   Therese C. MacKinnon   484
How Boys Become Men   Jon Katz   487
"Growing Up" Is Cumulative, Evolutionary and Never-Ending
    Brian Dickinson   490

Thanksgiving Is the Greatest Holiday   Robert C. Maynard   493
Go and Conquer the World   Michaela Otway   496
The Importance of Wearing a Safety Belt   Larissa R. Houk   499
Exposed Toes   Diane Riva   501
A Religion?   Henry Bousquet   504
A Bully Who Wore Bobby Pins   Amanda Beaulieu   506
Fear Not   Greg Andree   508
To Smoke or Not to Smoke   Charlotte Medeiros   510
Thoughts about Writing   Charlotte Medeiros   512

Appendix A: **Writing with a Computer** *515*

Appendix B: **Tips for ESL Writers** *521*

Appendix C: **Exploring the Dictionary** *541*

Rhetorical Index *547*

Index *555*

Preface

At some point during the eighth century B.C., the legendary Greek poet Homer first sang his epic poem about the adventures of the hero Odysseus. As his audience listened, Homer related the story of a journey so fantastic that the name of his poem—*The Odyssey*—came to signify a great journey.

Writing is also a great journey, a voyage through the world of ideas. That's why this text is entitled *Odyssey: A Guide to Better Writing,* Second Edition. The adventure that is writing begins with ideas jotted on paper or typed across a computer screen and ends with a completed piece of writing that expresses those ideas in simple, clear, complete, and correct terms. It is a journey of self-discovery, as we tap into our creativity and draw on our reserves of experience and knowledge. This journey brings us into contact with the world as we exchange information and react to what we learn from others. This text will prepare you for all the journeys—and all the promise—that writing holds.

Odyssey's approach is based on three fundamental premises about learning to write. The first is that **the best way to learn is to write.** The more people write, the more comfortable and confident they become with the process, and the more willing they are to practice and to strive to develop greater skill and fluency. Therefore, *Odyssey* immediately sets sail into the world of ideas by involving you in engaging writing activities.

The second premise is that **writing well requires both creativity and sound critical thinking.** Before you can effectively express your ideas about a subject on paper, you must understand that subject, be able to analyze it from different perspectives, recognize its significance, and articulate your ideas about it. *Odyssey* develops both creativity and critical thinking through a variety of writing exercises and also provides clear guidelines for using written language effectively. In addition, the text emphasizes the value of working with others to generate ideas and to assess and revise a piece of writing.

The third premise is that **good writing is the sum of engaging content and correct form.** Writing successfully means expressing ideas in a way that is universally accepted and understood by readers. For this reason, much of

Odyssey details how universally accepted guidelines of grammar and usage apply to writing situations.

▶ ORGANIZATION OF THE TEXT

Odyssey's organization ensures cumulative skill development and allows flexibility in course design. Part One, "Starting Out," consists of four chapters that focus on the stages of the writing process through progressively sequenced activities. Chapter 1, "Ensuring Success in Writing," discusses both the essential elements of writing (**writer, reader, topic, message,** and **means**) and the primary purposes of writing (to **inform, entertain,** and **persuade**). Chapter 2, "Generating Ideas through Prewriting," introduces five prewriting activities—**freewriting, brainstorming, clustering, branching,** and **idea mapping**—and discusses **journal writing** as a way to generate ideas and develop writing skills. Chapter 3, "Composing: Creating a Draft," takes students through the entire composing stage, from developing a topic sentence to completing a draft, showing how to distinguish between writer-centered and reader-centered ideas. Chapter 4, "Refining and Polishing Your Draft," illustrates the revision process: reassessing for **unity, coherence,** and **effective language;** seeking advice from an objective reader; redrafting; and then editing.

Part Two of *Odyssey,* "Using the Patterns of Paragraph Development," focuses on writing paragraphs featuring the rhetorical modes—narration, description, example, process, definition, comparison and contrast, cause and effect, and division and classification. Chapters 5 through 12 explain and illustrate the specific characteristics of each mode and discuss them as techniques writers use to fulfill a purpose. Chapter 13 covers argument, which *Odyssey* treats as a purpose.

The three chapters making up Part Three, "Moving On to the Essay," apply the principles presented in Part One to essay writing. Chapter 14, "Developing an Essay," uses a single essay to illustrate the processes of generating ideas, developing a thesis and supporting sentences, developing an introduction and a conclusion, and evaluating and adjusting the draft for unity, coherence, and effective language. Chapter 15, "Examining Types of Essays," focuses on ways to develop entire essays using the rhetorical modes. It explains and illustrates the characteristics of each mode in relation to the essay, again discussing argument as a purpose that employs a variety of modes. Chapter 16, "Answering Essay Questions," presents a simple, direct method for performing well on written examinations.

The chapters making up the next three parts of *Odyssey* all deal with aspects of grammar and usage that beginning writers find challenging. Each problem area is discussed in relation to the writing process, emphasizing the point made at the beginning of the text that effective writing is a synthesis of content and form.

The four chapters in Part Four, "Developing Sentence Sense," focus on writing correct sentences and avoiding sentence errors. The four chapters in Part Five, "Understanding Subjects and Verbs," focus on subject–verb agreement as well as different aspects of verb use. The seven chapters comprising Part Six, "Keeping Your Writing Correct," deal with other aspects of usage and mechanics.

Part Seven, "Connecting: Responding to Reading," is a brief anthology of fifteen readings, including pieces by professional writers such as Amy Tan and Deborah Tannen as well as works by student authors. The student writings are products of assignments like those presented throughout *Odyssey*. An introduction to the section provides guidelines for careful, analytical reading, and a brief annotated reading illustrates the principles outlined in the section. Each selection is accompanied by a set of questions that promote critical thinking, discussion, and writing.

Three practical appendices supplement the lessons in the text. Appendix A, "Writing with a Computer" is a brief introduction to the basic word processing functions that can help to make the writing process efficient and effective. Appendix B, "Tips for ESL Writers," intended for non-native speakers of English, covers selected aspects of grammar and usage that ESL students often find confusing. Appendix C, "Exploring the Dictionary," emphasizes good dictionary and vocabulary-building skills through use of a sample dictionary entry as well as stimulating exercises.

FEATURES IN THE TEXT

Odyssey includes a number of special features designed to make your voyage through the book both interesting and enlightening.

➤ Each chapter contains carefully sequenced sets of exercises that challenge you incrementally. **Exploration a** and **Exploration b** exercises check comprehension and provide practice with the concepts just presented. **Exploration c** exercises, many of which are collaborative, call for planning and composing short writings. **Challenge** sessions emphasize critical thinking, drafting, or revising; many of these activities are also collaborative. All the chapters in Parts Four through Six also include **Summary Exercises** that assess understanding of all the concepts presented in a particular chapter.

➤ The text includes a wide variety of engaging and challenging writing assignments. These **Discovering Connections** exercises are designed to stimulate imaginative and critical thinking. In Part One, several of the assignments employ a unique visual element to spark the kind of creative associations that lead to thoughtful, effective writing. In Parts Two through Six, the Discovering Connections assignments are presented in two segments, one calling for invention on a given choice of topics and the other calling for composing and revising a draft based on the work done for the first segment. In addition, the questions following each reading selection in Part Seven, "Connecting: Responding to Reading," ask for written responses to the ideas presented in the selection.

➤ **Exercises on grammar and usage** are presented in complete paragraph form, as unified discourse. This feature underscores the emphasis throughout *Odyssey* that content and form are interconnected and interdependent.

➤ The **arrangement of the text** allows for a focus on either paragraph writing or essay writing.

➤ The **rhetorical modes** are presented as techniques used by writers to fulfill the purpose of a piece of writing.

➤ **Argument** is treated as a purpose that encompasses several modes.

➤ **Collaborative activities** are identified with a special icon, like the one shown here.

➤ The **attractive full-color design** provides visual stimulation, and **full color charts** throughout the text graphically accentuate key relationships among parts of speech, sentence elements, and so forth.

➤ **Chapter Recaps** review terms presented in the chapter and offer visual summaries of key concepts.

➤ Realistic, engaging **writing samples** illustrate all aspects of content and form while modeling clear, effective writing.

➤ An **anthology of professional and student readings** encourages discussion and provides opportunities for active reading, critical thinking, and additional writing.

➤ Except for the four chapters in Part One, **each chapter is self-contained,** allowing maximum flexibility in terms of course design and presentation of material.

➤ **Three appendices** meet the needs of a spectrum of students. **Appendix A: Writing with a Computer** introduces basic word processing functions; **Appendix B: Tips for ESL Writers** presents additional grammar and usage tips for ESL students; and **Appendix C: Exploring the Dictionary** provides instruction in dictionary use.

➤ NEW IN THIS EDITION

From the moment that we began work on the first edition of *Odyssey: A Guide to Better Writing,* our goal has remained constant: to create the most accessible, practical, and effective basic writing text possible. With this goal in mind, once the first edition was published, we immediately began examining ways to improve it. We used and evaluated the text ourselves, asked our students what they thought and how we might adjust the text to meet their needs to an even greater degree, and queried colleagues across the nation for their reactions and suggestions. On the basis of this collective analysis, this second edition of *Odyssey: A Guide to Better Writing* features a number of significant changes.

For example, sentence errors remain among the most persistent problem spots for beginning writers, so we have doubled the amount of coverage and number of exercises in Chapter 18, "Fragments," and in Chapter 20, "Comma Splices and Run-On Sentences." This degree of coverage is unmatched in other basic writing texts.

Another aspect of writing that often creates difficulty for beginning writers is maintaining subject–verb agreement, so we have added an entire chapter dealing with this area of concern, Chapter 21, "Subject–Verb Agreement." Beginning writers also often face difficulties with dangling and misplaced modifiers. To address this need, we have significantly increased the coverage of these problem spots in a section entitled "Avoiding Dangling and Misplaced Modifiers," which appears in Chapter 26, "Adjectives, Adverbs, and Other Modifiers." And throughout the rest of *Odyssey*, we have added new examples and changed various individual exercises to ensure that our presentation remains fresh and engaging.

We have also made a number of changes in Part Seven, "Connecting: Responding to Reading." For instance, to the discussion of note taking and active reading, we have added a brief annotated reading that underscores the importance of these strategies while clearly illustrating these techniques. We have also added a number of stimulating and entertaining new readings, both by professional writers, including "Fish Cheeks" by Amy Tan and "Thanksgiving Is the Greatest Holiday" by Robert C. Maynard, and by student writers, including "Go and Conquer the World" by Michaela Otway, "The Bully Who Wore Bobby Pins" by Amanda Beaulieu, and "The Importance of Wearing a Safety Belt" by Larissa Houk.

Finally, Appendix C, "Exploring the Dictionary," has been revised and expanded. Now, in addition to the thorough, step-by-step analysis of a typical dictionary entry, this section includes several interesting, innovative exercises that make dictionary mastery fun and easy.

➤ SUPPLEMENT PACKAGE

A complete array of supplements is available to use with *Odyssey: A Guide to Better Writing*.

> ➤ The **Instructor's Annotated Edition** contains a special preface providing sample syllabi as well as valuable suggestions for organizing and managing a developmental writing classroom. Topics include ways to create a productive classroom atmosphere that puts students at ease and techniques for stimulating class discussion, working effectively in conferences, evaluating papers, and managing collaborative groups.

➤ A **Companion Website** has been created to provide additional exercise activities for the book. It can also be used for live chats, message boards, and e-mailing between students and between instructors and students. The website can be found at <http://www.abacon.com/kelly>.

➤ An **Interactive Companion CD-ROM,** which is keyed to the text, provides computerized versions of the textbook exercises as well as additional writing assignments and grammar exercises. This item is provided free to students upon request of their instructor.

➤ **The Allyn & Bacon Editing Exercises** accommodate a frequent request by instructors to provide even more grammar exercises in paragraph and essay contexts. This item is intended to provide students with additional practice in areas of common error. This item is provided free to students upon request of their instructor.

➤ A short booklet, **"Ten Habits of Highly Successful Students,"** provides instruction on important fundamentals for successful college learning in a number of skill areas such as critical reading, time management, and working with instructors. This item is provided free to students upon request of their instructors.

➤ The **Test Bank** includes a diagnostic test, two twenty-item tests for each chapter in Parts Four through Six, and a comprehensive mastery test.

➤ The **Computerized Test File** is an electronic version of the test bank items for PC or MAC.

➤ The **GrammarCoach Software Package** contains hundreds of exercises from which individualized drill and practice sessions can be generated. The attractive interactive format makes self-directed work on problem areas in grammar and mechanics engaging and enjoyable.

➤ The **Student Answer Key** enables students to check and correct their own work on text exercises.

➤ The new **Allyn & Bacon CompSite Web Page** (http://www.abacon.com) provides a wealth of resources for instructors and students, including hotlinks to other sites and opportunities for on-line exchanges with other *Odyssey* users.

➤ *A*CKNOWLEDGMENTS

We would like to acknowledge a number of people for their assistance and guidance as we worked on this second edition of *Odyssey: A Guide to Better Writing*. First, we thank John M. Lannon, University of Massachusetts, Dartmouth, and Robert A. Schwegler, University of Rhode Island, for their continuing support. They are wonderful teachers, wonderful writers, wonderful friends.

Many people at Bristol Community College also deserve our thanks for their support of our work. We salute our students, who have taught us so much over the years. In addition, we are grateful to our colleagues who have taken a serious interest in our work, including Cynthia Brenner, Rylan Brenner, Raymond Butts, Sally Cameron, Debra Deroian, David Feeney, Tom Grady, Penny Hahn, Diana McGee, and Jerry LePage. We also thank Jack Warner, Vice Chancellor of Higher Education for Massachusetts, for his friendship and ongoing support. We offer special thanks to Paul F. Fletcher, Professor Emeritus of English and retired Assistant Dean for Language, Humanities, and the Arts, from whom we learned so much about teaching and about treating students and colleagues with respect and kindness.

A number of talented professionals from around the country offered us suggestions that have helped us to shape this edition of *Odyssey*. They include Marie Connelly, Cuyahoga Community College Western Campus; Frances Secco Davidson, Mercer County Community College; Mary M. Greene, Tidewater Community College; Isabel Hansen, Black Hawk College; William T. Hope, Jefferson Community College; Claudia House, Nashville State Technical Institute; Kenneth P. Kerr, Wor-Wic Community College; David E. Rogers, Valencia Community College; and Josephine M. Van Wyk, Millersville University. Thanks also to James Vanden Bosch for his work on some of the exercises.

We are also grateful to the fine team at Allyn and Bacon who have worked so hard to make this second edition of *Odyssey* so attractive. Joe Opiela, Vice President, Humanities, deserves particular thanks for his unwavering confidence in *Odyssey* and in its authors. We also thank Lisa Kimball, Executive Marketing Manager, for her determination to ensure that as many people as possible have the chance to learn about *Odyssey*. Thanks also to Donna de la Perriere, Developmental Editor, for her efforts in marshaling the manuscript through the early stages of publication, and to Donna Simons, Production Administrator, for her outstanding work in transforming that manuscript into this final form. We are also grateful to Mary Varney, Editorial Assistant, Humanities, who did a wonderful job coordinating different aspects of this project, especially her work on permissions.

Finally, we would like to thank our friends and family for their constant support of us and our work.

Debbie Lawton would like to thank her Bradcliffe friends, Mary Beth, Judy, Tom, Barbara, and Michele, for offering a helping hand, a word of encouragement, or a smile whenever needed. Above all, she would like to thank her family for their support and love. Her children, Matthew and Amy, have brought her much joy as they have traveled toward adulthood. The person to whom she is most grateful is her husband, Kevin. His patience, confidence in her, and love have always been, and will continue to be, essential parts of her professional accomplishments and personal happiness.

Bill Kelly would first like to thank his parents, the late Mary R. and Edward F. Kelly, for their love and support. The sacrifices they made for their four sons ensured that the doors to an education and to the future beyond swung open for them. His in-laws, Flo and Leo Nadeau, deserve special thanks for their constant support, love, and interest in his work. Nicole C. and Jacqueline M. Kelly, his children, amaze and inspire him day after day with their respect and tolerance for others, with their intelligence, with their talents. No parent could be more blessed. But most of all, he thanks his wife, Michelle Nadeau Kelly.

For more than twenty-eight years, she has offered her unwavering support, encouragement, and love, and he looks happily forward to enjoying the new millennium in her company.

▶ AN INVITATION TO STUDENTS AND INSTRUCTORS

We would like to hear your reactions, comments, and suggestions regarding this text. Contact us directly at the following:

E-mail: wkelly@bristol.mass.edu
Fax: (508) 675-2294
Phone: (508) 678-2811, ext. 2948

or

c/o English Department
Bristol Community College
777 Elsbree Street
Fall River, MA 02720

About the Authors

William J. Kelly earned his Ph.D. in English from the University of Rhode Island. He also received an M.A. in English from Rhode Island College and a B.A. in English from Southeastern Massachusetts University (now the University of Massachusetts, Dartmouth). The youngest full professor in the history of Bristol Community College, he has been a classroom teacher since 1975. In addition to teaching writing and literature at Bristol for sixteen years, he previously taught junior high school and high school English in Fall River, Massachusetts. An active freelance writer since 1981, his credits also include a three-year stint as a weekly newspaper columnist. He has authored three other textbooks for Allyn & Bacon: *Models and Process: A Rhetoric and Reader; Beginnings: A Rhetoric and Handbook;* and *Strategy and Structure,* Second Edition. The Carnegie Foundation for the Advancement of Teaching and the Council for Advancement and Support of Education named him 1997 Massachusetts Professor of the Year. He is the first community college instructor ever to receive this prestigious award.

For twenty years, **Deborah L. Lawton** has been working to help community college students reach their goals. In her community college career, including five years as a student affairs professional and more than fifteen years as a teacher of writing, literature, and communications, she has learned of the dreams community college students have and the challenges they face. She is currently an associate professor of English and, as assistant dean, leads the division of language, humanities, and the arts at Bristol Community College. She holds an M.A. in English from Western Michigan University, a B.A. in English from the University of Massachusetts, Amherst, and an associate degree from Greenfield Community College in Greenfield, Massachusetts.

Odyssey
A Guide to Better Writing

part

one

Starting Out

1	Ensuring Success in Writing
2	Generating Ideas through Prewriting
3	Composing: Creating a Draft
4	Refining and Polishing Your Draft

Ensuring Success in **Writing**

 **O**VERVIEW: *UNDERSTANDING THE IMPORTANCE OF GOOD WRITING SKILLS*

Writing is a means of exploration and discovery. By opening this book, you have embarked on an exciting odyssey through the world of ideas. As you learn more about ways to express yourself, you'll also learn more about yourself and the world around you.

But just as important as these pleasures are the practical benefits you will gain along the way. Today, more than ever, being able to write well is a vital skill. People all over the world communicate, exchange information, and conduct business instantaneously across cyberspace. To make your messages clear and accurate for this new arena, you must have good writing skills.

Good writing skills will also help you in other, more traditional ways. When you express your ideas directly, completely, and correctly in school, you earn better grades. And when you write effectively on the job, you will earn the respect of colleagues and supervisors and ensure your success as a professional.

This chapter discusses the basic elements of writing:

➤ the five interacting components of writing—writer, reader, topic, message, and means

➤ the purposes of writing—to inform, to entertain, and to persuade

➤ RECOGNIZING THE DYNAMICS OF WRITING

Simply defined, *writing* is an act of communication. It is the act of using words to convey your ideas to someone else. You do the same thing when you speak, but writing is different in two major ways. First, writing is more *deliberate*—more fully thought out—than speech. Second, writing is more *precise*—more carefully crafted word by word for just the right effect.

In the act of writing, five components interact: (1) a writer, (2) a reader, (3) a topic, (4) a message, and (5) the means of expressing that message (written language). The *communication triangle* below shows how the five elements in the writing process interact.

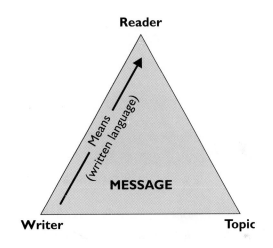

The *writer* begins by learning and thinking about a *topic.* The inside of the triangle represents the *message,* or what the writer understands and wants to communicate about the topic. However, to convey the message to a *reader,* the writer must use some *means* that the reader will understand: written language. If the reader understands the message, then the writer has communicated effectively.

Exploration 1a   Considering the Dynamics of Writing

1. What are the five interacting components in the communication triangle?

   The five interacting components is: a writer, a reader, a topic, a message, and the means.

2. What are two ways in which writing differs from speech? _____

   writing is more deliberate and precise than speech.

Exploration 1b   Exploring Your Attitudes about Writing

1. On the following lines, briefly explain why you enjoy the act of writing or why you dislike it. _Honestly, I dislike writing because I am not so skillful to write well, however, in compare with speaking my writing looks much better._

2. Which do you find easier, speaking or writing? Why? _Some times, speaking usually, is not as formal as writing. When people speak they help themselves to communicate effectively by using emotions or body language._

Exploration 1c   Using the Communication Triangle

1. In your own words, explain how writing involves exploration and discovery. _Through writing you can become deeply envolved with some ideas, that may be have never cross your mind, and find new ways to express yourself._

2. Look at the communication triangle on page 3. Think of all the things you understand about the topic *trees*. Using the means of written language, communicate a message about this topic to an imaginary reader.

   _____

   _____

   _____

   _____

   _____

Challenge 1   Analyzing Yourself as a Writer

1. On the lines provided, list three things that make you uncomfortable with writing. Then, put a ✓ next to the one that you consider your biggest obstacle to writing well.

   a feeling of unconfidence.

   usually not enough supporting details.

   unsubstantial

   spending too much time thinking about a topic.

2. Working with a partner, make two lists in the spaces provided below. On the left, list what you feel strong writing skills would enable you to do. Then, on the right, list problems caused by weak writing skills.

   Strong writing skills
   will allow me to . . .

   get better grades
   communicate
   by writing on
   apropriate level
   express my ideas
   directly and completely
   write effectively
   be successful

   Weak writing skills
   mean that I . . .

   will not be
   able to communicate
   though writing

3. On the following lines, list three things you would like to learn about the writing process.

   to generate ideas.
   to write fast.
   to be able write substantial essays.

UNDERSTANDING THE BASIC COMPONENTS OF WRITING

To understand what writing actually involves, it's important to understand the five components of the communication triangle more fully. When you write, of course, *you* are the **writer,** the person who explores the **topic,** or specific subject, you want to write about. You might do this by drawing on your own experiences, talking to others, or reading and doing research. To convey your understanding of the topic, you use supporting examples, details, and explanations to construct a **message.** The written language that you use to express your message is the **means.** And the audience that the paper is directed to, the person or persons whom you want to understand you, is the **reader.**

Imagine that you have written the following paragraph:

> In the last few years, no technological advance has had more impact on the way people communicate, pursue information, and conduct business than the Internet. With a few clicks of the computer mouse, people can contact anyone from a friend in the next house to a perfect stranger on the other side of the globe. They can search for information in major on-line libraries and from a wide variety of other sources. They also have the opportunity to communicate with nationally and internationally recognized experts, just by hitting a few keys on the keyboard. For both corporation and consumer, the Internet has forever changed the way business is conducted. Today everything from clothing to computers to vacation packages is available on-line, making the shopping experience simpler and cheaper for the companies and the customers.

You are the writer. The Internet is your topic. Your message is about the ways the Internet has influenced communications, information-gathering, and business. The specific words you have used to explain the Internet's various influences are your means. The person to whom you are directing this material is your reader.

FOCUSING ON THE READER

As a writer, you need to focus first and foremost on the reader. If your writing doesn't communicate to a reader, then it's not effective. It's that simple.

To communicate effectively, you first need to identify your reader. Sometimes you will know exactly who the reader is. For example, if you are writing a follow-up letter after a job interview, you know that the reader will be the person who interviewed you.

However, for much of the writing you'll do, your reader won't be so clearly identified. In these cases, you must try to imagine a reader. It may help to think of a specific person, someone you know slightly but not well. The danger in using someone close to you is that you share too much common knowledge. Unless you assume that you are writing to a stranger, you are likely to omit information necessary to communicate with your actual readers.

A second option is to focus on the average reader—someone who is like most of us. Most people know a little about many subjects. However, they don't often know detailed information about them. They don't know the hows or whys. Think of yourself before you learned about your subject. What kinds and amounts of information would you have needed to understand the subject?

For example, imagine that you have been weight training for months. Before you trained, you didn't realize that there are two kinds of weight training: (1) body building, which involves repeated routines of lifting small amounts of weight to sculpt the body, and (2) power lifting, which involves lifting increasingly larger amounts of weight to increase strength.

The average reader is like you before you walked into that gym. He or she needs to be given the kind of information that helped you understand weight training, which you now take for granted. Your message needs to include the kinds of details and examples that made it possible for you to understand the subject yourself.

The more personal or complex the topic, the more fully you will need to explain it. The average reader will need a good deal of direction from you to understand *as you do* why two members of your family no longer speak to each other, for example, or how acid rain develops.

Exploration 2a   Identifying Your Reader

1. In your own words, briefly explain why it's not a good idea to imagine a close relative or friend as your reader. _When you imagine a person close to you as your reader, message of your writing can be not complete and understandable._

2. What advantage is there in imagining your reader as a stranger? _Your message well include more detailed information, such as if you explain something to stranger._

Exploration 2b   Understanding Your Reader

1. Look again at the paragraph about the Internet on page 6. What kind of reader did the writer have in mind? Briefly describe that reader. _____

   There should be an average reader, _____ _____ most knowledge computer terminology

2. How are you and the average reader similar? How are you different?

   I am average reader for this topic; I am not a professional, but I have some basic knowlege about how a computer and internet.

Challenge 2   Evaluating the Needs of a Specific Reader

1. If the reader of the paragraph on the Internet had no access to a computer, how would this paragraph need to be changed? Working with a partner, make a list of information you would add. Write your list on a separate sheet of paper.
2. Now, on the same page, make a list of typical writing situations in which you know exactly who your reader is.

UNDERSTANDING THE PURPOSE BEHIND YOUR WRITING

People write to fulfill three main **purposes** or aims: *to inform, to entertain,* or *to persuade.* A paper explaining the effects of diabetes, for example, would inform. So would a paper spelling out how to build a stone wall.

A paper about a practical joke played on a friend would clearly entertain. Not all writing that entertains makes you laugh, however. A story about breaking your leg just before a marathon you'd trained for would also entertain because it would arouse your reader's interest and emotions.

An essay suggesting that world powers should work together to save South America's tropical rain forests would be persuasive. So would one suggesting that we should ban nuclear weapons for the sake of humanity. As a college writer, you'll frequently be called upon to prepare persuasive writings, or *arguments.* Writing that persuades can be particularly difficult to master. For this reason, Chapter 13 is devoted entirely to ways to develop an effective argument paragraph. In addition, a section of Chapter 15 explains ways to write an effective argument essay.

Often your purposes in writing overlap. An informative paper on diabetes might also entertain if it draws the reader in by describing specific cases. It might also be persuasive if it claims that more research money should be devoted to discovering better ways to control diabetes. Although one purpose may be primary, most papers fulfill more than one purpose.

Often students don't think much about the primary purpose of their writing because it is dictated by the assignment. However, it's always important to take a moment to identify that purpose, because purpose determines what you include and also influences the style and tone you adopt.

For example, imagine that your instructor asks you to write a paper that outlines some of the difficulties a first-semester college student might encounter. The primary purpose is to inform. If you instead write a paper in which you try to persuade your reader that first-semester students need more personal and academic support, the paper won't fulfill the primary purpose. Moreover, it won't meet the needs of your reader, who expects different content.

Exploration 3a   Understanding the Purposes for Writing

1. What are the three main purposes for writing? _to inform_
   to entertain , to pesuade
   _____

2. Why is it important to understand the purpose of a piece of writing?
   The purpose determines what
   you include in a writing and
   influences the style and tone of
   you adopt

Exploration 3b   Analyzing the Purpose of a Paragraph

1. Read the following paragraph to determine its *primary* purpose. On the lines below, write that purpose, and explain your answer briefly.

   According to recent statistics, more than 50 percent of all marriages in the United States end in divorce. This phenomenon has far-reaching implications, especially for the children of these broken families. In particular, many of these children experience trouble in school. Guidance counselors have reported cases of elementary school children who were formerly outgoing and affectionate becoming distant and cold. At the high school level, challenges to authority and physical aggression are

two of the most frequent signs. Overall, divorce usually spells at least a
temporary drop in classroom productivity.

Informative

2. What other purpose does the paragraph fulfill? Explain. _____

entertain purose.
the paragraph arouse emotions and
interest toward a problem of divorses

Exploration 3c   Listing Details That Are Appropriate to Purpose

1. Working with a partner, choose *one* of the following three subjects: *a New
   Year's Eve party, a job interview, a popular vacation destination.* Now, list different details you might include in a paper on this topic for each of the following purposes.

   a. Purpose: to inform *a job interview*
   what to wear, how to speak,
   how to anwer on questions, questions that
   are appropreate to ask,

   b. Purpose: to entertain
   New Year's party. Where? who was invited?,
   weather; descriptions

   c. Purpose: to persuade *a popular vacation destination*
   not expencive; very popular;
   clean; a lot of activities, climat.
   not so far.

2. Which of the papers for which you've listed examples would you find easi-

   est to write? Why? Which would you find hardest? Why? _____

   _____

_____

_____

_____

Challenge 3 Analyzing Writing Approach for a Specific Purpose

1. Working with a partner, make a list of the difficulties that a first-semester college student might face. _unfamiliar with rules;_ _difficulties to ajust new_ _learning stile; responsibilities_

_____

2. Briefly explain how you might present the difficulties on your list if the purpose of your paper is to entertain. _organisation;_

_____

_____

_____

DISCOVERING CONNECTIONS A

When you see this drawing, what do you think of? Do you think of sitting down in your favorite chair, relaxing, reading, talking with someone, or watching television? Do you focus on a particular coffee shop, diner, or restaurant that you frequent? Does it make you think of a particular person who always seems to have a cup in hand? Or does the symbol make you think of habits in general?

For this assignment, focus on the icon, and discover what you think about it. Using the examples in this chapter to guide you, jot down what you think the average reader would need to know in order to understand your thoughts. Also, write down what your primary purpose would be if you were to write a paper that used these thoughts. Save this work for later use.

DISCOVERING CONNECTIONS B

For this assignment, think of a first-time experience: a first day on a new job, a first date, the first day at a new school, or the first party you gave. Look again at the sample paragraph on page 6 and the paragraph in Exploration 3b on page 9. Then, write down examples and details for your own paragraph. What does your reader need in order to understand the experience? Also, indicate the primary purpose for your paper on this topic. Save this work for later use.

RECAP
ENSURING SUCCESS IN WRITING

New terms in this chapter	Definitions
➤ writer	➤ the person expressing ideas through the written word
➤ topic	➤ the subject of a paper
➤ message	➤ the supporting examples, details, and explanations that convey the writer's understanding of the topic
➤ means	➤ the written language used to express ideas
➤ reader	➤ the audience to whom a paper is directed
➤ purposes	➤ the intents or aims of a paper ➤ The three purposes of writing are to inform *Example* a paper explaining how political polls are conducted to entertain *Example* a paper recalling an embarrassing experience to persuade *Example* a paper asserting that physician-assisted suicide should be legalized

To write effectively, you must

➤ understand how the five components of writing—**writer, reader, topic, message,** and **means**—interact
➤ identify and focus on the **needs of the reader**
➤ recognize the **purpose of the writing**

Generating Ideas through Prewriting

2

OVERVIEW: *SEEING PREWRITING AS A WAY TO EXPLORE IDEAS*

As Chapter 1 discussed, writing is an act of discovery. As you write, you explore the world around you and your relationship to it. As you develop your writing skills, you also develop your creativity and powers of analysis. Through writing, you discover the significance of your ideas and explore the connections among them. This chapter will explore the most creative stage of writing: **prewriting.** For a writer, this stage is like the launch of an exciting journey to a new place.

In this chapter you will learn how to use the following prewriting techniques:

➤ freewriting
➤ brainstorming
➤ clustering
➤ branching
➤ idea mapping
➤ keeping a journal

➤ UNDERSTANDING PREWRITING

Actually, you have already begun your exploration of *prewriting*. In the exercises of Chapter 1, you thought of ideas for writing to communicate what you know about a topic. That activity actually represented an approach to prewriting.

Prewriting is the first stage in the writing process, which involves two more stages: *composing* and *revising*. Look at this illustration:

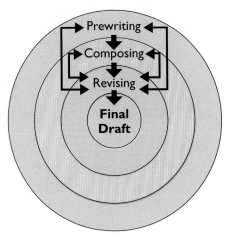

As the illustration shows, when you write, you begin with prewriting and proceed to composing and then to revising. However, notice that in the three outer circles, the arrows point both ways. That is because you may find it necessary to repeat certain steps. Before you hand in your final paper, you will complete several *drafts* or versions. Sometimes you may need to return to prewriting to generate new ideas along the way.

The real work for any piece of writing always begins with prewriting. In order to explain your understanding of a topic, you have to generate ideas that will express that understanding for your reader. Through prewriting, you can develop these ideas about your subject. Most writers use a number of informal prewriting activities, such as talking (either with other people or alone into a tape recorder), doodling, and thinking. However, experienced writers also use other, more specific techniques, including *freewriting, brainstorming, clustering, branching, idea mapping,* and *maintaining a journal.*

As you read about each technique, try it out. That way, you'll know which technique—or which combination of techniques—is best for you.

➤ FREEWRITING

Freewriting is a no-holds-barred prewriting technique that involves writing down all your ideas on a subject for a set period of time. Ten minutes is a typical period. Simply write everything that comes to your mind, even if it contains errors, drifts from the original subject, or doesn't immediately make sense. Don't stop, even if you get stuck. Instead, try different things to get your freewriting going again. For example, rhyme the last word you've written, or write "I can't think" until something different comes to mind. The strength of this method is its ability to help you overcome inhibitions and concerns and to get your ideas starting to flow.

If you use a word processor, you will discover that it is an excellent tool for freewriting. First, set up your program to triple space your document. If you'd like, darken the screen so that you cannot see what you write. This will make you feel less inhibited. Now, you can simply type away on your keyboard for ten minutes. When you are finished, print out what you have written. (For more information about using a word processor for writing, see Appendix A on page 515.)

A freewriting on a subject such as childhood might look like this:

> Childhood, let's see—don't remember much, guess memories start when I started school. Miss Lynch—that was her name, I liked her, the first teacher I can remember. Wonder where she is now? No worries then, not many, at least, no responsibilities—not like now. Kids have it made. My allowance, bought candy and the only work to do was sweep up and make my bed, OK what now, can't write, can't think!! OK was I happy then? little things made me happy, let's see, staying up late to watch TV or winning at cards with my sister. What else about childhood? guess mine wasn't too exciting, I wouldn't pay to watch a movie about it. Movies about kids now are weird. Either they're lost or abandoned or they're saving the world or making their parents look stupid. Am I getting off track? it doesn't matter, I guess. All right, childhood—what about kids today? Not easy for a lot of them now, latchkey kids, violence in school, no time to be a kid anymore.

As the highlighted areas indicate, there are many promising ideas in this freewriting. Incidentally, no matter what prewriting technique you use, *highlighting, underlining,* or *circling* your best ideas is important. That way you can easily find them later if you want to develop them as topics.

Although these promising ideas are in very rough form, they represent *potential* for constructing a good piece of writing later on. Then, you will need to develop these ideas by writing additional details about them and drawing connections among them.

Exploration 1a   Understanding Freewriting

1. In your own words, explain what freewriting is. _Prewriting_
still that help generate your ideas
on a subject during a set time.
_____

2. Which ideas in a freewriting should you highlight, underline, or circle? Why?
The promising ideas that obviously
help to develop topic.
Well connected ideas

Exploration 1b   Analyzing a Freewriting Example

1. Take another look at the sample freewriting on childhood on page 15. What detail especially interests you or makes you curious? Why? _____
Comparison of childhood now and
some time ago.
_____
_____

2. In your judgment, which detail or idea about childhood holds the most potential for development as a topic for writing? Why? _____
_____
_____
_____
_____

Exploration 1c   Practice with Freewriting

1. Now you can try freewriting. On a separate sheet of paper, freewrite for ten minutes on one of the following topics: *childhood, money, loneliness.*

2. Identify the ideas in your freewriting that show the most promise by circling, highlighting, or underlining them.

3. Answer the following questions on a separate sheet of paper:
   a. What do you like best about freewriting as a prewriting technique? Why?
   b. What specific idea or example in your freewriting has the most potential for development? List it on your paper, and then write three additional details about it.

Challenge 1 Evaluating Freewriting

1. Exchange your freewriting with a classmate. On the freewriting you receive, put a ✓ next to the ideas that you find the most interesting. Return the freewriting to the writer, and explain your choices. Put your own work aside for later use.

2. Will you use this prewriting strategy again? Explain. *Yes, I will. It definetely helps me to generate new ideas and clearly realize what I am going to write about.*

866-4835137 FBI

BRAINSTORMING

Brainstorming is a second creative technique for generating ideas. To brainstorm effectively, you should deliberately focus on a subject and then make a list of every idea that comes into your head. Brainstorming is an excellent technique when you are working with a partner or a group. Other people's ideas will start sparking your own creative thoughts, and soon you will find that the ideas come more quickly. A set time limit isn't necessary, although some people prefer to work with one. After brainstorming, you may have fewer notes on paper than you do when you freewrite, but the ideas you generate are likely to be more obviously connected.

You can also brainstorm with your word processor, again, if you wish, darkening the screen so that you cannot see what you write. Then type your list, letting your mind lead you easily from one idea to another. When you are finished, print out your list. (For more information about using a word processor for writing, see Appendix A on page 515.)

After you brainstorm, highlight, underline, or circle ideas that you think have potential as writing topics.

Here is a brainstorming on the subject of exercise:

> *Exercise—reasons to*
>
> *people should get in shape*
>
> *stay in shape*

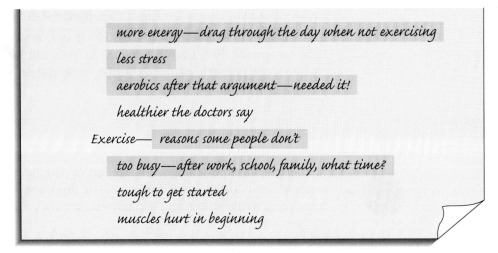

more energy—drag through the day when not exercising

less stress

aerobics after that argument—needed it!

healthier the doctors say

Exercise— reasons some people don't

too busy—after work, school, family, what time?

tough to get started

muscles hurt in beginning

Brainstorming generates a broad listing of loosely related ideas, in most cases more than can be used in one paper. As a result, you have a wide variety of possibilities for further development.

Exploration 2a   Defining Brainstorming

1. In your own words, explain brainstorming. _____

   _____

   _____

   _____

   _____

2. Name one way in which brainstorming differs from freewriting. _____

   In you freewriting you can
   write any idea that comes to you —
   not related to subject.

   _____

Exploration 2b   Analyzing a Brainstorming Example

1. Look again at the sample brainstorming on exercise. What item on the list

   would you like to learn more about? Why? _____

   the reasons for exercise

   _____

_____

_____

2. Which section of this brainstorming do you think holds the most promise

for further development? Why? _____

_____

_____

_____

Exploration 2c   Practice with Brainstorming

1. Now you can try brainstorming. On a separate sheet of paper, brainstorm on one of the following topics: *exercise, luck, relaxation.*
2. Go through your notes, and highlight, circle, or underline any ideas that are especially promising.
3. Answer the following questions on the same page:
   a. What do you like best about brainstorming as a prewriting technique? What do you like least? Explain.
   b. What single idea in your brainstorming seems most promising as a topic? List it, and add three details you could use to develop the idea.

Challenge 2   Evaluating Brainstorming

1. Exchange your brainstorming with a classmate. On the brainstorming you receive, put a ✓ next to the idea or area that you see as the most promising. Then return it to the writer, and explain your choice. Save your own brainstorming for later use.

2. Will you use brainstorming again? Explain. _____

_____

_____

_____

CLUSTERING

Clustering is a prewriting technique that graphically emphasizes connections among the ideas you develop. Begin by writing a general idea in the middle of the page and circling it. As you think of related ideas or details, write them down and circle each one. Then draw lines to connect the new ideas to the ideas from which they developed. Continue this process until you have thoroughly examined the subject. The result is a series of clustered ideas and examples, with lines showing how they relate to each other. Finally, review your work, and highlight or underline the ideas that hold the most promise.

Look at this clustering on the subject *sports*:

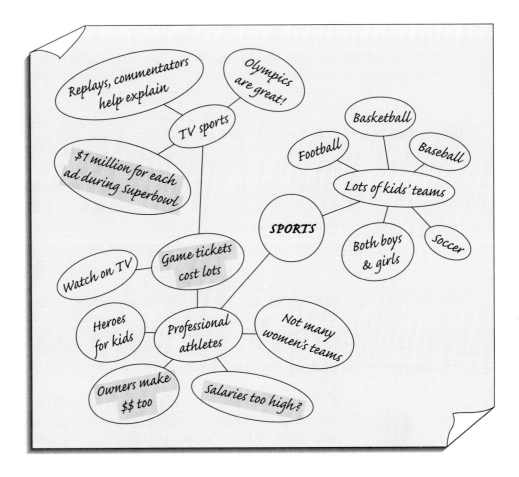

As this example shows, clustering emphasizes the connections among related ideas in the material you generate.

Exploration 3a   Defining Clustering

1. In your own words, explain clustering. _____

_____

_____

_____

_____

2. How is clustering similar to freewriting and brainstorming? How is it different? _____

_____

_____

_____

_____

Exploration 3b Analyzing a Clustering Example

1. Consider again the sample clustering on sports on page 20. Which cluster interests you most? Why? _____

_____

_____

2. What three questions would you ask the writer about the cluster you chose?

_____

_____

_____

_____

_____

Exploration 3c Practice with Clustering

1. Now you can try clustering. On a separate sheet of paper, create a clustering on one of the following subjects: *sports, humor, an ideal vacation spot.*
2. Circle, underline, or highlight the ideas or examples that interest you most.
3. On a separate sheet of paper, answer the following questions:
   a. What did you like best about clustering? What did you like least?
   b. What single idea holds the most potential for development? Write that promising idea, and add three details about it.

Challenge 3 Evaluating Clustering

1. Exchange your clustering with a classmate. On the paper you receive, put a ✓ next to the portion that you find most interesting. Return the clustering to the writer, and explain your choice. Save your own paper for later use.

2. Will you use clustering again? Explain. _____

_____

_____

_____

_____

_____

BRANCHING

Branching also visually emphasizes the connections among related ideas. Start by listing your topic on the left side of a piece of paper. Next, write ideas inspired by this topic to the right of it, and connect them to it with lines. As these new ideas lead to related thoughts and ideas, add these to the right again. Let your ideas branch out across the page, with lines showing relationships. Once you complete the branching, highlight, underline, or circle any promising ideas for later development.

Look at this branching on the subject of telephones:

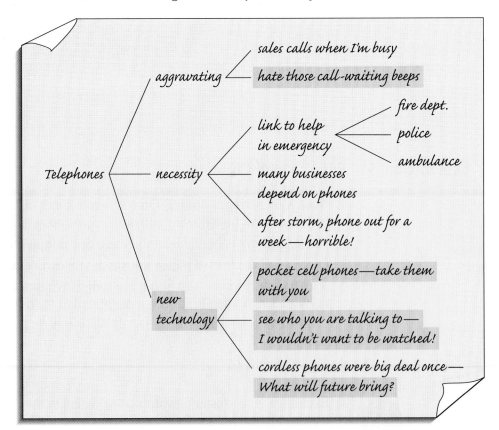

Branching leads you from one aspect of a topic to other, more specific aspects. As an added advantage, each "branch" holds an arrangement of related ideas. This focused organization allows you to concentrate on one area of your topic now and save the other areas for development later on.

Exploration 4a   Defining Branching

1. In your own words, explain branching. _____

    _____

    _____

    _____

    _____

2. How does branching differ from other prewriting techniques? _____

    _____

    _____

    _____

    _____

Exploration 4b   Analyzing a Branching Example

1. Which section of the sample branching on telephones on page 22 would

    you find easiest to develop further? Explain. _Highlighted_

    section is easiest to develop because

    all ideas are closely related

    _____

2. Which section would you find hardest to develop further? Explain.

    aggravating,

    not substantial

    _____

    _____

 **Exploration 4c** Practice with Branching

1. Now give branching a try yourself. On a separate sheet of paper, complete a branching on one of the following topics: *telephones, frustration, a holiday celebration.*

2. Highlight, circle, or underline the portions of your branching that might be further developed.

3. Answer the following questions on the same page:
   a. What did you like most about branching? What did you like least?
   b. What section in your branching holds the most promise for development? List it, and then add three details about this idea or section.

Challenge 4 Evaluating Branching

1. Exchange your branching with a classmate. On the branching you receive, put a ✓ next to the detail or example that holds the most interest for you. Return the branching to the writer, explaining your choice. Save your own branching for later use.

2. Will you use branching again? Explain. _____

_____

_____

_____

_____

 **IDEA MAPPING**

Idea mapping is a freewheeling prewriting technique that attempts to stimulate both hemispheres of your brain. When you idea map, you write words *and* create images such as icons, scribbles, sketches, and symbols. According to the theory underlying this technique, the words you include flow from the left side of your brain, the home of logic and analysis. The sketches and doodles you create arise from the right side of your brain, the home of creativity.

To try idea mapping, start anywhere on the page, writing a word or drawing a picture representing the general topic. Then let your mind range freely on the subject, recording your associations in images or words, as seems natural. After you finish, identify the ideas and images that have the most depth and meaning to you; highlight or circle them.

Here is an idea map on the subject of pollution:

The final step in idea mapping is to translate selected images into words. For example, you might translate the scribbled sketch of the smokestacks like this: "Right now, utility companies across the nation are polluting our air." You might change the image of the boom box into this form: "Last summer's Free Air outdoor concert was so loud, people could hear the music five miles away." The written version can serve as a resource for a paper.

Exploration 5a Defining Idea Mapping

1. Explain in your own words what idea mapping is. _____

   _____

   _____

   _____

   _____

2. Explain how idea mapping stimulates the hemispheres of your brain.

   _____

   _____

   _____

   _____

Exploration 5b   Analyzing an Example Idea Map

1. In the sample idea map about pollution on page 25, what image most interests or intrigues you? Why? _____

_____

_____

_____

_____

2. What words most interest or intrigue you? Why? _____

_____

_____

_____

_____

Exploration 5c   Practice with Idea Mapping

1. Look at the scene you see from your vantage point in the classroom, and create an idea map of your thoughts and feelings about the scene. Or, if you prefer, complete an idea map on one of the following subjects: *pollution, time, a first date.*

2. Highlight, circle, or underline the ideas in your map that you feel you can develop further. Remember—translate key images into words.

3. On a separate sheet of paper, answer the following questions:
   a. What do you like most about idea mapping? What do you like least?
   b. What particular image or idea on your map holds the greatest potential for later development? Write it down, and add three details about it.

Challenge 5   Evaluating an Idea Map

1. Exchange your idea map with a classmate. On the map you receive, put a ✓ next to the idea or image you'd most like to see developed. Return it to the writer with an explanation for your choice. Save your own idea map for later use.

2. Will you use idea mapping again? Explain. _____

_____

◢ MAINTAINING A JOURNAL

A **journal** is an idea book. How you set up your journal is up to you. It can be a notebook you devote entirely to this purpose or a separate section of another notebook. A computer file is also an ideal place for journal entries. Simply retrieve the file, and enter the date at the start of each new entry. (For more information about using a word processor for writing, see Appendix A on page 515.)

Several times a week, use journal writing to explore new ideas as well as familiar subjects. Use it to respond to discussions and books or articles you read for your classes. Use it to sort out your feelings about another person or an issue that is important to you.

As with any other activity, writing becomes easier the more you do it. Writing in your journal every day is one of the best ways to make writing seem as natural as talking and thinking. Make no mistake about it: This extra practice will translate into improved writing for you.

Here is a list of topics that you could write about in your journal:

music	confidence	the media	minimum wage
a perfect weekend	dreams	habits	If I were a professor, . . .
high school	deadlines	power	adult responsibilites
the class clown	getting respect	best teachers	best book I've read
security	anticipation	stress	favorite magazine
childhood	success	happiness	best movie of all time
stereotypes	fads	freedom	public transportation
the ideal climate	urban life	worst fears	a special possession
pride	ambition		

Here is a sample journal entry on the subject *time:*

Being late is a huge problem for me. Like what happened today. First I missed the bus, and the next one was ten minutes late. So of course I missed class—I hate to go in after the lecture starts. That seems rude. Went to the library to work on my history project instead and lost track of how late it was. I had to meet Gwen, and she hates to wait. By the time I got to work, I was

> *complaining to Steve that I need time off. Seems like I'm too busy and still not doing what I have to do. Get organized, he said. Easy for him to say—I wanted sympathy! Maybe a schedule is what I need—or a plan. Every night I can write what I need to do the next day, or at least the most important things. Maybe start earlier to get to school —wonder if I can find a ride instead of the bus? Would be nice to have a few minutes to do nothing for a change!*

Devote at least ten to twenty minutes to each journal writing session. After each one, reread what you've written, and highlight, circle, or underline any ideas that you might want to develop into papers in the future.

Which prewriting technique should you use? The answer, of course, depends on what works for you and makes you feel comfortable. The best way to find out is to explore each technique a few times. Then feel free to adapt or combine any of these techniques to suit your unique style.

Exploration 6a   Defining a Journal's Purpose

1. In what ways is writing in a journal similar to keeping a diary? How is it different? Explain. _____

   _____

   _____

   _____

   _____

2. How can writing in a journal help you improve your writing skills? _____

   _____

   _____

   _____

   _____

Exploration 6b   Analyzing a Sample Journal Entry

1. Take another look at the sample journal entry about time on pages 27–28. What portion of it do you find most interesting? Why? _____

_____

_____

_____

_____

_____

2. How is journal writing similar to the other prewriting techniques you've tried? How is it different? Explain. _____

_____

_____

_____

_____

_____

Exploration 6c   Practice with Journal Writing

1. Now try journal writing yourself. On a separate sheet of paper, write a page on one of the following topics: *pets, advertising techniques, televised sports.*
2. Reread your journal entry. Circle, underline, or highlight the material you would like to explore in greater detail.
3. What section holds the most promise? Why? On your paper, briefly explain.

Challenge 6   Analyzing Your Writing Rituals

1. As you worked on your journal entry, what did you notice about your writing habits or rituals? Is the time of day or the place where you write important to you? Do you need noise or silence? What do you use to write—pen, pencil, word processor? Begin your own journal by focusing on one aspect of your writing rituals, and then explore this subject for a page or so.

2. Now exchange your journal entry with a partner to compare answers.

DISCOVERING CONNECTIONS **A**

When you look at this icon, what comes to mind? Does it make you think of a letter you received recently or long ago? Who was it from? What was it about? Why do you remember it? Perhaps it makes you remember a letter you have written—or wished you had. Does it make you think instead of how communication has changed? Now that we have e-mail, does sending a letter seem old-fashioned?

Using the prewriting technique you find most comfortable, explore some of this subject's possibilities. Then highlight, underline, or circle the ideas that seem most promising. Save this material for later use.

DISCOVERING CONNECTIONS **B**

For this assignment, think of a pet peeve or annoyance you face regularly. Perhaps it's the person who takes the last cookie and leaves the empty bag in the cupboard. Perhaps it's the driver who keeps a turn signal on for several miles, or the individual who peppers every sentence with expressions such as, "You know what I mean?" Use the prewriting technique that you prefer to explore this topic. Make sure you mark the ideas that have the most potential. Save your work for later use.

RECAP

GENERATING IDEAS THROUGH PREWRITING

New terms in this chapter	Definitions
➤ prewriting	➤ the initial idea-generating stage of the writing process ➤ Prewriting techniques include freewriting, brainstorming, clustering, branching, idea mapping, and maintaining a journal.
➤ freewriting	➤ writing freely about a subject for a set period of time without stopping or worrying about correctness or completeness
➤ brainstorming	➤ focusing on a subject and listing all related ideas that come to mind
➤ clustering	➤ writing and circling an idea in the middle of the page, developing and circling related ideas around it, and drawing lines to connect related clusters of ideas

New terms in this chapter	Definitions
➤ branching	➤ listing a subject on the left side of the page, writing ideas inspired by that subject to the right, and connecting the branching ideas with lines
➤ idea mapping	➤ writing words and drawing images about a topic in a random manner across a page and then translating the images into words
➤ maintaining a journal	➤ writing several times a week in a separate notebook to explore or discover new ideas, respond to points raised in classes, or explore issues important to you

3

Composing: Creating a Draft

OVERVIEW: UNDERSTANDING COMPOSING

Chapter 2 discussed the first stage in the writing process, showing you various techniques for generating preliminary ideas. This chapter focuses on the next stage: **composing.** If prewriting is like the launch of an exciting journey, then composing is like the main leg of that journey. In this stage of the writing process, you focus your topic on a manageable point and organize your relevant ideas into a coherent message. You compose sentences that support, explain, or illustrate that topic.

At this stage, your goal is to translate your ideas into writing in a way that communicates them clearly to your reader. The following pages will discuss how to transform the prewriting material you have generated into a complete draft that meets your reader's needs. This will involve limiting your subject and identifying the strongest details, examples, and illustrations for support.

This chapter focuses on creating the two components that make up a paragraph:

➤ the topic sentence
➤ the supporting sentences

RECOGNIZING THE STRUCTURE OF A PARAGRAPH

A **paragraph** is a series of sentences that work together to develop one main idea. Paragraphs vary in length, depending on the point you are trying to make. Generally, they are between five and ten sentences long.

What is the role of the paragraph? One way of looking at paragraphs is as the *building blocks of essays*, the longer writings you will be expected to write as a college student. (For more on the essay, see Chapters 14 and 15.) As you move from paragraph to paragraph in an essay, you expand your discussion, covering your subject in detail.

For the types of paragraphs you will be practicing in the next several chapters, it's especially useful to think of paragraphs in another way: as a miniature version of an essay. Like an essay, a paragraph develops several items of support for its main idea. However, the scope of your discussion is more limited than it is in an essay.

The following figure shows how a paragraph is arranged:

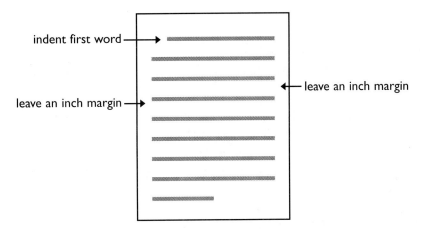

As the figure shows, the first line of a paragraph is *indented* about a half-inch on the paper. This provides a visual cue which tells the reader that a new idea is being introduced.

Now, look at this sample paragraph. Consider the structure of its content.

> *Today, the children's division of our library is much more attractive and accessible than it was when I was young.* For example, the staff has moved all the bookshelves against the wall and put a number of comfortable chairs throughout the room. Next to the librarian's desk, the staff has added three big aquariums, two hamster cages, and a glass case filled with lizards. It's Dinosaur Month now, so there are cutouts and pictures of dinosaurs hanging from the ceiling and taped to the walls. Best of all, the librarians encourage children to talk, ask questions, and browse through the books. The children are made to feel at home in the library, and that makes them more interested in reading.

ESL Note
See "Writing Paragraphs," especially the section on unity, and "Writing Essays" on pages 538–540.

The first sentence of this paragraph answers the reader's unstated question, "What's the point?" It is the **topic sentence,** the sentence stating the main idea. The other sentences are the supporting sentences. These are sometimes called the *body* of the paragraph. They elaborate on the topic through details and examples. Together, the supporting sentences communicate to the reader how the children's division of the library has changed.

Exploration 1a   Understanding Composing and Paragraphs

1. In your own words, briefly explain the differences between prewriting and composing. _____

   _____

   _____

   _____

   _____

2. What makes the topic sentence different from the other sentences in a paragraph? _____

   _____

   _____

   _____

Exploration 1b   Understanding the Structure of Paragraphs

1. The following passage runs two paragraphs together. After reading the entire passage, put a / at the point where the second paragraph begins. Then, on a separate sheet of paper, briefly explain why you feel the second paragraph begins at that point.

   It was so much fun last summer watching the traveling circus set up the big top. First, the twenty members of the circus crew spread out the yellow-and-white-striped canvas, half as long as a football field. They hammered enormous spikes into the ground and tied off one end of the tent. Next, they laid the main tent pole flat, with the center of the tent attached to the top of the 35-foot post. Once this was set, they put several more spikes along each side and tied these sections off. Then came what everyone was waiting for: the elephants. The canvas seemed almost to come to life as the elephants strained to pull up the pole. The handlers quietly urged the elephants on while the crowd cheered. After five minutes of work, the pole was up, and the crowd applauded while the elephants enjoyed their reward: an extra bale of hay and a shower.

_____

_____

_____

_____

2. Below are five topic sentences. Choose two of them. On your paper, list three ideas that you would use to support each. Use a prewriting technique if necessary to help generate ideas.

   a. Consumers have to be careful to avoid telemarketing scams.
   b. An insensitive teacher can have a terrible effect on young children.
   c. The families of Alzheimer's patients often suffer more than the patients themselves.
   d. The behavior of adults at youth league games is often offensive.
   e. The public is often more honest than the media would have us believe.

Exploration 1c   Practice Writing Topic Sentences

1. Paragraphs *a, b,* and *c* lack topic sentences. Read each passage, and then, on the lines after it, write a suitable topic sentence.

   a. For example, using the tools of a word processing program, you can easily produce attractive, error-free documents and letters. With money management software, you can keep track of all your financial transactions and plan for the future. If your computer has a CD-ROM player, you can choose from hundreds of entertaining and challenging games and programs for fun and learning. Even more exciting, by using a modem in combination with your computer, you can purchase a connection to the Internet and join the Cyberworld. There you can shop for everything from software to softballs, communicate with people around the globe, and find fascinating information about any topic you can imagine. Increasingly, the personal computer is becoming a one-stop business and entertainment center in American households.

   _____

   _____

   _____

   b. Rent takes a big chunk of my pay. I have to pay $350 a month. In addition, I have to pay for my utilities: heat, lights, electricity, and telephone. That's usually $175 a month. Then, I have to pay for food. Between the groceries I buy and the few meals I eat out, food costs me $300. My school expenses are enormous, too. I receive some aid, but I'm still responsible for $1,000 per semester plus the cost of books. At the end of the month, I have about $10 left.

_____

_____

c. Many of my jobs involve cutting lawns and raking. On some jobs, I also tend gardens. This means regular watering, weeding, and fertilizing of the flower beds, and turning the mulch. I also have to dig up and reseed any problem spots in the lawns. On most days in the spring and summer, I work ten hours straight.

_____

_____

2. Choose a paragraph (five to ten sentences long) from one of the readings in Part Seven. Identify the topic sentence of the paragraph. Then briefly explain the relationship between the topic sentence and its supporting sentences. Write the page number so you can find the paragraph again easily.

_____

_____

_____

_____

Challenge 1   Analyzing and Developing Supporting Details

1. Look again at the paragraph on page 33 about the children's division of the library. Working with a partner, explain on a separate sheet of paper how the rest of the sentences in the paragraph support or explain the topic sentence.

2. Choose one of the following topics. On a separate sheet of paper, list five ideas that could support it. Try your hand at a paragraph, putting your ideas into sentence form. Save the paragraph for later use.

   a. the perfect night out
   b. a dangerous activity
   c. dieting

FOCUSING A TOPIC

Sometimes you know right away what part of a subject you want to focus on. In many cases, however, you will need to work through and evaluate your prewriting material to decide your focus. (See Chapter 2 to review prewriting techniques.)

For instance, imagine you have been asked to write about nature. The general topic has some appeal to you. You like the outdoors and feel that too many people take for granted the beauty of the United States' forests, lakes, mountains, deserts, and oceans. However, nature is far too broad a subject to cover in a paragraph. You're not sure what aspect of the subject you want to deal with. Therefore, you do some brainstorming on the subject and end up with this:

> camping trips every summer
>
> swimming in Cosmo's Lake
>
> day trips hiking
>
> pollution, ruining environment
>
> that landfill outside of the city, ruining water
>
> smell is awful
>
> trash all over the city—really ugly mess
>
> my trip to the desert—so quiet and lonely
>
> cactuses and weird rock formations
>
> miles and miles of open road with no gas stations, etc.—
>
> scary
>
> rain forest—check notes from environment class!!
>
> destruction of one species of plant or animal a day
>
> reason for destruction—economic
>
> land only good for one or two years of farming
>
> affects weather in the rest of the world
>
> what cures are we missing out on—herbs, etc.
>
> zoos
>
> try to seem more natural
>
> elephants and lions in Regional Zoo given room to roam
>
> new plains section

As the highlighted areas show, the most promising material concerns the rain forest. Now you have a specific area to focus on: *the destruction of the rain forest.*

This area interests you, and you have things to say about it. Your concern now should be to *limit* your subject, or restrict its scope, enough that it can be covered well in a paragraph. In one paragraph, you could not fully explore the destruction of the rain forest. However, you could explore some of the effects of its destruction. Now you have limited your topic enough.

Exploration 2a   Understanding Topic Focus

1. What steps should you follow if you don't immediately know the specific

    idea you want to write about? _____

    _____

    _____

    _____

2. How do you select the prewriting details that you should focus on through

    the rest of the writing process? _____

    _____

    _____

    _____

Exploration 2b   Practice with Focusing a Topic

Select another area from the brainstorming on nature on page 37—one that interests you and could be developed. On the following lines, list this topic possibility. If it is too broad, narrow it to a subcategory that can be covered in a paragraph.

_____

_____

_____

_____

Challenge 2   Developing Your Own Limited Topic

Choose a prewriting technique and generate ideas for the topic *greeting cards.* Select the idea in your prewriting that interests you most. Then evaluate whether you can cover this subject in one paragraph. Add subcategories to the idea until you have limited the scope of your subject appropriately for a paragraph. Save this work for later use.

➤ WRITING A CLEAR, SPECIFIC TOPIC SENTENCE

After you limit, or focus, your subject, the next step is to develop a topic sentence that expresses your specific focus. Writers often place the topic sentence first in a paragraph. That way, readers know immediately what the paragraph will be about and in what direction it is heading. This is a good pattern to follow as you begin to develop your writing skills. Don't be surprised, though, if you occasionally find that the topic sentence fits better elsewhere in the paragraph, perhaps at the end or in the middle.

A typical topic sentence accomplishes two things: (1) it states the topic clearly, and (2) it suggests the direction or tone of the paragraph, often by revealing the writer's attitude toward it. Look again at the topic sentence from the paragraph about the children's library:

> **topic**   **writer's attitude or reaction**
> Today, *the children's division of our library* is *much more attractive and accessible than it was when I was young.*

The topic is the children's division of the library, and the writer's attitude or reaction expresses positive ways it has changed.

As this example shows, an effective topic sentence is more than a simple announcement of your intent. Never write "I am going to write about . . . " or "This paragraph will deal with . . . ." Instead, *directly* express the specific point you want to make about your subject.

An effective topic sentence is also clear and specific. Consider this version of the topic sentence about the children's library:

> **Weak**
> Today, the children's division of our library is very different.

This topic sentence is too vague to communicate the main point effectively. It suggests that the library has changed, but it doesn't indicate in what way things have changed or whether those changes are good or bad.

Now compare that weak version with the effective version, presented again here:

> **Clear and specific**
> Today, the children's division of our library is much more attractive and accessible than it was when I was young.

As you can see, this version is effective because it is clear and specific. It identifies the ways that the library has changed and indicates that those changes have been positive.

Your topic sentence is developed from your chosen prewriting details. It must encompass them and at the same time provide a direction for the paragraph. For example, look at the highlighted material in the brainstorming on nature (page 37). It relates to the destruction of the Brazilian rain forest. The details listed all relate to the harmful effects of this destruction: on world climate, on the rain forest land itself, and on many species of organisms. If you determine your attitude or reaction to this topic, you will be ready to formulate a topic sentence:

> **topic**   **attitude or reaction**
> *The destruction of the Brazilian rain forest has serious consequences for the whole world.*

This topic sentence is effective because it is clear and specific and because it answers the reader's implied question, "What's the point?"

Exploration 3a   Understanding the Topic Sentence

1. With most paragraphs, where will you place the topic sentence? Why?

   One of the most valuable things humanity has ever had is money, and through the centuries people's work was appraised by particular

2. In your own words, briefly explain the difference between a vague topic sentence and a clear, specific topic sentence. *amount of it.*

   Nowadays, money is driving force and power in the world; moreover, it is integral part and necessary thing in people's lives.

Exploration 3b   Analyzing and Revising Topic Sentences

1. In each of the following topic sentences, circle the topic, and underline the writer's attitude or reaction to it. Study the example first.

   Example   The (many costs of owning a car) make automobile ownership

   a luxury some students cannot afford.

a. Most people don't spend enough time planning for their future.

b. Poor highway design is a major reason for auto accidents.

c. Both major political parties in the United States seem out of touch with the average person.

d. Not all top high school athletes are poor students.

e. The fierce winter weather is particularly hard on the poor and elderly.

2. The following topic sentences are too general and vague. Working with a partner, rewrite them on the lines provided, making sure they clearly focus on a specific topic and express a definite attitude.

a. I enjoy physical activities.

Money is valuable for people because it

b. Being laid off is bad.

doesn't fall out of the sky, and they have to

c. Computers are amazing.

work most of their life to have it.

Exploration 3c   Evaluating Topic Sentences

1. Here are several potential topic sentences. Working with a partner, label the effective topic sentences with an *E* and the weak ones with a *W*.

_E_ a. Working in a nursing home has helped me learn the true meaning of dignity.

_W_ b. Housebreaking animals is necessary.

_W_ c. The best decision my uncle ever made was to get his general equivalency diploma (GED).

_E_ d. Oil spills are environmental nightmares that affect the world for years.

_W_ e. Many of today's movies are bad.

2. With the same partner, select one of the topic sentences that you identified as weak.

a. On a separate sheet of paper, rewrite it. Be sure it focuses clearly on a *specific* topic and expresses a definite reaction.

b. On the same paper, develop at least three supporting sentences for this topic sentence.

Challenge 3 Developing a Topic Sentence from Your Prewriting

1. In Challenge 2 (pages 38–39), you identified the most promising idea in a prewriting on greeting cards and focused it as a topic. Now, on a separate sheet of paper, write a draft topic sentence based on this limited topic.

2. On your paper, list at least three ideas that you could use as support for your topic sentence.

➤ PROVIDING THE BEST SUPPORT FOR THE TOPIC SENTENCE

After you have developed a clear, specific topic sentence, you need to develop additional sentences that will support, illustrate, or explain it. You can draw much of your raw material from the related prewriting ideas.

Imagine that you have developed the following freewriting on the subject of confidence:

confidence?? what I wish I had more of sometimes —always seem to feel that I can't do some things, like sports, pressure —tests, too, especially on essay tests—couldn't answer two questions on my sociology test yesterday, but I knew the answers, I freeze up, maybe test anxiety? always sick the night before even quizzes, just like before my meet last week actors, musicians must need a lot of confidence, teachers must have it too—they have to talk in front of people every day. For me that's the worst thing, thought I was going to throw up in speech class the other day when I had to give a 3-minute talk, I felt like I do when I'm at the foul line waiting to shoot with everyone looking at me I don't have confidence. Eileen—she has plenty of confidence, doesn't seem afraid of anything. Dating, that's another thing I don't have confidence in. I'm afraid people won't like me, I'm always sick before dates, just like before last week's math quiz, I was so afraid I was going to flunk that I couldn't concentrate, I made four really stupid mistakes and got a D—what a headache I always get after, too. Wish I could figure out the magic formula for confidence

From the highlighted portions, it's easy to see a main idea: A lack of self-confidence negatively affects your life. Here's a topic sentence that expresses this idea:

> My lack of self-confidence is keeping me from being as successful as I could be.

With your main idea clearly stated, you can look back at your prewriting with a selective eye. Which details and examples supply the best support for the topic sentence? First, group the highlighted areas into categories:

1. *sports examples:*
   sports, pressure
   just like before my meet last week
   I felt like I do when I'm at the foul line waiting to shoot with every-
      one looking at me
2. *school examples:*
   especially on essay tests—couldn't answer two questions on my
      sociology test yesterday, but I knew the answers, I freeze up
   test anxiety? always sick the night before even quizzes
   thought I was going to throw up in speech class the other day when
      I had to give a 3-minute talk
   just like before last week's math quiz, I was so afraid I was going to
      flunk that I couldn't concentrate. I made four really stupid mistakes
      and got a D
   what a headache I always get after, too
3. *social life examples:*
   Dating, that's another thing I don't have confidence in
   I'm afraid people won't like me, I'm always sick before dates

All these groups of information offer support for the idea that a lack of self-confidence is having a negative impact on your life. Which group offers the strongest and most complete support?

You probably chose the school examples, which are the most specific and detailed. If you were writing an essay instead of a single paragraph, you could use the other groups of examples to develop additional paragraphs. For a single paragraph, these school examples are probably the best choice.

Exploration 4a   Understanding How to Build Support for a Topic Sentence

1. How can grouping your prewriting ideas help you decide which details and
   examples to include in your paragraph? _Some times, people_
   can face the problem has to spend money.
   Some of the people spend money in casinos
   wasting it on games of chance, some of

2. Not all the ideas you develop during prewriting can be used in any one paragraph. What purpose can the other ideas serve? _____

then put their money on a savings account, and some of them think how to spend money more wisely to benefit from it.

Exploration 4b   Analyzing the Relationship between Topic Sentence and Body

1. Choose a paragraph of five to ten sentences from a reading in Part Seven, and identify its topic sentence.
2. On the lines that follow, explain the connection between this topic sentence and its supporting sentences. (Write the page number for the paragraph so you can locate it again easily.)

First of all, using some of this money I could cover my debts. For example I bought the new com. and furn., and during next 2 years

---

Exploration 4c   Developing an Effective Topic Sentence

1. Here is a list of details from an idea map on credit card purchases:

birthday presents	new coat
shoes	books
CDs	stereo equipment
graduation gifts	pants

   Working with a partner, arrange the details in related categories on a separate sheet of paper. Add more specific details as you wish.
2. After you and your partner identify the grouping with the most potential for development, pinpoint the topic they cover, and write a clear, specific topic sentence.

Challenge 4   Evaluating a Topic Sentence and Grouping Details

1. Exchange the topic sentence you drafted in Challenge 3 (page 42) with a partner. Check the topic sentence you receive to make sure it is clear and specific. Return the topic sentence and any suggestions for changes to the writer. Then make any necessary changes to your own topic sentence.

2. Using the example on confidence on page 43 to guide you, group the ideas from the prewriting you completed for Discovering Connections A or B at the end of Chapter 2 (page 30). Save this work for later use.

▶ **D**ECIDING ON THE MOST EFFECTIVE ARRANGEMENT

Once you select the details and examples that will best support your topic sentence, you must arrange them in a logical, effective order. Working with your prewriting material, you may find it helpful to divide your established, broad categories into smaller categories and consider their order. Your aim is to understand the relationships of the ideas to one another.

Here is the most promising material from the freewriting on confidence arranged into two groups:

Results in class from lack of confidence

- couldn't answer two questions on my sociology test yesterday, but I knew the answers
- just like before last week's math quiz, I was so afraid I was going to flunk that I couldn't concentrate. I made four really stupid mistakes and got a D

Physical effects from lack of confidence

- I freeze up
- always sick the night before even quizzes
- thought I was going to throw up in speech class the other day when I had to give a 3-minute talk
- what a headache I always get after, too

Now consider the effects of the order in which these details might be presented in an actual paragraph.

ESL Note

See "Writing Paragraphs" on pages 538–539.

In the diagram, the examples concerning the effects on schoolwork appear first, followed by the examples dealing with the effects on health. In paragraphs that discuss problems and their consequences, details are often presented in order of increasing importance, with the least important details first. Notice that the examples dealing with poor classroom performance are more specific. If they were presented last, the paragraph would build toward clearer, stronger supporting details. It would also emphasize academic problems most. Your decisions about how to order the details in a paragraph should depend on which kind of emphasis best suits your topic sentence. In any case, using this kind of diagram helps you to sort your ideas and to begin thinking about how to organize them.

Exploration 5a   Observing the Importance of Order in a Paragraph

1. Once you have grouped the ideas and examples in your prewriting, what should you do next? Why? _to pay for my education._
this very is more particu practical and beneficial. Our life change so fast, meanwhile, science and technologies develop rapidly, and this situation requires

2. How will arranging your supporting details in a logical order make your paragraph more effective? _deep and complete knowleges._
Most likely, only well educated person will have a chance to get a job wich involve with hes tech. and fin. pros. Therefore, speaking of money for my education is the appropriate way because good educ.

Exploration 5b   Identifying Strong Supporting Details

1. Take another look at the groups of information about lack of self-confidence in the diagram on page 45. Which group would you find easier to develop? Why? _is the key to success fate._

2. Of all the details listed, which do you think is the strongest? Why? _____
Wedding should be confortt

I'm sure, with 10.000 $, I could make my wp a. h.m are unforgettable, joyfal, and pleasant memories.

Exploration 5c   Practice in Arranging Supporting Details in Your Writing

1. Choose one of the groupings of details you created on credit card purchases in Exploration 4c (page 44). On a separate sheet of paper, arrange this list in an order you could use to support the following topic sentence: *Credit cards make it easy to spend more than you really want to.*

2. Exchange your list with a partner.
   a. On the list you receive, evaluate the order of the details and make any suggestions you think would help the writer develop a better paragraph. Return the list to the writer.
   b. After considering your reader's comments, make any changes you feel are necessary. Put this list aside for later use.

Challenge 5   Ordering Your Supporting Ideas

1. On a separate sheet of paper, arrange the prewriting information you grouped in exercise 2 in Challenge 4 (page 45) into ordered subcategories. Save this work for later use.

2. Develop one of the details from one of the categories into a supporting sentence. Write it on your paper.

▶ *M*AKING YOUR MATERIAL READER CENTERED

In order for your reader to understand your ideas, you must present them as **reader-centered writing.** In other words, you must express those ideas fully, in complete sentences, so that the average reader will understand them.

Prewriting ideas are generally not expressed completely or in correct sentence form. They are expressed as **writer-centered writing,** that is, in a raw, unpolished form that makes sense to you but not necessarily to another person.

To understand the difference between writer-centered and reader-centered material, think of your notes for one of your classes. In a psychology class, for example, you might have written the following notation:

Writer-centered

Prsnalty types/Jung—way you behave?

These words have a specific meaning to you because you were in class when your instructor presented the material, and you participated in the class discussion that followed. However, a reader who was not in that class might have trouble interpreting your notes.

Now, look at this reader-centered version of the same material:

Reader-centered

Carl Jung's theories about personality types raise some questions about the way we behave.

As you can see, this version expresses the ideas more thoroughly in complete sentence form. With the ideas spelled out this way, even a reader unfamiliar with psychology can understand what the note actually means.

Exploration 6a   Understanding Writer-Centered and Reader-Centered Writing

1. In your own words, briefly explain the difference between writer-centered and reader-centered information. _____

   In conclusion, I'd say that people should understand that money itself is simple pieces of paper and met. What

2. How do you change writer-centered material into reader-centered information? *really makes a different is the way of making a profit. You can't eat or wear money. Some people are trying to save more money, stocking it under the mattress & making saving accounts in the bank. But I*

Exploration 6b   Practice in Creating Reader-Centered Sentences

1. Make a copy of a page of notes you took for another class. Exchange this copy with a partner. On a separate sheet of paper, try to change the writer-centered notes you receive to reader-centered sentences.
2. Return the notes and your reader-centered version to the writer. Review the papers returned to you and circle any detail that your reader failed to understand. Explain what you meant to communicate.

Challenge 6   Evaluating Reader-Centered Sentences

1. Return to the material you developed in Challenge 4 (page 44) and Challenge 5 (page 47). On a separate sheet of paper, transform all of your writer-centered details into reader-centered sentences.

2. Exchange your reader-centered sentences with a partner. On the page you receive, put a + next to each sentence that is reader centered and a ✓ next to any sentence that is still writer centered. Return the page to the writer, and suggest a way to improve the sentences marked with a ✓. Save your own work for later use.

USING A READER EVALUATION CHECKLIST

The secret to success in writing is to meet the needs of your reader. In most cases, you can assume that your reader knows a little bit about many subjects but not necessarily a great deal about most subjects. Using a **reader evaluation checklist** is one way to make sure that your supporting information meets the needs of your reader.

To use the reader evaluation checklist below, simply insert the name of your topic in the blanks, and then write your answers to the questions.

Reader Evaluation Checklist

1. What does the average reader need to know about _____?
2. What does the average reader already know about _____?
3. What information would help the average person better understand _____?
4. What did I find the hardest to understand about _____ at first?
5. What helped me to figure out _____?
6. What's the best example or explanation I can give the average person about _____?

As you answer these questions, you will also focus on the examples or explanations that your reader will need to see your point.

Exploration 7a   Understanding Your Reader's Needs

1. In your own words, explain how much specialized knowledge you can expect your reader to possess about most topics. _____

*think that money exists for spending.
There are many ways to spend money
wisely to get profit, joy, and happiness in*

2. Briefly explain how using the reader evaluation checklist can help you

our life, so we should choos right ones.

meet the needs of your reader. _____

_____

_____

_____

Exploration 7b   Analyzing Your Readers' Needs

1. On the lines below, list three subjects that you know a great deal about and then three subjects that you wish you knew more about.

   I know a great deal about . . .   *I wish I knew more about . . .*

   a. _____   a. _____

   b. _____   b. _____

   c. _____   c. _____

2. Choose one item from each column in number 1, and then answer the following questions.

   a. What details would help you communicate to a reader what you know

      about the subject you understand well? _____

      _____

      _____

      _____

   b. What details would help you understand more about the subject you

      want to explore? _____

      _____

      _____

      _____

Exploration 7c   Evaluating How Well a Paragraph Meets Readers' Needs

1. Using the reader evaluation checklist on page 49, read and assess the following paragraph. Use the questions below the paragraph as guidelines.

   Coffee bars are gaining in popularity in cities and towns throughout the country. The trend began a while ago. The shops serve several varieties of coffee and food, and they offer a pleasant atmosphere. Some coffee bars have begun to include various activities to make patrons feel comfortable as they enjoy their favorite brand of coffee.

   a. Did the writer do a good job of providing information the average reader might not know?
   b. What did the writer assume the average reader *did* know?
   c. Are there areas on which the writer still needs to focus?

2. On a separate sheet of paper, write to the writer of the paragraph, suggesting ways to improve this paragraph.

Challenge 7   Rewriting a Paragraph to Meet Readers' Needs

1. Exchange the note you wrote to the writer in Exploration 7c with a partner. Using the comments to guide you, rewrite the paragraph on a separate sheet of paper.

2. Exchange your rewritten paragraph with a partner. Use the reader evaluation checklist on page 49 to assess the paragraph you receive. Make a note next to any point that still needs work, and return the paragraph to the writer.

▶ **D**EVELOPING A COMPLETE DRAFT

ESL Note
See "Writing Essays" on pages 539–540.

The final step in the composing stage of writing is developing a **complete draft.** This draft combines your topic sentence with selected reader-centered examples and details in the order you have chosen.

As you develop this initial version, remember that it doesn't have to be perfect. (The next chapter will show you how to revise, or refine and polish, your writing.) At this point, focus your energies on stating your ideas completely and clearly.

You should make your draft look clean and readable, too. If you have access to a word processor, learn how to use it. You'll find the flexibility of handling a computer file especially helpful in making changes as you revise. Whether you use a word processor or a typewriter, make sure to double-space to leave room to make corrections and additions. If you write by hand, write on every other line. Either way, you'll have room to make corrections and additions as you revise your work.

Here's a first draft of a paragraph on the effects of lack of self-confidence, based on the freewriting on page 42. Notice the addition to the topic sentence. The added words (underlined) reflect the specific focus of the paragraph:

> *My lack of self-confidence is keeping me from being as successful as I could be, <u>especially in school</u>* . Most of the time, I am so afraid that I'm not going to do well on a test or a quiz that I'm physically sick the night before. Even though I have studied for hours, I still can't relax. It's as if

my lack of self-confidence causes me to freeze up. After every test, I get a terrible headache, too. Last Wednesday I was so afraid I would mess up a simple three-minute presentation in speech class that I almost threw up. This lack of confidence has already affected my grades. On my sociology test yesterday, I couldn't complete two of the questions, even though I knew the answers. I was just too nervous. The same thing happened to me in math last week. I was so afraid I was going to flunk that I couldn't concentrate. As a result, I made four silly errors and got a D. I hope I can find a way to be more confident before I end up in real academic trouble.

As you can see, the writer-centered prewriting material has all been changed into reader-centered supporting sentences. They have been effectively arranged, as suggested on page 45, so that general examples lead to more specific ones, and academic results are emphasized (as the topic sentence suggests).

This draft can certainly be improved, but that is why we revise. Before you can revise, you need a solid beginning, and that's exactly what this paragraph represents.

Exploration 8a   Understanding the First-Draft Stage

1. What do you do in the final step of the composing stage of writing?_____

_____

_____

_____

2. What advantage is there in double-spacing your work? _____

_____

_____

_____

Exploration 8b   Analyzing a First Draft

1. Which aspect of the composing stage have you found easiest? Which is most difficult for you? Explain. _____

_____

_____

_____

_____

2. On the following lines, explain what you like most about the first draft paragraph on self-confidence. What do you think should be changed? _____

_____

_____

_____

_____

Exploration 8c   Evaluating a First Draft

1. Reread the model paragraph on self-confidence (pages 51–52). Which of the supporting sentences do you think is most effective? Why? _____

_____

_____

_____

2. On the following lines, list any examples in this first draft that need improvement. _____

_____

_____

_____

Challenge 8   Creating a First Draft

1. Through several Challenges in this chapter, you have been developing your prewriting from Discovering Connections A or B in Chapter 2 (page 30). Now write a clear, specific topic sentence for the subject you have developed from this prewriting. Let the model paragraph on self-confidence on pages 51–52 serve as a guide.

2. Identify your best details from the reader-centered sentences you developed in Challenge 6 (pages 48–49), and turn them into your supporting sentences for a first draft. Save your draft for later use.

DISCOVERING CONNECTIONS A

When you look at this icon, what ideas does it inspire? Does it make you think of something you need to throw away? Something you threw away that you now wish you had saved? What was it? Why do you feel this way? How about the expression, "One person's trash is another person's treasure"? Do people sometimes overlook the value in something they discard? Does the symbol instead make you think of society's wasteful habits or the mountains of trash that cities and towns accumulate every day?

For this assignment, focus on the icon, prewrite, choose and focus a topic, and compose a draft paragraph (at least five to ten sentences long). Follow the process outlined in this chapter, making sure that your writing is reader centered.

DISCOVERING CONNECTIONS B

For this assignment, focus on an influential individual that you know. Who is it? How did you meet this person? In what ways has this individual influenced you in the past? How does this individual influence you now? Is the influence positive or negative? After you prewrite, compose a paragraph (at least five to ten sentences long), following the steps outlined in this chapter. Concentrate on making your paragraph reader centered.

RECAP

COMPOSING: CREATING A DRAFT

New terms in this chapter	Definitions
➤ composing	➤ the stage of writing during which you focus on a topic and provide supporting ideas drawn from your prewriting material
➤ paragraph	➤ a series of sentences that work together to develop one main idea

New terms in this chapter	Definitions
➤ topic sentence	➤ the sentence stating the main idea, or topic, of a paragraph and setting the tone or direction for the writing ➤ The topic sentence expresses the topic, limits it to a manageable size, and usually reveals the writer's attitude or reaction to the topic. *Example* **topic** The new biography of former President Carter is **attitude or reaction** fascinating reading.
➤ reader-centered writing	➤ ideas expressed thoroughly and in complete sentence form so that they make sense to the reader
➤ writer-centered writing	➤ raw, unpolished ideas that provide enough clues to make sense to the writer but not necessarily to the reader
➤ reader evaluation checklist	➤ series of questions designed to help writers ensure that their supporting information meets their readers' needs
➤ complete draft	➤ the first complete version of a piece of writing, including a clear, specific topic sentence plus supporting sentences

The Process of Composing a Draft

Focus a topic.

↓   ↑

Create a **topic sentence.**

↓   ↑

Organize **prewriting ideas** and **examples.**

↓   ↑

Develop **supporting sentences.**

Refining and Polishing Your Draft

OVERVIEW: UNDERSTANDING THE REVISING STAGE

You can always be sure of one truth about writing: You won't write a masterpiece on the first try. The best writing you can do takes thought, time, and patience. A good first draft is only the beginning. Once you have completed a solid draft, you must *revise,* or refine and polish, your draft. This chapter explains how to revise a paragraph and turn something good into something even better.

Revising actually involves three interrelated steps: reassessing, redrafting, and editing. **Reassessing** means checking for *unity, coherence,* and *effective language.* It also means seeking feedback from an objective reader. **Redrafting** means rewriting to eliminate any problem spots and add needed material. You may need to reassess and redraft more than once in order to achieve the results you want. **Editing** means proofreading your final draft to eliminate any remaining errors. It represents the last leg of your writing odyssey.

This chapter outlines the way to refine and polish your first draft until it represents your best. You will learn that revising involves

➤ reassessing
➤ redrafting
➤ editing

REASSESSING: RESEEING YOUR WORK

By the time you complete a draft, you will probably feel that you've taken your paragraph as far as you can. Let a little time pass though, and you will undoubtedly find areas that still need work. Putting your initial draft away for a day or two will create a distance and enable you to *resee* your paragraph. When you look at it again with a fresh eye, you'll be better able to reassess it for unity, coherence, and effective language.

Maintaining Unity

Writing has **unity** when all the examples and details relate directly to the main idea. To make sure your writing is unified, eliminate any material that is not relevant to your topic.

Look at this paragraph about a fulfilling work experience:

> Last summer, I had a great experience working as a soccer coach for the day camp at a local boys and girls club. I was in charge of the indoor soccer games for the youngest group of campers, ages five to seven. Soccer is the world's most popular sport. In many countries, soccer is called football. So far, professional soccer hasn't been especially successful in the United States. During the first week of camp, I assigned the fifty kids to different teams and had practice games. They didn't really understand how to play the game, so I spent the first two weeks teaching them basic things like passing and playing defense. Then, for the rest of the summer, I was able to watch them as they improved and learned to love soccer. At the end of the summer, all the players gave me a plaque naming me "Most Valuable Coach." I never would have guessed that a simple summer job could have been so rewarding.

Which sentences are not directly connected to the writer's topic, a fulfilling experience as a soccer coach?

You probably identified the third, fourth, and fifth sentences. While these sentences are about soccer, they are irrelevant to the writer's summer experience. Once you eliminate them, the paragraph is unified.

Exploration 1a Defining the Revising Process

1. In your own words, explain the steps in revising. ———————

_____

_____

2. When you reassess a draft to see if it is unified, what are you looking for?

_____

_____

_____

Exploration 1b   Eliminating Unrelated Sentences

1. Check the following paragraph for unity. Circle any sentences that do not belong with the others.

    The city police should be investigated for the way they treated my daughter last weekend. At about 11 P.M., her car broke down near an on-ramp to the highway. The highway is very poorly lit. She put on her emergency blinkers and walked to the police station a half mile away. When she told the police what had happened, an officer asked to see her license and registration. When he saw that she was only sixteen, he arrested her for being out after the midnight curfew! Some police forces ought to do a better job of training their officers. In general, adults don't seem to realize that kids have lives, too. My daughter tried to explain that she would have been home before the curfew if her car hadn't broken down, but the officers on duty ignored her. I was out of town, so she had to spend the whole night in jail. When they released her the next morning, the police told her that she would have to pay $100 to get her car back.

2. Use the following lines to explain why the sentences you've circled do not

belong. _____

_____

_____

_____

Challenge 1   Assessing Unity in Your Writing

1. You completed a draft paragraph for Challenge 8 in Chapter 3 (page 53). Exchange that draft paragraph with a partner. Check the paper you receive for unity. Indicate for the writer any sentence that you think does not belong, and return the paragraph to the writer.
2. Check your reader's comments, and make whatever changes you feel are necessary to establish unity in your paragraph. Save your work for later use.

Providing Coherence

In order for a paragraph to communicate your ideas clearly to a reader, it must have **coherence.** Coherence is what makes a paragraph hold together. All of the paragraph's sentences should be arranged in a logical order and connected so that ideas flow smoothly.

Two elements give a piece of writing coherence: (1) transitions and (2) organization of sentences or order of ideas.

Transitions

Connecting your supporting sentences smoothly is a matter of supplying *transitions.* Writers use three techniques to relate sentences to one another.

1. Repeat key words and phrases or rename them with pronouns.
2. Substitute **synonyms,** words that have similar meanings, for key words.
3. Insert transitional expressions to connect ideas.

The repetitions and substitutions provide a thread of continuity that keeps the main idea uppermost in the reader's mind. Look at the italicized words in the following sentences.

> **Example**
>
> The *real estate developer* tried to convince the *city planning board* to allow *her* company to build homes around the *city reservoir.* The *board members* refused, saying that the danger of polluting the *water supply* was too great a risk.

In the first sentence, *her* renames the real estate developer. In the second sentence, *board members* is substituted for the *city planning board* named in the first sentence. At the same time, the synonym *water supply* is used in the second sentence to refer back to *city reservoir* in the first sentence.

Perhaps the most useful technique for showing the relationships among sentences is adding **transitional expressions** to connect ideas. Here is a listing of common transitional expressions:

> ### *Common Transitional Expressions to Illustrate or to Show Cause and Effect*
>
> | | | | |
> |---|---|---|---|
> | accordingly | consequently | indeed | particularly |
> | after all | for example | in fact | specifically |
> | as a result | for instance | of course | therefore |
> | because | for one thing | overall | thus |

Example

The extra police officers on the street haven't reduced the crime rate downtown. *In fact,* recent statistics show that things are now worse than they were a year ago.

> ### *Common Transitional Expressions to Add, Restate, or Emphasize*
>
> | | | | |
> |---|---|---|---|
> | again | finally | in conclusion | on the whole |
> | also | first (second, last, etc.) | in other words | too |
> | and | further | moreover | to sum up |
> | besides | in addition | next | |

Example

After the recent subway accident, federal investigators inspected all signal lights along the track. *In addition,* all train operators were forced to take tests for drug and alcohol use.

> ### *Common Transitional Expressions to Show Time or Place*
>
> | | | | | |
> |---|---|---|---|---|
> | above | beyond | lately | soon | until |
> | after | currently | now | then | when |
> | as soon as | earlier | once | there | whenever |
> | before | here | presently | to the left (or right) | where |
> | below | immediately | since | under | |

Example

The crowd sat quietly *until* the speaker walked on stage.

Common Transitional Expressions to Compare or to Contrast

although	despite	in the same way	similarly
and	even though	likewise	still
as	however	nevertheless	though
both (neither)	in contrast	on the other hand	whereas
but	in spite of	regardless	yet

Example

My friend Isaac can play the piano beautifully; *yet* he can't read a note of music.

Look again at the italicized transitional words in the example sentences above. As you can see, these words signal the connections between ideas. They are linking devices.

Consider the italicized and underlined words in the following paragraph:

> *Computerized listings of holdings* have made college libraries everywhere more accessible to *students*. The unwieldy card catalog has <u>now</u> been replaced with electronic files, and other valuable reference tools are on CD-ROM databases. <u>Because of</u> *these innovations, people* find it easier to locate the information *they* need *to write research papers.* <u>As a result</u>, *students* are less intimidated by the thought of *doing this kind of library work.*

As you can see, transition holds this paragraph together. For example, *these innovations* renames *electronic files* and *CD-ROM databases,* so it functions as a transition. *People* and *they* rename *students,* and *doing this kind of library work* refers back to *to write research papers.* In addition, <u>now</u>, <u>because of</u>, and <u>as a result</u> are transitional expressions; <u>now</u> relates two ideas in time, and <u>because of</u> and <u>as a result</u> signal a cause and effect relationship between ideas.

Exploration 2a   Understanding Coherence

1. What do you check for when you reassess your writing for coherence?

_____

_____

_____

_____

2. What techniques can you use to connect your sentences smoothly?_____

_____

_____

_____

Exploration 2b   Identifying Transitions

1. Return to the paragraph on a fulfilling work experience (page 57). Working with a partner, underline its transitional expressions, and circle any synonyms or renaming words.

2. Choose one of the transitional expressions you underlined, and, on the following lines, briefly explain how it connects ideas in the paragraph._____

_____

_____

_____

Exploration 2c   Using Transitions in Your Writing

1. Write a paragraph of at least five sentences about your favorite way to relax. Include several of the transitional expressions from one of the lists on pages 60–61.

2. Choose one of the sentences you have just written. On the lines below, briefly explain how its transition provides connection within the sentence or between sentences.

_____

_____

_____

Challenge 2   Evaluating Use of Transitions

1. Exchange the draft paragraph you completed in Challenge 8 of Chapter 3 (page 53) with a partner. Check the paper you receive for adequate use of transitions. Put a ✓ at any point where you feel a transition is needed, and return the paragraph to the writer.

2. Check your reader's comments, and make whatever changes you feel are necessary to connect your paragraph's sentences smoothly.

Organizing Sentences Effectively

The second element of coherence is organization. The order in which you present your ideas can affect how well your reader is able to see your point. Therefore, when you reassess, you should make sure your ideas are effectively arranged. Three common organizational plans for writing are *chronological order, spatial order,* and *emphatic order.*

Using Chronological Order Whenever you recall a series of events in the sequence in which they occurred, you use **chronological order,** or time order. In some cases, you deliberately break up chronological order by using a *flashback,* an episode presented out of sequence to help emphasize or explain some point.

Look at this paragraph about a border crossing from Mexico to the United States:

> Before I came to the place where I would cross the Rio Grande, I had to travel a long distance from our small village. When I arrived with my brother in a dirty border town, everyone was living in shacks and tents. I was frightened by the strange sounds, smells, and tough men there. My brother sewed his money in the cuff of his pants, and we found a safe place to wait for two days. Then our "coyote," the man who would take us across, came to get us in the middle of the night. We spoke only in whispers while he led us down to the edge of the water. I could see the dim shadows of other people hoping to cross, waiting huddled at the edge until their coyotes gave them a signal. Then our man motioned to us, and my breath fell away. He picked me up on his back and waded across the Rio Grande. After he put me down, I crouched and waited for my brother. I saw the coyote hoist him on his back and make his way across the river. When he arrived safely, I cried. We made our way to a ditch on the side of the road. We spent the rest of the night there, and then we headed off down the road to begin the search for my uncle.

In this paragraph, events are presented in the order in which they occur. Chronological order and transitional words help the reader keep the events straight. *Before* she reached the border town, the writer had to travel a long way. *When* she arrived with her brother, she was frightened. *Then* the coyote came to bring them to the water. *Then* he motioned and she lost her breath. *After* he put her down, and *when* her brother arrived, they slept in a ditch and *then* headed down the road.

Exploration 3a Understanding Order in Paragraphs

1. In your own words, briefly explain how a clear, logical ordering of ideas can

   improve your writing. _____

_____

_____

_____

2. On the following lines, briefly explain chronological order. _____

_____

_____

_____

Exploration 3b   Considering the Uses of Chronological Order

1. List three types of subjects that would be best organized in chronological

   order—for example, a first night at a new job. _____

   _____

   _____

   _____

2. Choose one of the subjects you listed in number 1 and, on the following

   lines, list at least three steps in that sequence of events. _____

   _____

   _____

   _____

Exploration 3c   Using Chronological Order in Your Writing

1. Working with a partner, arrange the following steps in the formation of a
   thunderstorm in chronological order. Number them *1, 2, 3,* and so forth.

   _____ Precipitation starts, causing updrafts and downdrafts within the
   cloud.

   _____ A cold air mass enters an area of warm air, pushing up the warm air.

   _____ The condensation causes a cloud to begin forming and heat to be
   released into the atmosphere.

   _____ The heat pushes the air higher yet, releasing more heat, condensing
   more water vapor so that the cloud grows.

_____ The violent up-and-down motion within the thunderhead forms storm cells.

_____ As the cloud grows, windspeed increases, forming an anvil-shaped cumulus cloud called a thunderhead.

_____ The thunderstorm is now mature; thunder, lightning, even hail, accompany heavy rains.

_____ The rising warm air reaches dew point and water condenses from the surrounding air.

2. On a separate sheet of paper, work with your partner to turn the steps above into a paragraph. Combine some sentences if you'd like. Make sure to provide transitions to connect ideas. Draw from the lists of transitional words on pages 60–61.

Challenge 3 **Evaluating the Use of Chronological Order**

1. Exchange the draft paragraph you worked on for Challenge 2 (page 62) with a partner. If chronological order has been used in the paper you receive, make sure the sequence is clear. Add any suggestions for your reader, and return the paper.

2. After considering your reader's comments, make whatever changes you think are necessary. Save your work for later use.

Using Spatial Order   When you need to explain where one thing exists in relation to other objects, you use **spatial order.** This method of arrangement is often used in description to help the reader visualize a scene. Objects, people, or places are viewed from top to bottom, left to right, near to far, in an orderly, natural way. Spatial order is discussed further in Chapters 6 (page 96) and 15 (page 200).

Look at this paragraph about the scene of a terrible accident:

> The worst accident I ever saw involved a school bus and several other vehicles. A small pickup truck had been traveling on one of the busier streets in the city, and a school bus was right behind the truck. Suddenly, a van in front of the truck came to a complete stop. With brakes squealing, the truck crashed into the back of the van. The driver of the bus couldn't avoid the truck, so the bus ended up on top of it. As a result of the impact, the passenger in the truck was thrown from the vehicle into the middle of the road. The driver of the truck was trapped inside the cab, which was wedged under the front of the bus. The scene was so horrible that it gave me nightmares for weeks.

In this paragraph, spatial order is used first to help you visualize where each vehicle is before the accident. A van is *in front of* the truck; a bus is *right behind* the truck. Then, through spatial order, the writer pictures the accident scene. The truck slams *into the back of* the van; the bus ends up *on top of* the truck, which is *wedged under the front* of the bus. The truck's passenger is thrown *into the middle of the road,* while the driver is trapped *inside the cab* of the truck. This organizational plan makes it clear what happened, why it happened, and what resulted.

Exploration 4a   Defining Spatial Order

Briefly explain spatial order.

_____

_____

_____

_____

Exploration 4b   Analyzing Spatial Order in a Paragraph

1. Read the following paragraph. Then, on the lines below it, explain the order in which the parts of the suit have been described.

The man's Armani suit gave graphic evidence of how difficult his ordeal in the woods had been. The jacket's left shoulder bore a long raveling pull, as though a thorny branch had wrestled with it. The right sleeve was torn almost completely off, and both cuffs were frayed and dirty. A large, purple stain had spread across the midsection of the vest. The pants legs of the suit, from the knees down, were so riddled with tears and holes that they looked shredded. The whole outfit could have been framed and enshrined in the hall of unlikely heroic survivals.

_____

_____

_____

_____

_____

2. Working with a partner, select transitional expressions that specify location to insert in the paragraph on page 66. Insert them in the space between lines where they fit best. Compare your work with that of another team, and discuss which versions work best.

Exploration 4c　Using and Evaluating Spatial Order Cues

1. Use spatial order to give a partner a tour of a room in your home. As you speak, have your partner sketch the room on a sheet of paper.
2. Switch roles, do the exercise again, and compare sketches. Then answer the following questions on your paper:
   a. How accurate are the sketches?
   b. What transitional expressions related to spatial order helped you and your listener visualize the scenes? Why?

Challenge 4　Evaluating Spatial Order in Your Writing

1. Exchange the draft paragraph you worked on for Challenge 3 (page 65) with a partner. If the paper you receive features spatial order, make sure the description progresses smoothly and logically. Return the paper to the writer, pointing out any problems that you had in visualizing the scene or the topic.
2. Consider the suggestions your reader has made, and then make the changes you feel are called for. Save your work for later use.

Ordering for Emphasis　Another way to organize your ideas is in **emphatic order,** or order of significance. Often this means building from less important to more important ideas. First identify which of your details and examples are stronger or more significant than the others. Then arrange them in the order that gives the most impact. In many cases, especially if you are trying to persuade readers, emphatic order means saving your strongest example for last. In this way, the examples build to a high point and sustain the reader's interest, much as a story or play does.

Look at this paragraph about a ban on smoking in all restaurants:

> Cigarette smoking should be banned in all restaurants. For one thing, the odor of smoke is unappetizing and unattractive. In some cases, it can even affect the taste of the food. In addition, trying to confine smoke in designated smoking areas just doesn't work. The smoke travels into the surrounding sections of the restaurant, disturbing the people in these areas. However, the most compelling reason of all to ban smoking in restaurants is the health risk. Research has proven that cigarette smoking causes cancer and other serious respiratory problems. Therefore, it makes sense to restrict smoking as a way to encourage smokers to quit or at least to reduce their smoking. Furthermore, a ban

protects nonsmokers from inhaling secondhand smoke, which has been proven to be as dangerous as smoking itself. Banning smoking in restaurants would therefore benefit everyone.

The paragraph begins with a strong reason for a ban on smoking in restaurants (the unpleasant odor), followed by a stronger reason (the ineffectiveness of smoking areas). These build up to an even stronger reason (the health risks for smokers and nonsmokers alike). As you can see, emphatic order sustains the reader's interest as it accentuates the topic sentence.

Exploration 5a   Defining Emphatic Order

1. In your own words, briefly explain emphatic order. _____

   _____

   _____

   _____

2. Why is emphatic order effective in persuasive writing? _____

   _____

   _____

   _____

Exploration 5b   Identifying Transitions That Emphasize Importance

1. Read the following paragraph. Working with a partner, underline transitional expressions and phrases that help you to see the relative importance of each point in the argument.

(1) Everyone who drives or rides in a car should be required by law to wear a seat belt. (2) One important reason is that seat belts prevent injuries in minor crashes because they keep the driver and passengers from bouncing around on impact. (3) Even more important, not wearing a seat belt in a car equipped with air bags can lead to serious injuries. (4) Recent studies have shown that unless you are wearing a seat belt, the sudden expansion of an air bag can slam you up against the roof of the car. (5) Most important of all, children without seat belts are particularly vulnerable because they are generally

too small to brace themselves for any crash. (6) Seat belts keep children from being thrown against the windshield or out of the car in the most serious crashes.

2. On the following lines, briefly explain how the transitional expressions help emphasize the importance of the supporting material. _____

_____

_____

_____

_____

Exploration 5c Writing and Organizing Reasons in Emphatic Order

1. Working with a partner, choose one of the following statements and develop a list of at least three reasons for or against it. Write down your reasons on a separate sheet of paper.
   a. Family members should have the right to terminate life support for patients who have been declared brain dead.
   b. People convicted of drunk driving should lose their licenses for five years.
   c. Only high school students with a C average or better should be allowed to participate in extracurricular activities.
2. Now arrange your reasons in emphatic order.

Challenge 5 Evaluating Your Use of Emphatic Order

1. Exchange the draft paragraph you worked on for Challenge 4 (page 67) with a partner. If the paragraph you receive is arranged in emphatic order, make sure the sentences are ordered well to stress the point of the topic sentence. If you think the order might need adjusting, let the writer know.
2. Consider your reader's suggestions, and adjust your own paper accordingly. Save your work for later use.

Choosing Effective Language

When you reassess, you must also reevaluate the language you've used. Your choice of words plays a direct role in how effectively your ideas come across for your reader. Therefore, it's important to make sure that you use **effective language** that is both specific and concise.

Keeping Your Writing Specific

To help your reader picture things as you picture them, you must keep your language *specific*, that is, detailed and to the point. When you think of *sports car*, for example, the image of a particular car probably comes to mind. However, *sports car* is a general expression; it can conjure up any of dozens of different images in the reader's mind. What details does your reader need to see the car as you see it?

To communicate clearly, make such general terms *specific*. For example, replace the general expression *sports car* with a more specific description, such as *shiny new, forest-green Mazda Miata*. This specific language gives your reader an exact picture of what you mean.

Look at this paragraph from writer and poet Maya Angelou's autobiographical narrative, *The Heart of a Woman*. She describes the first time she read her work at the Harlem Writers Guild.

> I read the character and set description despite the sudden perversity of my body. The blood pounded in my ears but not enough to drown the skinny sound of my voice. My hands shook so that I had to lay the pages in my lap, but that was not a good solution due to the tricks my knees were playing. They lifted involuntarily, pulling my heels off the floor and then trembled like disturbed Jello. Before I launched into the play's action, I looked around at the writers expecting but hoping not to see their amusement at my predicament. Their faces were studiously blank. Within a year, I was to learn that each had a horror story about a first reading at the Harlem Writers Guild.

Which specific details help you picture this scene?

You probably identified particular details, such as *blood pounded in my ears* and *skinny sound of my voice*, which bring the scene to life. Other specific details include the involuntary movement of her knees *pulling my heels off the floor* and the *studiously blank* faces of her listeners.

Keeping Your Writing Concise

When you reassess, you also need to make sure your writing is *concise*—brief but clear. One way to keep your writing concise is to eliminate deadwood. Deadwood means unnecessary words and expressions that are like junk food—they can fill up your paper, but they have no value and add no real meaning. For example, nonspecific words like *a lot, definitely, extremely, quite, really, somewhat,* and *very* combined with weak, vague terms such as *good* or *bad* may make your paper longer, but they do not help you communicate.

At the same time, concentrate on choosing the best word or two to express your meaning. The English dictionary is filled with words of precise meaning and almost endless variety. Don't specify "a closed-roof car with two or four doors seating four to seven people" when *sedan* will do. Moreover, don't use two or more words when one will do to say the same thing. The following lists suggest ways to turn inflated phrases into more concise expressions:

Convert these wordy expressions . . . into these concise words

due to the fact that	because
a large number of	many
in the near future	soon
prior to	before
completely eliminate	eliminate
come to the realization that	realize
with the exception of	except for
in order that	so
at the present time	now
take action	act
the month of January	January
give a summary of	summarize
mutual cooperation	cooperation
make an assumption	assume

What parts of the following paragraph need to be made more concise?

> The most definitely traumatic experience I can remember is when I was thirteen and had to attend my grandmother's wake. I had lived with her for the first ten years of my life, so I was really devastated when she passed on to her reward. To show the proper respect to her memory, I told my mother I wanted to go to her wake. I didn't know how upsetting it would be due to the fact that I had never been to a wake. When I got to the funeral home, the fragrance of the flowers was very overpowering. I looked to the front and saw the casket with what looked like a wax statue of my grandmother in it. As I stood there, I felt my head start to spin and my eyes go out of focus. The next thing I knew, I was outside in the hallway, with my mother and my aunt leaning over me and crying. That's when I came to realize that I had fainted.

As you can see, several sentences need to be made more concise. In the first sentence, *definitely* can be eliminated, as can *really* in the second and *very* in the fifth. *Due to the fact that* in the fourth sentence can be changed to *because,* and *came to realize* in the last sentence can be shortened to *realized.* In the second sentence, the phrase *passed on to her reward* is overinflated; the simple word *died* communicates more directly. Here is the more concise version which makes the same point more directly:

> The most traumatic experience I can remember is when I was thirteen and had to attend my grandmother's wake. I had lived with her for the first ten years of my life, so I was devastated when she *died.* To show the proper respect to her memory, I told my mother I wanted to go to her wake. I didn't know how upsetting it would be *because* I had never been to a wake. When I got to the funeral home, the fragrance of the flowers was overpowering. I looked to the front and saw the casket with what looked like a wax statue of my grandmother in it. As I stood there, I felt my head start to spin and my eyes go out of focus. The next thing I knew, I was outside in the hallway, with my mother and my aunt leaning over me and crying. That's when I *realized* that I had fainted.

Exploration 6a   Defining Specific and Concise Language

1. On the lines below, briefly explain how to make writing specific. _____

_____

_____

_____

2. What are two strategies you can use to make your writing more concise?

_____

_____

_____

Exploration 6b   Identifying Overly General Language

Read the following paragraph. Working with a partner, underline the details that are too general. Then, on the lines on page 73, make up details, and write more specific versions of these sentences.

(1) My favorite job was at Mac and Al's Diner. (2) I worked every weekend for almost three years when I was in high school. (3) On Friday nights, I started at 5 P.M. and worked until 1 A.M. (4) On Saturdays and Sundays, I worked from 6 A.M. to 3 P.M. (5) I never knew what to expect when I went to work. (6) Sometimes I'd be the dishwasher. (7) Other times the boss would have me do other

things. (8) I loved the people I worked with. (9) They were great. (10) Many of the customers were there so often, they seemed like family. (11) One couple met at the diner and came in every Saturday night for a big steak dinner. (12) When they finally got married, they invited the entire staff at the diner. (13) Mac and Al closed the place down that day so we could attend the wedding.

_____

_____

_____

_____

_____

_____

_____

Exploration 6c   Practice in Writing Specific, Concise Language

1. Transform the following general words into concrete, specific images:

   a. an accident

   _____

   b. a book

   _____

   c. a car

   _____

2. On the lines provided, make the following sentences more concise.

   a. A large number of tourists head to New England during the month of October.

   _____

   b. The weather forecast calls for really warm temperatures in the near future.

   _____

c. Michelle eventually came to the realization that cutting class definitely had the potential to create problems for her.

Challenge 6   Evaluating the Effectiveness of Language in Your Writing

1. Exchange the draft paragraph you worked on for Challenge 5 (page 69) with a partner. Check the paragraph you receive to make sure the language is specific and concise. Put a ✓ next to any area that you think needs revision, and return the paragraph to the writer.

2. After considering your reader's suggestions, make any changes you feel are necessary. Save your work for later use.

Getting Feedback from an Objective Reader

An especially helpful step in reassessing is to seek feedback from an objective reader. Anybody who can be counted on to read your work without bias and respond intelligently and honestly to it—a classmate, a family member, a friend—is a potential reader.

You might suggest that your objective reader use the following reader assessment checklist. This series of questions will guide your reader through an evaluation of your writing. Even more important, the answers will help you to see how effectively you communicate.

Reader Assessment Checklist

1. Do you understand the point I am making? (topic sentence)
2. Do I stick to that point all the way through? (unity)
3. Are all my ideas and examples clearly connected and easy to follow? (coherence)
4. Are the words I've used specific and concise? (effective language)
5. What changes do you think I should make?

Exploration 7a   Understanding the Function of Feedback

1. Who is a suitable candidate to provide feedback on your paper? _____

_____

_____

2. How can the feedback you receive from an objective reader help you improve your paragraph? _____

_____

_____

_____

Exploration 7b   Evaluating the Feedback Process

1. What do you find most difficult about providing feedback to another writer?

   _____

   _____

   _____

2. Which of the questions on the reader assessment checklist do you think is

   most important? Why? _____

   _____

   _____

   _____

   _____

Exploration 7c   Practice in Evaluating and Revising

1. For Exploration 3c on page 64, you arranged a draft paragraph explaining how a thunderstorm starts. Working with a partner, use the reader assessment checklist on page 74 to evaluate the paragraph. List your answers on a separate sheet of paper.
2. Working with your partner, revise the paragraph, using the evaluation to guide you.

Challenge 7   Evaluating a Partner's Draft

1. Make a copy of the draft you worked on for Discovering Connections A or B at the end of Chapter 3 (page 54). For this assignment, work with a reader who has not previously seen your paper. Complete the following steps with the draft you receive:
   a. Put a + next to the topic sentence if it provides a clear direction. Put an ✗ next to it if the main point isn't clear.
   b. Now, check the paragraph for unity and coherence. Underline any section or sentence that disrupts the unity of the paragraph, and put a ✓ at

any point where additional transition would help. Note any problems with the order of the sentences.

c. Check the paragraph for effective language. Circle any vague words and deadwood. Write suggested substitutes above the words. Return the draft to the writer.

2. After evaluating your reader's comments, make any adjustments you feel are needed in your own paragraph. Save your work for later use.

REDRAFTING

After you have identified what still needs work in your writing, the next step is *redrafting,* or writing a new version or draft of your paper. In this second draft, you'll fill the gaps and correct the flaws you've discovered.

Here is a paragraph dealing with environmental concerns:

> Many of the things we use every day are adding to the growing environmental problems in our country. What we are currently doing doesn't affect us for just today, either. Even if we were to start acting responsibly now, the problems would take hundreds of years to clean up.

A reassessment of this paragraph shows that it is unified, coherent, and organized, but it is far too general and lacks supporting details. For instance, what *exactly* are we doing to complicate our environmental problems? In what *specific* ways are our present habits going to affect our future? What *particular* steps might we take to begin acting more responsibly?

Now look at this more specific version:

> Many of the things we use every day are adding to the growing environmental problems in our country. *For example, without active recycling programs in place, many plastic and glass items that are used only one time end up taking valuable space in landfills.* What we are currently doing doesn't affect us just for today, either. *Many people still don't realize that some disposable items take more than 200 years to break down and that some Styrofoam packing and cups will last almost forever.* Even if we were to start acting responsibly now *by recycling and severely limiting our use of plastics,* the problems would take hundreds of years to clean up. *As it is, landfills across the country continue to swell. Fed by our wastes, they tick away like timed-release environmental bombs, leaking hazardous waste into our water supply.*

As you can see, the added sections (in italics) clearly improve the paragraph. This new material *specifies* the ways that our environmental problems are compounded and the steps we must take to improve the situation.

Redrafting is different with every paper you write. With some papers, you'll need to make minor adjustments in several areas. With other papers, you may have to concentrate to a greater degree on one particular point. No matter what you need to add, correct, or remove, however, remember that your goal for redrafting is always the same: to improve your paper.

Exploration 8a Defining Redrafting

1. Briefly explain what redrafting involves. _____

   _____

   _____

   _____

2. Why is this step of revising important? _____

   _____

   _____

   _____

Exploration 8b Practice Evaluating a Paragraph Draft

1. Read the following paragraph, and then evaluate it using the reader assessment checklist on page 74. Write your evaluation on a separate sheet of
   paper.

   > Television programming today is uninspired and boring. For exam-
   > ple, none of the comedies are original. The plots are simply recycled
   > versions of earlier comedy shows. Even fairly good shows like *Friends*
   > or *Frasier* stoop to cheap gags like mistaken identities or being locked
   > out of an apartment. The dramas are even worse. *ER* is simply an up-
   > dating of *St. Elsewhere*. The late night talk shows all feature similar
   > routines and the same celebrities selling the same movies, books, or
   > television shows.

2. On the same sheet of paper, redraft the paragraph, making changes you
   think will improve it.

 Challenge 8 Analyzing Feedback and Redrafting

1. Compare your suggestions for changes in the paragraph from Exploration 8b with those of a partner. After comparing answers, adjust your own
   list to include good points your partner noted.
2. On a separate sheet of paper, redraft this paragraph again, incorporating the
   suggestions you added to your list.

▶ *E*DITING

Once you have eliminated the weaknesses in your draft, you are ready for the final step in revising: *editing.* When you edit, you polish that draft to correct errors in your use of English. This means you need to *proofread,* to identify and eliminate any errors in grammar, spelling, and punctuation.

Developing a Personal Proofreading System

The secret to effective proofreading is timing. Plan your time so that you proofread your paper when you are rested. That way, fatigue and familiarity with content won't cause you to see what you *meant to write* rather than what you *have actually written.* When you are tired, for example, you may see *receive* even though you've actually misspelled it as *recieve.*

Also, concentrate on the types of errors that most often appear in papers. Focus on the following proofreading checklist, and you'll eliminate most of the mistakes that trouble writers and distract readers.

Proofreading Checklist
1. Have I eliminated all sentence fragments (*frag*)?
2. Have I eliminated all comma splices (*cs*)?
3. Have I eliminated all run-on sentences (*rs*)?
4. Is the spelling (*sp*) correct throughout?
5. Is the verb tense (*t*) correct throughout?
6. Do all subjects agree with their verbs (*subj/verb agr*)?
7. Do all pronouns agree with their antecedents (*pro/ant agr*)?

Of course, this checklist doesn't cover all of the errors writers make. You may have trouble with some other aspect of writing such as double negatives or apostrophe use. Don't worry if you don't yet understand why some of these errors occur. Other chapters in this book will explain how to watch for and eliminate them. The Sentence Skill Locator on the inside back cover shows you where to look for help.

The secret to effective proofreading is to tailor your checklist to suit your own needs. Concentrate on the items listed above that you find most difficult; add others that especially trouble your writing. Then you'll have your own personal proofreading checklist that focuses on your particular areas of concern.

Teaming up with a proofreading partner is another way to eliminate errors in your paper. Once you have proofread your paper, exchange it with another reader. This proofreading partner will not be as invested or involved with the writing as you are and so may be better able to find any remaining errors. You can perform the same duties for your partner. The result will be better papers for both of you.

Using Computer Tools to Your Advantage

If you are using a word processor or computer, you probably have an additional proofreading tool: the spell check command. This function checks your spelling against the computer's dictionary and points out words that appear to be misspelled. Sometimes the computer offers a list of words that you might have intended rather than the misspelled word. To eliminate the error, simply select the correctly spelled version. If the computer doesn't offer a possibility, look the word up to find the correct spelling, and then make the changes yourself.

Don't trust the computer to find all your spelling errors, however. Imagine that you have written this sentence: "Suddenly the room became deathly *quite*." The computer doesn't read and reason as you do, so it won't be able to tell that you meant to write *quiet,* not *quite.* Therefore, take full advantage of the spell checker on your computer, but do a final check yourself to make sure, for example, that you don't use *dose* when you really mean *does.*

Exploration 9a Defining Editing

1. In your own words, explain what editing involves. _____

_____

_____

_____

2. What advantage do you gain by allowing some time to pass before you

proofread? _____

_____

_____

_____

Exploration 9b Analyzing Your Proofreading Strengths and Weaknesses

1. Of the areas of concern noted in the proofreading checklist on page 78, which one has given you the most trouble in the past? Why do you think you have difficulty with this area?

_____

_____

_____

_____

2. Which of the areas of concern highlighted in the proofreading checklist troubles you least? Why do you think you find this area easy? _____

_____

_____

_____

Exploration 9c Practice in Editing a Paragraph

1. Proofread the following paragraph. Correct the errors that you find. In the margin beside each error, write the abbreviation from the proofreading checklist on page 78 to identify the type of error (*frag, sp,* and so forth).

The hardest thing I ever has to endure was my parents' divorce. I was ten when it happened, I had always thought I had the perfect family, but I was wrong. A few days before Christmas, my mother sat down in front of my brother and me and told us that my father was moving out to live with another woman. Every kid wants to have someone they can look up to, and for me that used to be my father. But when I saw how sad my mother looks, I hated my father I wished he were dead. He kept calling the house to talk with me, but I wouldn't talk to him. Two years later, after the divorce was final. I met him by accident downtown. When he seen me, he started to cry and said he was sorry. I couldn't forgive him then and I can't forgive him now. He ruined my prefect family.

2. Working with a partner, compare your editing. Make a note of any errors that you originally missed. Then check your answers against the corrected version on page 81.

Challenge 9 Editing Your Paragraph

1. After you proofread the draft you worked on for Challenge 7 (pages 75–76), exchange your draft with a partner. On the paragraph you receive, put a ✓ before any error you see, and then return the draft to the writer.
2. After evaluating your reader's corrections, make all necessary corrections.

DISCOVERING CONNECTIONS A

When you see this drawing, what comes to mind? Do you think of a recent success in your life? What was it? Did you have to overcome some obstacle to achieve it? Or does the drawing make you think of the opposite, of a time that you hoped for success but didn't achieve it? What happened?

For this assignment, choose some aspect of this topic, prewrite on it, and develop a draft paragraph (at least five to ten sentences long). Then, following the process outlined in this chapter, revise the draft.

DISCOVERING CONNECTIONS B

For this assignment, think of a traumatic incident you experienced or witnessed. What happened? Who was involved? When and where did it occur? What caused it? How did you react? How has it affected you since? Prewrite to gather ideas, and then compose a draft paragraph (at least five to ten sentences long) on the subject. Then revise the draft, following the process outlined in this chapter.

Corrected Version
Exploration 9c, Number 1

t & subj/verb agr   The hardest thing I ever ~~has~~ *had* to endure was my parents' divorce. I was ten

cs   when it happened, I had always thought I had the perfect family, but I was

wrote. A few days before Christmas, my mother sat down in front of my brother

and me and told us that my father was moving out to live with another woman.

pro/ant agr   Every kid wants to have someone they *he or she* can look up to, and for me that used to

t/vs   be my father. But when I saw how sad my mother ~~looks~~ *looked*, I hated my father. I

wished he were dead. He kept calling the house to talk with me, but I wouldn't

frag   talk to him. Two years later, after the divorce was final, I met him by accident *saw*

t   downtown. When he ~~seen~~ me, he started to cry and said he was sorry. I

cs/sp   couldn't forgive him then , and I can't forgive him now. He ruined my ~~prefect~~
                                                  perfect

family.

RECAP

REFINING AND POLISHING YOUR DRAFT

New terms in this chapter	Definitions
➤ revising	➤ the stage of writing during which you refine and polish a draft ➤ Revising means (1) reassessing, (2) redrafting, and (3) editing.
➤ reassessing	➤ looking closely at a draft to find and correct errors and weaknesses
➤ redrafting	➤ creating a new version of a piece of writing by correcting problems and incorporating new material
➤ editing	➤ polishing and proofreading a piece of writing to eliminate errors in grammar, spelling, and punctuation
➤ unity	➤ quality achieved in writing when all sentences relate to the main idea
➤ coherence	➤ quality achieved in writing when sentences hold together well ➤ Coherence comes from logical order and connections that show how ideas interrelate.
➤ synonyms	➤ words with similar meanings
➤ transitional expressions	➤ words that connect ideas and show relationships between them
➤ chronological order	➤ organization in sequence on the basis of time
➤ spatial order	➤ organization based on location of parts in relation to a whole
➤ emphatic order	➤ organization based on order of significance, or importance
➤ effective language	➤ language that communicates well because it is specific (detailed) and concise (brief but clear)

The Process of Revising

❶ Reassess	➡	❷ Redraft	➡	❸ Edit
Check for ➤ unity ➤ coherence ➤ effective language Seek feedback from objective reader	⬅	Add new material Improve existing material Delete irrelevant material	⬅	Proofread for errors in ➤ spelling ➤ grammar ➤ punctuation

part

two

Using the Patterns of Paragraph Development

5 Narration

6 Description

7 Example

8 Process

9 Definition

10 Comparison and Contrast

11 Cause and Effect

12 Division and Classification

13 Argument

Narration

OVERVIEW: TELLING YOUR STORY

"Once upon a time . . . ." This is the traditional way to begin fairy tales, but people use variations of the same words to tell true stories, too. In both cases, the people telling the story are using the same technique: *narration.*

Narration is actually one of several techniques or *modes* you can use to write. If you've looked ahead in the book or through the table of contents, you've seen the names of the other modes: *description, example, process, definition, comparison and contrast, cause and effect,* and *division and classification.* Each enables you to approach and cover a topic in a different way.

The next eight chapters will look at each of these modes one by one. They will help you learn the characteristics of each and become used to using them.

Most writing uses a combination of modes to communicate ideas to readers. One mode will dominate, and one or more of the others will support it. For example, comparison and contrast would dominate in a paragraph examining two forms of government. However, cause and effect might also be used to explain how each type of government evolved, and process might be used to explain how each functions.

In Chapter 13, we will look at *argument.* Argument refers to the purpose of a piece of writing, not to a single mode or technique. As you learned in Chapter 1, one of the three main purposes of writing is to persuade. Argument is writing that persuades.

In this chapter, you'll learn how to use narration. Whenever you relate a series of events or incidents, you are using **narration.** For instance, a story about a near-drowning would be narration. So would a paper about a prank or the discovery of an unplanned pregnancy.

This chapter will explore the basic requirements for writing an effective narrative paragraph:

➤ providing a topic sentence that establishes a context

➤ explaining the events in the story in chronological order

➤ recognizing the most effective point of view

Once you have mastered these basics, you will begin to understand how to write narratives of more than one paragraph as well.

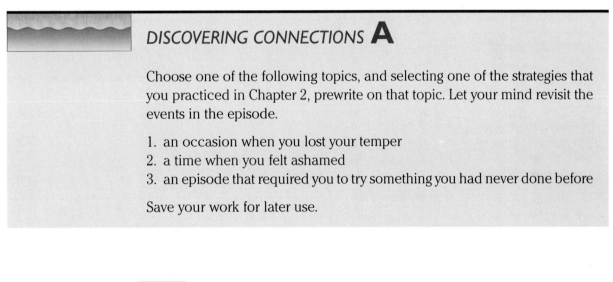

DISCOVERING CONNECTIONS A

Choose one of the following topics, and selecting one of the strategies that you practiced in Chapter 2, prewrite on that topic. Let your mind revisit the events in the episode.

1. an occasion when you lost your temper
2. a time when you felt ashamed
3. an episode that required you to try something you had never done before

Save your work for later use.

WRITING A CLEAR TOPIC SENTENCE THAT ESTABLISHES A CONTEXT

ESL Note
See "Sentence Basics" on page 521 and "Word Order" on page 524.

In order to help readers understand the point of a narrative paragraph, the writer must establish a clear direction, or point, for the story he or she is about to tell. The part of the paragraph that provides this needed direction is the topic sentence. The topic sentence establishes a context for the sequence of events that follows. In other words, it sets the scene and orients the reader. As Chapter 3 showed, a typical topic sentence pinpoints both the *topic* and your *attitude* or *reaction* to it. In the narrative paragraph, the topic is the incident, or story. Your reaction is the "spin," or slant, you put on the events you relate.

Look at the topic sentence in this narrative paragraph about a woman who was laid off from her job:

> For Shirley Vroman, getting caught in a corporate downsizing squeeze proved to be a beautiful gift in an ugly package. Two months ago, Vroman was laid off from her job as a salesperson for a national cosmetics chain. Although she had made a decent living in that line of work, she had never really enjoyed it. So although she was shocked and scared when she got her pink slip, it took only a few days for her to realize that this was an opportunity in disguise. Vroman worked up her courage and went to the Ferber Employment Agency. A placement specialist there helped Vroman redo her resume and sent her off to an interview the next day. Vroman landed the job: selling paper products. "My boss and my customers both teach me things every day about publishing, advertising, printing, and other industries," says Vroman. "Now I feel I have a job that I can keep and enjoy for years to come."

As you can see, the topic sentence *For Shirley Vroman, getting caught in a corporate downsizing squeeze proved to be a beautiful gift in an ugly package* provides a clear direction for the reader. It not only pinpoints the topic (being laid off) and attitude (upbeat about an unexpectedly pleasant result), but it also reveals the point of the narrative (something positive can come out of an event that at first seems totally negative). This topic sentence prepares the reader well for the sequence of events that describe Vroman's experience.

Exploration 1a   Defining Narration

1. In your own words, explain narration. _____

   _____

   _____

   _____

   _____

2. What role does the topic sentence play in a narrative paragraph? _____

   _____

   _____

   _____

   _____

   _____

Exploration 1b   Analyzing a Topic Sentence for a Narrative Paragraph

Reread the example paragraph about being laid off on page 86. On the lines below, briefly explain how the topic sentence sets the direction and context for the actions described in its supporting sentences.

_____

_____

_____

_____

_____

_____

Challenge 1   Preparing to Write a Narrative Paragraph

Prewrite on the subject of a first date. Then plan a sequence for the details you select as promising. Finally, write a topic sentence that establishes an appropriate direction and context. Save your work for later use.

RELYING ON CHRONOLOGICAL ORDER

Another way to help readers understand the point of a narrative paragraph is to arrange the sequence of events in your story in *chronological* order, that is, as they occurred in time. This way, the reader can "see" them as they actually happened. For further discussion, see "Using Chronological Order" on page 63.

Sometimes, though, writers will interrupt the time sequence to present a **flashback,** an event that occurred further back in the past. Flashbacks can provide important background information. Imagine you were writing about how you overcame terrible stage fright in a public speaking course. Including a flashback about the incident that caused your fear to develop in the first place—forgetting your lines in the first-grade play—would make it easier for your reader to understand how hard it was to overcome your anxiety later on.

Note the use of chronological order in the following narrative paragraph about a talent-show performance, taken from Amy Tan's novel, *The Joy Luck Club.*

> And I started to play. It was so beautiful. I was so caught up in how lovely I looked that at first I didn't worry how I would sound. So it was a surprise to me when I hit the first wrong note and I realized

> something didn't sound quite right. And then I hit another and another followed that. A chill started at the top of my head and began to trickle down. Yet I couldn't stop playing, as though my hands were bewitched. I kept thinking my fingers would adjust themselves back, like a train switching to the right track. I played this strange jumble through two repeats, the sour notes staying with me all the way to the end.

Telling the events in order of occurrence makes it easier to understand the story. First, the narrator begins to play the piano. Then she hits a wrong note, followed by other wrong notes. She realizes that her fingers are not playing the correct keys, yet she continues to play until she reaches the end of the piece. Each event in the paragraph leads to the next.

When you write a narrative, you will find certain transitional expressions helpful to show the sequence of events. Some of them are listed below.

■ *Transitional Expressions for Narratives*

after	during	later	soon
before	first (second, etc.)	meanwhile	then

➤ **C**HOOSING THE MOST EFFECTIVE POINT OF VIEW

Any time you tell a story, you select a **point of view,** or storyteller's perspective. Often when you use narration, you will write from a *first person point of view*, especially with stories from your experience. In other words, you will tell how you participated in the episode, using *I, me,* and so on. At other times, you will write from a *third person point of view*, as if you were an observer rather than a participant. Your focus will be on others, so you will use *he, she, her, him, they,* and so on.

Take a look at this narrative excerpt about a childhood recollection, taken from "God in the Doorway," an essay by author Annie Dillard:

> One cold Christmas Eve I was up unnaturally late because we had all gone out to dinner—my parents, my baby sister, and I. We had come home to a warm living room, and Christmas Eve. Our stockings drooped from the mantel; beside them, a special table bore a bottle of ginger ale and a plate of cookies.
>
> I had taken off my fancy winter coat and was standing on the heat register to bake my shoe soles and warm my bare legs. There was a commotion at the front door; it opened, and cold wind blew around my dress.
>
> Everyone was calling me. "Look who's here! Look who's here!" I looked. It was Santa Claus. Whom I never—ever—wanted to meet. Santa Claus was looming in the doorway and looking around for me. My mother's voice was thrilled: "Look who's here!" I ran upstairs.

The use of the first person pronouns *I, we, me,* and *my* makes it clear that this excerpt concerns an incident in which the writer was a participant.

Now, consider this paragraph from Peter Griffin's biography of Ernest Hemingway, *Less Than a Treason.* It describes Hemingway's first encounter with flying.

> Ernest first saw the plane from the window of the taxi he and Hadley took to the field. It was a silver biplane with a tiny cabin with portholes, and a seat for the pilot in the rear. Ernest bought the tickets at a counter in the plane shed, and had them checked by an attendant who stood just ten feet away, by the door to the field. Then, with cotton stuffed into their ears, Ernest and Hadley climbed aboard the plane and sat one behind the other. The pilot, a short, little man with his cap on backwards, shouted contact, and the mechanic gave the propeller a spin.

relative clause

In this case, the paragraph is related from the third person point of view. In other words, the writer is not a participant but a witness.

Exploration 2a Understanding Chronological Order and Point of View

1. How does chronological order help a reader to understand a story?

   _____

   _____

   _____

   _____

   _____

2. Briefly explain the difference between first person and third person point of view. _____

   _____

   _____

   _____

   _____

   _____

   _____

Exploration 2b Listing Events in a Narrative Paragraph

Turn again to the sample narrative about a childhood recollection on page 88. Working with a partner, list and number the sequence of events.

_____

_____

_____

_____

_____

Exploration 2c Revising a Narrative Paragraph to Use Flashback

Ernest Hemingway was excited about the prospect of flying before he actually took the flight described in the paragraph on page 89. Try to imagine an event that would have aroused his interest in flying. Then, on a separate sheet of paper, rewrite the paragraph, including a flashback that describes this earlier, imaginary event.

Challenge 2 Writing a Narrative Paragraph

Using the notes you completed for Challenge 1 (page 87), draft a narrative paragraph of at least 100 words that deals with a first date.

DISCOVERING CONNECTIONS B

1. In Discovering Connections A on page 85, you chose a topic for a narrative paragraph and completed your prewriting. Now using the points in this chapter as a guide, develop a paragraph of at least 100 words that tells your reader the series of events involved in the experience.
2. Exchange your paragraph with a partner. If you completed the paragraph for Challenge 2 above and you feel this is better, use it for this exercise instead. Evaluate the paragraph you receive, using the narrative paragraph checklist on page 91. Write your answers on a separate sheet of paper, and then return the paragraph and your assessment to the writer.
3. Using your reader's comments to guide you, revise your own paragraph.

Narrative Paragraph Checklist

1. Does the topic sentence establish a context?
2. Is the material arranged in chronological order?
3. Is the point of view used to present the paragraph appropriate?
4. In your judgment, the best part of this paragraph is _____ . Explain.
5. Which detail or example would be even better if it were expanded? Why?

RECAP

NARRATION

New terms in this chapter	Definitions
➤ narration	➤ the writing technique used to relate a series of events or incidents
➤ flashback	➤ a past event deliberately presented out of sequence to provide background information
➤ point of view	➤ the perspective a writer uses to tell a story ➤ Using *first person point of view* makes the writer a participant (I, me, my, mine). *Example* Suddenly, I heard a car stop outside my window. ➤ Using *third person point of view* makes the writer an observer (she, he, they, him, her, his, them, their, it, its). *Example* The old woman stood up and reached for her cane.

Writing a Narrative Paragraph

Focus on a subject that includes a **sequence of events.**

↓   ↑

Develop a **topic sentence** that establishes a **context** for the reader.

↓   ↑

Present the events through **chronological order.**

↓   ↑

Choose the most effective **point of view—first person** or **third person.**

Description

OVERVIEW: CREATING A PICTURE IN WORDS

Whether you are telling a story or writing an essay for a class assignment, your words are a camera lens through which your reader views the experiences or situations you are presenting. One of the best techniques for bringing the view in the lens into focus is description.

Whenever you attempt to paint a picture in words of a scene, an individual, an experience, or an object, you are using **description.** A paragraph detailing the destruction caused by a hurricane would call for description. Description would also logically be used to bring an article about an outdoor rock concert to life for readers.

This chapter will explore the basic requirements for writing an effective descriptive paragraph:

➤ providing a topic sentence that previews your description
➤ drawing upon sensory details
➤ relying on both objective and subjective description
➤ considering spatial order

Once you have mastered these basics, you will also begin to understand how to write longer essays that use description.

DISCOVERING CONNECTIONS A

Select one of the following topics. Then, following one of the strategies that you practiced in Chapter 2, prewrite on that topic. Consider sensory details and location of parts of the scene (or person).

1. an accident scene
2. a nightclub, stadium, workplace, or other facility after closing
3. the best-looking person you've ever met

Save your work for later use.

PREVIEWING THE FOCUS OF DESCRIPTION THROUGH THE TOPIC SENTENCE

Your reader depends on you to clarify early on what your paragraph will be about. Your descriptive paragraph will create a vivid impression of an object, person, or place in the reader's mind. To begin it, you need a topic sentence that previews what will be described and suggests your point of view. That way your reader can make sense of the specific details and examples that follow.

Consider the italicized topic sentence in this paragraph about a beautiful sunset:

The most beautiful sunset I ever witnessed occurred when I was hiking in the woods surrounding Lake Wampsutta. One Saturday afternoon last fall, four of my friends and I hiked for three hours through the pungent pine trees surrounding the lake where we hold our annual camping trip. Our destination was a secluded area along the shoreline of the lake. When we arrived, we unloaded our gear and set up camp. By the time we had finished, the bright sunlight was starting to fade, so we walked down to the lakeside. As we sat on an old log, we looked west and saw the sun—a brilliant orange globe nesting in pink-streaked clouds against an almost violet sky. The sun seemed to sink into the greenish black water, as a broad stripe of shimmering gold reflected light spread out toward us across the surface of the lake. I had never seen anything so breathtaking in my whole life.

The italicized topic sentence tells readers that the paragraph will describe a sunset. It also tells them that the writer thought the sunset was beautiful, and it sets the scene by mentioning woods surrounding a lake. Then, the body of the paragraph provides the details and examples that make the scene come alive.

► USING SENSORY DETAILS

Vivid experiences create vivid memories. Think for a moment of the aroma the last time you walked into a bakery or of the sensation the last time you plunged into a swimming pool on a hot summer day. **Sensory details**—what you perceive by seeing, hearing, tasting, smelling, and touching—enable you to communicate these experiences to your reader. To write sensory details, choose concrete language that draws in the five senses.

Look at this paragraph from "Blackberries," a short story by Welsh poet and fiction writer Leslie Norris.

> The boy put the blackberry in his mouth. He rolled it with his tongue, feeling its irregularity, and crushed it against the roof of his mouth. Released juice, sweet and warm as summer, ran down his throat[;] hard seeds cracked between his teeth. When he laughed[,] his father saw that his mouth was deeply stained. Together they picked and ate the dark berries, until their lips were purple and their hands marked and scratched.

Sensory details, such as the feeling and texture of the berry in the boy's mouth, the taste of the juice when he crushes the berry, and the sensation of the hard seeds cracking between his teeth, make the experience vivid for the reader.

Exploration 1a   Defining Description

1. Briefly define description. _____

   _____

   _____

   _____

   _____

2. What are sensory details? How do they help you write effective description?

   _____

   _____

   _____

   _____

Exploration 1b   Identifying the Role of the Topic Sentence

Reread the paragraph about eating blackberries. How does the topic sentence prepare you for the details that follow?

_____

_____

_____

_____

_____

Exploration 1c   Identifying Sensory Details

Review the paragraph about a beautiful sunset on page 93. Working with a partner, make a list on a separate sheet of paper of the various sensory details in the paragraph. Beside each detail, write the sense or senses to which it appeals.

Challenge 1   Prewriting for a Descriptive Paragraph

Prewrite on the subject of a special day or a memorable event in your life. Try to focus on sensory details you remember vividly. Save your work for later use.

RELYING ON OBJECTIVE AND SUBJECTIVE DESCRIPTION

There are two basic types of descriptive writing. **Objective description** focuses on actual details and sensations. **Subjective description** focuses on the impressions those details and sensations create within the writer. Most writing uses a combination of objective and subjective details. Only rarely is a paper completely objective (as a lab report is) or completely subjective (as an essay dealing with a religious experience or hallucination would be).

Consider the details in this paragraph about being caught in a sudden summer rainstorm:

> Last summer, I went into downtown Springfield for a big job interview and got caught in a sudden rainstorm. As I left the subway station, I could smell dust in the air. It was a peculiar odor, sharp and sweet, like

dried hay. Then the temperature dropped suddenly. My shirt felt clammy, and I felt a chill run up my neck. Within a minute, the sky darkened and then exploded in a jagged bolt of light. Half a second later, there was a roaring, crackling sound that seemed to shake the skyscrapers all along Fifth Avenue. Finally, with a hiss that grew louder moment by moment, the rain began. By the time I reached the office for my interview, I was drenched. I felt angry and embarrassed that I hadn't thought to bring an umbrella. I blushed when I thought of how foolish I'd look to the interviewer.

This paper uses objective and subjective description to capture the numerous sensations that accompanied this thunderstorm. The odor in the air, the change in temperature, the flash of the lightning, the roar of the thunder, and the splash of the rain are all examples of objective description. The writer's clammy, chilled feeling and the anger, frustration, and embarrassment resulting from being caught in the storm are examples of subjective description. Together, these two types of description create a vivid sense of what the sudden storm was like for the writer.

➤ USING SPATIAL ORDER

Writers often rely upon **spatial order** to organize descriptive writing. Spatial order locates the described elements logically in relationship to each other. It directs the reader's attention, for example, from left to right, from near to far, or from top to bottom. Presenting the details in a logical spatial order helps your reader to visualize the scene as it actually exists.

Study the order of details in this descriptive paragraph about a unique eating establishment:

> The most unusual restaurant in town is a place called PastaWorks, Inc. It is set up to resemble the inside of a broken-down factory. Near the main entrance, there are several gigantic machines, each running from floor to ceiling, made of enormous spinning gears. The dining area is spread out behind the machines. This part of the restaurant is wide open, like the inside of a warehouse. Overhead, huge fans and pipes billowing steam hang from the ceiling. The strangest part of the room is the back wall. About twenty feet up is the front half of a real delivery truck. The wall is painted so that it looks as if the truck had crashed right through the wall. On the floor underneath the truck lies a jumble of bricks and truck parts.

Here, spatial order helps the reader bring this unusual place into focus. The description proceeds in an orderly way from the front entrance to the back wall: The gigantic machines are near the entrance, the dining area is behind the machines, the fans and steam pipes are hanging from the ceiling, and the nose of the delivery truck is about twenty feet up on the back wall.

Where spatial order is used to organize a descriptive paragraph, transitional expressions that show location help your reader. A few of these transitions are shown below.

> ### Transitional Expressions Showing Location
>
> | | | |
> |---|---|---|
> | above, below | in front of, behind | toward, away |
> | close, far | next to, near, between | up, down |

Exploration 2a Understanding Types of Description and Spatial Order

1. Briefly explain the difference between objective and subjective description.

   _____

   _____

   _____

   _____

   _____

2. How can spatial order make it easier for your reader to understand your

   description? _____

   _____

   _____

   _____

   _____

Exploration 2b Analyzing Spatial Order in a Paragraph

Reread the paragraph on the thunderstorm on pages 95–96. Working with a partner, make a list on a separate sheet of paper of the spatial details that guide the reader through the description.

Exploration 2c Working with Descriptive Details

1. Look again at the paragraph about the thunderstorm. Which details—

   objective or subjective—did the most to catch your attention? Why? _____

   _____

_____

_____

_____

2. Working with a partner, make a list of three subjective details to add to the

paragraph on page 96 about the unusual restaurant. _____

_____

_____

_____

_____

_____

Challenge 2   Writing a Descriptive Paragraph

Using the prewriting material you completed for Challenge 1 on page 95, complete a paragraph of at least 100 words that deals with a special day or memorable event. First, outline a plan for your paragraph, deciding on the best order for your details.

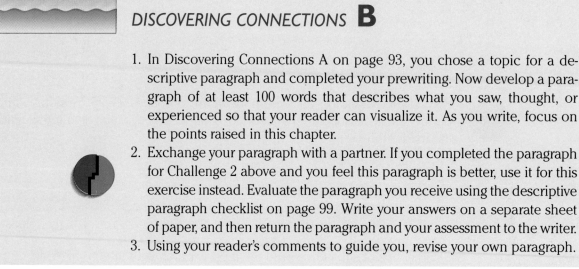

DISCOVERING CONNECTIONS **B**

1. In Discovering Connections A on page 93, you chose a topic for a descriptive paragraph and completed your prewriting. Now develop a paragraph of at least 100 words that describes what you saw, thought, or experienced so that your reader can visualize it. As you write, focus on the points raised in this chapter.
2. Exchange your paragraph with a partner. If you completed the paragraph for Challenge 2 above and you feel this paragraph is better, use it for this exercise instead. Evaluate the paragraph you receive using the descriptive paragraph checklist on page 99. Write your answers on a separate sheet of paper, and then return the paragraph and your assessment to the writer.
3. Using your reader's comments to guide you, revise your own paragraph.

Descriptive Paragraph Checklist

1. Does the topic sentence preview the description?
2. Does the paragraph use sensory details? List them.
3. Does it make effective use of both objective and subjective description? Write an *S* above every use of subjective description and an *O* above every use of objective description.
4. Is it effectively arranged in spatial order or some other order? Explain.
5. In your judgment, what is the best part of this paragraph? Explain.
6. Which detail or example would be even better if it were expanded? Why?

RECAP

DESCRIPTION

New terms in this chapter	Definitions
➤ description	➤ the writing technique used to paint a picture in words of a scene, individual, object, or experience
➤ sensory details	➤ information perceived through sight, sound, taste, smell, and touch
➤ objective description	➤ writing that focuses on actual details and sensations *Example* The restaurant featured wood paneled walls and candlelit tables.
➤ subjective description	➤ writing that focuses on the impressions that details and sensations create within the writer *Example* The atmosphere in the restaurant was warm and cozy.

Writing a Descriptive Paragraph

Develop a **topic sentence** that previews the object to be described in the paragraph.

↓ ↑

Include **sensory details** to bring the scene into focus.

↓ ↑

Use a combination of **objective** and **subjective description.**

↓ ↑

Present the details through **spatial order** when appropriate.

7

Example

 **O**VERVIEW: *LEARNING TO ILLUSTRATE YOUR POINT*

You've probably said it hundreds of times yourself: "For example, ..." We use examples when we want to be sure our point or statement is fully understood. In fact, in writing, **example** is the use of specific instances to illustrate, clarify, or back up a point.

As a writing technique, example is valuable. Well-chosen examples help you make your point powerfully. A paragraph outlining the difficulties involved in hunting for a job could be developed through example. A paragraph about the duties of a pet owner might also use example.

This chapter will explore the basic requirements for writing an effective example paragraph:

➤ providing a topic sentence that clearly states the point you will illustrate

➤ choosing examples that are specific

➤ selecting examples that are relevant

Once you have mastered these basics, you will also begin to understand how to write longer essays that use example.

DISCOVERING CONNECTIONS A

Select one of the following topics. Then, employing one of the strategies that you practiced in Chapter 2, prewrite on that topic. Concentrate on useful, effective illustrations or examples.

1. annoying advertisements
2. diets
3. fads

Save your work for later use.

PROVIDING A TOPIC SENTENCE THAT STATES THE POINT YOU WILL ILLUSTRATE

In an example paragraph, the topic sentence identifies the general idea to be clarified and illustrated through the examples the writer develops. It should clearly state the point to be illustrated.

Look at this paragraph from a psychology textbook by Carol Tavris and Carole Wade:

> Even the simplest gesture is subject to misunderstanding and offense. The sign of the University of Texas football team, the Longhorns, is to extend the index finger and the pinkie. In Italy and other parts of Europe this gesture means a man's wife has been unfaithful to him— a serious insult! Anita Rowe, a consultant who advises businesses on cross-cultural customs, tells of a newly hired Asian engineer in a California company. As the man left his office to lead the first meeting of his project team, his secretary crossed her fingers to wish him luck. Instead of reassuring him, her gesture thoroughly confused him: In his home country, crossing one's fingers is a sexual proposition.

As you can see, the topic sentence indicates the focus of the paragraph: the possibility of misunderstanding a gesture. The sentences that follow it supply two specific examples of misunderstood gestures.

Incidentally, note that when you use example, you often use the transitional expressions *for example* and *for instance*. They are good cues for you to use because they remind you of the commitment you have to your reader: to provide a convincing illustration of your point.

Also, note each example may require several sentences of explanation. The authors of this paragraph include two sentences to explain their first example of a misunderstood gesture and three sentences to explain the second example. Another possible plan is to discuss only one example thoroughly to make the main point. In this case, of course, all the supporting sentences would explain that one example.

Exploration 1a   Defining Example

1. Explain how example is used as a writing mode. _____

   _____

   _____

   _____

   _____

2. Why are *for example* and *for instance* good transitional expressions to use

   in an example paragraph? _____

   _____

   _____

   _____

   _____

Exploration 1b   Analyzing the Topic Sentence and Details in an Example Paragraph

Working with a partner, list the examples used to support the topic sentence in the paragraph about misunderstood gestures on page 101. Write each example below. Next to each example, explain how it supports the topic sentence.

_____

_____

_____

_____

_____

_____

Challenge 1   Preparing to Write an Example Paragraph

Prewrite on the subject of bad habits. Focus your topic, mark your best examples, and write a clear topic sentence. Save your work for later use.

PROVIDING SPECIFIC EXAMPLES

Specific means detailed and particular. Writing **specific examples** means providing enough information so that your reader understands their meaning and significance. Generally, the more specific information you supply, the more convincing your examples are.

Imagine you are writing a paragraph about problems in today's schools, such as poor reading skills, lack of discipline in the classroom, students' personal difficulties, and unmotivated teachers. Supplying statistics or specific background about each of these examples would help your reader understand the problems. Simply stating that all of these things are problems would be less helpful and convincing.

In some example paragraphs, you may make a strong presentation based on a single example. Consider this paragraph about agoraphobia, the abnormal fear of open spaces:

> When you have agoraphobia, the everyday things that people take for granted become major problems. For example, taking a ride in a car, even to the corner store, becomes a heart-pounding nightmare. You get in the car, and your heart begins to race. You're covered with a cold sweat, and you feel faint. As you move farther from home, the feelings intensify. Your heart pounds so hard you can hear it in your ears, you can't breathe, and you feel certain that you are going to die. The feeling starts to lessen only when you return to your home, a refuge which might as well be your prison.

Here, a single example, a trip to the corner store, is described in detail in terms of the physical effects for the agoraphobe: a racing and pounding heart, cold sweats, lightheadedness, and breathing difficulties. These details create vivid support for the point raised in the topic sentence that agoraphobia radically alters day-to-day living for those afflicted with it.

ENSURING THAT YOUR EXAMPLES ARE RELEVANT

Relevant means appropriate and connected. **Relevant examples** are directly associated with the topic. For a paper on frustrating household chores, examples such as dusting, vacuuming, and washing windows would be relevant. These tasks are all frustrating because the work is mindless and must be repeated so frequently. However, an example about sweeping up at work would not be relevant. Although this task may indeed be frustrating, it is an on-the-job duty, not a household chore.

ESL Note
See "Writing Paragraphs" on pages 538–539.

Consider this paragraph by N. L. Gage and David C. Berliner. As you read, relate each example to the topic sentence.

> How do expert physicists differ from novices? One difference is that experts take more time than novices in studying a problem. But once they start to work, they solve problems faster than novices do. The experts also seem more often than novices to construct an abstract representation of the problem in their minds. That is, in their working memory they hold mental representations of the blocks, pulleys, inclined planes, levers, or whatever they need to solve a problem. Expert physicists also tend to classify new problems more frequently. They may decide a problem is a type-X problem, to be solved by using the laws of inclined planes. Or they may see the problem as belonging to the type that deals with forces, pulleys, and blocks, which are always solvable by using some version of Newton's second law, $F = MA$ (Force = mass × acceleration).

As you can see, the topic sentence indicates for the reader that the paragraph will discuss the differences between experienced physicists and novices (beginners). The examples that follow the topic sentence are all relevant because they all concern things that experienced physicists do to a greater degree than novices.

Exploration 2a   Considering Specific and Relevant Examples

1. How does making examples specific help to make an example paragraph more effective? _____

    _____

    _____

    _____

    _____

2. What makes examples relevant? _____

    _____

    _____

    _____

    _____

Exploration 2b   Explaining Relevance in an Example Paragraph

Look again at the sample paragraph about agoraphobia on page 103. Working with a partner, explain why the detailed example is relevant.

_____

_____

_____

_____

_____

_____

_____

Exploration 2c Developing Specific Examples

Reread the examples of problems in today's schools given on page 103. Working with a partner, develop a list of additional examples of problems in U.S. public schools today. Choose one example, and list several ways you could provide specific support for it.

Challenge 2 Writing an Example Paragraph

Review the prewriting material and topic sentence on bad habits you developed for Challenge 1 on page 102. Make sure your examples are specific and relevant. Draft an example paragraph of at least 100 words that develops this topic.

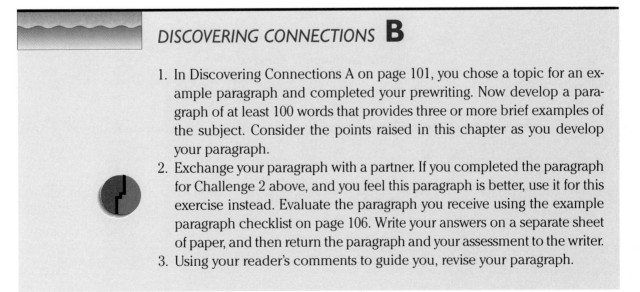

DISCOVERING CONNECTIONS **B**

1. In Discovering Connections A on page 101, you chose a topic for an example paragraph and completed your prewriting. Now develop a paragraph of at least 100 words that provides three or more brief examples of the subject. Consider the points raised in this chapter as you develop your paragraph.
2. Exchange your paragraph with a partner. If you completed the paragraph for Challenge 2 above, and you feel this paragraph is better, use it for this exercise instead. Evaluate the paragraph you receive using the example paragraph checklist on page 106. Write your answers on a separate sheet of paper, and then return the paragraph and your assessment to the writer.
3. Using your reader's comments to guide you, revise your paragraph.

Example Paragraph Checklist

1. Does the topic sentence clearly state the point to be illustrated?
2. Does the paragraph provide specific examples? Underline any example that you feel needs to be made more specific.
3. Are all the examples relevant? Put an * next to any example that you feel is not directly connected to the main idea of the paragraph.
4. In your judgment, what is the best part of this paragraph? Explain.
5. Which detail or example would be even better if it were expanded? Why?

RECAP

EXAMPLE

New terms in this chapter	Definitions
➤ example	➤ the writing technique that uses specific instances to illustrate, clarify, or back up the point being made
➤ specific examples	➤ illustrative material that is detailed and particular
	Example In the center of the room was *the old, dusty, mahogany roll-top desk.*
➤ relevant examples	➤ illustrative information that is appropriate and directly connected
	Example The *household chores* I find most annoying are *dusting, vacuuming,* and *washing windows.*

Writing an Example Paragraph

Identify the **subject** that you wish to **illustrate.**

↓ ↑

Provide a **topic sentence** that indicates the **specific idea** to be **illustrated.**

↓ ↑

Keep all examples **specific.**

↓ ↑

Make all examples **relevant.**

Process

VERVIEW: EXPLAINING "HOW TO" OR "HOW IT HAPPENS"

Whenever you explain how to do something or how something occurs, you are using **process.** There are basically three types of process writing. The most common type is *a set of instructions* (sometimes called a *how-to* writing). For instance, you have probably read instructions about how to assemble a toy or how to fill out a job application. The second type is *process analysis,* which explains such matters as how thunderstorms form or how some aerosol sprays destroy the ozone layer of the earth's atmosphere. The third type is *process narrative,* which explains how you did something, such as how you performed a lab experiment or organized a neighborhood crime watch.

This chapter will explore the basic requirements for writing an effective process paragraph:

➤ including a topic sentence that clearly states the procedure or technique

➤ using the imperative mood (you) when it's appropriate

➤ dividing the process into simple, logical steps

➤ relying on linear order

Once you have mastered these basics, you will begin to understand how to write longer papers involving process.

DISCOVERING CONNECTIONS A

Select one of the following topics. Then, using one of the strategies that you practiced in Chapter 2, prewrite on that topic. Concentrate on steps in the process.

1. how to cook your favorite food
2. how to unwind after a hard day
3. how to do a push-up

Save your work for later use.

➤ 1 NCLUDING A TOPIC SENTENCE THAT CLEARLY STATES THE PROCESS

Before you write a topic sentence for your process paragraph, you will have already limited your subject. This means you will have narrowed your focus to a process that can be adequately explained in a brief space. Therefore, your topic sentence will clearly state the specific process—procedure, technique, or routine—to be explained and take a direction that covers all the steps to be explained in the rest of the sentences.

Study the relationship of the topic sentence and the body of the following paragraph about the process of photosynthesis:

> *Photosynthesis is the quiet but profound process carried out each day in green plants around the world—an energy conversion process that makes life on earth possible.* Before the process can begin, the plant must assemble its raw materials: carbon dioxide and water. Terrestrial plants take in carbon dioxide through tiny openings in their leaves and draw water up through their root systems. In the first stage of photosynthesis, pigments called chlorophylls absorb light energy. This absorption produces a tiny electric current which converts the sunlight energy into high-energy chemicals. Then, the plant uses the energy in the chemicals to drive reactions forming starch and sugars out of carbon dioxide (CO_2) and water (H_2O). As the molecules of CO_2 and H_2O are broken down, oxygen gas is released into the atmosphere. This oxygen replaces that used up by animal respiration. At the same time, the process also uses up the CO_2 we produce when we breathe. In addition, the starch and sugars made by the plant form the basis for all food chains. Truly, photosynthesis is the mainstay of life on earth.

The topic sentence tells you that the paragraph is about how plants convert energy through the process of photosynthesis. Phrases like *quiet but profound* and *makes life on earth possible* clearly show the writer's respect for the importance of the process. The rest of the sentences explain the process step by step and clarify its importance.

USING THE IMPERATIVE MOOD: YOU

When you are writing instructions, it makes sense to address the reader directly, using the **imperative mood.** An *imperative* is a command. When you use the imperative mood, the unstated subject is *understood* to be the person reading the piece. For example, when you write, "Close the window when you leave the room," you are actually directing the reader to close it. In essence, you are saying, "*You* close the window when *you* leave the room."

Note the use of the imperative mood in this paragraph on how to insert a contact lens:

> Inserting a contact lens is a simple process. First, take the lens out of the fluid it is stored in and rinse it off. Next, place the cleaned lens on the tip of your right index finger. Check the edge of the lens to make sure the lens hasn't turned inside out. It should look like the top of an opened umbrella. Using your left index finger, pull down gently on your lower right eyelid to expose more of the white of the eye. Then carefully place the lens over the iris, or colored part, of your eye. Blink once to make sure the lens is securely in place. If you can see clearly through that eye, repeat these steps for your other eye.

As you can see, the steps of the process are written in the imperative mood. The subject is actually *you,* the person who is performing the steps, but the word *you* is never stated.

Exploration 1a Defining Process

1. In your own words, briefly explain process. _____

   _____

   _____

   _____

   _____

2. Why should you use the imperative mood when writing a set of directions?

   _____

_____

_____

_____

Exploration 1b   Relating the Parts of a Process Paragraph

Briefly explain the connection between the topic sentence and the support-ing sentences in the paragraph explaining photosynthesis on page 108. What does each accomplish?

_____

_____

_____

_____

_____

_____

Challenge 1   Preparing to Write a Process Paragraph

Prewrite on how to shave, iron a pair of pants, or apply makeup. As you list in-formation, think of your reader. Ask questions such as *What are the steps? Have I left out anything a novice would need to know?* Save your work for later use.

➤ DIVIDING THE PROCESS INTO SIMPLE, LOGICAL STEPS

The key to successful process writing is to separate the process into small, manageable steps and then to spell out these steps in detail. For example, al-though the process of circulating blood through the human body is highly complex, you can describe it fairly accurately in four basic steps: (1) The heart pumps oxygenated blood to body tissues through the arteries and capillaries. (2) The veins carry the blood back to the heart. (3) The heart pumps the blood to the lungs to be oxygenated again. (4) The blood returns to the heart to be circulated through the body again. Breaking the process down into discrete steps, each with its own function, makes the complex process easier for the reader to understand.

Consider the presentation of steps in this paragraph explaining how to water ski:

> If you follow these steps, water skiing will feel as natural as walking. First, prepare yourself to be towed. Once you're in the water, insert your feet in the rubber boots attached to the skis. Take a firm overhand grip on the handle of the tow bar, and then lean back slightly so that the tips of the skis are out of the water. The flotation belt or jacket will keep you from sinking below the surface of the water. Now you are ready to signal the driver to take out the slack in the tow rope. As the boat moves slowly forward, let the tow rope run between the ski tips. Keep the ski tips parallel and pointed out of the water. Next, bend your knees slightly, as if you were crouching, and signal the driver that you are ready. When the boat begins to accelerate, maintain that slight crouch until the boat picks up speed and you have your balance. It will pull you out of the water. Gradually straighten your legs, lean back a little, and enjoy the ride.

This paragraph breaks down the process of water skiing into distinct, easily completed steps. Each step is explained in specific detail. With the process presented this way, a reader should be able to follow these directions successfully.

RELYING ON LINEAR ORDER

Effective process writing often depends on **linear order,** or the arrangement of steps in order of their occurrence. Writing about the process of taking a photograph with a 35-millimeter camera would call for linear order: (1) adjust the focus; (2) change the setting to allow the proper amount of light through the lens; (3) push the shutter button to take the picture. Unless the steps are performed in this order, the photograph would probably not turn out well.

Consider the order of the steps in this paragraph explaining how to adjust the hand brakes on a bicycle:

> An important part of regular bicycle maintenance is tightening the hand brakes. To do so, you'll need an adjustable wrench, a pair of pliers, and a third-hand tool. This tool, a U-shaped metal device with a handle that you feed through the spokes and over each brake shoe, holds the brake shoes against the rim of the wheel. After the third-hand tool is in place, use the wrench to loosen the anchor bolt nut, which locks the cable into the brake assembly itself. Pull on the end of the cable with a pair of pliers. When the cable seems tight enough, use the wrench to retighten the anchor bolt nut while continuing to maintain pressure on the cable with the pliers. Once the bolt is tight, let

go of the cable, remove the third-hand tool, and recheck the brakes. If they need further adjustment, repeat the steps until you are satisfied. With a little trial and error, you'll have the improved fingertip brake control you are looking for.

As you can see, linear order plays an important role in this paragraph. In order to complete this complicated task successfully, you must follow the steps in the order in which they are presented. If you do any of them out of order—for example, if you pull on the cable before you've unloosened the anchor bolt nut—then you won't be able to complete the next steps.

Process writing places events in time order sequence. Therefore, transitional expressions that signal that order help your reader. See the list below for transitions useful in a process paragraph.

Transitional Expressions for Process Writing

Beginning	Continuing				Ending
begin by	as soon as	second step, etc.	until		finally
initially	next	then	while		last

Keep in mind that if you are explaining an unusual or specialized process, you may need to define special terms. In the paragraph above, the writer describes and gives the purpose for the *third-hand tool*. Without this orientation, the reader might very well be unable to find or to use this essential tool. Also, note that the writer first lists the equipment needed to tighten the hand brakes. In any how-to process paragraph, you will need to specify the materials or tools needed to carry out the process. Logically, this information should come right after the topic sentence so that the reader does not need to interrupt the process to get supplies.

Exploration 2a   Understanding Organization in a Process Paragraph

1. Why is it important to divide a process into small, manageable steps?

   _____

   _____

   _____

   _____

   _____

2. Briefly explain linear order. _____

   _____

   _____

_____

_____

 Exploration 2b   Explaining Order in a Process Paragraph

Reread the paragraph on water skiing on page 111, and then briefly explain how linear order helps the reader understand how to water ski.

_____

_____

_____

_____

_____

_____

Exploration 2c   Practice Enumerating Steps in a Process

1. Take another look at the sample paragraph on pages 111–112 about adjusting the hand brakes on a bicycle. Working with a partner, list the steps that make up the process on a separate piece of paper.
2. With your partner, list on your sheet the steps involved in tying a shoelace or hanging a picture.

Challenge 2   Writing a Process Paragraph

Using the ideas you developed in Challenge 1 on page 110, complete a paragraph of at least 100 words on how to shave, iron a pair of pants, or apply makeup.

DISCOVERING CONNECTIONS **B**

1. In Discovering Connections A on page 108, you chose a topic for a process paragraph and completed your prewriting. Now develop a paragraph of at least 100 words that explains how to perform the action. Use the points presented in this chapter as a guide.

Continued

2. Exchange your paragraph with a partner. If you completed the paragraph for Challenge 2 on page 113 and you feel this paragraph is better, use it for this exercise instead. Evaluate the paragraph you receive using the process paragraph checklist below. Write your answers on a separate sheet of paper, and then return the paragraph and your assessment to the writer.

3. Using your reader's comments to guide you, revise your own paragraph.

Process Paragraph Checklist

1. Does the topic sentence clearly state the procedure or technique to be presented?
2. Does it use the imperative mood (you)?
3. Is the process divided into simple, logical steps? Do you feel any step should be further subdivided to make it easier for the reader to perform the process? Put a ✓ next to any step that needs to be divided.
4. Are the steps presented in linear order? Underline any step that is out of linear order, and then draw a line to the spot in the paragraph where it actually belongs.
5. In your judgment, what is the best part of this paragraph? Explain.
6. Which detail or example would be even better if it were expanded? Why?

RECAP

PROCESS

New terms in this chapter	Definitions

➤ process	➤ the writing technique that explains how to do something or how something occurs
	
	➤ Three types of process writing include
	  1. *a set of instructions* (how to do something)
	  2. *process analysis* (how something is done or occurs)
	  3. *process narrative* (how you did something)

➤ imperative mood	➤ designating verb usage that expresses commands ➤ The subject of the sentence in the imperative mood is understood as the reader (you) rather than stated directly. *Example* *(You)* Move your books and papers into the other room, please.

New terms in this chapter	Definitions
➤ linear order	➤ an arrangement of steps in the order of their occurrence

Writing a Process Paragraph

Write a clear **topic sentence** that specifies the process to be explained.

↓   ↑

Directly address the reader through the **imperative mood** when it's appropriate.

↓   ↑

Present the process in **simple, logical steps.**

↓   ↑

Introduce the steps in **linear order.**

Definition

OVERVIEW: MAKING MEANING CRYSTAL CLEAR

No matter what topic you are writing about, your job is to communicate your ideas about that topic clearly and precisely. One writing mode that is especially helpful for this task is **definition.** Using definition, you can specify the meanings of actions, ideas, places, and things.

For example, a paragraph using the definition mode could spell out the qualities of a good boss. This mode would also be a natural choice to explain the meaning of strength as an emotional and spiritual quality displayed by a family coping with the loss of a child.

This chapter will explore the basic requirements for writing an effective definition paragraph:

➤ providing a topic sentence that highlights the term to be defined
➤ understanding the elements of an effective definition
➤ recognizing all the possible meanings of the term defined

Once you have mastered these basics, you will also begin to understand how to write longer papers involving definition.

DISCOVERING CONNECTIONS A

Select one of the following topics. Then, relying on one of the strategies that you practiced in Chapter 2, prewrite on that topic. Focus on defining qualities of the term.

1. charisma
2. stress
3. a slob

Save your work for later use.

PROVIDING A TOPIC SENTENCE THAT HIGHLIGHTS THE TERM TO BE DEFINED

An effective definition paragraph begins with a topic sentence that highlights the term to be defined. In fact, the topic sentence of a definition paragraph is often a brief definition itself. For example, if you were defining your view of what an *optimist* is, you might begin this way:

> An optimist is a person who sees good even in the worst situations and believes that, somehow, things will always work out for the best.

As you can see, the topic sentence provides a brief definition of the term, setting the direction for the sentences that will follow.

Look at this paragraph about the Jurassic Period:

> *Thanks to the movie* Jurassic Park, *the Jurassic is the best known of the three periods in the Mesozoic Era, which began some 225 million years ago.* Often called the Age of the Dinosaurs, the Jurassic Period began about 190 million years ago, when the huge reptiles began to dominate the land. In addition, the Jurassic saw the emergence of flying reptiles and birds. In fact, it was a time of great abundance and diversity of life on earth. Fossils of many forms of both plant and animal life dating from the Jurassic give evidence of a warm, moist climate that was fairly uniform around the world. The earlier Mesozoic period, the Triassic, which gave birth to the early dinosaurs as well as other reptiles, paved the way for the Jurassic abundance. The last Mesozoic period, the Cretaceous, acts as a footnote to the Jurassic; beginning around 136 million years ago, it saw an end to the dinosaurs, as small mammals made their appearance.

The topic sentence clearly states the term to be defined: the Jurassic Period. It also begins to define the Jurassic Period by mentioning a movie that is probably familiar to readers. Then it relates the period to a larger measure of time, the Mesozoic Era. The sentences that follow develop this definition further: The period's location in time is given; some of its dominant life forms are mentioned; its climate is described; and it is placed in relation to other periods of the Mesozoic Era.

➤ UNDERSTANDING THE PATTERN OF AN EFFECTIVE DEFINITION

A dictionary definition follows a simple pattern. It first identifies the general class to which the term belongs. Then it gives the special, or distinguishing, characteristics that set the word apart.

> **class**   **distinguishing characteristics**
> A derby is a *hat* with a *round crown made of stiffened felt.*

Paragraphs that define should also follow this **pattern of an effective definition.** However, most definition paragraphs call for greater elaboration. Especially with abstract subjects such as fear, you will need to express personal interpretation or experience. For such words, in addition to class and distinguishing characteristics, you should also provide specific, concrete examples and details for support.

Consider the elements of definition in the following paragraph on slapstick humor:

> Among the most popular types of comedy is slapstick humor, which involves violent acts such as hitting, punching, slapping, slipping, and falling down. The appeal of this type of humor is difficult to understand. Hit your own thumb as you work on some project, and you might bleed, swear, or pass out. Watch a television comedian hit her thumb with a hammer, and you'll probably laugh. Everyone knows that a person could slip on a banana peel and be seriously hurt, maybe even die; yet people still laugh when they see an actor slip on a banana peel and fall down.

The elements of an effective definition are at work here. The first sentence indicates that slapstick humor is part of a large class: comedy. Then it lists characteristics that make slapstick different from other types of humor. The rest of the paragraph provides specific details and examples of this type of comedy. Also, note that this definition raises an important question about the thing it defines: Why do we find slapstick humor funny? Raising this kind of question makes writing interesting and engaging.

Exploration 1a Defining Definition

1. Briefly explain definition. How is a dictionary definition different from a definition paragraph? _____

   _____

   _____

   _____

   _____

2. What role does the topic sentence play in a definition paragraph? _____

   _____

   _____

   _____

   _____

Exploration 1b Identifying the Elements of Definition

In each sentence of definition below, underline the word that is being defined. Then circle the class to which the word belongs, and double underline the distinguishing characteristics that set it apart. Study the example first.

> *Example*   A diplomat is a (government representative) who conducts
>
> relationships involving trade, treaties, and other official
>
> business with the government of another nation.

1. A judge is an elected (or sometimes appointed) public official who has the authority to hear and decide cases in a court of law.

2. A gecko is a tropical lizard with soft skin, a short, stout body, a large head, and suction pads on its feet.

3. A monopoly involves ownership or possession that gives exclusive control of a service or commodity in a market, making it possible to fix prices and strangle free competition.

4. The nuclear family is a social unit that consists of parents and the children they raise.

5. A democracy is a government in which the people hold ruling power through elected officials.

Exploration 1c   Developing Supporting Details for a Definition Paragraph

1. On page 117, the following topic sentence is given: *An optimist is a person who sees good even in the worst situations and believes that, somehow, things will always work out for the best.* Working with a partner, list details that could develop this definition more fully. Write the list on a separate sheet of paper.
2. Turn the details that you and your partner generated into sentences to support the topic sentence.

Challenge 1   Preparing to Write a Definition Paragraph

Prewrite on the subject of maturity. Focus on your best defining details. Then draft a topic sentence. Save your work for later use.

RECOGNIZING THE FULL EFFECT OF THE TERM DEFINED

Preparing an effective definition paragraph may also mean taking into account all the possible meanings for the term you are defining. To do this, you need to consider both the **denotation,** or literal meaning of the word, and its **connotations**—all the associations that also come with the word.

For example, the denotation of *clever* is its literal meaning, quick-witted and intelligent. When we say a child is clever, that is a compliment. When we say a politician or a criminal is clever, we are implying something negative. It is important to keep these kinds of connotations in mind when you are writing a definition paragraph.

Consider the following paragraph written about a friend's frankness:

My friend Roscoe is wonderfully frank. No matter what, you know he will be honest with you if you ask for an opinion. If you ask him how your hair looks, and he says it looks nice, you know he sincerely means it. However, you shouldn't ask his opinion if you don't want to know it. If he thinks your hair looks awful, he'll say so and make no excuses for it.

Here, the writer defines *frank*, which means "open and honest in expressing what one thinks or feels," as a positive quality of his friend Roscoe. However, had the writer been hurt because of a comment from Roscoe, he or she might have described him as *blunt* or *tactless*, words with similar meanings but negative connotations.

Exploration 2a Distinguishing between a Word's Denotation and Its Connotations

Explain the difference between a word's denotation and its connotations.

_____

_____

_____

_____

_____

_____

Exploration 2b Using Connotations of Words to Create an Attitude

For each pair of synonyms, write a + beside the word with a positive connotation and a – beside the word with a negative connotation. Then write a sentence using each word so that its meaning and your attitude toward it are clear. Study the example first.

> **Example**   __–__ miserly   __+__ thrifty
>
> *The miserly old man was so stingy that he deserved his lonely life.*
>
> *My thrifty grandfather at last saved enough to buy me that fishing rod I wanted.*

1. _____ stubborn   _____ persistent

_____

_____

2. _____ quaint   _____ outlandish

_____

_____

3. ____ ideals ____ illusions

_____

_____

4. ____ dog ____ cur

_____

_____

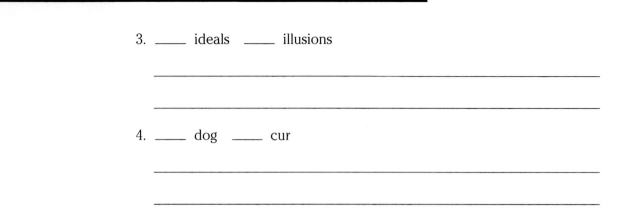

Challenge 2 Writing a Paragraph of Definition

For Challenge 1 on page 120, you completed a prewriting on the subject of maturity. Drawing on this material, write a paragraph of at least 100 words defining maturity. Consider the pattern of definition and the connotations of words as you write.

DISCOVERING CONNECTIONS **B**

1. In Discovering Connections A on page 117, you chose a topic for a definition paragraph and completed your prewriting. Now develop a paragraph of at least 100 words that defines that subject. Use the points laid out in this chapter as a guide.
2. Exchange your paragraph with a partner. If you completed the paragraph for Challenge 2 above and you feel this paragraph is better, use it for this exercise instead. Evaluate the paragraph you receive using the definition paragraph checklist below. Write your answers on a separate sheet of paper, and then return the paragraph and your assessment to the writer.
3. Using your reader's comments to guide you, revise your own paragraph.

Definition Paragraph Checklist

1. Does the topic sentence highlight the term to be defined?
2. Does it include the elements of an effective definition? What are they?
3. Does it take into consideration both the denotation and connotations of the term?

4. Underline any examples or details that are too general or too abstract to be effective. Suggest a concrete example that might be used instead.
5. In your judgment, what is the best part of this paragraph? Explain.
6. Which detail or example would be even better if it were expanded? Why?

RECAP
DEFINITION

New terms in this chapter	Definitions
➤ definition	➤ the writing technique used to specify the meanings of both concrete and abstract objects, ideas, events, or persons
➤ pattern of an effective definition	➤ two-step method of defining by first identifying the general class to which the term belongs, then listing its distinguishing characteristics

word	class	distinguishing characteristic

Example   A *convertible* is a *car* with a *retractable top.*

➤ denotation	➤ the direct, specific meaning of a word, as listed in the dictionary
➤ connotations	➤ the additional subjective meanings a word suggests, deriving from the associations or emotional overtones it has

Writing a Definition Paragraph

Choose a topic whose meaning needs **clarification** or **delineation.**

↓   ↑

Provide a **topic sentence** that indicates the term to be defined.

↓   ↑

Focus on the **elements of an effective definition.**

↓   ↑

Consider the **denotation** and **connotations** of the term you are defining.

10

Comparison and Contrast

OVERVIEW: EXPRESSING SIMILARITIES AND DIFFERENCES

We often make decisions after considering alternatives. For this reason, it's important to master the writing technique that examines alternatives, known as **comparison and contrast.** To compare is to examine *similarities;* to contrast is to examine *differences.* When you use comparison and contrast, you organize your explanation of one thing in terms of another, on the basis of common points.

A piece of writing that discusses the similarities and differences between two rock groups or political figures uses comparison and contrast. This mode would also be useful to explore the similarities and differences between two civilizations or two characters in a play. In fact, this mode of writing is often required in essay exams.

This chapter will explore the basic requirements for writing an effective comparison and contrast paragraph:

➤ providing a topic sentence that specifies the subjects and indicates the focus

➤ establishing a basis for comparison

➤ arranging ideas effectively

Once you have mastered these basics, you will also begin to understand how to write longer papers featuring comparison and contrast.

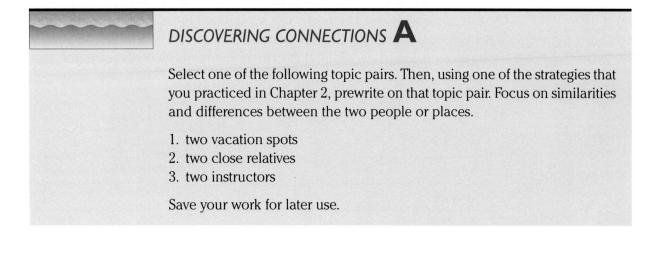

DISCOVERING CONNECTIONS A

Select one of the following topic pairs. Then, using one of the strategies that you practiced in Chapter 2, prewrite on that topic pair. Focus on similarities and differences between the two people or places.

1. two vacation spots
2. two close relatives
3. two instructors

Save your work for later use.

PROVIDING A TOPIC SENTENCE THAT SPECIFIES BOTH SUBJECTS AND INDICATES THE FOCUS

The topic sentence of a comparison and contrast paragraph specifies the two subjects to be examined. It also indicates whether the focus is on similarities or differences.

Consider this paragraph from a textbook on macroeconomics by Stephen L. Slavin:

> The big difference between the old Soviet economy and our own is what consumer goods and services are produced. In our economy, the market forces of supply and demand dictate what gets produced and how much of it gets produced. But a government planning agency in the Soviet Union dictated what and how much was made. In effect, central planning attempted to direct a production and distribution process that works automatically in a market economy.

Notice that the topic sentence names the subjects under discussion (the old Soviet economy and our own) and also indicates that the paragraph will contrast the two systems.

ESTABLISHING YOUR BASES FOR COMPARISON

Whenever you use comparison and contrast, you need to establish your **bases for comparison.** In other words, once you have chosen your subjects and your focus, you must specify the characteristics or elements you are going to examine.

For example, in a paragraph examining two brands of personal computers, you might examine *purchase price, warranties, types and availability of software,* and *ease of use.* Once you have established these bases of comparison, the next step is to discuss each brand in relation to these features. To be sure you include comparable information for both brands on every point, you may find it helpful to construct a planning chart first.

	Computer 1	Computer 2
Price		
Warranty		
Software		
Ease of use		

Look at this paragraph dealing with breast feeding versus bottle feeding:

> In many ways, breast feeding is much better than bottle feeding for babies. Formula certainly gives babies the basics in terms of vitamins and minerals. However, breast milk includes all these vitamins and minerals as well as special antibodies that combat common illnesses. In addition, some researchers have suggested that bottle feeding is less desirable because there is often minimal physical contact between the child and the person holding the bottle. They point out that breast feeding creates close physical and emotional bonds, so it is better for the infant's psychological well-being and strengthens the mother–child relationship. Overall, then, breast feeding seems the ideal way to keep a baby happy, healthy, and well-adjusted. In addition, it saves the cost of purchasing bottles and formula, so it is better for parents as well.

In this paragraph, the bases for comparison are clear. Both alternatives are examined in terms of nutrition and health, bonding between mother and child, and cost.

Exploration 1a   Defining Comparison and Contrast

1. In your own words, explain comparison and contrast. _____

_____

_____

_____

_____

2. What does *bases for comparison* mean? _____

_____

_____

_____

_____

Exploration 1b   Analyzing a Topic Sentence and Bases of Comparison

1. Take another look at the paragraph on page 126 about breast feeding versus bottle feeding. Explain what two pieces of information about the paragraph are supplied by the topic sentence.

_____

_____

_____

_____

_____

2. Working with a partner, list on a separate sheet of paper the bases for comparison in the paragraph on page 125 about our economy versus the old Soviet economy.

Challenge 1   Preparing to Write a Paragraph of Comparison or Contrast

Prewrite on the similarities or differences between two types of music or two political figures, actors, or professional athletes. Decide on several sound bases for comparison. Construct a planning chart like the one on page 126.

ARRANGING YOUR IDEAS EFFECTIVELY

When you write a comparison or a contrast paragraph, you can choose between two organizational plans. When you choose the **block format,** you first examine all the elements of subject A and then examine all the same elements in the same order for subject B. For example, say you used the block method to contrast two bosses for whom you've worked. You would first examine one boss in terms of how well he or she understood the job, how realistic he or she was, and how fairly this boss distributed work among the workers. Then you would examine the same criteria in the same order for the second boss.

The other method of arrangement is the **alternating format.** With this format, you switch back and forth between subjects as you examine each point. For example, you would first analyze how well boss 1 understood the job and then how well boss 2 understood the job. Next, you would discuss how realistic boss 1 was and then how realistic boss 2 was, and so on.

Notice the organizational plan of this paragraph which contrasts baseball and softball:

> Even though the rules for both games are the same, baseball and slow-pitch softball are definitely different games. Baseball is played on a large diamond. Softball, however, is played on a smaller field, more like a little league field. A baseball is pitched fast, up to ninety miles per hour in the major leagues, and overhand. In contrast, a slow-pitch softball is lobbed underhand. Because of the speed of the pitching and the variety of pitches, a .300 batting average for a baseball player is good. Because a softball is pitched more slowly, though, batting averages of .500 or more are common. Also, in baseball, players are allowed to steal bases. In softball, however, a runner can't leave the base until the ball is hit.

As you can see, this paragraph is arranged in the alternating format. First, the writer describes the size of the playing field for baseball and then for softball. Next, the writer compares the speed and style of pitching for both games, a typical batting average for baseball and then for softball, and base running rules in baseball and then in softball.

Now, take a look at the following paragraph from an astronomy textbook by Jay M. Pasachoff:

> Venus and the Earth are sister planets: their sizes, masses, and densities are about the same. But they are as different from each other as the wicked sisters were from Cinderella. The Earth is lush; it has oceans and rainstorms of water, an atmosphere containing oxygen, and creatures swimming in the sea, flying in the air, and walking on the ground. On the other hand, Venus is a hot, foreboding planet with temperatures constantly over 750 K (900°F), a planet on which life seems unlikely to develop. Why is Venus like that? How did these harsh conditions come about? Can it happen to us here on Earth?

This paragraph is arranged in the block fashion. First, the writer discusses various characteristics of Earth, and then he notes the contrasting characteristics of Venus. For information on using these formats in an essay, see "Using Comparison and Contrast to Develop an Essay" on page 211 in Chapter 15.

Transitional expressions are a great help to readers as they follow your organizational plan. A paragraph of comparison will, of course, use different sorts of transitions than a paragraph of contrast. The list below shows some of the transitional expressions you will find useful for each of these techniques.

Transitional Expressions Showing Contrast		*Transitional Expressions Showing Comparison*	
although	however	also	just as
but	on the other hand	both, neither	like
in contrast	unlike	in the same way	similarly

Exploration 2a   Distinguishing between Block and Alternating Format

Briefly explain the difference between the block format and the alternating format for comparison and contrast writing.

_____

_____

_____

_____

_____

_____

Exploration 2b   Practice in Formatting Bases of Comparison

1. For the subjects listed below, five types of differences are listed. Number the points of difference in column two so that they match up with the appropriate points of difference in column one.

Fish	*Whales*
1. vertical tail fins	_____ 20 feet to 100 feet long
2. gills take oxygen from water	_____ thick layer of blubber below skin
3. young develop from eggs released into water	_____ horizontal tail fins
4. up to 10 feet long	_____ lung breathers, must surface often
5. body covering of protective scales	_____ give birth to live young, feed them milk

2. Now on a separate piece of paper, describe how you would develop a paragraph contrasting whales and fish. Would you use alternating or block format? Explain your choice.

Exploration 2c   Revising and Evaluating Format

1. Review the sample paragraph on breast feeding versus bottle feeding (page 126). Working with a partner, identify the type of format the writer uses.

_____

_____

_____

2. With your partner, try reformatting the paragraph to use the other format. Now read your version out loud. Which format is more effective? Use the lines below to explain.

_____

_____

_____

_____

Challenge 2   Writing a Paragraph of Comparison or Contrast

Using the prewriting material you generated for Challenge 1 (page 127), complete a paragraph of at least 100 words that compares or contrasts two types of music or two political figures, actors, or professional athletes.

DISCOVERING CONNECTIONS B

1. In Discovering Connections A on page 125, you chose a topic for a comparison or contrast paragraph and completed your prewriting. Now develop a paragraph of at least 100 words that examines the similarities or differences between the subjects you chose. As you organize your plan and write your paragraph, remember the points raised throughout this chapter.

2. Exchange your paragraph with a partner. If you completed the paragraph for Challenge 2 and you feel this paragraph is better, use it for this exercise instead. Evaluate the paragraph you receive using the comparison and contrast paragraph checklist below. Write your answers on a separate sheet of paper, and then return the paragraph and your assessment to the writer.
3. Using your reader's comments to guide you, revise your own paragraph.

Comparison and Contrast Paragraph Checklist

1. Does the topic sentence specify the subjects and indicate the focus?
2. Does the paragraph establish bases for comparison? Make sure that each characteristic or element is discussed in equal detail for each subject. Put an * at any point where an element or characteristic is missing, and write *amplify* above any point that should be discussed in greater detail.
3. Are the ideas arranged effectively? Would the paragraph be more effective if the ideas were arranged differently or a different format were used? Explain.
4. In your judgment, what is the best part of this paragraph? Explain.
5. Which detail or example would be even better if it were expanded? Why?

RECAP
COMPARISON AND CONTRAST

New terms in this chapter	Definitions
➤ comparison and contrast	➤ the writing technique that examines similarities and differences between subjects ➤ *Comparison* may be used to develop similarities between subjects; *contrast,* to develop differences.
➤ bases for comparison	➤ the aspects, characteristics, or elements to be examined for both subjects in a paragraph of comparison and contrast
➤ block format	➤ a method of arranging elements for comparison and contrast in which all ideas about one subject are presented first, followed by all ideas about the second subject
➤ alternating format	➤ a method of arranging elements for comparison and contrast in which each of the elements or characteristics is discussed for both subjects on a point-by-point basis

Continued

Writing a Comparison and Contrast Paragraph

Choose subjects with evident **similarities** or **differences.**

↓   ↑

Provide a topic sentence that specifies the **focus—comparison** or **contrast.**

↓   ↑

Determine the **bases for comparison.**

↓   ↑

Consider either the **block format** or the **alternating format** to arrange your ideas.

The Block
Format

Introduction

Subject A
Point 1
Point 2
Point 3

Subject B
Point 1
Point 2
Point 3

Conclusion

The Alternating
Format

Introduction

Point 1
Subject A
Subject B

Point 2
Subject A
Subject B

Point 3
Subject A
Subject B

Conclusion

Cause
and **Effect**

OVERVIEW: EXPLAINING REASONS AND CONSEQUENCES

Nothing happens without a reason or without some kind of consequence. When you explain why things happen and what occurs when they do, the technique you use is **cause and effect.** *Cause* is *why* something occurred; *effect* is the *result* of what occurred. Because effects always have causes and causes always lead to effects, in writing, you rarely find one without the other. Often, however, the bulk of the writing focuses on one or the other.

Paragraphs about scientific topics often use a cause and effect structure. For example, a paragraph explaining the recent increase in certain antibiotic-resistant bacterial infections would call for a cause and effect approach. So would a writing dealing with the results of a severe drought.

This chapter will explore the basic requirements for writing an effective cause and effect paragraph:

➤ providing a topic sentence that focuses on either cause or effect

➤ distinguishing between direct and related causes and effects

➤ avoiding oversimplification of causes and effects

Once you have mastered these basics, you'll be prepared to use cause and effect to write longer papers.

DISCOVERING CONNECTIONS A

Select one of the following topics. Then, following one of the strategies that you practiced in Chapter 2, complete a prewriting on that topic.

1. a friendship you value (explain why you value it, or what caused it to develop)
2. leaving home to live independently (discuss results)
3. the attitude you have about politics (explain why you have this attitude)

Save your work for later use.

PROVIDING A TOPIC SENTENCE THAT FOCUSES ON CAUSE OR EFFECT

An important function of your topic sentence is to make clear whether you will focus on cause or on effect. Consider the following paragraph on the Civil War:

> *Although the debate over the causes of the Civil War is still raging, most historians believe that economic considerations played a dominant role in the conflict.* Before the secession, or the withdrawal, of the Southern states from the federal union, the North and the South had close economic ties. The South produced cotton that was woven into thread and fabric in the mills of the North. Other products, such as rice and tobacco, were also vital to the North's economy. Of course, the anti-slavery movement played an important role in motivating the North to declare war against the South. However, the threat to Northern pocketbooks probably weighed more heavily on the minds of politicians and merchants than did the injustices of slavery.

The topic sentence specifies that the paragraph will focus on the economic causes of the Civil War. That is, the Civil War is the effect; economic factors are primary reasons for that conflict. The body of the paragraph then explores those economic considerations.

Remember—transitional phrases will help you to clarify which of your supporting statements express causes and which express effects.

Transitional Expressions That Indicate Cause		*Transitional Expressions That Indicate Effect*	
because	since	as a result	if
cause	so that	consequently	therefore
reason	unless	effect	thus

➤ **D**ISTINGUISHING BETWEEN DIRECT AND RELATED CAUSES AND EFFECTS

Some causes and effects are more directly connected than others. For example, the primary cause of an automobile accident might be bad weather. However, excessive speed and lack of experience on the part of the driver may be contributing factors. You must distinguish between **direct causes** and **effects** and **related** ones so that you don't overstate a particular cause and effect relationship.

You must also make sure not to confuse cause and effect with **coincidence,** which refers to events, ideas, or experiences that occur at the same time but purely by accident. For example, just because the power went off in your next door neighbor's apartment while you were using your hair dryer, you cannot assume that one event necessarily caused the other.

Look at this example of a well-constructed cause and effect paragraph from a chemistry textbook by Cynthia Hahn:

> When a hot object is placed in contact with a cold object, energy is transferred from the hot object to the cold object by means of heat flow. The *temperature* of the hot object *decreases* because its *internal energy decreases.* The *temperature* of the cold object *increases* because its *internal energy increases.* The amount of energy lost by the hot object is equal to the amount of energy gained by the cold object. You know that heat flows spontaneously from hot object to cold, but not from cold to hot.

The opening sentence explains how energy is transferred from a hot object to a cold one. The direct cause of the heat transference, which the other sentences in the paragraph explain further, is a change in the internal energy of the objects. A decrease in internal energy of the hot object leads to an equal increase in the internal energy of the cold object.

Exploration 1a   Defining Cause and Effect

1. Briefly explain cause and effect writing. _____

_____

_____

_____

_____

2. What is the difference between a coincidence and a true cause and effect relationship? Briefly explain below; then provide an example of each.

_____

_____

_____

_____

_____

_____

Exploration 1b   Listing Causes and Effects

1. For each cause listed below, write as many effects, or consequences, as you can. Write your consequences in sentence form on a separate sheet of paper. Study the example first.

   Example   Cause: The drinking age is lowered to eighteen.

   Effect 1: The number of fatal car accidents involving teenagers doubles.

   Effect 2: The rate of teen alcoholism increases.

   Effect 3: Rates of truancy and unemployment among teens increase.

   a. Cause: World population doubles in size.
   b. Cause: You accept a job in another state.

2. For each effect listed on page 137, provide as many causes as you can. State these reasons in sentence form on your paper. Study the example first.

   Example   Effect: By 1900, bison nearly became extinct.

   Cause 1: In the late nineteenth century, hunters killed hundreds of thousands of bison for thrills or just for their tongues.

   Cause 2: In the late nineteenth century, settlers took over much of the bison's grassland habitat.

   Cause 3: In the late nineteenth century, smaller bison populations could not reproduce quickly enough to replace herd members killed by hunters.

a. Effect: The water supply in many communities is polluted and unsafe to drink.
b. Effect: Average life expectancy of United States citizens has increased.

Exploration 1c Planning for a Cause and Effect Paragraph

Working with a partner, exchange your work from Exploration 1b. Review one another's causes and effects. Place a ✓ beside the topic for which your partner has provided the strongest support. When you get your own work back, look at the list of supporting causes or effects that your partner has checked. Decide on an appropriate order of presentation for these causes and effects. Save your work for later use.

Challenge 1 Prewriting for a Cause and Effect Paragraph

Prewrite on the rise to popularity of a type of clothing, music, or dance. Explore reasons for the fad or for the effects it had.

A VOIDING OVERSIMPLIFICATION OF CAUSES AND EFFECTS

When you write about causes and effects, be sure to avoid **oversimplification** of either one. Rarely does an event or situation have a single cause or a single effect.

Think of a serious problem like juvenile delinquency. If you were to state that children whose parents are lenient will end up as juvenile delinquents, you would be *oversimplifying* a situation that is quite complex. Certainly a lack of discipline in childhood can contribute to bad behavior later in life. But to claim that one situation automatically leads to the other would not be accurate. Other outcomes are possible. (We all know people who were raised in undisciplined environments but who became solid citizens. We all also know individuals who had strict upbringings but still ended up in trouble.)

Consider this paragraph from a history textbook by Donald Kagan, Steven Ozment, and Frank M. Turner. It explains the social and economic consequences of the Black Death in Europe.

> As the number of farm laborers decreased, their wages increased and those of skilled artisans soared. Many serfs now chose to commute their labor services by money payments or to abandon the farm altogether and pursue more interesting and rewarding jobs in skilled craft industries in the cities. Agricultural prices fell because of lowered demand, and the price of luxury and manufactured goods—the work of skilled artisans—rose. The noble landholders suffered the greatest decline in power from this new state of affairs. They were forced to pay

more for finished products and for farm labor but received a smaller return on their agricultural produce. Everywhere their rents were in steady decline after the plague.

As this paragraph shows, the labor shortage in Europe following the bubonic plague led to a number of effects: an increase in wages; a migration from the farms to the cities; a decrease in agricultural prices and an increase in the cost of luxury and manufactured goods; and a decline in the power of noble landowners.

Exploration 2a   Understanding Complexity in Cause and Effect

Why is a paragraph that explores only one cause or effect likely to be an over-simplification?

_____

_____

_____

_____

_____

_____

Exploration 2b   Developing Adequate Causes

1. In the discussion on page 137, the subject of the causes of juvenile delinquency is raised. Working with a partner, make a list on a separate sheet of paper of possible causes of juvenile delinquency.
2. On the same sheet of paper, write a topic sentence and turn the causes of delinquency that you and your partner have identified into supporting sentences.

Exploration 2c   Writing a Topic Sentence and Supporting Sentences

Working with a partner, review the strongest list of causes or effects that you identified in Exploration 1c on page 137. Have you oversimplified any of your causes or effects? Add further support or revise any unclear reasons or consequences. Then write a topic sentence that specifies the focus of your paragraph. Turn your list of causes or effects into smoothly connected supporting sentences using transitions such as *because* or *as a result.*

Challenge 2   Composing a Cause and Effect Paragraph

For Challenge 1 on page 137, you completed a prewriting on how a type of clothing, music, or dance became popular or on what resulted from the fad. Now compose a cause and effect paragraph of about 100 words on this subject.

DISCOVERING CONNECTIONS B

1. In Discovering Connections A on page 134, you chose a topic for a cause and effect paragraph and completed a freewriting. Now develop a paragraph of at least 100 words that explains what led to the subject or what happened because of it. Make sure to consider the points raised in this chapter as you write your paragraph.

2. Exchange your paragraph with a partner. If you completed a paragraph for Challenge 2 above and you feel this paragraph is better, use it for this exercise instead. Evaluate the paragraph you receive, using the cause and effect paragraph checklist below. Write your answers on a separate sheet of paper, and then return the paragraph and your assessment to the writer.

3. Using your reader's comments to guide you, revise your own paragraph.

Cause and Effect Paragraph Checklist

1. Does the topic sentence focus on either cause or effect?
2. Does the paragraph distinguish between direct and related causes and effects? Underline any details that seem like coincidences rather than true causes or effects.
3. Does the writer provide a sufficient number of causes or effects to support the main idea? If you feel more specific details are required, write "I'd like to know more about _____" in the margin next to the appropriate sentence or passage.
4. In your judgment, what is the best part of the paragraph? Explain.
5. Which detail or example would be even better if it were expanded? Why?

RECAP
CAUSE AND EFFECT

New terms in this chapter	Definitions
➤ cause and effect	➤ the writing technique that explains why things happen (**cause**) and what occurs when they do (**effect**)
➤ direct causes	➤ primary or main reasons
➤ direct effects	➤ primary or principal results
➤ related causes or effects	➤ contributing reasons or results
➤ coincidence	➤ events, ideas, or experiences that occur by accident at the same time
➤ oversimplification	➤ error in reasoning that causes one to overlook the complexity in a cause and effect relationship
	Example "She doesn't want a career because her mother was never home when she was a child."

Writing a Cause and Effect Paragraph

Identify a **subject** that focuses on the **reasons for** or the **results of** an event or phenomenon.

↓ ↑

Establish the **focus**—**cause** or **effect**—in a clear topic sentence.

↓ ↑

Be sure the reader will understand the differences between **direct** and **related** causes and effects in your paragraph.

↓ ↑

Provide details to convey the **complexity** of the cause and effect relationship you are describing.

Division
and **Classification**

OVERVIEW: *ANALYZING THE WHOLE IN TERMS OF THE PARTS*

Writing often involves simplifying complex subjects in order to communicate clearly about them to a reader. Two important techniques for this purpose are **division** and **classification.** Although division and classification are separate processes, they are usually discussed together and often appear together in writing. Both processes involve analysis, looking at something large or complex by breaking it down into parts. *Division* refers to the separation of a subject into component parts. *Classification* refers to the arrangement of component parts into groups on the basis of some principle or characteristic.

A paragraph about bad drivers, for example, could use division and classification. The writer could divide the types into *slow drivers, fast drivers, rude drivers,* and *careless drivers* and then discuss examples of each type. A paragraph about putting together a home audio system could also use division and classification, discussing various *receivers, dual cassette decks, CD players,* and *speakers.*

This chapter will explore the basic requirements for writing an effective division or classification paragraph:

➤ providing a topic sentence that defines the scope of the discussion and indicates an emphasis on either division or classification
➤ establishing a logical method of analysis
➤ maintaining a consistent presentation
➤ using distinct and complete groupings

141

Once you have mastered these basics, you'll be prepared to use division and classification to write longer papers.

DISCOVERING CONNECTIONS A

Choose one of the following topics. Then, employing one of the strategies that you practiced in Chapter 2, complete a prewriting on this subject. Think of categories, or types, within the topic as you write.

1. college students
2. parties
3. television commercials

Save your work for later use.

➤ S PECIFYING SCOPE AND EMPHASIS THROUGH A TOPIC SENTENCE

In a division or classification paragraph, the topic sentence specifies the scope of the subject that the writer will examine. It also often indicates whether the emphasis in the paragraph will be on division or classification.

Consider this paragraph about being a health-care worker:

> *The work of a certified nurse's assistant can be divided into four basic tasks.* First, you must wash and dress the patients. Then you must feed the patients and make sure they all take their medications. Next, you must get the ones who can walk or be moved around in a wheelchair out of bed and to the activity room. Last, and most important, you must talk with and listen to patients. A nursing care facility is home for these people, and they need to have as normal a life as they can.

As you can see, the topic sentence spells out a broader category for the paragraph: the work of a certified nurse's assistant. In addition, the topic sentence indicates that the paragraph will use division: The broad subject *work* will be presented as four basic tasks.

A typical topic sentence for a classification paragraph will name the large group to be divided and then specify the *basis of classification.* This is the principle or characteristic used for making subdivisions or *classes.* The topic sentence may also name the classes, as in the following example:

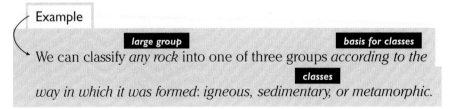

Example

We can classify *any rock* into one of three groups *according to the* [large group] [basis for classes]
way in which it was formed: igneous, sedimentary, or metamorphic. [classes]

ESTABLISHING A LOGICAL METHOD OF ANALYSIS

Whether your focus is on division or classification, you need to establish a logical method of analyzing the group or subject you choose. Any subject can be presented in a variety of ways. You need to choose divisions or categories that will enable your reader to understand your subject.

Imagine that you are writing about the role that the local hospital plays in your community. You could approach this subject from a number of directions. For example, you might examine the hospital as a full-service health-care center, using division to discuss first its *emergency department,* then its *inpatient treatment section,* its *diagnostic testing center,* and then its *rehabilitation clinic.* If you instead planned to examine how the hospital functions as a business, you might establish these subdivisions: *marketing department, billing and customer service area, volunteer services,* and *fund-raising committee.*

Look at this paragraph about government spending:

> The way the federal government spends money is ridiculous. My economics instructor explained that only 5 percent of the money it collects is allotted for combined spending on social services, assisted housing, public health programs, and unemployment compensation. In addition, only 9 percent is devoted to a combination of assistance programs such as food stamps, aid to families with dependent children, and supplemental security income. On the other hand, more than 20 percent is spent on defense, even though we aren't at war with anyone.

In this paragraph, the writer uses division to support the paragraph's broad argument about government spending. The method of analysis is clear and logical. The writer looks at government spending in three main areas: *social programs, assistance programs,* and *defense programs.*

Certain words and phrases will help you to stress the divisions or classifications you establish in your paragraph. The list below gives you some possibilities.

■ *Transitional Expressions That Show Division or Classification*

can be categorized (classified)	the first type (kind), second type, etc.
can be divided	the last category

Exploration 1a   Understanding Division and Classification

1. In your own words, explain division and classification. How do they differ?

_____

_____

_____

_____

_____

2. Briefly explain the meaning of *logical method of analysis.* _____

_____

_____

_____

_____

Exploration 1b   Identifying the Basis of Classification

Each group of things, places, or people below has been classified according to a principle or characteristic. This principle or characteristic is the basis of classification. On the blank line, write a phrase that explains the basis of classification. Next, see if all the classes fit this basis properly. Some groups have an item that does not belong. Cross it out. Study the example first.

> **Example**   *plants*   a. full sunlight   b. partial sunlight   c. ~~blooming~~
> d. shade
>
> basis of classification: *amount of light required to thrive*

1. *cereals*   a. oat-based   b. corn-based   c. wheat-based   d. cooked

   basis of classification: _____

2. *movies*   a. action   b. comedy   c. R-rated   d. Western

   basis of classification: _____

3. *sports icons*   a. "bad boys"   b. basketball stars   c. record-holders
   d. grand old legends

   basis of classification: _____

4. *travel accommodations*   a. bed and breakfast   b. resort lodge   c. motel
   d. hotel

   basis of classification: _____

5. *Westward expansion*   a. airplane   b. wagon train   c. railroad
   d. horseback

   basis of classification: _____

Exploration 1c Developing Classes for a Classification Paragraph

Working with a partner, choose one of the classified groups in Exploration 1b. Change or add to the list of classes if you wish. Add explanations, descriptive details, or examples, making sure they are parallel for each class. Save your work for later use.

Challenge 1 Prewriting for a Division or Classification Paragraph

Complete a prewriting on the tasks involved in performing your job or in completing assignments for one of your courses. Think in terms of the divisions or classes into which your topic may be organized. Save your work for later use.

*M*AINTAINING A CONSISTENT PRESENTATION

As you decide on the focus of your division or classification paragraph, it's also important to maintain **consistency** in the component parts or classes you establish. Maintaining a **consistent presentation** means establishing divisions or classes on a set basis. You must not introduce an unrelated category.

Imagine you were writing a paragraph about your expenses. You would be likely to discuss such items as *rent, food, clothing, savings,* and *entertainment.* You wouldn't discuss an upcoming raise or an expected tax return because these are *sources of income,* not *expenses.*

Take a look at this well-constructed classification paragraph about reinforcement from a psychology textbook by Zick Rubin, Letitia Anne Peplau, and Peter Salovey:

> **Reinforcement** is the process of using rewards—or reinforcers—to strengthen particular responses. A *reinforcer* is any event that strengthens the response it follows—that is, that increases the likelihood of that response occurring again. One of the most important challenges for anyone trying to teach something to an animal or person is to figure out just what things are reinforcing to that individual. Some things, such as food, water, and affection, seem to be naturally reinforcing; these are called **primary reinforcers.** Other things or events become reinforcing as a result of their association with primary reinforcers; these are called **secondary reinforcers.** Secondary reinforcers play a big part in shaping our behavior. Think of all the behaviors we engage in to earn awards, pats on the back, and grades. We have learned that the awards, pats, and grades are rewarding because they tend to go along with other more basic rewards, such as affection and esteem.

As you can see, this paragraph divides reinforcers into two similar categories: primary reinforcers and secondary reinforcers. It defines and explains each type through closely related examples: Food and water are primary reinforcers; awards and pats on the back are secondary reinforcers. Therefore, both the types it establishes and the details about those types are consistent.

➤ USING DISTINCT AND COMPLETE GROUPINGS

As you develop a division and classification paper, you also need to use **distinct and complete groupings.** When a grouping is *distinct,* it is clearly distinguished from others. When it is *complete,* it is expressed in full detail.

Imagine that you are writing a paragraph on community theater that focuses on the people who attend the plays. If you were to divide these people into only two groups—family members of the cast and other people from the community—the second category would be too general. Your groupings would be incomplete. In fact, *other members of the community* is actually composed of several groups: senior citizens, community leaders, college students, families with young children, and so forth. None of these groupings overlap; each one has a distinctive set of members. In order to make your analysis complete, you would want to be sure that these categories did not overlook anyone who attends the plays.

Consider the way this paragraph classifies types of workers. Are the groupings distinct and complete?

> In every job I've ever had, I have found that the workers can be classified into four groups. The first group consists of the self-appointed bosses. They are workers, just like the rest of us, but they take it upon themselves to tell fellow workers how to do their jobs. Sometimes they even make unsolicited reports back to the real supervisor. Then there are the avoiders. This type of worker does anything possible to avoid working hard. Avoiders leave work undone and call in sick or leave early on the busiest of days, so that their coworkers have to work even harder. Avoiders do just enough work to keep themselves from being fired. The next group is the complainers. These workers put in a solid day's work, but they make co-workers miserable and worsen morale by whining and criticizing. Finally, there is the most important group: the doers. This group of workers is what keeps a business going. Doers carry out all the tasks assigned to them completely and effectively, without complaining. It's a good thing there are more doers than any other group, because no company can survive without them.

In this paragraph, the groupings are both distinct and complete. The writer classifies workers into four groups: *self-appointed bosses, avoiders, complainers,* and *doers.* Each group is explained in detail to bring the portraits into focus for the reader.

Exploration 2a Understanding Consistency, Distinctness, and Completeness in Groupings

1. What is a consistent presentation? _____

   _____

   _____

   _____

   _____

2. In your own words, briefly explain how to keep groupings in a division or classification paragraph distinct and complete. _____

   _____

   _____

   _____

   _____

Exploration 2b Explaining Consistency, Distinctness, and Completeness in Groupings

1. Take another look at the paragraph about types of workers on page 146. Are the groupings consistent? Why or why not? _____

   _____

   _____

   _____

2. Reread the paragraph about reinforcement on page 145. Explain why the classes it presents are distinct and complete. _____

   _____

   _____

   _____

Exploration 2c   Creating Consistent, Distinct, and Complete Groupings

1. Working with a partner, choose one of the following subjects, and divide it into groups or types you might observe: people at a mall, kinds of commercials, types of bosses. Also, write the basis for your classification.

_____

_____

_____

_____

_____

_____

2. Exchange your paper with another team. Evaluate whether the classes are consistent, distinct, and complete. Return the paper, with your suggestions, to its writers.

Challenge 2   Writing a Division and Classification Paragraph

Using the prewriting material you developed for Challenge 1 on page 145, draft a paragraph of at least 100 words on the tasks involved in your job or in completing assignments for one of your courses.

DISCOVERING CONNECTIONS **B**

1. In Discovering Connections A on page 142, you chose a topic for a division or classification paragraph and completed your prewriting. Now develop a paragraph of at least 100 words that analyzes the subject by dividing or classifying it. As you develop your paragraph, consider the points raised in this chapter.
2. Exchange your paragraph with a classmate. If you completed the paragraph for Challenge 2 above and you feel that this paragraph is better, use it for this exercise instead. Evaluate the paragraph you receive, using the division and classification paragraph checklist on page 149. Write your answers on a separate sheet of paper, and then return the paragraph and your assessment to the writer.
3. Using your reader's comments to guide you, revise your paragraph.

Division and Classification Paragraph Checklist

1. Does the topic sentence define the scope of the discussion and indicate an emphasis on either division or classification?
2. Is a logical, consistent method of analysis maintained throughout?
3. Should any details or examples be further subdivided? If so, underline them.
4. Are the elements used distinct and complete? If you think any of the material needs to be made clearer or more specific, write, "I'd like to know more about _____" in the margin next to it.
5. In your judgment, what is the best part of this paragraph? Explain.
6. Which detail or example would be even better if it were expanded? Why?

RECAP
DIVISION AND CLASSIFICATION

New terms in this chapter	Definitions
➤ division and classification	➤ writing techniques used to break down a subject (**division**) or group ideas (**classification**) for analysis so that the subject is easier to grasp
➤ consistent presentation	➤ using the same principle of division or classification for all the parts of a topic under discussion and providing parallel elements of description or analysis for each
➤ distinct and complete groupings	➤ categories for classification or division that are clearly distinguished from others and expressed in full detail

Writing a Division or Classification Paragraph

Indicate your subject and your focus—**division** or **classification**—in a clear **topic sentence.**

↓ ↑

Choose a **logical method of analysis.**

↓ ↑

Keep your **presentation consistent.**

↓ ↑

Make all **categories distinct** and **complete.**

13

Argument

OVERVIEW: UNDERSTANDING PERSUASION

As noted in Chapter 5, **argument** refers to the purpose of a piece of writing. Argument is not a writing technique or a mode. It is writing that uses a combination of modes to *persuade* readers to accept a point of view.

A paragraph asserting that English should be the national language of the United States would be argument. So would one maintaining that public high schools have no right to impose student dress codes.

This chapter will explore the basic requirements for writing an effective argument:

➤ expressing a clear stance on the issue in a topic sentence
➤ providing sufficient support
➤ using a tone that is reasonable and convincing
➤ avoiding errors in logic
➤ arranging your support in emphatic order

Once you have mastered these basics, you'll be ready to write multi-paragraph arguments.

DISCOVERING CONNECTIONS A

Choose one of the following topics. Then, following one of the strategies that you practiced in Chapter 2, prewrite on the subject. Consider your position on the topic and your reasons for your conclusion.

1. warning labels on books, tapes, CDs, or video games
2. a required "C" average for college students to participate in sports
3. home confinement or other alternative sentencing for first-time criminal offenders

Save your work for later use.

➤ *P*ROVIDING A TOPIC SENTENCE THAT EXPRESSES A CLEAR STANCE ON THE ISSUE

The topic sentence of an argument paragraph should state clearly the **stance** you are taking on the issue, whether you are *in favor of* or *against* the point being raised. For example, imagine you were writing a paragraph about term limits for U.S. Senators and members of the House of Representatives. If you were writing to *oppose* term limits, you might write a topic sentence like this one:

> Imposing term limits on members of Congress would damage our system of government.

And if you were writing to *support* term limits, you might write a topic sentence like this one:

> The lack of term limits for members of Congress is a threat to the democratic process.

In either case, your reader would be aware of the issue and your opinion on it.

Consider the stance set forth by the topic sentence in this paragraph about a controversial aspect of adoption:

> *Adopted children should be able to read through their sealed adoption files and make contact with their biological parents if they choose.*

Many adoptees feel that something is missing in their lives. They feel an emotional gap that can only be filled by learning more about their biological parents. Also, adoptees should have the same rights as everyone else to learn about their heritage, race, and ethnicity. Most people consider this kind of knowledge important. If their adoption records remain sealed, how can adoptees gain a full understanding of their own background? However, the most important reason for unsealing adoption records is medical. Researchers have proven that many diseases and medical conditions, such as diabetes and heart disease, tend to run in families. Therefore, without a full medical history of their biological relatives, some adoptees may actually be at medical risk.

In this paragraph, the topic sentence provides a clear direction for the reader. Both the issue and the writer's stance are explicitly stated: Adoptees should have full access to their adoption records. As a result, the reader is prepared for the supporting sentences that follow.

➤ *D*EVELOPING SUFFICIENT SUPPORT THROUGH SOUND REASONS

There is no set rule about the amount of information needed to develop a sound argument. Think of a subject about which you are undecided. How much support would *you* need to see before you would accept that position? It's likely that you would require several solid supporting details and examples before you would be convinced. Your reader demands the same of you, so as a general guideline, include *at least* three points, or reasons, to support your stance.

As you develop your reasons with details and examples, it's important to recognize the relationship between fact and opinion. A **fact** is a verifiable truth. It's a *fact* that driving on icy roads is dangerous. There is no room for discussion. An **opinion,** however, is a belief. It may be founded on impressions, experiences, or a person's base of knowledge. It's an *opinion* to say that the failure to treat icy roads means that city or town officials aren't concerned about the danger. The validity of an opinion depends upon its basis, that is, how well it is supported by fact. To develop support for your opinion, incorporate facts wherever possible in your examples.

To help develop your argument, make a list of points that support your position and a list of points that someone opposed to the argument might raise. The value of the first list is obvious: These are the points that will form the framework for your argument. However, the second list is also important. By answering some of these points, you may be able to refute them completely or turn them to your advantage.

Imagine, for example, that you are interested in developing a paper in favor of banning television ads for beer and alcohol. Here is a list of reasons for and against the ban:

In favor of the ban

➤ Commercials exert pressure on young people to drink.
➤ They misrepresent what happens when people drink.
➤ Since cigarette commercials have been banned, the number of smokers has dropped.

Against the ban

➤ People need to take responsibility for their own actions.
➤ Some of the commercials are entertaining.
➤ A ban is a form of censorship.

The points in favor of the ban are valid, so you could feel comfortable including them in your essay.

However, you could also adapt and use the first and last points from the list *against* the ban. Yes, it's true that people should be responsible enough to make wise decisions concerning alcohol. And it's also true that banning anything is an infringement on our personal rights. But the government frequently imposes rules when it's obvious that people can't be trusted to act properly on their own. For instance, government officials have established speed limits and other traffic guidelines to ensure the safety of the public, although these laws may infringe on personal rights. Furthermore, the ban would be limited to television advertising. Alcohol companies, like cigarette manufacturers, could still advertise in newspapers and magazines, so they would still have an avenue to reach the public.

Now, look at an argument paragraph based on this material:

> Television ads for alcoholic beverages should be banned. For one thing, these commercials exert pressure on viewers, especially young people, to drink. They imply that the only way to be cool is to drink. In addition, these commercials misrepresent the effects of drinking. The people in them never get into fights, engage in unsafe sexual activities, or get behind the wheel of a car. In real life, however, these events are frequent consequences of drinking. It's true that banning these TV ads is a form of censorship and that people should take personal responsibility for their actions. However, the rate of alcoholism in the United States shows that many people aren't willing or able to take responsibility for themselves when it comes to drinking. Thus, the ban is justified to help protect society. A recent article in *Newsweek* reported that banning TV commercials for cigarettes in the 1960s contributed to a reduction in the number of people smoking. If a ban on commercials for alcoholic beverages were half as successful, there would be a lot more sober people and a lot less heartache caused by alcohol.

As you can see, examples in favor of the ban and against it are incorporated into the paragraph, resulting in an effective argument.

Incidentally, whenever you draw information from a document or individual to support your argument, you must indicate its source for your reader. In most argument paragraphs you will write, you can acknowledge your source with a simple text explanation: "According to a recent report in *U.S. News & World Report,* the number of reported rapes on college campuses nationwide has risen dramatically."

However, for longer, more formal assignments, you will need to provide more specific **documentation** for your sources, including such details as the title, date of publication, publisher, pages involved, and so on. Ask which style of formal documentation your instructor prefers. The reference section of your college library will have guidelines for several different styles. For most assignments in English or other humanities disciplines, your instructor will want you to use the guidelines of the Modern Language Association (MLA). The guidelines of the American Psychological Association (APA) are generally used in education, the social sciences, and the natural and physical sciences.

Exploration 1a   Understanding Argument

1. What makes argument different from the writing techniques (*narration, description, definition,* etc.) that you have studied in the last several chapters?

_____

_____

_____

_____

2. What gauge could you use to decide if you have provided enough support

   for your argument? _____

_____

_____

_____

3. Why should you think through the points of the opposing argument as you

   develop your plan for an argument paragraph? _____

_____

_____

_____

_____

Exploration 1b   Explaining the Stance and Reasons in an Argument Paragraph

1. Find the topic sentence in the argument paragraph about banning television ads for alcoholic products on page 153. Explain its role in the paragraph.

_____

_____

_____

_____

2. How many reasons are given to prove the writer's case? Summarize them on the lines given. _____

_____

_____

_____

_____

_____

Exploration 1c   Analyzing Fact and Opinion and Developing Persuasive Reasons

1. On a separate sheet of paper, list three facts. Then underneath each fact, write an opinion about that fact.

2. Look again at the paragraph about adoption on pages 151–152. Working with a partner, develop on a separate sheet of paper a list of reasons to support the opposite point of view. Then list as many facts as you can to support those reasons.

Challenge 1   Prewriting for an Argument Paragraph

Prewrite on the idea of a ban. For example, take a stand on the issue of banning certain books in U.S. public schools or on banning the expression of ideas that some groups in society find objectionable. Save your work for later use.

➤ USING A REASONABLE, CONVINCING TONE

Another factor that will affect your reader's acceptance of your point of view is your **tone,** the attitude you express about your subject. If your tone is sarcastic, superior, or patronizing, you may alienate a reader who might otherwise be swayed to agree with your point of view. On the other hand, if your tone is sincere and respectful, you'll enhance the chance that your point of view will be favorably received.

One way to make your writing convincing is by avoiding absolute terms. For instance, it is better to say that alcoholics rarely can control their drinking without help or support from a group such as Alcoholics Anonymous than it is to say that they *never* can. Below is a list of more moderate terms that you can substitute for absolute language.

Absolute Word	*Moderate Substitute*
all	most
always	frequently
every	many
never	rarely

It is also important to avoid personally attacking or insulting opponents of your argument (see Argument *ad hominem,* page 157). With an emotionally charged subject like gun control, for example, it's easy to understand how sentences such as these might appear in an early draft:

> Most people who buy handguns do so for personal protection. *However, a person would have to be stupid not to know* that handguns are statistically more likely to be stolen or to cause accidental injury than to be used effectively for protection.

The message in these sentences is valid, but the name-calling is insulting to both the opponents of the writer's position and readers who are merely poorly informed about this issue.

Now, consider this version of the sentences:

> Most people who buy handguns do so for personal protection. *However, many people are unaware* that handguns are statistically more likely to be stolen or to cause accidental injury than to be used effectively for protection.

The message is the same in the second version, but the simple change in phrasing eliminates inflammatory name-calling. Instead, the writer is providing information in an objective tone that is much more likely to make poorly informed readers want to learn more about the issue.

➤ USING SOUND LOGIC

To persuade a reader, an argument must use logical reasoning that leads to a valid conclusion. You can establish such a *line of reasoning* by engaging in one of two reasoning processes: induction or deduction. Although the goal of these two reasoning processes is the same, they come at the subject from opposite directions.

With **induction,** you move from a series of specific instances or pieces of evidence to a general conclusion. Physicians employ inductive reasoning in diagnosing an illness. For example, a dermatologist might conclude that a patient's skin rash is a form of eczema because every other rash like this one that she has examined has proven to be eczema.

An answer reached in this way involves an *inductive leap.* Although this diagnosis is a reasonable conclusion based on the evidence, it isn't the only possible valid explanation. The rash may closely resemble eczema, but it may actually be the result of another condition. The more specific instances backing it up, the more likely the conclusion is sound.

Deduction, in contrast, involves reasoning from a general statement to a specific conclusion. Say, for example, you know that flat, low-lying inland areas are especially vulnerable to tornadoes. You also know that your cousin lives in a flat, low-lying inland area. You could therefore conclude that your cousin's neighborhood is a likely target for a tornado.

Use of sound logic will strengthen your argument. Faulty logic or **logical fallacies,** like those described in the table below and on page 158, will weaken it.

Avoid Logical Fallacies

Fallacy	Examples of Fallacious Logic	Instead Use Sound Logic
Argument *ad hominem* (Latin for "argument to the man")		
Attacking the person	That film critic criticizes sex and violence in films, but he was accused of assault and battery while in college.	Respond to the opposing positions.
Bandwagon approach		
Urging acceptance because "everybody does it"	Everybody is against the idea of allowing that historic house to be demolished.	Cite objective, qualified authorities.
Begging the question		
Assuming as fact what must be proven	NASA's call for increased funding in these hard times is more proof that these scientists care about nothing but their pet programs.	Provide relevant, documented evidence.

(Continued)

Avoid Logical Fallacies (continued)

Fallacy	Examples of Fallacious Logic	Instead Use Sound Logic
Circular reasoning		
Restating your opinion and calling it a reason	She is the best candidate because of all of them, she is superior.	Give real reasons.
Creating a red herring		
Diverting attention to an unimportant point	Congress is trying to indict the President in the sale of arms to an enemy nation, yet these same legislators misuse the Congressional gymnasium.	Provide compelling evidence.
Either/or reasoning		
Suggesting only two alternatives when many possibilities exist	Unless we completely change the way we conduct presidential elections, we'll never attract good candidates.	Explore all relevant possibilities.
Hasty generalization		
Making an assumption based on insufficient evidence	Two of my friends have had trouble with that brand of stereo equipment, so that company obviously doesn't make very good products.	Base conclusions on many objective facts.
Non sequitur (Latin for "it does not follow")		
Linking two unrelated issues	Homeless people aren't working, and potato chips are getting so expensive I can't afford them.	Think through relationships using logic.
Oversimplification		
Wrongfully reducing a complex subject	Sex education classes will eliminate teenage promiscuity.	State all important aspects; admit inconsistencies.
Post hoc, ergo propter hoc (Latin for "after this, therefore because of this")		
Assuming cause–effect relationship between two things that occurred by coincidence	The killer had just eaten at a fast-food restaurant, so something in the food must have triggered his aggression.	Check your thinking for irrational statements.

Find the logical fallacy in this paragraph on banning some material on the Internet:

Censoring the discussion of certain topics on the Internet is wrong for several reasons. First, censorship of any sort is a violation of the First Amendment to the U.S. Constitution, which guarantees U.S. citizens freedom of speech. Banning particular words and subjects from websites violates this right. Second, many proponents of a ban are seeking censorship because the ideas being communicated are offensive to their religious beliefs. However, the United States was established on the principle of the separation of church and state. No religion must be allowed to dictate what is correct or moral for the majority. If we allow these extremists to decide what is acceptable and what isn't, before long we won't have any rights left. Third, and most important, restricting the flow of knowledge of any sort is counterproductive to society at large. Censoring an important means of worldwide communication creates the possibility that ignorance and hatred might prevail over peace and understanding.

You probably identified the seventh sentence, indicating that failing to stop this act of censorship will lead to an elimination of all our rights. This is a case of *either/or reasoning*. True, if a ban is established, we do face a limitation on *one* right, but it will not lead to a complete elimination of the First Amendment, nor will it affect the other freedoms we enjoy in the United States. Removing the sentence will improve the paragraph, for it will then be wholly based on logical reasoning.

ARRANGING YOUR SUPPORT IN EMPHATIC ORDER

Most often writers arrange ideas in an argument paragraph in emphatic order. Using *emphatic order* means arranging your details and examples so that each one has an impact that matches its relative importance. (Emphatic order is discussed at length on pages 67–68.) Your initial point should be lively enough to spark and hold your reader's interest and to begin cultivating acceptance of your point of view. Each point should grow increasingly stronger so that your argument builds to a forceful, convincing conclusion.

Read this argument paragraph about condom availability in college rest rooms. Consider the ordering of its reasons:

> Condom machines should be installed in all college rest rooms. Sometimes sexually active students are too self-conscious to buy condoms in a store, but they're not likely to skip sex because they don't have condoms. As a result, these students will be putting themselves and their partners at risk for unwanted pregnancies. Recent government statistics indicate that the number of pregnancies among unwed partners continues to climb at an alarming rate. The availability of condoms would help to cut down on that rate. However, the most important reason to install condom machines is the threat of AIDS. It's an indisputable fact that unprotected sex can lead to the transmission of AIDS, a deadly, incurable disease. Using condoms can stop the spread of AIDS. If having condom machines in campus rest rooms can save one life, then we should start installing them today.

As you can see, the supporting sentences are arranged in emphatic order. The initial reason—that some students won't actively seek a condom because of embarrassment—is a strong one. It adds credence to the stance that condoms should be freely available to college students for their own protection. The next two points add to the strength of the argument. The final point—that having condoms available may save lives—is the strongest support of all, and a fitting conclusion.

Transitional phrases can help guide your readers through your line of reasoning and highlight the emphatic order. The list below gives some of these transitions.

Transitional Expressions for Argument

To Establish Reasons	To Answer the Opposition	To Conclude
first (second, third, etc.)	some may say	therefore
most important	on the other hand	thus

Exploration 2a   Understanding Tone and Logical Reasoning

1. Explain how you can establish a reasonable, convincing tone in an argument paragraph. _____

   _____

   _____

   _____

   _____

2. Define and distinguish between induction and deduction. _____

   _____

   _____

   _____

   _____

Exploration 2b   Practice Eliminating Logical Fallacies

1. Turn again to the list of logical fallacies on pages 157–158. Working with a partner, choose three of the categories on the list. On a separate sheet of paper, write additional examples for them.

2. Exchange papers with another team. Evaluate the statements you receive. Mark statements that do not illustrate the specific fallacy as intended. Then for each fallacy, write a contrasting statement that is logical, factual, and reasonable. Return the papers to their writers.

Exploration 2c   Writing and Evaluating Arguments

1. Reread the sample paragraphs on censoring material on the Internet (page 159), and on the installation of condom machines in college rest rooms (pages 159–160). First, decide which topic interests you more. Then imagine you hold a point of view that opposes the view expressed by the writer. On a separate sheet of paper, make a list of reasons to support your stance.

2. Exchange your list with a partner. Evaluate the list you receive. Put a + beside strong, convincing reasons. Label any logical fallacies with the appropriate phrase (*begging the question, non sequitur,* and so forth), using the list on pages 157–158 as a guide.

3. Return the paper to its writer. Adjust your own list as needed.

Challenge 2   Writing an Argument Paragraph

Working from the prewriting material you generated for Challenge 1 on page 155, complete a paragraph of at least 100 words in which you either support or reject a ban on the topic you chose there.

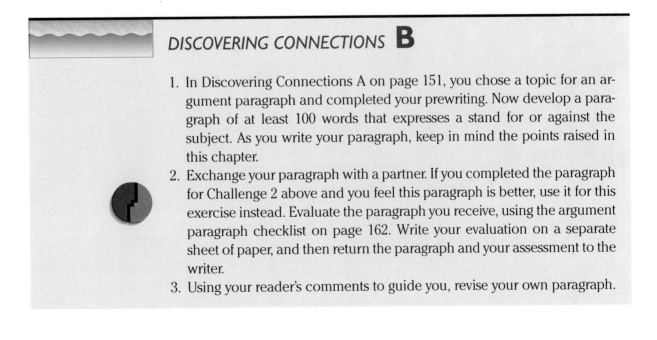

DISCOVERING CONNECTIONS **B**

1. In Discovering Connections A on page 151, you chose a topic for an argument paragraph and completed your prewriting. Now develop a paragraph of at least 100 words that expresses a stand for or against the subject. As you write your paragraph, keep in mind the points raised in this chapter.

2. Exchange your paragraph with a partner. If you completed the paragraph for Challenge 2 above and you feel this paragraph is better, use it for this exercise instead. Evaluate the paragraph you receive, using the argument paragraph checklist on page 162. Write your evaluation on a separate sheet of paper, and then return the paragraph and your assessment to the writer.

3. Using your reader's comments to guide you, revise your own paragraph.

Argument Paragraph Checklist

1. Does the topic sentence clarify the writer's stance on the issue?
2. Are there sufficient examples and details to support the stance?
3. Is the tone reasonable, sincere, and serious? Put a ✓ next to any places where you see a problem in tone.
4. Is the presentation logical? Underline and label any logical fallacies.
5. Is material effectively arranged in emphatic order or some other method of arrangement? Explain.
6. In your judgment, what is the best part of this paragraph? Explain.
7. Which detail or example would be even better if it were expanded? Why?

RECAP
ARGUMENT

New terms in this chapter	Definitions
➤ argument	➤ writing that seeks to persuade a reader to accept the writer's point of view
➤ stance	➤ the position taken on a subject—the writer's opinion
➤ fact	➤ a verifiable truth *Example* The city is in the process of tearing down several historic buildings.
➤ opinion	➤ a belief based on impressions, experiences, or knowledge base ➤ In argument, opinions must be backed up by facts. *Example* The city should be trying to preserve historic buildings instead of tearing them down.
➤ documentation	➤ the process of acknowledging the source of supporting information taken from another document or individual
➤ tone	➤ the attitude you express about your subject
➤ induction	➤ a system of reasoning that moves from specific examples to a general conclusion
➤ deduction	➤ a system of reasoning that moves from general premises to a specific conclusion

New terms in this chapter	Definitions
➤ logical fallacies	➤ common errors in reasoning: argument *ad hominem*; bandwagon approach; begging the question; creating a red herring; either/or reasoning; hasty generalization; *non sequitur*; oversimplification; *post hoc, ergo propter hoc*; circular reasoning

Writing an Argument Paragraph

Use the topic sentence to **express a clear stance** on the issue.

↓   ↑

Include **sufficient support.**

↓   ↑

Maintain an **effective tone.**

↓   ↑

Keep your presentation **logical.**

↓   ↑

Consider **emphatic order** to arrange the supporting material.

Moving On
to the Essay

14	Developing an Essay
15	Examining Types of Essays
16	Answering Essay Questions

14

Developing
an **Essay**

▶ **O**VERVIEW: *COMPARING THE PARAGRAPH AND THE ESSAY*

The preceding chapters focused on writing paragraphs as a way to develop your skills. However, both in college and in your profession, you will more often be asked to prepare longer pieces of writing. Most college writing requires that you deal with subjects in greater detail than is possible in a single paragraph. The main difference is in *scope*. A paragraph can deal with a subject in a limited way. An **essay** can cover numerous facets of a subject, exploring many different angles of interest.

What you have learned up until now will be very helpful in tackling these assignments. Paragraphs are the building blocks of essays, and writing an essay involves the same basic steps as writing a paragraph does.

In this chapter, you will learn the steps in the process of writing an essay:

➤ prewriting—exploring a topic, generating ideas, identifying a focus, and developing a thesis

➤ composing—turning the most promising ideas into supporting topic sentences, creating support for each topic sentence, and arranging the material into paragraphs, including an introduction and a conclusion

➤ revising—reassessing your draft for unity, coherence, and effective language; redrafting to eliminate any weaknesses; and editing to eliminate any remaining errors

DISCOVERING CONNECTIONS A

Later in this chapter, you will read an essay about a first day on the job. Before you read this essay, prewrite on one of your own first-time experiences—perhaps on a job, at camp, on a date, or at college. Then highlight the most promising ideas and save your work for later use.

UNDERSTANDING THE STRUCTURE OF AN ESSAY

An essay consists of three parts: an *introduction,* a *body,* and a *conclusion.*

The Introduction

The **introduction** of an effective essay is usually a single paragraph that clearly states the subject and focus of the paper. It also engages readers' interest and motivates them to continue reading.

The most important element in the introduction is the **thesis,** which is similar to the topic sentence of a paragraph. This statement reveals the subject of the essay, focuses the main point, and often suggests the structure that the essay will follow.

The Body

The **body** of an essay is the series of paragraphs through which a writer develops the thesis and provides support for it. There is no set number of paragraphs for an effective body. How many you provide will depend on the subject and focus of your paper. Each paragraph must contain the elements discussed in earlier chapters: (1) a clear topic sentence that specifies the subject and your perspective on it and (2) supporting details that relate to your topic sentence. In addition, the details should be arranged in a logical order.

The Conclusion

The **conclusion** of an essay—usually a paragraph—brings the paper to a logical and appropriate end. Often the conclusion sums up the *significance* of the essay. It strengthens the overall message expressed by the thesis and the supporting information. Although most conclusions do not introduce new ideas, often they raise issues that readers may want to pursue.

The following figure shows the structure of an essay. Note that the arrows between paragraphs point in both directions. Each paragraph must relate both to the thesis and to the paragraph that comes before it.

The Structure of an Essay

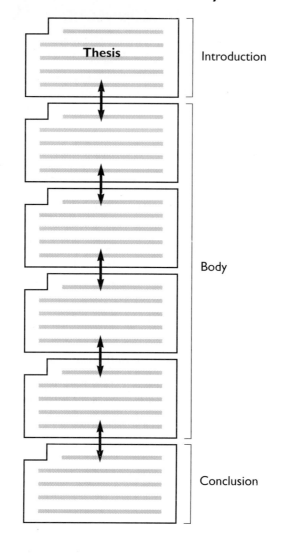

UNDERSTANDING THE ROLE OF THE THESIS

Every essay needs a thesis, a signpost in sentence form declaring the central idea or opinion to be developed in the entire essay. Like a topic sentence, an effective thesis generally focuses the essay using two elements: a topic and the writer's perspective on it.

The thesis statement should pinpoint the topic specifically, as the following example does:

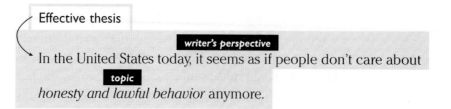

Effective thesis

writer's perspective
In the United States today, it seems as if people don't care about
topic
honesty and lawful behavior anymore.

The reader knows immediately that the essay will focus on honesty and that the writer feels that honesty is not valued by our society. Often, the thesis also sets up an expectation for the structure that the writer will use. Here, it is logical to expect that the writer will develop the body by providing examples of dishonest and unlawful behavior that goes unpunished.

The way a thesis is worded also helps the writer establish the purpose for writing.

> **Effective thesis**
>
> **topic**   **writer's perspective**
>
> *Computer education* should begin in U.S. schools as soon as children can recognize numbers and letters.

Here, the topic and the writer's perspective are clearly stated. In addition, readers know immediately that the writer's purpose is to persuade them. Most likely, the writer will construct the essay by presenting convincing reasons and examples.

Now consider the following elements that weaken a thesis. Perhaps considering the ways you should *not* express your idea will help you to choose the right words to express it.

➤ *Do not announce your intent.* Phrases such as *I want, I plan, I intend,* or *this paper concerns* are both unnecessary and uninteresting.

> **Poor thesis**
>
> I want to talk about how people no longer seem interested in being honest.

➤ *Avoid expressing your thesis as a statement of fact.* A fact is verifiable truth. By itself, it leaves little room for discussion or debate. You might use facts to support other points in your paper, but as a thesis, a fact gives your readers little reason to be interested in what you are about to say.

> **Poor thesis**
>
> Honesty is the quality of being truthful in all dealings.

➤ *Remember—a thesis is not a title.* First of all, a title is generally not a sentence. Second, a title's purpose is to provide a broad hint of your paper's subject matter. It cannot be expected to do the job of the thesis.

> **Not a thesis**
>
> Honesty: The Disappearing Virtue

Exploration 1a Understanding the Parts of an Essay

1. In your own words, explain the role of each part of the essay. _____

   _____

   _____

   _____

   _____

2. Briefly explain the role of the thesis in an essay. _____

   _____

   _____

   _____

   _____

Exploration 1b Making Weak Theses Effective

Working with a partner, turn each of the following sentences or titles into an effective thesis. Study the example first.

> *Example*   The Hovel Where I Grew Up
>
>   *Although the house where I spent my childhood was a shack, I*
>
>   *have many good memories of the days I spent playing there.*

1. The metric system is a system of measurement based on units of ten.

   _____

   _____

2. I plan to show that having a good educational experience in kindergarten can have an enormous impact on a child's self-image.

   _____

   _____

3. Tabloids like the *National Enquirer* sell millions of copies a week.

   _____

   _____

4. The Ideal Occupation

_____

_____

5. I want to show that insurance companies shouldn't be allowed to terminate coverage for people who face extraordinary medical bills.

_____

_____

➤ *E*XAMINING AN EFFECTIVE ESSAY

Read the following essay:

Lost and Confused: My First Day in the Hospital Halls

(1) Any change is difficult to handle. Beginning a new job is no different, especially when the new job involves more responsibility than the last one. My first day as a dietary aide at City Hospital was such an ordeal, I don't think I'll ever forget it. By the end of that first workday, I was so frustrated and embarrassed that I never wanted to return.

(2) At 6:45 on that first morning, half an hour before my shift officially started, I entered the imposing building and headed to the first floor, where the kitchen and cafeteria are located. In spite of my nervousness, I found my time card and punched in. I then introduced myself to the woman sitting at the desk next to the time clock and asked her where I should go next. She told me to report to Mr. Javits in the kitchen.

(3) Just as I was beginning to think I would make it through the day, I met Mr. Javits, and I became convinced that I wouldn't. First, he looked at me and yelled, "Who the hell are you?" After I explained that I was a new dietary aide, he quickly assigned me to set up and deliver morning meals to the entire cardiac unit. Mr. Javits warned me that any mistake in preparation or delivery of the meals could have serious consequences for the patients. By the time he finished talking, my shirt was soaking wet.

(4) My first round of deliveries was a disaster. The cardiac unit was being renovated, and the painting crew had removed the room numbers. I figured that once I identified one room, I would be able to find the rest easily. The rooms weren't arranged sequentially, however, so I had to personally identify all the patients and go through their menu choices with them. As a result, I fell behind schedule at each room. I began to know what salmon must feel like as they try to swim upstream.

(5) The worst was yet to come. When I returned to the cafeteria with the trays, Mr. Javits was waiting for me. He began yelling and demanding to know where I had been. As I pointed to the notice on the wall

announcing the renovation of the cardiac floor, I accidentally bumped Mr. Javits' hand and spilled his cup of coffee over the front of his uniform. At this point, I felt that the end of the day would never come.

(6) The lunch shift was almost as bad as the breakfast shift. This time, Mr. Javits assigned me to the orthopedic area. To distribute the meals, I had to travel the length of the hospital and take two different sets of elevators. By the time I collected the trays and returned them to the cafeteria, I was late again. My shift was scheduled to end at 2:30, and it was almost 3 P.M. Fortunately, Mr. Javits had already left.

(7) After this kind of start, it is hard to believe that I soon became an expert on the hospital. Within a couple of days, I knew my way around the building. After a month, Mr. Javits even put me in charge of training new workers. I also found out that most of my co-workers had had similar experiences on their first day working in the hospital cafeteria. Like me, they had been completely intimidated at the prospect of something new.

This essay illustrates all the required elements. Its *title* suggests the focus of the essay that follows. Its *introduction* has a clear *thesis:* "My first day as a dietary aide at City Hospital was such an ordeal, I don't think I'll ever forget it." This thesis is fully developed through the *body*—five paragraphs that detail what that first day was like. It closes with a *conclusion*—a final paragraph that restates the topic and implies the significance of the experience.

How did the essay come to be in this form? The rest of this chapter will walk you through the process of writing an essay by showing how this one was developed.

Exploration 2a   Explaining the Parts of a Model Essay

1. Briefly explain how the introduction in the essay about the first day on the

   job prepares the reader for the body to follow. _____

   _____

   _____

   _____

   _____

2. For each of the paragraphs in the body, summarize the details that support the thesis.

   (2) _____

   _____

   (3) _____

(4) _____

_____

(5) _____

_____

(6) _____

_____

3. How does the conclusion sum up the significance of this experience?

_____

_____

_____

_____

_____

➤ **E**XAMINING THE PROCESS OF WRITING AN ESSAY

ESL Note
See "Writing Essays" on pages 539–540.

The process you follow to write an essay is similar to the process you follow to write a paragraph, except you're able to explore the subject in greater depth. In Chapter 2, you discovered which *prewriting* technique—or which combination of techniques—you prefer to develop examples and details about your subject. You also use prewriting to focus, or *narrow*, the subject of your essay. Most writers start with a fairly general subject and then narrow the scope until they have a manageable topic.

Once you have this focus, you can draft your thesis. With essay writing, think of your thesis as the bridge from prewriting to composing. With your focus in sentence form, you are ready to refine and organize the ideas and examples you've generated during prewriting into supporting paragraphs. When you write an essay, instead of writing one series of sentences that support your topic, you develop a series of paragraphs that present, explain, and reiterate the thesis.

Once you have completed a draft of your essay, you revise, or refine and polish your draft: You assess its unity, coherence, and use of language. Then you redraft to address any problem spots. Finally, you edit to eliminate any remaining errors. The figure illustrates this process. As the two-way arrows show, you may need to repeat steps in the process to create a draft that is ready for editing.

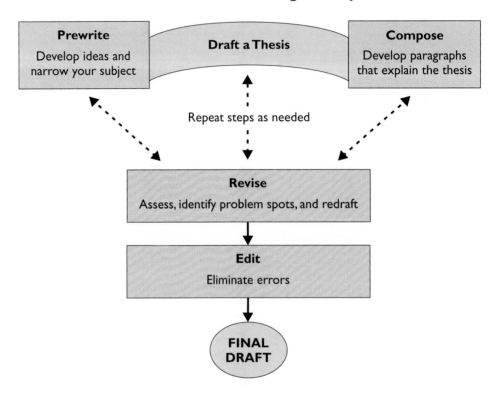

The Process of Writing an Essay

You've already seen the final draft of the essay "Lost and Confused: My First Day in the Hospital Halls." Below, we will retrace the author's writing process to see how that essay developed. We'll also look at examples of other student essays along the way.

Prewriting: Generating Ideas and Developing a Thesis

Here is the student's freewriting on the subject of first-time experiences:

first-time experiences? OK what do I remember about first-time experiences? school—can't even remember most of elementary school, like I was asleep until about seventh grade. first date—nothing special about that. Wait, how about that first day of work at the hospital? I was so screwed up. I messed up my first shift because the room numbers were missing and I came back really late. Then I had to go way across the hospital for the lunchtime delivery and pretty much got lost. Dolores Couch started work the next day but she quit after a week—I wonder what ever happened to her? Man that was an awful first day—I even spilled coffee all over Mr. Javits —never saw anybody jump straight up like that!! How the hell did I do that? OK, now I remember, I was trying to show him the sign that explained about the repainting and I hit his arm, sometimes I'm so uncoordinated. I was just so nervous, scared, and, what's the word I want? confused—worried? no—intimidated. Didn't see a single person I knew, including the person who hired me, she was on a day off. Mr. Javits, the "yeller," "Who the hell are you," he screamed the first time I met him, after a month or so, his attitude changed a lot, although he still yells when he is upset about something, but who doesn't? Sweating so much the whole time with him yelling at me about all the responsibilities. At the end of the day, I just wanted to go home and never come back.

The writer has highlighted the most useful ideas and details in the prewriting. This process helped evolve the idea for a focus on the trauma of the first day at the new job.

Once a focus for the essay has been identified, the next step is to write a thesis. In this instance, the writer chose the *first day on a new job* as the topic, and then expressed the viewpoint suggested by prewriting details: The first day was an unforgettable ordeal. Here's the resulting thesis:

Thesis

My first day as a dietary aide at City Hospital was such an ordeal, I don't think I'll ever forget it.

DISCOVERING CONNECTIONS   **B**

For Discovering Connections A on page 167, you completed a prewriting on one of your own first-time experiences and highlighted the most promising ideas. Now, drawing from this material, develop a thesis. Save your work for later use.

Composing: Creating the Draft

Once the thesis is developed, the composing stage of essay writing begins. At this point in the process, you work the most promising ideas from prewriting into the paragraphs that will form the body of the essay.

Focusing on the Most Promising Material

First, make a clear list of your best ideas. Then arrange the ideas in the way that will best express or support the thesis. The episode described in the freewriting concerns a first day at work. Therefore, it makes sense to list the events in chronological order, that is, in the order in which they actually occurred on that day. (See Chapter 4, page 63, for more on chronological order.)

The writer of this essay recalled the chronological order of the events that day as follows:

1. How about that first day of work at the hospital?
   I was so screwed up.
   Man that was an awful first day.
2. I was just so nervous, scared.
   Confused—worried?
   No—intimidated.
   Mr. Javits, the "yeller." "Who the hell are you," he screamed the first time I met him.
   Sweating so much the whole time with him yelling at me about all the responsibilities.
3. I messed up my first shift because the room numbers were missing and I came back really late.
4. I was trying to show him the sign that explained about the repainting and I hit his arm.
   I even spilled coffee all over Mr. Javits.
5. Then I had to go way across the hospital for the lunchtime delivery and pretty much got lost.
6. At the end of the day, I just wanted to go home and never come back.

Notice that closely related ideas have been grouped together. As Chapter 3 discussed, this ordering and grouping of ideas is a step towards making your presentation clear for your readers. In essay writing, grouping helps you construct a tentative blueprint for your paragraphs.

Once you have identified and arranged your ideas, the next step is to express them, using details, examples, and illustrations. As Chapter 1 explained, it is important to keep your readers' needs in mind as you do this. Because you understand the material, it's easy to forget that your reader doesn't have the same background and frame of reference.

The secret to meeting your reader's needs is to ask yourself this question: *What did I need to know in order to understand what I am writing about?* Using the reader evaluation checklist on page 49 will also help you zero in on your reader's needs.

An essay allows room for far more detail than a paragraph. However, you must also be sure that your content is reader centered, not just longer. As Chapter 4 explained, your writing must contain specific language and details and be expressed in complete sentence form.

DISCOVERING CONNECTIONS C

Review the ideas and thesis you generated in Discovering Connections A (page 167) and B (page 176). Then organize the details you have chosen in a logical order, grouping related ideas. Compose a paragraph for each group of supporting details. Be sure each supports the thesis. Use the list in the preceding section as a guide. Save your work for later use.

Considering Introductions and Conclusions

An essay is incomplete without two important specialized paragraphs: (1) the introduction, to draw readers in and prepare them for the direction your essay will take, and (2) the conclusion, to summarize and bring the piece to a logical and appropriate end.

Introductions   Writers employ a number of devices or techniques to engage readers' interest in an introduction. One technique is to use an **anecdote,** a brief, entertaining story that emphasizes the thesis.

Imagine a paper discussing the media's intrusion into the lives of people in the news. The introduction to this paper might include the following story about a victim of the media:

> When my friend Cerene opened the newspaper one morning last year, she saw a story that made her physically sick. There, on page two, was a story about her father's arrest for tax evasion. Included in the

story were her name and age. What the story didn't mention was that Cerene's parents had been divorced four years earlier. Her father hadn't contacted her or provided any financial support in all that time. These facts didn't stop the newspaper from dragging her name into the story, even though she had nothing at all to do with her father or his legal troubles. Cerene was perfectly innocent, yet she still had to face the embarrassment of seeing her name published in an unflattering situation. The media shouldn't be able to drag anyone's name into a story that doesn't genuinely involve that person.

Another technique is to use relevant facts or statistics:

> A recent *USA Today* poll found that 75 percent of all Americans think the media focus too much on the private lives of news makers.

To show the reader what direction the essay will take, the next sentence could state that the discussion will focus on examples from politics, business, show business, and sports.

Still another technique is to begin the introduction with a relevant saying or quotation:

> My grandmother's favorite expression was, "Keep your nose out of other people's business, and they'll keep their noses out of yours."

Another technique is to begin with a **rhetorical question.** This type of question is designed not to be answered, but to provoke thought or discussion:

> How would you like to suffer a personal loss and then read all the personal details in the paper the next morning?

Placing the thesis in the first or second sentence of your introduction enables your reader to understand the point of the essay right from the start. Regardless of where you place your thesis, however, keep in mind that your introduction should suggest the direction or structure of the essay.

Conclusions   The conclusion of an essay represents the writer's last word on the subject. It may restate or summarize the essay's message. Often it then adds a final thought or a question for the reader to consider. However, conclusions should not present detailed new information. The body of the essay is the place to develop thoughts and ideas fully. In your conclusion, sometimes an anecdote that embodies the point of the paper is a good choice. At other times, a relevant question or quotation will be the best way to conclude your essay. Whatever technique helps you bring your essay to an effective close is a good choice for that particular situation.

Here is an effective conclusion for a paper discussing the media's intrusion into the lives of people in the news:

> No one is saying that news reporters shouldn't have the right to publish or broadcast the news. But they do have a responsibility to make sure that the material they broadcast or publish is actually news and not gossip. Everybody has the right to personal privacy, even public figures, and the media should respect this right.

Exploration 3a   Understanding Composing for an Essay

1. How does the thesis act as a bridge between prewriting and composing?

   _____

   _____

   _____

   _____

2. What advantage do you gain by grouping promising ideas that you develop for your essay during prewriting? _____

   _____

   _____

   _____

   _____

Exploration 3b   Understanding Techniques for Introductions and Conclusions

1. List at least three techniques that can be used in introductions or conclusions. _____

   _____

   _____

   _____

2. Select one of these techniques. Explain how it helps to draw readers in and prepare them to read the essay or to bring the essay to a satisfactory close.

   _____

   _____

_____

_____

_____

Understanding the Relationship between Topic Sentences and the Thesis

As Chapter 3 indicated, the main sentence in any paragraph is called the *topic sentence.* An essay is a multi-paragraph writing, so it contains several topic sentences, each of which is directly connected to the thesis.

Here again is the thesis from the paper about honesty in the United States:

> In the United States today, it seems as if people don't care about honesty and lawful behavior anymore.

As the thesis indicates, the rest of the essay deals with different examples of dishonest or illegal behavior. For example, the first paragraph of the body discusses regular violations of drug laws. The next paragraph explains employee pilferage, and the next one discusses political corruption. The final paragraph of the essay discusses dishonesty on Wall Street. The conclusion then restates the significance of the thesis—that in all areas of life, society no longer values honesty as it once did.

The figure on page 181 illustrates the relationship between the thesis and the topic sentences of this essay. As the figure shows, each of the topic sentences deals with some form of dishonesty or unlawful behavior. In terms of the relationship between the thesis and these topic sentences, *dishonesty or unlawful behavior* represents the *common thread,* the element that all the paragraphs have in common. This thesis indicates that honesty is no longer valued. Each topic sentence directly supports, illustrates, or explains this thesis by presenting a different aspect of dishonesty.

 Challenge 1   Relating Thesis and Topic Sentences

Review the final draft of the essay about the first day at a new job on pages 171–172. Find the topic sentence of each paragraph. Working with a partner, show the relationship between the thesis, the topic sentences in the body, and the topic sentence in the conclusion. Create a figure like the one on page 181.

Developing a Solid First Draft

Once you have organized selected details into a list like the one on page 176, then it's time to develop a solid first draft of the essay. Using your list to guide

The Relationship between Topic Sentences and the Thesis

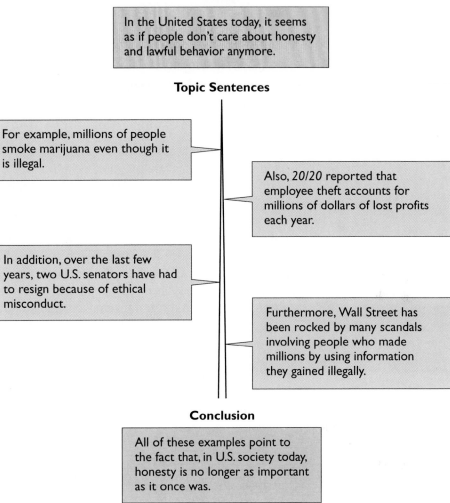

Thesis

In the United States today, it seems as if people don't care about honesty and lawful behavior anymore.

Topic Sentences

For example, millions of people smoke marijuana even though it is illegal.

Also, *20/20* reported that employee theft accounts for millions of dollars of lost profits each year.

In addition, over the last few years, two U.S. senators have had to resign because of ethical misconduct.

Furthermore, Wall Street has been rocked by many scandals involving people who made millions by using information they gained illegally.

Conclusion

All of these examples point to the fact that, in U.S. society today, honesty is no longer as important as it once was.

you, you should be able to compose an introduction, body, and conclusion, all expressed in complete sentence form.

Here is the *first draft* of the paper on the disastrous first day at work:

Lost and Confused: My First Day in the Hospital Halls

(1) Any change is difficult to handle. My first day as a dietary aide at City Hospital was such an ordeal, I don't think I'll ever forget it.

(2) Really early, I headed to the first floor, where the kitchen and cafeteria are located. I introduced myself to the woman sitting at the desk next to the time clock. She told me to report to Mr. Javits in the kitchen.

(3) I was beginning to think I would make it through the day. I met Mr. Javits, and I became convinced that I wouldn't. He looked at me and

yelled, "Who the hell are you?" He quickly assigned me to set up and deliver morning meals to the entire cardiac unit. Mr. Javits warned me that any mistake in preparation or delivery of the meals could have serious consequences for the patients. My shirt was soaking wet.

(4) A month later I met his wife. Two people couldn't be more different than Mr. Javits and his wife. Unfortunately, she died last year.

(5) My first round of deliveries was a disaster. The room numbers were missing, so I had to go through menu choices with each patient, and I fell behind schedule at each room. I was late returning from my lunch time deliveries.

(6) Mr. Javits was waiting for me when I returned from my breakfast deliveries, and he was really mad. I accidentally bumped Mr. Javits' hand and spilled his cup of coffee over the front of his uniform. At this point, I felt that the end of the day would never come.

(7) Mr. Javits assigned me to the orthopedic area for the lunch shift. Just getting to that part of the hospital was hard. The hospital was founded over 100 years ago. All together there are more than 400 employees. By the time I collected the trays and returned them to the cafeteria, I was late again. Fortunately, Mr. Javits had already left.

(8) Within a couple of days, I knew my way around the building. I also found out that most of my co-workers had had similar experiences on their first day working in the hospital cafeteria.

This first draft contains the essential elements: a thesis, ideas expressed in sentence form, and paragraphs arranged into an introduction, body, and conclusion. However, it is in rough form. It needs to be reexamined and then refined through revising.

DISCOVERING CONNECTIONS D

For Discovering Connections C on page 177, you developed supporting sentences for the thesis you had created earlier. Now compose a first draft of an essay on that topic. Don't forget to include an introduction and a conclusion. Save this first draft for later use.

Revising: Turning Something Good into Something Better

Once a draft of an essay is completed, it is a good idea to take a break. If you allow a day or so to pass before moving on to the revising stage, you will bring a fresh eye to this crucial part of writing. As Chapter 4 illustrated, revising actually involves three steps: reassessing, redrafting, and editing.

The first step, *reassessing*, involves reexamining the essay for several factors:

1. *Unity*   All examples and details must relate directly to the thesis.
2. *Coherence*   All the material should have clear transitions and be arranged in a logical order.
3. *Effective language*   Ideas should be expressed in words that are specific and concise.

Revising for Unity

A successful essay is one in which all of the elements work together to support the thesis. When you reassess a draft, examine each component to make sure it is directly connected to your main idea. For example, look again at paragraph 4 of the first draft essay about the initial day on a new job:

> A month later I met his wife. Two people couldn't be more different than Mr. Javits and his wife. Unfortunately, she died last year.

The essay's main point is that the first day of a new job was difficult. This paragraph does not relate to the main point, although the information is interesting and informative. Therefore, to maintain unity, this paragraph must be eliminated.

Individual sentences within a paragraph can also lack unity. Each one should relate both to the paragraph's topic sentence *and* to the thesis of the essay. Take another look at paragraph 7. Which material isn't unified?

> Mr. Javits assigned me to the orthopedic area for the lunch shift. Just getting to that part of the hospital was hard. The hospital was founded over 100 years ago. All together there are more than 400 employees. By the time I collected the trays and returned them to the cafeteria, I was late again. Fortunately, Mr. Javits had already left.

You probably identified the third and fourth sentences, which concern the background of the hospital rather than a first day at work. These sentences aren't directly related to the story, so they must also be eliminated to maintain unity.

DISCOVERING CONNECTIONS E

Check the draft you completed for Discovering Connections D (page 182) to make sure it is unified. First, be sure that all of your paragraphs relate to the thesis. Then be sure that every sentence within each paragraph relates to the paragraph's topic sentence. Cross out any sentences or paragraphs that do not belong in your essay.

Revising for Coherence

An effective essay is one in which one idea flows smoothly on to the next. This quality, called *coherence,* is achieved (1) by providing adequate *transitions* between paragraphs and between sentences and (2) by *organizing* your ideas in a logical order.

Transitions   As Chapter 4 showed, transitions help establish a smooth flow of ideas. Both *synonyms* and *common transitional expressions* help show relationships among your ideas. (See pages 60–61 for lists of transitions.) When you reassess a draft, examine it closely for any gaps or points where the flow between sentences or paragraphs should be improved.

Consider again paragraph 3 from the draft about the first day at work:

> I was beginning to think I would make it through the day. I met Mr. Javits, and I became convinced that I wouldn't. He looked at me and yelled, "Who the hell are you?" He quickly assigned me to set up and deliver morning meals to the entire cardiac unit. Mr. Javits warned me that any mistake in preparation or delivery of the meals could have serious consequences for the patients. My shirt was soaking wet.

There are a number of problems with coherence in this paragraph. For example, the paragraph itself begins abruptly. In addition, no transitional expressions sustain the flow between the sentences. They read more like a list of sentences than a coherent paragraph.

Now look how much better the paragraph reads with transitions added:

> *Just as*
> I was beginning to think I would make it through the day, I met Mr.
>   *First, he*
> Javits, and I became convinced that I wouldn't. He looked at me and
>   *After I explained that I was a new dietary aide, he*
> yelled, "Who the hell are you?" He quickly assigned me to set up and de-
>
> liver morning meals to the entire cardiac unit. Mr. Javits warned me that
>
> any mistake in preparation or delivery of the meals could have serious
>   *By the time he finished talking, my*
> consequences for the patients. My shirt was soaking wet.

Challenge 2   Assessing the Need for Transitions in a Rough Draft

Working with a partner, assess the need for transitions in the paragraphs (other than paragraph 3) of the first draft essay on pages 181–182. Put a ✓ next to places where transitions are needed.

DISCOVERING CONNECTIONS F

Reassess the draft you completed for Discovering Connections D (page 182) to make sure you have used transitions effectively. Insert transitional expressions where they are needed to help the flow of ideas. Save your changes to use later, when you redraft.

Proper Organization   The second element of coherence is logical order. A successful essay is organized in such a way that the reader can easily follow it. Chapter 4 discussed several methods of establishing order:

1. *Emphatic order*   arranging points according to their importance
2. *Spatial order*   arranging descriptive details on the basis of their physical relationship with each other
3. *Chronological order* arranging events on the basis of order of occurrence

Notice that "Lost and Confused: My First Day in the Hospital Halls" uses chronological order.

When you reassess a draft, check the arrangement to make sure it is consistent and logical. If the essay features spatial order, reevaluate the presentation to make sure that the reader is able to visualize the scene. If the essay follows emphatic order, check the presentation to ensure that it sustains the reader's interest and effectively accentuates the thesis. If the writing is arranged in chronological order, look closely at the sequence of events, making sure each event is presented in the order in which it actually occurred. For example, take another look at paragraphs 5 and 6 of the sample draft. Is there a problem with sequence in this passage?

> My first round of deliveries was a disaster. The room numbers were missing, so I had to go through menu choices with each patient, and I fell behind schedule at each room. I was late returning from my lunch time deliveries.
>
> Mr. Javits was waiting for me when I returned from my breakfast deliveries, and he was really mad. I accidentally bumped Mr. Javits' hand and spilled his cup of coffee over the front of his uniform. At this point, I felt that the end of the day would never come.

You probably noticed that the last sentence in paragraph 5 discusses events *after* lunch, and then paragraph 6 talks about an event *before* lunch. To keep the chronological order consistent, it is necessary to move the discussion of the incident after lunch so that it *follows* the paragraph about the event in the morning.

Challenge 3   Assessing Logical Order in a Rough Draft

Working with a partner, list the sequence of events presented in the first draft of "Lost and Confused: My First Day in the Hospital Halls" (pages 181–182). Are any events out of sequence? Place a ✓ beside them on your list.

DISCOVERING CONNECTIONS **G**

Reassess the draft you completed for Discovering Connections D (page 182) to make sure it is organized logically. In the margin, draw an arrow from any sentence that is not in the proper order to the place it should be moved. Note any other errors in logic that may affect the structure of your essay. Save your notes to use later, when you redraft.

Revising for Effective Language

A successful essay is one in which the language captures the meaning the writer intends. When you reassess a draft, look for any spots in which the language is vague, general, or unclear. Then replace this weak language with specific and concise terms. If they will help to re-create the experience or clarify your point, you should include additional examples or details.

Here is a paragraph written by novelist Chaim Potok. It describes a softball team composed of young Hasidic Jews. See if you can identify the details that help the reader visualize the scene:

> There were fifteen of them, and they were dressed alike in white shirts, dark pants, white sweaters, and small black skullcaps. In the fashion of the very Orthodox, their hair was closely cropped, except for the area near their ears from which mushroomed the untouched hair that tumbled down into the long side curls. Some of them had the beginnings of beards, straggly tufts of hair that stood in isolated clumps on their chins, jawbones, and upper lips. They all wore the traditional undergarment beneath their shirts, and the tzitzit, the long fringes appended to the four corners of the garment, came out above their belts and swung against their pants as they walked. These were the very Orthodox, and they obeyed literally the Biblical commandment *And ye shall look upon it,* which pertains to the fringes.

Chances are that you identified details such as *white shirts, dark pants, white sweaters, small black skullcaps,* and *untouched hair that tumbled down into the long side curls.* What other details help to create a clear, specific picture of these young men?

Now consider again paragraph 2 from the first draft of "Lost and Confused: My First Day in the Hospital Halls" (pages 181–182):

> Really early, I headed to the first floor where the kitchen and cafeteria are located. I introduced myself to the woman sitting at the desk next to the time clock. She told me to report to Mr. Javits in the kitchen.

As you can see, this paragraph fails to create a clear picture for the reader. *Really early* is not concise or specific, so it does little to help the reader understand what was happening. Nor is there specific information about where the event takes place or how the writer was feeling. The reader needs this kind of information in order to understand the experience fully.

Now consider this version:

> *At 6:45 on that first morning, half an hour before my shift*
> *officially started, I entered the imposing building and*
>   ~~Really early, I~~ headed to the first floor, where the kitchen and cafete-
> *In spite of my nervousness, I found my time card and punched in. I then*
> ria are located. I introduced myself to the woman sitting at the desk next
> *and asked her where I should go next.*
> to the time clock, She told me to report to Mr. Javits in the kitchen.

The sentence now opens with specific, concise phrasing: *At 6:45 on that first morning, half an hour before my shift officially started.* It also contains specific details about the hospital itself (*the imposing building*), about the writer's feelings (*In spite of my nervousness*), and so on. With these changes, the language in the paragraph is far more effective.

Challenge 4   Assessing Use of Effective Language in a Rough Draft

Working with a partner, check the effectiveness of the language in the other paragraphs in the first draft of "Lost and Confused: My First Day in the Hospital Halls" (pages 181–182). Circle or highlight any words that are too vague or too general to be effective. Discuss possible replacements.

DISCOVERING CONNECTIONS H

Reassess the draft you completed for Discovering Connections D (page 182) to make sure you have used language effectively. Replace any wordy or vague language with specific, concise phrases; add details as needed to allow readers to understand the experience fully. Save your changes to use later, when you redraft.

Seeking Help from an Objective Reader

In addition to reassessing your draft yourself, it's always a good idea to get feedback from an objective reader. Choose someone who will respond honestly and intelligently to your work. Your reader will find the following reader assessment checklist useful in responding to your first draft.

Reader Assessment Checklist

1. Do you understand the point I am making? Does my thesis statement clearly state the topic along with my perspective on it? (thesis)
2. Do I stick to that point all the way through? Does the topic sentence of each paragraph relate to the thesis? (unity)
3. Are all my ideas and examples clearly connected and easy to follow? (coherence)
4. Are the words I've used specific and concise? (effective language)
5. Are my introduction and conclusion effective?
6. What changes do you think I should make?

Exploration 4a   Understanding Effective Revision

1. List three elements you should reassess in a first draft. _____

_____

_____

_____

2. Why is it a good idea to give yourself a break between the composing and revising stages of writing? _____

_____

_____

_____

_____

3. How can an objective reader help you improve your essay? _____

_____

_____

_____

_____

Challenge 5   Providing Feedback on a Student Essay

Working with a partner, select a student essay from Part Seven. Pretend that a classmate has written this essay and has asked for your reaction. Use the reader assessment checklist on page 188 to review and evaluate it.

Redrafting

Once you have identified the weaknesses in an essay, it's time to address these problems by *redrafting*. This involves more than changing a word here and there. When you redraft, you need to rethink your essay and then create a new draft that may be quite different from your first draft.

When you redraft, you make the adjustments that you noted were necessary to achieve unity, coherence, and specific language. You also *amplify*, adding examples or details to fill in any gaps that you and your objective reader have discovered. This additional material brings the scene or information into better focus for the reader.

DISCOVERING CONNECTIONS ▌

Revise the draft you completed for Discovering Connections D (page 182). Incorporate the lessons you have learned in this chapter and the changes you made as you completed the last several Discovering Connections exercises.

Editing: Eliminating Errors

The final step in revising an essay is *editing*. To edit is to eliminate any grammatical or spelling errors through proofreading. It's important to be well-rested when proofreading so that you don't overlook obvious errors.

As you proofread, use the following proofreading checklist, which includes several of the most common errors, to identify specific problems in your essay. Next to each item is the abbreviation commonly used to mark this error when it appears in a paper. The inside back cover of this book includes a more complete list of errors and abbreviations.

Proofreading Checklist

1. Have I eliminated all sentence fragments (*frag*)?
   (*See Chapter 18 for more on sentence fragments.*)
2. Have I eliminated all comma splices (*cs*)?
   (*See Chapter 20 for more on comma splices.*)

Continued

3. Have I eliminated all run-on sentences (*rs*)?
   (See Chapter 20 for more on run-on sentences.)
4. Is the spelling (*sp*) correct throughout?
   (See Chapter 29 for more on spelling.)
5. Is the verb tense (*t*) correct throughout?
   (See Chapters 22, 23, and 24 for more on verb tense.)
6. Do all subjects agree with their verbs (*subj/verb agr*)?
   (See Chapters 21 and 25 for more on subject–verb agreement.)
7. Do all pronouns agree with their antecedents (*pro/ant agr*)?
   (See Chapter 27 for more on pronoun–antecedent agreement.)

You may find few or no problems in some of these categories, and you may find other errors not listed here. Using this list and the one on the inside back cover, compile a list that focuses on the areas that most trouble you. Make your own *personal proofreading list,* and use it each time you write an assignment, a paper, or even a letter.

It's also a good idea to work with a proofreading partner, who can look for errors with a fresh perspective. If you are working on a computer or word processor, take full advantage of the *spell check* function. Just make sure to do one more reading after the program proofreads your paper. A computer doesn't reason as you do. If you write *hole* when you actually mean *whole,* the computer won't correct it because *hole* is a correctly spelled word.

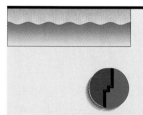

DISCOVERING CONNECTIONS J

1. Exchange the final draft you completed for Discovering Connections I (page 189) with a partner. Using the proofreading checklist above, check the essay you receive. Identify any errors you see in the paper, using the abbreviations presented in the checklist and on the inside back cover of this book. Then return the paper to the writer.
2. Correct any errors your proofreading partner identified in your essay.

LOOKING AGAIN AT THE FINAL DRAFT

Remember the final draft of "Lost and Confused: My First Day in the Hospital Halls" you saw earlier on pages 171–172? Here it is again, this time in annotated form. The various notations point out how the essay has changed from first draft to final draft.

Lost and Confused: My First Day in the Hospital Halls

Any change is difficult to handle. Beginning a new job is no different, especially when the new job involves more responsibility than the last one. My first day as a dietary aide at City Hospital was such an ordeal, I don't think I'll ever forget it. By the end of that first day, I was so frustrated and embarrassed that I never wanted to return.

> Details and examples have been added.

At 6:45 on that first morning, half an hour before my shift officially started, I entered the imposing building and headed to the first floor, where the kitchen and cafeteria are located. In spite of my nervousness, I found my time card and punched in. I then introduced myself to the woman sitting at the desk next to the time clock and asked her where I should go next. She told me to report to Mr. Javits in the kitchen.

> The material has been made more specific.

> Transitions and details have been added.

Just as I was beginning to think I would make it through the day, I met Mr. Javits, and I became convinced that I wouldn't. First, he looked at me and yelled, "Who the hell are you?" After I explained that I was a new dietary aide, he quickly assigned me to set up and deliver morning meals to the entire cardiac unit. Mr. Javits warned me that any mistake in preparation or delivery of the meals could have serious consequences for the patients. By the time he finished talking, my shirt was soaking wet.*

> Transitions have been added.

> Specific details and transitions have been added.

> Unrelated information has been eliminated to maintain unity.

My first round of deliveries was a disaster. The cardiac unit was being renovated, and the painting crew had removed the room numbers. I figured that once I identified one room, I would be able to find the rest easily. The rooms weren't arranged sequentially, however, so I had to personally identify all the patients and go through their menu choices with them. As a result, I fell behind schedule at each room. I began to know what salmon must feel like as they try to swim upstream.*

Additional details and transitions have been supplied to explain the difficulty of the job.

An example has been added to illustrate the frustration.

Out-of-sequence material has been repositioned.

The worst was yet to come. When I returned to the cafeteria with the trays, Mr. Javits was waiting for me.

Transition and detail have been added.

He began yelling and demanding to know where I had been. As I pointed to the notice on the wall announcing the renovation of the cardiac floor,   I accidentally bumped Mr. Javits' hand and spilled his cup of coffee over the front of his uniform. At this point, I felt that the end of the day would never come.

Details have been added to explain what led to spilling the coffee.

The lunch shift was almost as bad as the breakfast shift. This time, Mr. Javits assigned me to the orthopedic area. To distribute the meals, I had to travel the length of the hospital and take two different sets of elevators. * By the time I collected the trays and returned them to the cafeteria, I was late again. My shift was scheduled to end at 2:30, and it was almost 3 P.M. Fortunately, Mr. Javits had already left.

A topic sentence and a transition have been added.

Additional details have been supplied to explain how involved the task actually was.

Unrelated information has been eliminated to maintain unity.

Additional information has been supplied to emphasize the frustration.

Transition has been added to ease the reader into the conclusion.

After this kind of start, it is hard to believe that I soon became an expert on the hospital. Within a couple of days, I knew my way around the building. After a month, Mr. Javits even put me in charge of training new workers. I also found out that most of my co-workers had had similar experiences on their first day working in the hospital cafeteria. Like me, they had been completely intimidated at the prospect of something new.

Additional information has been supplied to explain the experience more completely.

As the notes show, composing this final draft involved making a significant number of changes. Often writers must work through several drafts before they feel satisfied with the results.

Exploration 5a   Understanding the Redrafting Process

1. Briefly explain how redrafting can help you improve an essay. _____

   _____

   _____

   _____

   _____

2. Explain the difference between redrafting and editing. _____

   _____

   _____

   _____

   _____

3. What specific types of errors would you add to your own proofreading

   checklist? _____

   _____

   _____

   _____

Challenge 6 Evaluating a First Draft Essay

1. Read the following first draft essay on home shopping. Then, working with a partner, answer the questions that follow on a separate sheet of paper.

The Home Shopping Phenomenon

(1) Home shopping has become a popular alternative for busy shoppers of the '90s.

(2) There are a couple of different home shopping networks. All the shows seem to work the same, a host introduces the product, describes it, and posts the price. Then a phone number is flashed. You can get a good deal on collectibles and sports memorabilia.

(3) The home shopping networks sells designer clothing, including outerwear and shoes. Occasionally, a fashion designer comes on to discuss the clothing while fashion models walked around displaying them.

(4) Celebrities come on to sell her own brands of fragrances or jewelry. Cheap rings, bracelets or necklaces can cause allergic reactions. The celebrities chat with the hosts and encourage viewers to buy.

(5) What makes it all especially convenient is that you never have to leave your couch to shop. When you see what you want on the screen, you dial the 1-800 number, give a credit card number, and the item is on its way to your door. No crowded mall parking lots, no long lines at the registers.

(6) In today's fast-paced world, it's often hard to find time to go out shopping, especially during the holiday season.

a. Evaluate the introduction and conclusion. In what way would you suggest they be changed?

b. Which paragraph in this draft supplies the best support? Explain why.

c. Turn again to the reader assessment checklist (page 188) and the proofreading checklist (pages 189–190), and use them to assess and edit this first draft. On a separate sheet of paper, make a list of problem spots and errors that need to be addressed.

2. Imagine that the writer has asked you to write a critique (a short paragraph of around ten sentences) in which you indicate (a) what is good in the essay and (b) what still needs work. On a separate sheet of paper, write that critique.

RECAP
DEVELOPING AN ESSAY

New terms in this chapter	Definitions
➤ essay	➤ a multi-paragraph writing that deals more extensively with a subject than a paragraph does
➤ introduction	➤ a paragraph that opens an essay, providing a clear thesis and engaging the reader

New terms in this chapter	Definitions
➤ thesis	➤ the sentence in the introduction that specifies the main idea of the essay
➤ body	➤ the series of paragraphs that provide support and illustration for a thesis
➤ conclusion	➤ a paragraph that closes the essay, summarizing the essay's point and bringing it to a logical and appropriate end
➤ anecdote	➤ a brief, entertaining story, often used to make a point ➤ An anecdote may be used effectively in an introduction or a conclusion.
➤ rhetorical question	➤ a question designed not to be answered, but to provoke thought or discussion ➤ A rhetorical question may be used effectively in an introduction to engage readers.

The Process of Writing an Essay

Prewrite on a **topic.**
Identify a **focus.**
Develop a **thesis.**

Arrange the most promising prewriting ideas in a logical order and turn them into **supporting sentences.**
Develop the supporting sentences into **paragraphs.**
Write paragraphs for an **introduction** and **conclusion.**

Reassess your draft for **unity, coherence** (transitions and organization), and **effective language.**
Redraft to eliminate any weaknesses identified in reassessing.
Edit to eliminate any **grammatical** or **spelling errors.**

15

Examining Types of Essays

As the previous chapters pointed out, your writing is effective when it fulfills a purpose and communicates ideas to the reader. Chapters 5 through 12 showed how to communicate your ideas in paragraphs using various techniques or *modes: narration, description, example, process, definition, comparison and contrast, cause and effect,* and *division and classification.* Most writers use a number of these modes in combination when they compose an essay. This chapter explores ways to use different combinations to suit different purposes.

In this chapter, you will learn how to use the modes to write

➤ narration essays

➤ description essays

➤ example essays

➤ process essays

➤ definition essays

➤ comparison and contrast essays

➤ cause and effect essays

➤ division and classification essays

➤ argument essays

THE RELATIONSHIP BETWEEN YOUR PURPOSE AND THE MODES

It's important to understand the connection between your purpose and the modes. As Chapter 1 explained, people write to fulfill one of three purposes: to *inform*, to *entertain*, or to *persuade*. The modes are your means to fulfill the purpose you choose. In most essays, one mode will dominate, with other modes providing additional support.

Open your favorite magazine, and read a few of the articles. Perhaps one article reports recent findings about fat consumption and heart disease. In this case, the writer's primary purpose is to *inform* readers about the data linking diet and heart disease. Another article might take a lighthearted look at the shopping habits of U.S. families. In this case, the writer's primary purpose is to *entertain*. Of course, not all writing that entertains is intended to make you laugh. For example, a story about a small village raising money to send a promising young musician to college would not be funny, but it would entertain you. Finally, the primary purpose of an article asserting that nuclear power plant construction should be halted until safety concerns are addressed would be to *persuade*.

Look closely at the articles, and you will also see the modes in action. For example, the article about the scientific research would feature *cause and effect* as its primary mode to link coronary disease to diet. It would also feature such modes as *example* to develop specific case studies and *definition* to explain the terms used in the article.

The essay about people's shopping habits would have *division and classification* as a primary mode to explain how different people approach shopping differently. It would also include such modes as *description* to create images of the shoppers in action and *narration* to follow them as a video-camera might.

The essay about nuclear power plants would feature *example* as the primary mode to illustrate the dangers at specific nuclear power plants. It might also feature *process* to show how nuclear power plants generate electricity. In addition, it would include *cause and effect* to show how radiation leakage could affect nearby residents' health. Finally, it could include *description* to show in vivid terms the destruction that could result from a nuclear accident.

The rest of this chapter will examine ways to use the modes to develop essays. Remember—although an assignment might call for one particular mode, you will actually use a combination of modes to fulfill your purpose.

USING NARRATION TO DEVELOP AN ESSAY

As Chapter 5 explained, writing that relates a series of events is *narration*. For example, if you were writing a paper about a special day you recently enjoyed with your family, narration would be a natural choice. Like narrative paragraphs, **narrative essays** are usually arranged in *chronological order*. In addition, narrative writing is often presented from *the first person point of view* (using *I, me, my*), although it may be written in the *third person* (using *he, she, her, him, they*). In order to be effective, a narrative essay must also be *unified* and include plenty of specific details for support.

Examining a Narrative Essay

Take a look at this narrative essay about a special day:

The Fourth of July, My Favorite Day

(1) The old saying, "Everybody loves a party," certainly applies to my family. We observe many traditions associated with holidays, but the celebration we enjoy on the Fourth of July is the best. First, we have a big cookout for family and friends, followed by an afternoon of volleyball, croquet, and whiffle ball. Then we all walk the half mile to Washington Park to see the fireworks display. Last year I was in charge of organizing the Fourth of July festivities, and my family agrees that it was one of the best celebrations we've had in years.

(2) I actually started my preparations on July 3. I spent about an hour at the supermarket picking up two dozen hamburgers, three dozen hot dogs, buns, disposable plates and cups, and snack items. After I finished my shopping, I rounded up all the equipment for the games and then set up the volleyball net and croquet wickets. Finally, I checked the gas grill to make sure that I had plenty of fuel for the cookout.

(3) On the morning of the Fourth, I got out of bed early and prepared two big bowls of garden salad and two additional bowls of fresh fruit salad. I knew I needed plenty of food because, in addition to my parents and sisters and brother, my guests included six of my friends from school and their dates. My friends and their dates began arriving about noontime, just when I was firing up the grill.

(4) The next two hours were hectic for me, as I cooked nearly two dozen hamburgers and almost three dozen hot dogs. When I finally had a chance to eat at about 2:30 P.M., all the salad and the hamburgers were gone, so I ate what was left: three well-done hot dogs. I was so hungry that I don't think I ever enjoyed a meal more.

(5) We spent the next three hours playing games. First, we played a volleyball game the way we traditionally play on the Fourth, with the women against the men. We all started out laughing, but after the women scored the first few points, the men began to take the game seriously. Three of the women had played on a championship high school volleyball team, however, so it didn't make any difference how hard the men played. We still managed to beat them. For croquet and whiffle ball, we had mixed teams, and by the end of the afternoon, everybody was worn out and ready for a few more sodas, some snacks, and a little relaxation.

(6) After everyone had eaten again and rested, it was time for the best part of our annual Fourth of July celebration: the fireworks. At 8:30 P.M. we had our own little parade from my house to Washington Park about a half a mile away. When we arrived at the park, we placed our blankets end to end on the ground and enjoyed the fireworks. This night was the first time in four years that it hadn't been rainy or foggy on the Fourth. As a result, we had the chance to enjoy the best fireworks display anyone could remember.

(7) For most people, the Fourth of July isn't as big a holiday as Thanksgiving or New Year's Eve. But when it comes to traditions, I'll take our Fourth of July celebration over all other festivities. It's a day filled with great food, great friends, and great fun.

Challenge 1 Analyzing the Sample Narrative Essay

Refer to the sample narrative essay above to answer each question.

1. Reread the introduction of the essay. Underline the thesis.

2. Underline the topic sentences of paragraphs 2 through 6. In an essay, each topic sentence relates back to the thesis, but it also serves as a building block for its own main idea. Work with a partner to analyze the role of these sentences. On a separate sheet of paper, explain (a) how each topic sentence in the essay is related to the thesis and (b) how each one is developed by its supporting paragraph information.

3. On the same sheet, list transitional expressions that help establish the sequence of events.

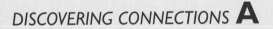

DISCOVERING CONNECTIONS A

1. Using the essay above to guide you, write a narrative essay on a special day of your own or on one of the following topics:

   a. a time when you witnessed a crime
   b. the best phone call you ever received
   c. a family (or school, team, or club) reunion
   d. a time you were caught in a lie
   e. an accident you witnessed

2. Exchange your draft with a partner. Evaluate the essay using the narrative essay checklist on page 200. Write your answers on a separate sheet of paper, and then return the essay and your assessment to the writer.

3. Using your reader's comments to guide you, revise and redraft your narrative essay.

Narrative Essay Checklist

1. Does the introduction set the scene for the sequence of events to follow?
2. Is a *first person* or *third person* point of view used consistently?
3. Does the paper follow chronological order? If a flashback has been used, has the switch in time been made clear for the reader?
4. Is the essay unified, with all supporting ideas and examples related to the main idea? Circle any material that isn't unified.
5. Are there enough specific details and examples to guide the reader? Put a ✓ next to any spot that you'd like to know more about.
6. In your judgment, what is the best part of this essay? Explain.

➤ USING DESCRIPTION TO DEVELOP AN ESSAY

As Chapter 6 showed, writing that uses words to paint a picture of a scene, individual, or experience is *description*. Effective description emphasizes specific sensory details. For example, a descriptive essay about an unusual experience would bring its unique nature to life using carefully crafted details of particular sensations and scenes. **Descriptive essays** often combine both *objective* description (observable details and sensations) and *subjective* description (the impressions that the details and sensations create within the writer). In addition, descriptive writing often uses *spatial order* to organize details for the reader.

Examining a Descriptive Essay

Take a look at this descriptive essay about an unusual experience:

Bright Lights, Loud Music: Not *Your Average Planetarium Show*

(1) If someone invited you to a planetarium show, what would you expect? You are probably thinking of seeing pictures of stars and constellations. You may even be thinking, "Boring!" At first, that's what I thought when two friends invited me to a show at the Hayden Planetarium in New York City, but I was mistaken. On that night my eyes and ears were exposed to more sensation and stimulation than they had ever been exposed to at one time.

(2) I was on vacation visiting friends who go to school in New York City, and they told me that we were going to the planetarium that evening. I had been to other planetarium shows before, and I had always enjoyed seeing images of the various constellations projected on the inside of a dome. I was a bit surprised, though, that my friends, two of the wildest people I have ever met, had picked such a tame adventure. After all, it was Friday night, and we were in one of the most exciting cities in the world.

(3) When we arrived at the planetarium at 8:30, I began to wonder exactly what was going on. About 300 people, most of them under twenty-five, were just starting to stream through the doors under the sign that said "Genesis Laser Show." Like the other planetariums I had been in before, this one had rows of soft seats that reclined so that people could comfortably look up at the ceiling. I settled into my seat just as the lights began to dim, and a display of the various constellations appeared on the ceiling.

(4) That's when I got my second surprise of the night. The constellation on the ceiling suddenly disappeared, plunging the planetarium into darkness. Then a series of speakers practically exploded with a tune by the rock group Genesis. Suddenly, rows of red, blue, and yellow lasers projected a series of brilliantly colored designs that moved to the beat of the music all across the inside of the domed ceiling.

(5) The music was so loud that I felt as if I were on stage with the group. I could feel each beat of the drum reverberate right through my body. I felt as if I was completely surrounded by the music through all fifteen of the songs.

(6) But what I was hearing was nothing compared to what I was seeing. The designs pulsed and glowed and blinked all across the dome. Even if I tried to close my eyes, the light seemed to break through my eyelids. It was as if those lasers had some magical power to force me to keep looking. It was like being able to look at the sun without having to worry about burning your eyes. The light was brilliantly bright, yet cool and comfortable at the same time.

(7) Finally, after forty-five minutes, the music stopped, the lights came on, and the crowd filed out the double doors into the hot July night. I felt exhausted but exhilarated at the same time. Outside, the bright street lights and the blaring New York City traffic seemed mild compared to what I had just experienced.

(8) An evening that I expected to be merely calm and pleasant turned out to be a true adventure for my ears and eyes. Now every time I hear a song by Genesis on the radio, I immediately think back to one of my favorite vacation memories, a night filled with sound and light.

Challenge 2   Analyzing the Sample Descriptive Essay

Refer to the sample descriptive essay above to answer each question.

1. Reread the introduction of the essay. Underline the thesis.

2. Working with a partner, analyze paragraphs 2 through 7 of the essay. On a separate piece of paper, explain how each one develops this thesis. Rate these six paragraphs according to how effectively they use description: 1 = very effective; 2 = somewhat effective; 3 = not effective.

3. Working with the same partner, bracket each sentence of description in paragraphs 3 through 7. In the margin, write *S* next to each sentence of subjective description; write *O* next to each sentence of objective description.

4. Does the essay use spatial order? On your paper, explain where and how it is used.

DISCOVERING CONNECTIONS B

1. Using the sample descriptive essay to guide you, write an essay on an unusual experience of your own or on one of the following topics:

   a. a normally busy place, now deserted
   b. a physical injury or bout with illness
   c. the feeling of being alone
   d. a unique restaurant, deli, bakery, or bar
   e. what you see in a painting or photograph

2. Exchange your draft with a partner. Evaluate the essay using the descriptive essay checklist below. Write your answers on a separate sheet of paper, and then return the essay and your assessment to the writer.
3. Using your reader's comments to guide you, complete the final draft of your descriptive essay.

Descriptive Essay Checklist

1. Does the introduction engage the reader? Does the thesis prepare you for the event to be described?
2. Does the essay include effective use of both objective and subjective description?
3. Are the paragraphs arranged so that the reader can picture the scene being painted? Explain.
4. Does each paragraph feature a number of specific, concrete sensory details to support the thesis?
5. In your judgment, what is the best part of this essay? Explain.
6. Which detail or example would be even better if it were expanded? Why?

➤ USING EXAMPLE TO DEVELOP AN ESSAY

As Chapter 7 discussed, the *example* mode uses specific instances to illustrate, clarify, or back up some point you've made. An **example essay** would be a natural choice for detailing why you would or wouldn't want to go through an experience a second time. When you write an essay that relies heavily on this technique, make sure that the examples you include are *relevant* and *specific*. In addition, *amplify*—provide enough examples to develop your main idea fully. Don't forget to take advantage of the transitional expressions *for instance* and *for example* to alert your reader that a specific example is to follow.

Examining an Example Essay

Consider this example essay about the prospect of going through high school a second time:

No Second Chances, Please

(1) You've probably seen a movie or television show about someone who goes back to experience high school all over again. On the screen, the central character, with all the knowledge he or she has now, always seems to have a great time. Personally, I can't believe anybody in real life would ever want to go back to high school a second time. Who would want to experience the worst stage of life twice?

(2) One thing that made high school so difficult was the fear of not being accepted by the right group of kids. Right from the beginning of freshman year at my high school, the popular kids seemed to band together, and the rest of the students tried to get this group to accept them. For example, the "in-crowd" of twenty or so students congregated every morning in the corridor outside the cafeteria doors. It was pitiful to watch other students who would stand next to these popular kids and try to get their attention. Some of these kids wanted to be in this group so badly that they began to dress, wear their hair, and talk like the in-crowd. For the chosen few that made up this popular group, this part of high school was fine. However, for the rest of the crowd that didn't measure up, high school sometimes seemed like four years of disappointment.

(3) Another difficult part of high school was trying out for an athletic team. The top athletes at my school were all set. They had experience or pure talent, so naturally the coaches focused on them. What happened to the hard-working athletes who couldn't score as many baskets or hit a softball as well as these superstars? As anyone who has been to high school knows, most of these marginal athletes ended up sitting on the bench or being cut from the teams completely. Who would want to go through this kind of frustration again?

(4) Dating was another horrible part of high school. I always seemed to be attracted to someone who didn't even know I was alive. Meanwhile, the only people who asked me out were the guys who made me wish I *wasn't* alive. Getting a prom date was definitely the worst part of dating. It was the same scene for both my junior and senior prom. Would my dream date call, or would I finally have to break down and beg a friend to go with me? You couldn't pay me enough to go through that torture again.

(5) By far the toughest part of high school was dealing with the constant peer pressure. During their high school years, many students are unsure of themselves. They don't have enough self-esteem to accept themselves as they are. Instead, they try to act in a way that they think will make them acceptable to others, even if the things they do aren't good for them. Many students become sexually active or use drugs or alcohol, not because they want to, but because they feel pressured to conform. In my own case, for instance, I even let my schoolwork slide during my senior year because I was afraid my friends would make fun of me for being a successful student.

(6) Most people have plenty of good memories of high school, and as time passes, it gets easier to overlook the difficulties of this period in life. However, for many people, high school was four years of worries and frustrations. As far as I'm concerned, having to go back to high school would be more like cruel and unusual punishment than fun.

Challenge 3   Analyzing the Sample Example Essay

Refer to the sample example essay above to answer each question.

1. Working with a partner, analyze paragraphs 2 through 5 of the essay. On a separate piece of paper, summarize the example each presents to support the thesis that high school is "the worst stage of life."

2. Working with the same partner, analyze each example. On your paper, list the number of the paragraph that you find most effective. Explain why its example is effective.

DISCOVERING CONNECTIONS **C**

1. Using the example essay to guide you, write an essay on something that you would like or not like to experience a second time or on one of the following topics:

   a. college challenges
   b. dating complications
   c. proper manners
   d. superstitions
   e. duties as a pet owner

2. Exchange your draft with a partner. Evaluate the essay using the example essay checklist below. Write your answers on a separate sheet of paper, and then return the essay and your assessment to the writer.

3. Using your reader's comments to guide you, complete the final draft of your example essay.

> ### *Example Essay Checklist*
>
> 1. Does the introduction spell out the concept or principle to be illustrated?
> 2. Are all the examples directly connected to the thesis? Put a ✓ next to any example that you feel is not relevant.
> 3. Are all the examples specific? Put an * next to any example that you feel needs to be made more specific.

4. Are there enough examples to support the thesis? Write *for example* or *for instance* next to any passage that you think could use another example.
5. In your judgment, what is the best part of this essay? Explain.
6. Which example would be even better if it were expanded? Why?

➤ **U**SING PROCESS TO DEVELOP AN ESSAY

Chapter 8 introduced *process,* the writing technique used to explain how to do something, how something occurs or is done, or how you did something. For instance, an essay explaining a method of problem solving would clearly be a **process essay.** When you are explaining how to do something, you should use the *imperative mood* to address the reader directly. The imperative mood is usually not appropriate for other types of process writing. If you were writing an essay explaining how acid rain affects the environment or an essay detailing how you investigated your family history to create a family tree, you would not address the reader directly. Many process essays are organized in linear order, using transitional words such as *first, next, then, afterward,* and so on. Be sure that each step describes a small and manageable part of the task, and that you warn your reader about any particularly difficult or potentially confusing steps.

Examining a Process Essay

Consider this essay, which explains the process of problem solving using the scientific method:

The Science of Solving Problems

(1) Everybody needs to solve problems, large and small. Scientists have developed an orderly and systematic approach to problem solving called the scientific method. This enables researchers to seek answers to problems through a set sequence of logical steps. The application of this method has made possible many of the technological advances that have profoundly influenced our lives. However, we can also benefit from applying the steps of the scientific method to solve everyday problems.

(2) The first step in the method is to recognize and clearly state the problem. A clear, objective statement permits you to begin thinking of options. For example, if you consistently overdraw your checking account each month, you could state the problem as "How can I better balance my income with my expenditures each month?"

(3) The second step in the method is to gather all available information related to your problem. In the case of your checking account, your checkbook record and monthly statements from the bank would clearly

show how much money had been deposited in the account, how much had been drawn out to pay checks, and to whom you had written the checks. If you had a job, you would also have a record of income from your employer.

(4) After you have gathered your information, the next step is to propose a solution you think would work. In scientific terms, this is called forming a hypothesis. For example, suppose that your checkbook records show that over the past six months you have written checks totaling a fourth of your income for clothing and entertainment. Your hypothesis might be stated in this way: "Each month I spend more on clothing and entertainment than I can afford."

(5) Once you have formulated your hypothesis, the real work begins. The fourth step in the scientific method is pinpointing evidence either to prove or to disprove your hypothesis. Scientists test their hypotheses through carefully controlled experiments. They test one variable at a time and control all the others. Your own experiment could involve limiting your clothing and entertainment expenditures for one month. For example, you might decide that you will write checks totaling no more than $100 (one-sixth of your income) for clothing and entertainment during that month. If you also kept all your other check writing similar to that in other months, then you could see whether changing your clothing and entertainment spending made a difference.

(6) The next step in the scientific method is to record and analyze the data from the experiment. For instance, you might construct a chart to compare the checks you wrote each month before the experiment with those that you wrote during the experiment:

	February	March	April	May (experimental month)
Deposit of paycheck	+ $600	+ $600	+ $600	+ $600
My share of the rent	– $200	– $200	– $200	– $200
Groceries/meals out	– $155	– $135	– $174	– $140
Car insurance	– $87	– $87	– $87	– $87
My share of utilities	– $55	– $53	– $49	– $48
Clothing/entertainment	– $150	– $175	– $140	– $98
Balance	– $47	– $50	– $50	+ $27

This information clearly shows that limiting your clothing and entertainment expenditures does indeed make a difference in keeping your checking account balance positive.

(7) The final step in the scientific method is stating your conclusion. If your results support your hypothesis, then you can restate the hypothesis as a conclusion. Usually, a single experiment is not enough to justify a firm conclusion. Scientists repeat their experiments several times to be sure the results are always similar. For example, you might limit your clothing and entertainment expenses for six months to be sure it made a critical difference. Then, based on your data, you could state a conclusion such as, "With my current income and obligations, I cannot afford to spend more than $100 a month for clothing and entertainment."

(8) Your conclusion would hardly be as earth-shattering as Sir Isaac Newton's conclusions about gravity, force, and motion, but it would be based on sound procedure and logic. Then if you had the determination and discipline to act on your conclusion, you could be proud of having used the scientific method to solve your problem.

Challenge 4   Analyzing the Sample Process Essay

Refer to the sample process essay above to answer each question.

1. Working with a partner, find and underline the thesis in the introduction.
2. What are the steps in the scientific method of problem solving? List them in order on a separate sheet of paper.
3. Find and underline transitional expressions that help establish linear order in the essay.
4. With your partner, evaluate each step in the process. Do you need more information about any steps? What questions would you ask the writer to get the information you need?

DISCOVERING CONNECTIONS D

1. Using the sample process essay to guide you, write your own essay that tells how to carry out a process such as changing a flat tire. If you prefer, write on one of the following:

   a. how to build a campfire
   b. how a natural phenomenon—a thunderstorm, a tornado, a tsunami (tidal wave)—occurs
   c. how to make a bed
   d. how to balance a checkbook
   e. how you conducted a study or experiment

2. Exchange your draft with a partner. Evaluate the essay using the process essay checklist below. Write your answers on a separate sheet of paper, and then return the essay and your assessment to the writer.
3. Using your reader's comments to guide you, complete the final draft of your essay.

Process Essay Checklist

1. Does the introduction identify the procedure or technique to be presented?
2. Is the reader addressed directly through the imperative mood (you)? Is it appropriate for this essay? Why?

Continued

3. Are the steps presented in linear order? Underline any step that is out of order, and then draw an arrow to the spot in the essay where it actually belongs.
4. Is each step simple and clear? Put a ✓ next to any step that you think should be divided or explained further.
5. In your judgment, what is the best part of this essay? Explain.
6. Which detail or example would be even better if it were expanded? Why?

USING DEFINITION TO DEVELOP AN ESSAY

Chapter 9 introduced *definition*, the writing technique used to identify the essential characteristics or qualities of an object, location, or individual. An essay setting forth the qualities of a truly considerate person, for example, would use definition. To write a **definition essay**, you need to recognize the *elements of an effective definition*: The term is placed in its appropriate class and then differentiated from the other elements in its class. In general, you should provide a *working definition* in the introduction and then build an *extended definition* throughout the body of the paper. This is done by supplying *clear, specific,* and *detailed* examples and illustrations. At the same time, take into consideration both the *denotation*, the literal meaning of the term, and its *connotations*, additional subjective or emotional impact it will have on readers. In addition, you should present the material you include in an order that enhances understanding.

Examining a Definition Essay

Look at this essay, which defines "truly considerate people":

Truly Considerate People: A Rarity

(1) Probably no one would disagree with the wisdom of the old saying, "Treat others as you'd like to be treated yourself." At the same time, however, it seems as though few people actually follow this adage. Today, rudeness and lack of consideration for others seem to be accepted as normal behavior. Every day, people curse at each other in the workplace and slam doors in people's faces. They sneak their cars into a parking space another driver has waited for patiently and perform hundreds of other rude, inconsiderate, and impolite acts. That's why, when you come across a truly considerate person, an individual who is pleasant, thoughtful, polite, and concerned, you notice right away.

(2) First of all, truly considerate people are pleasant. If you take the subway or bus on a regular basis, you know that finding people with this characteristic is rare. From the person who sells the tickets to the people

sitting on either side of you, most of the faces you see each day wear expressions that would scare little children. However, just about every day, you meet a few smiling faces, individuals who take a moment to say, "Hi" or "Good morning." Truly considerate people don't groan or complain if a delay is announced. They simply grin, say something like, "Oh well, what can you do?" and wait patiently for the bus or train to arrive.

(3) Truly considerate people are also thoughtful. At school, for example, most people don't even look to see if anybody is behind them when they get to a door. Instead, they open the door, walk through, and let the door close. If you are heading out of a building with your arms full of books and supplies, and you happen to be behind the typically thoughtless individual, it's your tough luck. The door slams, and you're left to struggle to open the door. Truly considerate people are too thoughtful to let that happen. When they are in front of you, they always make sure to hold the door. If they happen to see you struggling because somebody else was thoughtless, they'll go out of their way to open the door for you.

(4) In addition, truly considerate people are always polite. If your job involves serving the public, you may sometimes work an entire shift without hearing the words "Please" and "Thank you." When some people go out to eat, for example, they demand to be seated immediately and make a scene if their service isn't as fast as they'd like. Truly considerate people are easy to recognize in these situations, too, because of their gracious attitude. They are the individuals who say, "Excuse me" before they ask when they'll be seated. If they have been waiting a while for their orders to be taken, truly considerate people wait until a server is walking by the table to ask calmly when someone will take their order. Moreover, if an order has to be returned, truly considerate people ask if the waiter or waitress would please correct the order, and end their comments with a smile and a "Thank you."

(5) Furthermore, truly considerate people show concern for those around them. Unfortunately, many people that you come across each day don't possess this characteristic. For example, one of my neighbors walks three miles a day through a heavily traveled part of the city. Last week, while she was walking past North Park, she tripped and fell. She hit her head, scraped her hands, and cut her knees. She said there was a Little League baseball game going on in the park, and she is sure that several people in the stands saw her fall. However, none of those people came to help her. Finally, after several minutes passed, a woman who was driving by stopped, helped my neighbor up, and gave her a ride to the local clinic so she could be checked for broken bones. Truly considerate people notice when others around them need help, and then they do their best to provide that help, even if it means inconveniencing themselves.

(6) In today's world, rude and inconsiderate people seem to be everywhere, making life unpleasant for themselves and everyone around them. Luckily, almost every crowd has at least a couple of people whose caring behavior stands out like an oasis in a desert. These people truly are treating others as they want to be treated themselves. Now you know what to call these people: truly considerate.

Challenge 5   Analyzing the Sample Definition Essay

Refer to the sample definition essay on pages 208–209 to answer each question.

1. Find and underline the thesis statement in the first paragraph. On a separate sheet of paper, write the term that is defined and the writer's working definition of it.

2. Working with a partner, analyze paragraphs 2 through 5. First, underline the topic sentence in each. Then study the way each topic sentence is developed. On your paper, summarize the way each paragraph develops or extends the definition.

3. Why are the supporting paragraphs presented in this order? On your paper, explain why you think the writer organized the paper in this way. Would you change the order? Tell how and explain why.

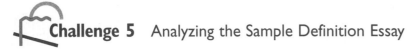

DISCOVERING CONNECTIONS **E**

1. Using the essay on pages 208–209 to guide you, write an essay on your definition of good manners or on one of the following topics:

   a. a sports (or music, surfing, dance, computer, religious) fanatic
   b. a perfect date
   c. true charity
   d. success
   e. a masterpiece of literature, music, or art

2. Exchange your draft with a partner. Evaluate the essay using the definition essay checklist below. Write your answers on a separate sheet of paper, and then return the essay and your assessment to the writer.

3. Using your reader's comments to guide you, complete the final draft of your definition essay.

'Definition Essay Checklist

1. Does the introduction introduce the term or principle to be defined?
2. Does the essay begin with a working definition and then develop an extended definition?
3. Does the extended definition reflect both the denotations and connotations of the term defined?
4. Are the supporting details and examples clear and specific? If you find any that are too general or too abstract, suggest a way to clarify or sharpen them.

5. Are the supporting paragraphs effectively arranged in an appropriate order? Explain.
6. In your judgment, what is the best part of this essay? Explain.
7. Which detail or example would be even better if it were expanded? Why?

USING COMPARISON AND CONTRAST TO DEVELOP AN ESSAY

As Chapter 10 discussed, the writing technique that focuses on examining alternatives is called *comparison and contrast. Comparison* means examining similarities, and *contrast* means examining differences. For example, an essay evaluating two ways to afford to drive a new car would call for comparison and contrast. In your college courses, you will often be called on to explain how two people, objects, or phenomena are alike or how they are different. With most comparison and contrast essays, restrict your focus to *two subjects* that have some common ground. In addition, be sure you have an adequately developed *basis of comparison* using at least three points.

To arrange a **comparison and contrast essay,** use either a *block format* or an *alternating format.* For the block format, include a thesis in your introduction, and then present the first point, the second point, the third point, and so on for Subject A. Afterward, examine the first point, the second point, and the third point for Subject B.

For the alternating format, examine the two subjects at the same time. In other words, after the introduction, address the first point for Subject A and Subject B, then the second point for Subject A and Subject B, then the third point for Subject A and Subject B, and so on. This method is helpful for longer papers. It may be hard for a reader to keep all the points for Subject A in mind while reading the second half of such a paper. See page 132 for illustrations of both the block and alternating formats.

Examining a Comparison and Contrast Essay

Here's a comparison and contrast essay by student Michael Goes that compares the costs of purchasing versus leasing for the same vehicle:

The Car Question: To Buy or to Lease?

(1) Should you buy or lease your next new car? Ultimately, this is a personal decision, but it should be based on a knowledge of the costs involved. Many people assume incorrectly that leasing is a more expensive option. However, for the average driver who puts 12,000 miles or less on the odometer each year, the cost of each option is about the same.

(2) Let's look first at the typical costs involved in buying a new car with a loan from a bank. For the purposes of our comparison, we'll assume that you are about to buy under the following terms:

Purchase price	$20,000
Term of loan	36 months
Compound interest rate	6 percent annual percentage rate (APR)

(3) A bank usually requires a down payment of 20 percent, which in this case will amount to $4,000. Your 36 equal monthly payments for the remaining $16,000 at 6 percent APR interest would be $486.75 each. At the time you make the purchase, you are required by law to pay 5 percent sales tax on the entire $20,000, which amounts to $1,000. The figures below show your total investment at the end of three years. When you have paid off your loan, then, at long last, you receive the title from the bank and officially own the car.

Down payment	$ 4,000.00
Monthly payments ($486.75 × 36)	17,523.00
Sales tax	1,000.00
Total investment	**$22,523.00**

(4) If you're a typical American, however, at the end of three years and 36,000 miles, you start thinking that it is time for a new car. Of course, in order to afford that new car, you have to unload this one first. When you look in the industry guides, you discover that your $20,000 vehicle has depreciated by about 40 percent over three years. It's now worth $12,000, so you place an ad in your local paper and sell it. The income from that sale lowers your total investment. If you divide your adjusted total investment by 36, you can see the amount you paid each month for driving the car:

Total investment	$ 22,523.00	
	−12,000.00	sale income
Adjusted total investment	**$10,523.00**	
	÷ 36	
Net monthly expense	**$ 292.30**	

(5) With these calculations in mind, let's now examine the costs involved in a typical 36-month leasing arrangement for the same car. When you enter into a lease, you agree to drive no more than a certain number of miles (usually 12,000 a year) during a specific amount of time—36 months for our purposes. To calculate a lease payment, you must first consider three factors: the capitalized cost of the car, which is equivalent to the purchase price; the term of the lease; and a lease factor, or interest rate. For our comparison, we will use the following numbers:

Capitalized cost	$20,000
Term of lease	36 months
Lease factor	.0025, or ¼ of one percent (equal to 6% APR)

(6) The leaseholder calculates your monthly payments based on the *depreciation amount,* or the difference between the capitalized cost and the projected value of the car at the end of the lease. As we saw earlier, the projected value for your car in 36 months is $12,000. The difference

between the capitalized cost ($20,000) and the projected value ($12,000) is an $8,000 depreciation amount. Your payments must cover this $8,000 depreciation amount plus the leaseholder's borrowing costs.

(7) To understand how a lease payment is calculated, think of the payment as two separate loans. The first loan is for the depreciation amount plus the lease factor. For your car, this would be $8,000 at the lease factor of .0025. Payments for this portion would be divided into 36 equal installments of $243.37 each. The other loan is to pay the interest on the projected value of the car after the lease terminates. For our example, we are assuming a 6 percent annual interest rate on the $12,000 projected value, or $60 a month. In addition, your sales tax would be 5 percent of your monthly total, or $15.16 per month. When we tally all of these numbers, your total monthly payment would be as follows:

Depreciation loan	$243.37
Interest on projected value	60.00
Sales tax	15.16
Net monthly expense	**$318.53**

Now you can figure your total investment. At the end of the lease term, you will have made 36 payments of $318.53, so your total is as follows:

Investment per month	$ 318.53
	× 36
Total investment	**$11,467.08**

(8) As you can see, you would actually spend only $944.08 more overall (the difference between $11,467.08 and $10,523.00), or $26.23 more per month (the difference between the net monthly expenses of $318.53 and $292.30), to lease the car than you would to purchase it. If you choose to lease, you can invest the $5,000 that you would have used on a down payment and sales tax. You could also invest the $168.22 you save each month (the difference between the $486.75 monthly payment to purchase and the $318.53 to lease). Even at a conservative 4 percent rate of return, over a 36-month period you would earn just about enough money to cover the difference between the overall cost of buying and leasing. In addition, when your lease runs out, you can simply return the car to the leaseholder and sign another agreement for a new car.

(9) When you compare all of the costs in a systematic way, you can see that the myths about leasing are not true. For the average driver, leasing is no more expensive than purchasing a car. Moreover, leasing eliminates the hassle of having to resell a car. As with most purchasing options, taking the time to do some simple math can help you make a more informed decision about buying versus leasing.

Challenge 6 Analyzing the Sample Comparison and Contrast Essay

Refer to the sample comparison and contrast essay above to answer each question.

1. In his introduction, what point does Goes make about leasing a car versus buying it? What does the introduction tell you about the purpose of this essay? Write your answers on a separate sheet of paper.

2. Working with a partner, analyze paragraphs 2 through 8. What bases of comparison does Goes use to compare buying and leasing? List the bases of comparison on your paper.

3. Still working with a partner, identify the format Goes uses to arrange his essay. On your paper, prepare a diagram like the one on page 132 in Chapter 10 to illustrate his organizational plan.

DISCOVERING CONNECTIONS **F**

1. Using the essay just presented to guide you, write a comparison or contrast essay on two other purchasing options or on one of the following topics:

   a. the typical family today versus the typical family twenty-five years ago
   b. two jobs you've held
   c. two dates you've gone on
   d. two politicians, musical groups, or professional athletes
   e. two religions

2. Exchange your draft with a partner. Evaluate the essay using the comparison and contrast essay checklist below. Write your answers on a separate sheet of paper, and then return the essay and your assessment to the writer.

3. Using your reader's comments to guide you, complete the final draft of your comparison or contrast essay.

Comparison and Contrast Essay Checklist

1. Does the introduction specify the essay's focus and the subjects to be compared or contrasted?
2. Does the essay concentrate on two subjects?
3. Is a basis for comparison established and followed? Make sure that each characteristic or element is discussed in detail for each subject. Put a ✓ at any point where an element or characteristic is missing, and write *amplify* above any point that should be discussed in greater detail.
4. Has the block format or the alternating format been used to arrange the paragraphs? Would the essay be more effective if it were arranged differently, for example, using block format instead of alternating format or vice versa?
5. In your judgment, what is the best part of this essay? Explain.
6. Which detail or example would be even better if it were expanded? Why?

➤ USING CAUSE AND EFFECT TO DEVELOP AN ESSAY

Cause and effect, the writing technique you use to focus on what led to something or what happened as a result, is discussed in Chapter 11. Cause is *why* something occurred, and effect is the *outcome* or *consequence* of an occurrence. An essay in which you discuss how a new job has changed your life would be a cause and effect essay.

For a **cause and effect essay,** remember that most events or experiences have *more than one* cause and *more than one* effect. Therefore, don't oversimplify. Furthermore, be sure that any cause and effect relationships you suggest aren't actually *coincidence*—events that occur close to the same time by accident. Finally, arrange the various causes or effects you present in a logical order.

Examining a Cause and Effect Essay

Look at this essay about the various consequences of advancing to a more responsible job:

More Than a Promotion

(1) When I was about ten years old, I spent two weeks at my cousin's house just outside of Chicago. One day we went into the city with my aunt to see the department store that she managed. She showed us around the store and then took us up to her office. I sat quietly watching her make phone calls and instruct her staff on what she wanted done that day. After half an hour, I knew I wanted to do just what she did for a living when I grew up. Six months ago, I got my chance to fulfill my dream when I was made the night and weekend manager at a large drug store. Almost overnight, I went from simply doing my job as a part-time clerk to keeping the ten people I supervise happy and productive. The many changes my promotion has brought about have definitely made me a different person.

(2) One way the promotion has changed my life is financial. When I was a clerk, I worked twenty hours a week at $7 an hour with no benefits. After taxes, my weekly pay was about $115. As a manager, I work at least forty hours a week for a weekly salary of $500, and I have full insurance coverage. Since I've become a manager, I have been able to buy a car and save money on a regular basis. With a little luck, I should be able to afford to move out of my mother's house and into my own apartment in six months or so.

(3) My new responsibilities have also helped build up my self-confidence. At first, I almost didn't take the job because I wasn't sure I could handle the responsibility. My supervisor convinced me to take it by telling me that she wouldn't have recommended me if she didn't feel I was capable. After the first few weeks on the job, I found out something about myself that I had never realized. Not only was I able to

handle responsibilities such as motivating other workers, setting work schedules, and doing the payroll, but I was actually good at all these things. Because of these successes, I'm more confident whenever I face a new task.

(4) Taking the promotion has also meant I had to grow up a lot. For one thing, I had to learn to budget my personal time. As a manager, I work almost twice as many hours as I did when I was a clerk. Furthermore, managers often have to attend meetings at night or on weekends and do paperwork at home. No longer do I have time to ride around with my friends. I also can no longer do things like call in sick when I just don't feel like working. A clerk might be able to get away with that, but a manager can't. Managers are paid to be responsible.

(5) I've also had to adjust to a new relationship with the people I supervise. Before, I was one of them, but now I'm their boss. I have to make decisions about such things as who has to work Friday and Saturday nights and who gets extra hours when business is good. I now also have to evaluate them every four months to see who gets merit raises and who doesn't. Some of the people I was friendliest with when I was a clerk barely talk to me now because I won't play favorites when it comes to schedules and raises. I sometimes feel guilty when I have to give someone a bad evaluation for job performance or lack of punctuality. I know that when I was a clerk, I sometimes was lazy and showed up late or left a few minutes early. But I'm a manager now, and I have a responsibility to make sure that my company is getting its money's worth.

(6) I've been a manager for four months now, and I can honestly say that I enjoy the job far more than I ever expected to. I like earning more money, and the idea that people are willing to put their trust in me has made me more confident overall. I also like the fact that I've learned to take responsibility. I know that, overall, this job has helped to make me a better person.

Challenge 7   Analyzing the Sample Cause and Effect Essay

Refer to the sample cause and effect essay above to answer each question.

1. What event is the focus of this cause and effect essay? Does the essay explore the causes for this event or the consequences of it? Write your answers on a separate sheet of paper.

2. Working with a partner, analyze paragraphs 2 through 5 of the essay. First, underline the topic sentence of each paragraph. Then, on your paper, write the specific changes that occurred in the writer's life.

3. Imagine that the focus of this essay was on causes, not effects. Consider the causes of the promotion—diligence at work, a positive attitude, natural leadership ability, and a supervisor's confidence. Working with your partner, write a cause and effect paragraph that focuses on these causes. (Remember—your thesis should state the effect and reveal that you will explore the causes.)

DISCOVERING CONNECTIONS **G**

1. Using the essay "More Than a Promotion" to guide you, write an essay on the cause(s) or effect(s) of a change in employment, schools, or personal relationships. If you prefer, choose one of the following topics:

   a. your interest in music, art, or sports
   b. an automobile, motorcycle, or bicycling accident you were involved in or witnessed
   c. a major environmental disaster like an oil spill from an ocean-going tanker, a volcanic eruption, a forest fire, or an earthquake
   d. lack of consumer confidence in a product or company
   e. cheating in high school or college

2. Exchange your draft with a partner. Evaluate the essay using the cause and effect essay checklist below. Write your answers on a separate sheet of paper, and then return the essay and your assessment to the writer.
3. Using your reader's comments to guide you, complete the final draft of your cause and effect essay.

Cause and Effect Essay Checklist

1. Does the introduction indicate a focus on either cause or effect?
2. Are the cause and effect relationships supported with enough examples and details to avoid oversimplification? If you feel more specific details are required, write "I'd like to know more about _____" in the margin next to the poorly explored passage.
3. Does the essay distinguish between direct and related causes and effects? Underline any details that seem like coincidences rather than true causes or effects.
4. Are the supporting paragraphs effectively arranged in a logical order?
5. In your judgment, what is the best part of this essay? Explain.
6. Which detail or example would be better if it were expanded? Why?

USING DIVISION AND CLASSIFICATION TO DEVELOP AN ESSAY

Chapter 12 discussed the writing techniques you use to analyze a complex subject. *Division* is separation of a subject into its component parts. *Classification* is arrangement of the subcategories into *groups* on the basis of some principle or characteristic. An essay in which you discuss different types of horror movies would use both division and classification. When you write a **division and classification essay,** choose a logical *method of classification,* and keep the groupings as *distinct* and *complete* as possible.

Examining a Division and Classification Essay

Look at this essay about the various types of horror movies:

Spine-Chilling Choices

(1) *Entertainment Weekly* recently reported that the movie business continues to thrive, with Americans spending several million dollars every week on movie tickets and video rentals. At this moment, many of those consumers are preparing to watch their favorite type of movie: a good horror movie. As every connoisseur of this type of entertainment knows, horror movies fall into several categories, each of which has its own special appeal and pattern.

(2) First of all, there are the classic horror movies involving mad scientists or ghosts, vampires, werewolves, and other assorted mythical creatures. *Dracula, Frankenstein, The Mummy, The Howling,* and *The Fly* are all examples of this type of horror movie. Most horror classics contain more spooky locations, weird happenings, loud screaming, and dramatic music than blood and guts.

(3) Another type of horror movie is the science fiction horror movie. This kind of movie combines horror with such science fiction themes as experiments gone wrong or prehistoric creatures awakening. Sometimes, however, the creatures in the movie develop as a result of radioactive fallout or toxic waste, or they arrive here from another planet. *King Kong, Godzilla, C.H.U.D., The Blob, Alien,* and *Invasion of the Body Snatchers* are examples of the sci-fi horror movie. These movies are filled with action as well as destruction, either of whole cities or towns or of the human race itself.

(4) A third type is the action horror movie. This kind of horror movie features some real creature that suddenly begins to attack human beings. The most famous action horror movie is *Jaws,* a movie about a series of attacks by a great white shark. *Arachnophobia,* a movie about armies of spiders attacking people, is another example. Other films in this class have featured tarantulas, ants, bees, and alligators. Action horror movies take advantage of the natural fear that most people have of these creatures.

(5) Then there are the slice-and-dice horror movies. These movies usually feature crazed killers who stalk and use knives, axes, saws, and sledge hammers to murder a series of innocent victims. *Friday the 13th, Halloween, Nightmare on Elm Street,* and *The Texas Chain-Saw Massacre* are all good examples of slice-and-dice horror movies. These movies terrify audiences through massive amounts of gore that seems to ooze and drip right through the screen.

Thesis

(6) Finally, there is the type of horror movie that many people think is the most frightening: the supernatural horror movie. These movies usually involve forces or individuals from another dimension who try to destroy or harm us. Sometimes the force is Satan, but other times it is simply some unnamed evil power. Movies like *The Exorcist, The Omen, Poltergeist, Phantasm,* and *The Shining* are all good examples of this type of movie. The terror in these movies results less from bloody gore than from various special effects that suggest what the evil force looks like or can do. Basically, supernatural horror movies take advantage of our fear of the unknown.

(7) As you can see, horror movies are not all the same. Each type is designed to scare people, but each does it in a different way. Some use horrible monsters; others use rivers of blood; and some use a nameless, faceless, evil power. Considering the number of horror movies that are released each year, it's obvious that people love being scared out of their wits, no matter how it's done.

Challenge 8   Analyzing the Sample Division and Classification Essay

Refer to the sample division and classification essay above to answer each question.

1. Find and underline the thesis statement in the first paragraph. Then, on a separate sheet of paper, list the essay's subject and the classes into which it is divided.

2. Find and underline the topic sentences of paragraphs 2 through 6. Working with a partner, analyze these paragraphs. On your paper, name each class of horror film and describe the elements of each type that are discussed.

3. Working with a partner, identify another category of horror movies or subdivide one of the existing categories. Then write a paragraph that illustrates or explains this new classification.

DISCOVERING CONNECTIONS H

1. Using the essay "Spine-Chilling Choices" to guide you, write a division and classification essay on types of fiction or sitcoms, or on one of the following topics:

   a. types of rock 'n' roll music
   b. kinds of shoppers at the mall
   c. types of responsibilities a first-year college student faces
   d. types of indoor sports
   e. kinds of clothing in your closet

2. Exchange your draft with a partner. Evaluate the essay using the division and classification essay checklist below. Write your answers on a separate sheet of paper, and then return the essay and your assessment to the writer.

3. Using your reader's comments to guide you, complete the final draft of your essay.

Division and Classification Essay Checklist

1. Does the introduction specify the focus of the discussion and indicate an emphasis on either division or classification?
2. Are the elements distinct and complete? If you think any divisions or classes need to be subdivided further to make them clearer or more specific, write, "I'd like to know more about _____" in the margin next to them.
3. Does the essay feature a logical, consistent method of analysis throughout?
4. Are the supporting paragraphs presented in an effective order?
5. In your judgment, what is the best part of this essay? Explain.
6. Which detail or example would be even better if it were expanded? Why?

WRITING AN ARGUMENT ESSAY

As Chapter 13 explained, *argument* isn't a writing technique or a mode. It is writing that uses a combination of modes to persuade. An **argument essay** takes a firm stand on an issue and then attempts to convince readers to agree with that stand. For example, an essay suggesting that child beauty pageants are harmful to participants would be an argument because its purpose would be to convince readers to accept the writer's viewpoint.

When you write an argument essay, it's important to make your stance on the issue clear in the introduction. In the body, supply at least three convincing reasons why readers should agree with you. Back up each reason with sound support. Should you draw any of your supporting information from a document or individual, always acknowledge your source. Also, adopt a reasonable tone; avoid an emotional or condescending view. It's often better to use qualifying terms such as *most, rarely,* and *frequently* rather than absolute ones such as *all, never,* and *always.* In addition, make sure that your argument essay has a logical line of reasoning and that you have avoided the errors in logic known as *logical fallacies.* See the list of logical fallacies on pages 157–158. Finally, be sure to arrange your points in a logical order, such as order of importance.

Examining an Argument Essay

Look at this argument essay about child beauty pageants:

The Beast Is the Beauty Contest

(1) On Christmas Day, 1996, six-year-old JonBenet Ramsey was murdered in Boulder, Colorado. Shortly after her tiny body was discovered, the story of her brief life became public, especially details about her involvement in child beauty pageants. Within a few weeks, the spotlight was turned on the pageants themselves. The public quickly learned that at these events, held in nearly every state across the United States, children as young as ten months old don makeup and fancy clothing to compete for crowns and titles. Despite the large number of people who claim that these events are a form of innocent fun and recreation, these reports clearly indicate that children's beauty pageants can have a negative and lasting effect on their young participants.

(2) Proponents of child beauty pageants, including promoters and parents of contestants, compare these events to other childhood pastimes such as Little League or playing "dress-up." They argue that the competitions can help youngsters develop poise and self-confidence. A lucky few, they point out, even earn scholarships or launch careers in acting or modeling. However, these people are ignoring the fact that the lessons these competitions teach are damaging to a child's future.

(3) The first lesson children learn is that personal appearance is everything. The "dressing-up" that they do in these pageants is far from innocent play. Right from the start, they see that the right hairstyle, the most stylish outfit, the perfect makeup win the prizes. How you look, not who you are, is what is truly important in this world. Unfortunately, this harmful attitude may stay with a child well into adulthood, coloring the way she interacts, forms relationships with others, and values herself.

(4) Those who compare beauty pageants with Little League are also forgetting that beauty, unlike a sport, cannot be developed and improved through practice. If a child's appearance does not conform to society's standards for beauty, then winning the competition is out of the question. Children who fail at these events may learn to feel unattractive, rejected, and worthless before they even have a chance to develop an adult body. Moreover, even those who enjoy success as children may run into trouble when they reach adolescence. When they grow taller or heavier, or when they develop acne, they may no longer meet society's standards for beauty. If they have based their sense of self-worth on their appearance, then these children are in danger of developing disorders such as depression, anorexia, or bulimia.

(5) The most damaging aspect of child beauty pageants, however, is that children learn to display themselves as sex objects before they can possibly understand what sexuality is all about. As the news reports have shown, many of the contestants have to appear before adult judges in elaborate makeup, scaled-down versions of provocative dresses, and

bathing suits. They also learn to flirt and use their bodies to attract attention. In a world in which sex crimes against children make daily headlines, such practices are deeply disturbing and potentially harmful.

(6) Although it is tempting to argue that child beauty pageants should be banned, that is not a good long-term solution. Instead, parents should think carefully about the lessons and values that children are likely to learn from these events. If parents really considered the consequences of those lessons, then the competitions might die a natural death. Vermont, for example, recently failed to produce a Miss America candidate because the women in that state refused to enter a contest that judges people on looks and other superficial qualities.

(7) If parents do not want their children to grow up thinking that appearance is all that matters, then they should keep their children away from activities that twist and exploit a child's natural desire for attention. Beauty contests are far more likely to make children, like poor JonBenet, the victims of adult desires than to deliver the fame and fortune they seem to promise.

Challenge 9   Analyzing the Sample Argument Essay

Refer to the sample argument essay above to answer each question.

1. Find the thesis statement in the first paragraph. Write it on a separate sheet of paper.

2. Working with a partner, analyze the paragraphs in the body of the essay. How many reasons does the writer give to support this thesis? On your paper, list each reason.

3. Analyze the support given for each reason. Which is most convincing to you? Which reason is least convincing? Working together, brainstorm further support for this reason (or develop an alternative reason) and revise or replace this paragraph.

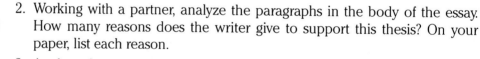

DISCOVERING CONNECTIONS

1. Using the essay "The Beast Is the Beauty Contest" to guide you, write an argument essay taking a stance on whether beauty contests—for adults or children—are harmful. If you prefer, choose one of the following topics instead, and write an argument essay in which you support or refute it:

   a. There should be a law requiring the use of helmets for bicyclists and in-line skaters.
   b. Dress codes should be imposed in public schools.
   c. Attendance should be mandatory in college classrooms.
   d. People receiving government assistance should be required to perform community service in return.
   e. A C average should be a minimum requirement for high school and college students who wish to participate in sports.

2. Exchange your draft with a partner. Evaluate the essay using the argument essay checklist below. Write your answers on a separate sheet of paper, and then return the essay and your assessment to the writer.
3. Using your reader's comments to guide you, complete the final draft of your argument essay.

Argument Essay Checklist

1. Does the introduction clarify the stance on the issue?
2. Are there at least three reasons, properly documented if necessary, to support the stance?
3. Is the tone throughout the essay respectful and concerned? Put a ✓ next to any sentence in which the tone seems inappropriate.
4. Is the presentation logical? Underline any errors in logic.
5. Does the essay feature qualifying terms rather than absolute ones when appropriate?
6. Are the supporting paragraphs effectively presented in emphatic order or some other method of arrangement? Explain.
7. In your judgment, what is the best part of this essay? Explain.
8. Which detail or example would be even better if it were expanded? Why?

RECAP

EXAMINING TYPES OF ESSAYS

New terms in this chapter	Definitions
➤ narrative essay	➤ a multi-paragraph writing that relates a sequence of events in story fashion
➤ descriptive essay	➤ a multi-paragraph writing that uses concrete, sensory language to re-create a scene, situation, or individual
➤ example essay	➤ a multi-paragraph writing that uses specific instances to illustrate, clarify, or back up a thesis
➤ process essay	➤ a multi-paragraph writing that spells out how to do something, how something is done, or how you did something
➤ definition essay	➤ a multi-paragraph writing that specifies the characteristics or elements of some object, location, or individual
➤ comparison and contrast essay	➤ a multi-paragraph writing that examines similarities and differences between two or more subjects

Continued

New terms in this chapter	Definitions
➤ cause and effect essay	➤ a multi-paragraph writing that considers reasons leading to some situation or condition or the outcomes or consequences of an event or phenomenon
➤ division and classification essay	➤ a multi-paragraph writing that analyzes a complex subject either by separating it into its component parts or by grouping its parts into categories ➤ Some division and classification essays use both approaches.
➤ argument essay	➤ a multi-paragraph writing that takes a firm stand on an issue and then attempts to convince readers to agree with that stand

The Relationship between the Purpose of an Essay and the Modes

Determine the *purpose* of the writing task	Choose your *main* mode	Employ *supporting* modes
Example topic: What is sexual harassment? purpose: to **inform**	Identify the characteristics of sexual harassment using **definition.**	Support your definition using **example, cause and effect,** and **comparison and contrast.**

Answering Essay Questions

OVERVIEW: LAYING THE FOUNDATION FOR ANSWERING ESSAY QUESTIONS

An **essay question** is a specific writing assignment given as part of an examination. It calls for a clear, concise multi-paragraph response within a limited period of time.

   Answering an essay question isn't all that different from completing other writing tasks. Your goal is the same: to work through the writing process and to communicate to your reader what you know about the question.

This chapter covers some basic steps toward ensuring success on essay exams:

➤ preparation
➤ anticipation
➤ rehearsal

APPROACHING AN ESSAY QUESTION

The secret to writing a successful answer to an essay question grows out of your approach to the material you have absorbed in class. As the following

225

figure shows, you can improve your chances of doing well by following three simple steps in this process: *preparation, anticipation,* and *rehearsal.*

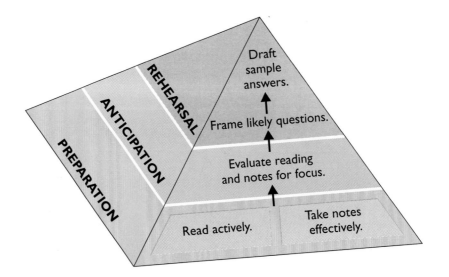

The three steps are closely connected. Preparation gives you the foundation you need for both anticipation and rehearsal, and anticipation gears you up for rehearsal.

Preparation

The best way to *prepare* yourself to answer essay questions is to apply yourself in your coursework. Learn the information you will need during an exam by (1) reading actively and (2) taking effective classroom notes.

Active Reading

To get the most out of your assigned reading, read *actively.*

➤ Read the introduction and conclusion to each chapter for an overview of the material.

➤ Preview all headings and subheadings in the selection. They highlight main ideas in the chapter.

➤ Read any *charts, boxed areas,* or *lists.* They summarize important information.

➤ If the material belongs to you, highlight or underline information you judge to be important—*specific* names, dates, distances, conditions, and so on.

➤ Look for any *definitions* and information presented *in order (first, second, third,* and so on). Be alert for *transitional expressions* and words like *important, crucial,* and *vital* that signal important material will follow.

➤ Write any points that you feel are especially important in the *margin* or in your *notebook.*

➤ Use the material you have highlighted or underlined to prepare a *summary,* a greatly reduced version of the original, expressed in your own words.

Effective Note-Taking

To take effective notes, follow these guidelines:

➤ Filter what you hear in class. Concentrate on recording information that is new to you or that you are unsure of.
➤ Assume that any material your instructor puts on the board is important.
➤ Listen when your instructor uses words like *important, vital, crucial,* and so on. These words are clues to what the instructor feels it is necessary for you to know.
➤ Focus on definitions and material the instructor repeats or presents in sequence (*first, second, third*).
➤ Keep your notes as neat and orderly as possible, writing on every other line.
➤ Use abbreviations or your own personal shorthand system.
➤ Reread your notes an hour or so after the class is over and flesh out, clarify, and tie together the information.
➤ Write a summary, interpretation, or analysis of the material.

Exploration 1a   Understanding Active Reading and Effective Note-Taking

1. Look at the suggestions for active reading on page 226. Are you an active reader? Explain what changes you should make in your reading habits to read more effectively.

   _____

   _____

   _____

   _____

2. Review the guidelines for effective note-taking above. On the following lines, list two of these things that you currently do. Then list two that you *should* do. Explain how doing these things could help you get more from class discussions and lectures.

   _____

   _____

   _____

   _____

Challenge 1   Analyzing Note-Taking Techniques

1. When you take notes in class, how do you keep pace with your instructor's comments? On a separate sheet of paper, list several note-taking techniques that you find helpful.

2. Exchange your explanation of your note-taking techniques with a partner, and then compare techniques. If your classmate has successfully used a technique that you haven't tried yet, add this technique to your own list, and try it in your next class.

Anticipation

In addition to learning your course material, it is wise to think strategically about an upcoming essay exam. Begin by evaluating your notes and readings to identify the topics your instructor might use for essay questions. To *antici-pate* these essay questions, consider the following guidelines:

➤ Focus on the ideas you've identified as important in your reading.
➤ Note the focus of any questions or checklists your instructor has provided or discussed.
➤ Reconsider your classroom notes, paying particular attention to material that your instructor described as *important, crucial, vital,* and so on or that he or she repeated several times.
➤ Discuss important ideas with your classmates. This will help you clarify your own thinking, and it may provide additional perspectives on those ideas.

Exploration 2a   Understanding Anticipation

On the lines below, list two ways you could identify likely essay question topics for a specific class you are taking.

_____

_____

_____

_____

Challenge 2   Anticipating Likely Essay Topics

1. Make a copy of your most recent notes from another course you are currently taking. Then, on a separate sheet of paper, summarize the key points and explain how they are interrelated.

2. Exchange the copy of your notes and the page that summarizes and clarifies this information with a partner. Examine the material you receive. If you feel that some of the notes need to be further explained or emphasized, put a ✓ next to them. Then return the material to the writer.

3. Using your summary and edited notes, list the topics that would be likely to appear on an essay exam for the course you have chosen.

Rehearsal

Once you have identified the information you feel is likely to be included on the examination, you should *rehearse.* In this context, rehearsal means creating several **practice questions,** or the type of query that might appear on an exam, and then drafting answers.

Drawing Up a Practice Question

Imagine, for instance, that you are studying for an essay examination in your introductory sociology class. Over the last two weeks, you've discussed a great many topics in relation to substance abuse. One of the areas you've identified as important in your reading and in your notes is the current controversy concerning alcoholism. The controversy is over whether alcoholism should be classified as a *social problem* rather than as an *illness.*

If you were to write a practice question about how such a change would affect alcoholics and society at large, it might look like this:

> There is currently a move by major insurance companies to have the surgeon general reclassify alcoholism as a social problem rather than an illness. Discuss the effects that such a change might have on alcoholics and on society in general.

Answering a Practice Question

To write an answer for a practice question like the one above, you would follow the steps of the writing process in an abbreviated fashion:

Prewriting

Read the question fully, making sure you understand what points you are to cover.

Decide what mode or modes are called for to shape your answer.

Jot down any ideas that you might be able to use to answer the question.

Budget your time—decide what percentage of your total test time you would be willing to spend answering this question, given its relative importance.

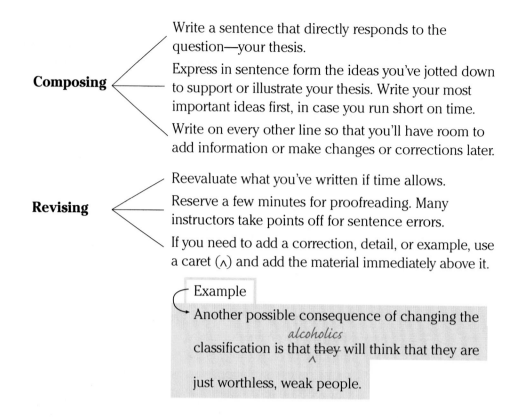

Composing
- Write a sentence that directly responds to the question—your thesis.
- Express in sentence form the ideas you've jotted down to support or illustrate your thesis. Write your most important ideas first, in case you run short on time.
- Write on every other line so that you'll have room to add information or make changes or corrections later.

Revising
- Reevaluate what you've written if time allows.
- Reserve a few minutes for proofreading. Many instructors take points off for sentence errors.
- If you need to add a correction, detail, or example, use a caret (∧) and add the material immediately above it.

Example

Another possible consequence of changing the
                                      alcoholics
classification is that ~~they~~ will think that they are
                              ∧

just worthless, weak people.

Examining an Answer to a Practice Question

To get a better idea of how the writing process works for exam questions, first look again at the practice question concerning what might happen if alcoholism were reclassified as a social problem:

> There is currently a move by major insurance companies to have the surgeon general reclassify alcoholism as a social problem rather than an illness. Discuss the effects that such a change would have on alcoholics and on society in general.

A good essay question clearly indicates what the writer must do. This question clearly asks you to discuss the *effects* of reclassifying alcoholism as a social problem. In your answer, you must point out and explain changes that might occur. First, take a few minutes to generate a list of possible changes, like the one below:

Changes because of new classification of alcoholism

Society thinking that alcoholics are weak people, not sick—stigma
Alcoholics will deny their drinking problems
Destroy their self-esteem—they'll give up hope—won't seek any help

> *Society has to support alcoholics who can't or won't work*
>
> *Insurance won't pay for rehab centers anymore—alcoholics*
> *can't afford treatment on their own*

ESL Note

See "Writing Essays" on pages 539–540.

As you can see, some of these changes can be grouped together. The first two, for example, are closely related. The last two also form a group. Once you see that you have three main points, you can decide on a logical order. For this essay, emphatic order would be best, moving from the least important point to the strongest one. (See pages 67–68 for more on emphatic order.) If you are pressed for time, however, it might make sense to move from the most important to the least important point, in case you are not able to finish your answer. Think "on your feet" during the actual test, and make the most logical choice given your circumstances.

To compose an essay from your list of changes, you would rely primarily on *cause and effect*, the mode that examines reasons and consequences. (See Chapters 11 and 15 for more on cause and effect.) To a lesser degree, you would use *comparison and contrast* to discuss attitudes before and after the change in classification. (See Chapters 10 and 15 for more on comparison and contrast.) You might also use *definition*, to focus on what alcoholism is, and *description*, to paint a picture through specific details and examples. (See Chapter 6 for more on description and Chapter 9 for more on definition.)

Here is the preliminary information from the list of changes, organized and expressed in sentence form:

> *If the surgeon general of the United States reclassifies alcoholism as a social problem rather than an illness, the effects on alcoholics and society in general will be major and negative. First, insurance companies won't have to pay for people to go to alcohol rehabilitation centers. Places like the Betty Ford Clinic have a great success rate, but the average person can't afford to pay the thousands of dollars it costs to stay there for a month of treatment. As a result, many alcoholics and their families won't be able to get the help they need. If these nonrecovering alcoholics are working, their companies will continue to have workers who are not as effective or productive as they could be. If these alcoholics are unemployed, they won't be getting any help, and society will have to continue supporting them and their families through welfare.*

> *Second, one of the principal reasons that alcoholism is so difficult to treat is that people deny that they have a drinking problem. Denial has been common because of societal attitudes toward drinkers. For years alcoholism was thought to be the result of moral weakness—a kind of character flaw. With alcoholism classified as a disease, people have begun to understand that alcoholics are driven physiologically by something they can't control. If the classification is changed, many people will once again begin to think that alcoholics are moral weaklings instead of sick people—raising the denial quotient again.*
>
> *A third possible consequence of changing the classification is that alcoholics will think that they are worthless. This is the worst thing that could happen to these people. In order for alcoholics to recover, they must develop better self-esteem. But how can alcoholics think well of themselves if society tells them that their alcoholism is their fault? As a result, many alcoholics may be convinced that their situation is hopeless and that their lives are ruined.*

This answer is effective because it clearly describes three major effects that might result if alcoholism were reclassified from a disease to a social problem. It uses a logical order to move from the least significant to the most significant problem. It is unified, containing only points that relate to the thesis. And finally, it is expressed in complete, correct sentences.

Challenge 3   Developing and Answering Essay Questions

1. Imagine that you are preparing for an essay examination in one of your courses. Go through the reading you have done and your relevant classroom notes. On a separate sheet of paper, list the key information that appears in both your reading and your notes.

2. From this list of material, develop three essay questions. Write each question on a separate sheet of paper.

3. Prepare answers of 200 to 300 words for each question. Write each answer immediately under the appropriate question.

4. Exchange your questions and answers with a partner. Evaluate the material you receive, using the essay answer checklist below. Return the answer and your assessment to the writer.

5. Correct the problem spots your reader has identified in your answers.

Essay Answer Checklist

1. Does the essay answer directly address the question being asked? Make a note in the margin next to any point that does not relate to the question.
2. Should any section of the answer be amplified? Put a ✓ next to the section that needs more explanation.
3. Are there any mistakes in spelling or usage? Circle any errors.

RECAP
ANSWERING ESSAY QUESTIONS

New terms in this chapter	Definitions
➤ essay question	➤ a specific writing assignment given as part of an examination that calls for a clear, concise multi-paragraph response within a limited period of time
➤ practice question	➤ an essay question that a student creates to rehearse for an exam ➤ Formulate practice questions by identifying key topics in readings and notes.

The Process of Preparing for an Essay Exam

Prepare
Read actively.
Take thorough classroom notes.

↓

Anticipate
Review readings and notes.
Identify key points and discuss them with classmates.

↓

Rehearse
Prepare practice questions.
Complete sample answers.

part

four

Developing Sentence Sense

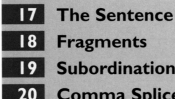

17 The Sentence

18 Fragments

19 Subordination and Coordination

20 Comma Splices and Run-On Sentences

17

The Sentence

ESL Note
See "Sentence Basics" on pages 521–523 and "Word Order" on pages 524–526.

OVERVIEW: UNDERSTANDING SENTENCE BASICS

To be a **sentence,** a group of words must contain a subject and a verb and express a complete thought. The subject is the doer of the action or the person, place, or thing that is being described. The verb describes the action or the condition of the subject. No single skill is more important to your success as a writer than learning to recognize and construct complete sentences.

In this chapter, you will discover how to identify and use

➤ action verbs, linking verbs, helping verbs, verb phrases, and compound verbs

➤ simple subjects, complete subjects, and compound subjects

DISCOVERING CONNECTIONS A

Using one of the techniques you practiced in Chapter 2, prewrite on one of the following topics: cameras in the courtroom, getting in shape, tourists. Save your work for later use.

UNDERSTANDING VERBS

In most sentences, the subject precedes the verb. However, when you're identifying the components in a sentence, it makes more sense to look for the verb before the subject. By definition, a **verb** is a word that shows action or a link between the subject and another word that renames or describes it.

A verb that describes what the subject did, does, or might do is called an **action verb:**

> Example
>
> Charlie *played* the guitar at the party last night.

> Example
>
> We *enjoyed* his performance.

Not all verbs are action verbs. A **linking verb** links the subject and a word that identifies or describes it; it indicates a state of being. Study these common linking verbs and the examples which follow:

Common Linking Verbs

forms of *to be* (am, is, was, were, will be, might have been, etc.)	feel become appear	look seem taste, smell

> Example
>
> In high school, Charlie *was* a drummer in the stage band.

> Example
>
> Ashley *seems* happy with her choice.

Was is a linking verb because it connects *Charlie* with a word that identifies him: *drummer.* The linking verb *seems* links *Ashley* with the descriptive word *happy.*

To identify the verb in a sentence, try asking yourself *what word describes action or shows a connection between two things?*

Sometimes the verb in a sentence is composed of more than one word. These verbs may be either verb phrases or compound verbs. A **verb phrase** is a *main verb* plus a *helping verb,* as the italicized words in the following examples show:

> Example
>

> Helen *is cleaning* the banquet room.

Example

> | helping verb | main verb |
>
> Krista *had bought* several sweaters last month.

Study the list of common helping verbs shown here:

■ *Common Helping Verbs*

am	been	do	have	must	were
are	can	does	is	shall	will
be	could	had	may	should	would
being	did	has	might	was	

A **compound verb** consists of two or more verbs connected by *and* or *or*, which share the same subject. Study the italicized verbs in the following examples:

Example

> During the rainstorm, the house lights *blinked* and *flickered*.

Example

> Aunt Gabriella *was, is,* and always *will be* a staunch Democrat.

Exploration 1a   Identifying Verbs

Underline the verbs in the following sentences. In the space above each, label the verb *A* (action) or *L* (linking). Remember—some verbs may be phrases or compound; check to be sure you have underlined the whole verb. Study the example first.

> *A*
>
> *Example*   Attitudes toward women <u>have changed</u> in recent years.

(1) Many women have fought for women's rights in this century. (2) In the early 1900s, for example, Margaret Sanger bravely challenged vice laws and distributed information about birth control. (3) She researched and wrote *Family Limitation,* a book with contraceptive information. (4) Such an educational tool for family planning never had been available to the general public before. (5) Sanger was arrested and served time in jail because of her activism. (6) The availability of safe, legal birth control today is a result of her crusade for reform.

Exploration 1b Using Verbs in Your Writing

Choose ten of the following verbs, verb phrases, and compound verbs. Use them to write ten sentences on a separate sheet of paper.

pass and dribble	has found	records	opens
scurries	decays	celebrated	protested
had called	are discussing	jogs	have thought
have moved	study or fail	mix	triumphed

Challenge 1 Identifying and Evaluating Verbs in an Essay

1. Working with a partner, choose a selection from Part Seven that you would both like to read. Then, reading the essay together, identify verbs that the author has used in ten sentences.
2. On a separate piece of paper, copy these sentences, and label the verb(s) in each: *action* or *linking*. Also label any *verb phrases* or *compound verbs*.
3. Share the sentences with your classmates. Which of the action verbs that you have identified are the most effective? Why?

➤ RECOGNIZING SUBJECTS

The second crucial component of a sentence is the **subject,** the noun or pronoun performing the verb's action or being described. A **noun** names a person, place, or thing, and a **pronoun** substitutes for a noun. To find the subject, first find the verb, and then ask yourself *who or what is doing the action or being discussed?*

What are the verbs and the subjects in the sentences below?

> **Example**
> That movie received a great review.

> **Example**
> The bus will be late because of the accident downtown.

In the first example, the verb is *received.* Now ask *who or what received a great review?* The subject is *movie.* In the second example, the verb is *will be.* Ask *who or what will be late because of the accident downtown?* The subject is *bus.*

Most sentences have both a simple subject and a complete subject. The **simple subject** is an individual word that identifies who or what is doing the action or being discussed. The **complete subject** is that simple subject plus any words or phrases that describe or modify it. A **modifier** is a word or a group of words that describes a noun or pronoun, telling *which one* or *what kind.*

In the sentences below, both the verbs and complete subjects are identified. Find the simple subject of each sentence.

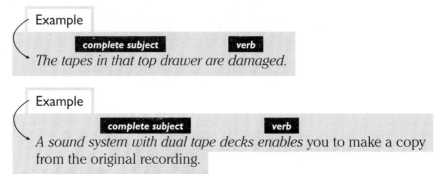

Example

complete subject   verb
The tapes in that top drawer are damaged.

Example

complete subject   verb
A sound system with dual tape decks enables you to make a copy from the original recording.

In the first sentence, the simple subject is *tapes.* In the second sentence, it is *sound system.*

It is important to be able to identify the simple subject because the verb must *agree with* or match the simple subject. The problem is that modifiers in the complete subject can mislead you into selecting the wrong verb form. This is especially true if the words are in a **prepositional phrase.** A prepositional phrase begins with a *preposition* and ends with a noun or pronoun called the *object of the preposition.* The preposition *relates* that noun or pronoun to another word in the sentence, often by indicating location, direction, or time. Here is a list of common prepositions:

Common Prepositions

about	behind	during	on	to
above	below	except	onto	toward
across	beneath	for	out	under
after	beside	from	outside	underneath
against	besides	in	over	unlike
along	between	inside	past	until
among	beyond	into	since	up
around	but (except)	like	than	upon
as	by	near	through	with
at	despite	of	throughout	within
before	down	off	till	without

Consider again the examples above, this time with the prepositional phrases italicized:

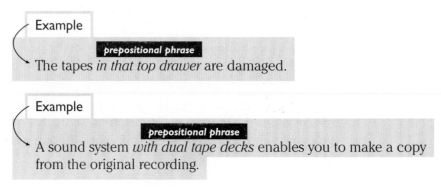

Example

prepositional phrase
The tapes *in that top drawer* are damaged.

Example

prepositional phrase
A sound system *with dual tape decks* enables you to make a copy from the original recording.

In the first sentence, the preposition is *in,* and the object of the preposition is the singular word *drawer.* In the second, the preposition is *with,* and the object of the preposition is the plural word *decks.* Writers sometimes make the mistake of making the verb agree with the object of the preposition rather than with the simple subject. Remember—*an object cannot be a subject.* Therefore, be careful to identify the simple subject.

Sometimes the answer to the question *who or what is doing the action or being discussed?* is a **compound subject.** Compound subjects consist of two or more nouns or pronouns, usually connected by *and* or *or.* These subjects may cause confusion for writers, who must decide whether the subject is singular or plural.

> **Example**
> *Dana or Rebekka* answers the phone in the office after 5 P.M.

> **Example**
> *Squirrels, birds, and opossums* live in the tree behind the cafeteria.

In the first sentence, the verb is *answers,* and the answer to the question *who or what answers?* is the compound subject, *Dana* or *Rebekka. Or* implies a choice. Only one person answers the phone, so the verb is singular. In the second sentence, the verb is *live,* and the answer to the question *who or what live?* is the compound subject, *squirrels, birds,* and *opossums. And* implies addition, making the subject plural. All of these animals live in the tree, so the verb is plural.

Exploration 2a   Distinguishing between the Simple and the Complete Subject

Underline the complete subject, and circle the simple subject in the sentences below. Remember—the simple subject is the specific noun or pronoun that is doing the action or being discussed. Study the example first.

Example   The (crowd) in the streets waited impatiently for the

beginning of the fireworks display.

(1) Sports championships on television attract huge viewing audiences. (2) The NCAA Final Four Basketball tournament in April is one such ratings-boosting program. (3) Tennis fans can cheer for their favorite players in the popular Wimbledon tournament during July. (4) The glitzy Super Bowl with its hours of pregame shows attracts the most armchair quarterbacks all year. (5) However, the traditional favorite of many couch potato fans is still October's World Series.

Exploration 2b   Finding the Simple Subjects in Sentences with Compound Subjects

Each of the sentences in the following paragraph has a compound subject. Underline the simple subject within each portion of the compound subject. Study the example first.

> *Example*   Good <u>books</u> and positive <u>attitudes</u> are the backbone of a good education.

(1) High <u>expectations</u> and good <u>performance go</u> hand in hand. (2) Responsible <u>parents</u> and dedicated <u>teachers expect</u> children to do well in school. (3) Their high <u>expectations</u> and judicious <u>monitoring are</u> usually <u>answered</u> by student success. (4) With low expectations for their success, both exceptional <u>students</u> and average <u>students have</u> less motivation to do well. (5) <u>Children develop</u> feelings of self-worth and a sense of confidence in proportion to the degree of faith that adults have in them. (6) Of course, both grade-school <u>children</u> and young <u>adults will respond</u> more to praise than to constant criticism. (7) Young <u>people</u> and mature <u>adults</u> alike <u>need</u> to feel successful in order to feel good about themselves.

Challenge 2   Using Compound Subjects in Your Writing

1. Below is a list of compound subjects. Choose ten of these subjects, and on a separate piece of paper, write a sentence using each one. Add modifiers if you wish.

heat and humidity	a shovel and rake
swimming or sailing	soccer and football
red meat, eggs, and cheese	travel and tourism
hardcovers and paperbacks	Macintosh and Gateway
wind and rain	my father and mother
winning or losing	breakfast and lunch

2. Exchange sentences with a partner. Underline the verbs in each sentence; then return the draft to its writer. Do all of your sentences have a verb that agrees with the subject? If not, revise your sentences to be sure they are correct and complete.

DISCOVERING CONNECTIONS **B**

1. In Discovering Connections A on page 236, you prewrote on one of three suggested topics. Now, using this prewriting material as your basis, work your way through the rest of the writing process, and complete a draft essay of about 500 words on this subject.
2. Exchange your draft with a partner. Using the material in this chapter to guide you, check the draft you receive. Make a note in the margin to indicate errors in subject–verb agreement, and mark any word groups in which a subject or a verb is missing. Return the draft to its writer.
3. Revise your essay, correcting any errors your partner noted.

SUMMARY EXERCISE

In each sentence, underline the complete subject, and circle the simple subject. For sentences with compound subjects, circle the simple subject within each portion of the compound subject. Double underline each verb, verb phrase, or compound verb.

(1) Honor students are not always the smartest students in class. (2) They probably organize, plan, and prepare the most effectively, however.

(3) Organized students purchase necessary tools for their classes. (4) The items and equipment at the top of their shopping list might include an assignment notebook and calendar, highlight markers, and folders. (5) A pocket dictionary and computer disks are other useful tools.

(6) Successful students with job or family commitments have scheduled manageable study time in advance. (7) They have analyzed their time needs for study and balanced their schedules. (8) Study schedules must be flexible and realistic. (9) Emergencies can happen and may interrupt work on assignments. (10) A list of assignments and due dates is an excellent planning tool. (11) Less serious students do the fun, easy assignments first. (12) Successful students, however, complete the assignments in a logical order. (13) They tackle challenges a step at a time.

(14) Preparation also leads to good grades. (15) One good study technique is called prereading. (16) Smart students preview the textbook materials before the lecture. (17) Introductions, chapter highlights, and review sections often emphasize key points. (18) Successful students read assignments on time, take good class notes, and anticipate test questions. (19) This preparation before the day of a test repays them with good scores as well as better learning.

(20) Good grades are within your reach. (21) Your effective study habits are the key.

RECAP

THE SENTENCE

New terms in this chapter	Definitions
➤ sentence	➤ a series of words containing a subject and verb and expressing a complete thought
➤ verb	➤ a word or words that describe the action or the condition of the subject
➤ action verb	➤ a word or words expressing action completed by the subject *Example* Marcel *held* the door for his sister.
➤ linking verb	➤ a word or words connecting the subject with other words that identify or describe it ➤ The most common linking verbs are the forms of *to be*. *Example* Katherine *is* an excellent athlete.
➤ verb phrase	➤ a main verb plus one or more helping verbs *Example* Karen *has been taking* dancing lessons for five years.
➤ compound verb	➤ two or more verbs connected by a conjunction and relating to the same subject *Example* Shannon *cooked* and *served* the meal.

New terms in this chapter	Definitions
➤ subject	➤ the noun or pronoun that is the doer of the action or the focus of the verb ➤ Find the subject by answering the question *who or what is doing the action or being discussed?* *Example* Paul enjoyed the party.
➤ noun	➤ a word that names a person, place, or thing *Example* The *river* overflowed its banks.
➤ pronoun	➤ a word that substitutes for a noun *Example* *He* loves to tell ghost stories.
➤ simple subject	➤ the noun or pronoun that answers the question *who or what is doing the action or being discussed?*
➤ complete subject	➤ the simple subject plus any words or phrases that describe or modify it *Example* The *books on that shelf* are best-sellers.
➤ modifier	➤ a word or group of words that tells you *which* or *what kind* when used with a noun or pronoun *Example* *My older, wiser* sister gave me *some good* advice.
➤ prepositional phrase	➤ a group of words beginning with a preposition and ending with a noun or pronoun that is the object of the preposition ➤ The subject of a sentence can *never* be in a prepositional phrase. *Example* The clothes *on the floor* are dirty.
➤ compound subject	➤ two or more nouns or pronouns connected by a conjunction and acting as the subject for the same verb *Example* Our wonderful *friends* and our dear *neighbors* collected money to help us after the fire.

The Basic Elements of a Sentence

Subject ——————— Verb

Expression of a Complete Thought

18

ragments

OVERVIEW: RECOGNIZING AND WRITING COMPLETE SENTENCES

In order for your reader to get a full understanding of what you mean, you must make sure you eliminate any sentence fragments. A **sentence fragment** is an incomplete piece of a sentence. It lacks one or more of the elements required for a sentence: a subject, a verb, or other words needed to express a complete thought. Sentence fragments are serious errors. Since they do not convey complete ideas, fragments can leave readers guessing about the meaning you intended.

In this chapter, you will learn how to avoid and correct fragments created by

➤ omitting a subject or a verb

➤ mistaking a phrase for a sentence

➤ mistaking a subordinate clause for a sentence

➤ mistaking an appositive for a sentence

DISCOVERING CONNECTIONS **A**

Using one of the techniques you practiced in Chapter 2, prewrite on one of the following topics: cable television, local or national museums or monuments, sloppy people. Save your work for later use.

CORRECTING FRAGMENTS WITH MISSING SUBJECTS OR VERBS

ESL Note
See "Sentence Basics" on page 521.

In order for a group of words to be a sentence, it must contain a subject and a verb. When you are checking your own sentences, first identify the verb. If you cannot find an action or linking verb, the group of words is a fragment. Look at the following group of words:

> Fragment
>
> The apartment building with the mural on the side.

There is no verb here, only a noun and its modifiers, so this group of words is a fragment. To change it to a sentence, add a verb and complete the thought:

> Revised
>
> The apartment building with the mural on the side *burned* down.

Sometimes a group of words has a subject and a word or group of words that seems to be a verb but in fact cannot function as a verb. These words, called **verbals,** are verb forms that can't communicate a complete action or meaning.

Look at the verbals in the following groups of words:

> Fragment
>
> The police officer *looking* for the robbery suspects.

> Fragment
>
> She *spoken* on the phone an hour earlier.

> Fragment
>
> Eddie *to run* the New York Marathon again.

All three groups of words are fragments because they contain verbals, not verbs. To make them into sentences, substitute true verbs for the verbals.

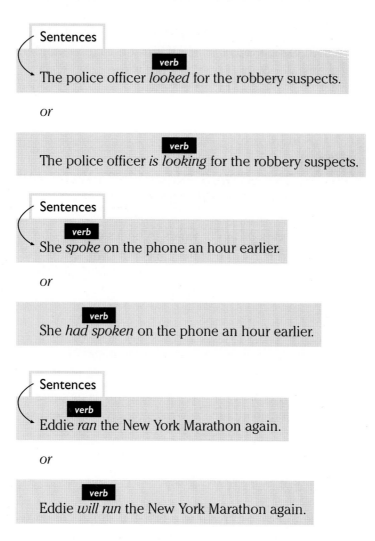

Sentences

[verb]
The police officer *looked* for the robbery suspects.

or

[verb]
The police officer *is looking* for the robbery suspects.

Sentences

[verb]
She *spoke* on the phone an hour earlier.

or

[verb]
She *had spoken* on the phone an hour earlier.

Sentences

[verb]
Eddie *ran* the New York Marathon again.

or

[verb]
Eddie *will run* the New York Marathon again.

See Part Five for more on using verbs correctly.

Even if a group of words has a verb, it's not a sentence unless it also has a subject. As the previous chapter showed, the subject is the word or group of words that answers the question *who or what is doing the action or being discussed?* If no word answers the question, then there is no subject, and the group of words is a fragment.

Consider the following group of words:

Fragment
Told Sally's boss about Sally's excellent computer skills.

This group of words is not a sentence. There is a verb—*told*—but if you ask *who or what told,* there is no answer.

To correct this fragment, simply add a subject:

Sentence

subject

Professor Tessier told Sally's boss about Sally's excellent computer skills.

Exploration 1a Correcting Fragments with Missing or Incomplete Verbs

The following groups of words are fragments because they contain verbals, not verbs. Correct each fragment by (1) crossing out the misused word and writing an appropriate verb above it or (2) adding a verb. There is more than one way to correct the fragment. Study the example first.

Example The dry cleaner ~~pressing~~ *pressed* my good white shirt.

(1) My aunt Julia ~~baking~~ *bakes* the most delicious sweets. (2) The whole family ~~to gather~~ at her home every Sunday evening for dessert. (3) She ~~serving~~ *need* hot apple pie, rich chocolate cake, or creamy pudding. (4) We ~~eating~~ *eated* and ~~visiting~~ *visited* for a couple of hours. (5) This tradition ~~being~~ *is* our family's favorite weekend activity.

Exploration 1b Correcting Fragments with Missing Subjects or Verbs

The following groups of words are fragments because they lack a subject, a verb, or a helping verb. On the lines provided, write an appropriate subject or verb, and complete the thought. Label your added portions *S* or *V*. Study the example first.

Example Wildflowers *bloomed* (V) by the roadside.

1. ___*He*___ picked the robber from a police lineup.

2. Shirley ___*was*___ running after the bus.

3. _____ is a good gift to give if you don't know the recipient very well.

4. The cookbook ___*is*___ the complete recipe in Spanish.

5. The chocolate roses ___*are*___ melting in the hot midday sun.

Exploration 1c   More Practice Identifying and Correcting Fragments

The following passage contains several fragments. Underline the fragments, correct the fragments by adding a subject or a verb, and rewrite the paragraph on a separate piece of paper.

(1) One of history's most horrific periods *was* represented in the United States Holocaust Memorial Museum. (2) The museum's mission is to educate visitors about the Nazis' anti-Semitism and racism in the 1930s and 1940s. (3) The first exhibits *was* tracing the rise of Hitler's brutal regime. (4) Visitors hearing and watching speeches by Hitler and other Nazi officials. (5) Photographs of hundreds of people who later died in concentration camps lining the walls. (6) Containers along the walkway are filled with personal belongings such as luggage, shoes, razors, and toothbrushes. (7) *It* Becomes personal and not just words in a history book. (8) The exhibits are also intended to inspire visitors. (9) The last floor of the museum ~~to~~ contain accounts and testimonies of survivors and rescuers. (10) Before they leave the museum, visitors can pause in the Hall of Remembrance and reflect on this time in history and on its lessons.

Challenge 1   Writing Supporting Sentences for a Paragraph

Working with a partner, compose at least five sentences to support one of the topic sentences listed below.

1. Knowledge of a second language is important in today's global economy.
2. Reading a book is more satisfying than watching a movie based on that book.

Exchange your sentences with another writing team. Check the paper you receive for fragments. Write *frag* in the margin beside each fragment you find. Return the paper to its writers. Make any corrections needed to your paper.

CORRECTING PHRASE FRAGMENTS

A *phrase* is a group of two or more related words that lacks a subject–verb combination. As the previous chapter indicated, two common types of phrases are *verb phrases* (page 237) and *prepositional phrases* (page 240). When a phrase is left to stand alone, it is a **phrase fragment.**

Look at the following groups of words:

Fragment
Will soon be sleeping.

Fragment
Inside the house.

The first example is a verb phrase, and the second is a prepositional phrase. They both lack a subject–verb combination, so both are fragments.

To correct phrases that are incorrectly used as sentences, you need to supply the missing elements, as these versions show:

Sentence
The baby will soon be sleeping.
subject

Sentence
The missing necklace was found inside the house.
subject   verb

Exploration 2a   Identifying and Correcting Phrase Fragments

The following sentences contain several fragments resulting from phrases used incorrectly as sentences. Underline these fragments. Then, on a separate piece of paper, rewrite the paragraph, turning the fragments into sentences. Use the example to guide you.

Example   Under the porch.

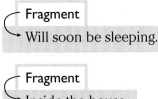

The frightened kitten hid under the porch.

(1) Being a musician demands a lot of dedication. (2) Have to practice hours daily. (3) Some musicians keep an unusual schedule. (4) Until the early morning hours. (5) Then they sleep until the afternoon. (6) Family life becomes difficult. (7) With this work schedule. (8) Sometimes musicians face weeks without employment. (9) Through all this, musicians keep playing. (10) Have a need to bring the joy of music to their audiences.

Exploration 2b   Rewriting Phrases as Sentences

On a separate sheet of paper, turn the following verb phrases and prepositional phrases into sentences by adding subjects or verbs or both and completing the thoughts. Study the example first.

> *Example*   over the lake
>
> *The sun dawning over the lake was beautiful.*

1. throughout the school
2. inside my shoe
3. were hiking
4. on the subway
5. have been told
6. behind first base
7. will go soon
8. through the picture window
9. are learning how
10. was canceled

Challenge 2   Identifying Subjects and Verbs

Exchange the sentences that you and a partner wrote for Challenge 1 on page 250 with another pair of students. Underline the subjects and verbs in each of the sentences, and return the paragraph. Make revisions that are necessary to eliminate any fragments in your own work.

➤ CORRECTING SUBORDINATE CLAUSE FRAGMENTS

Even if a group of words contains a subject and a verb, it is still a fragment if it does not express a complete thought. For example, a **subordinate clause fragment** contains a subject and a verb, but it cannot stand on its own. It must be joined to a *main clause* to express a complete thought. It is called *subordinate* because its purpose is to explain or describe a main clause.

Look at these subordinate clause fragments:

Fragment

After the *candidates arrive.*
subject verb

Fragment

That *Allen saw* outside the bus station.
subject verb

Both examples have subjects and verbs, but neither one expresses a complete thought. Each leaves the reader waiting for more information.

To correct this type of fragment, you have a couple of choices. You could add or delete words so that the clause makes sense on its own:

Sentence
The candidates arrive by limousine.

Sentence
Allen saw Lila outside the bus station.

In the first sentence, *after* has been deleted, and *by limousine* has been added. In the second sentence, *That* has been deleted, and *Lila* has been added. Both groups of words are now sentences. Furthermore, the meaning of both groups of words has changed considerably.

You can also choose to correct this type of fragment by adding a main clause to the subordinate clause. Together, they should express a complete thought:

Sentence
After the candidates arrive, *the mayoral debate will begin.*

Sentence
The car that Allen saw outside the bus station *was broken down.*

These changes make the meaning of the original clauses clearer and more specific. They do not alter the meaning as the preceding corrections do.

Exploration 3a   Identifying Subordinate Clause Fragments

The following passage contains several subordinate clause fragments. Underline these fragments.

Example   The crowd waiting to see the new movie was huge. Because the reviews had been so positive.

(1) In the twenty-first century, books, magazines, and newspapers might be produced on disks and read on computers. (2) If this is the wave of the future, (3) The benefits will outweigh the drawbacks. (4) First, the environment

will benefit from this new technology. (5) <u>Because fewer trees will have to be cut to make paper.</u> (6) Also, landfills will not be overwhelmed with piles of paper. (7) <u>Which take years to decompose.</u> (8) Electronic books will be easy to carry, too. (9) <u>Since a disk weighs very little.</u> (10) Students will be able to carry all of their books in their pockets.

Exploration 3b   Rewriting Subordinate Clauses as Sentences

On a separate sheet of paper, turn the following subordinate clauses into sentences by adding a main clause. Check your work for correct use of capitals and punctuation. Study the example first.

> *Example*   even though the class had ended
>
> *The students continued their discussion, even though the class had ended.*

1. who plans to ride to the game on the team bus
2. whenever a false alarm is sounded
3. which hung on a chain around her neck
4. until I get a haircut
5. so that I can improve my keyboarding skills
6. unless management agrees to give them a raise
7. although it won two Academy Awards
8. in order that my wife and I could both attend the concert
9. because the neighborhood parents petitioned the school department
10. since it wasn't my fault

Exploration 3c   Identifying and Correcting Subordinate Clause Fragments

The following passage contains several subordinate clause fragments. Underline these fragments. Then, on a separate piece of paper, rewrite the paragraph, turning the fragments into sentences. Study the example first.

> *Example*   Who has a quick temper.
>
> *My boss, who has a quick temper, should learn how to relax.*

(1) Sweetgrass basket making is a historic craft. (2) Which dates back to the late 1600s in this country. (3) When slaves from West Africa were brought to South Carolina, (4) They brought their skills in cultivating rice. (5) The Africans made and used bulrush baskets to winnow the rice. (6) Their knowledge was essential to plantation owners. (7) Because the Europeans had little experience with growing rice. (8) Slave women made durable, pliable household baskets. (9) Since sweetgrass was easier to work with than heavy bulrush, (10) The women chose this plentiful grass to work with. (11) The techniques they used to craft the baskets are the same ones their ancestors in Africa used. (12) Although more and more coastal farmers started to cultivate rice, (13) The craft of sweetgrass basket making stayed locally in and around Charleston, South Carolina. (14) Who learned the techniques of basketry from their mothers and grandmothers, still make and sell their beautiful baskets from stands along the highways. (15) The baskets are not only useful and durable, but they are also decorative pieces of art with a historic tradition.

Challenge 3   Analyzing and Completing Sentences

To make sure each of the sentences you revised in Exploration 3c expresses a complete thought, ask a partner to read your completed revision aloud, pausing for a few seconds after the period at the end of each sentence. Note any groups of words you hear that can't stand on their own. Turn these groups of words into complete sentences. Repeat this process for your partner.

CORRECTING APPOSITIVE FRAGMENTS

An **appositive** is a word or group of words that is meant to rename or explain another noun or pronoun. Some appositives contain subjects and verbs. But like subordinate clauses, appositives don't express complete thoughts on their own.

Look at the following appositives:

Fragment

subject	verb

The spot where the *roof had begun* to leak.

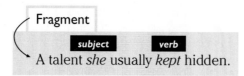

Fragment

subject   verb

A talent *she* usually *kept* hidden.

Both groups of words have subjects and verbs, but both are fragments because they don't express complete thoughts.

To eliminate this kind of fragment, you can change the order of the words to express a complete thought:

Sentence

subject   verb

The *roof had begun* to leak at that spot.

Sentence

subject   verb

She usually *kept* that talent hidden.

Alternatively, you can join the fragment with a main clause so that it expresses a complete thought:

Sentence

Rich's bed was in the corner, the spot where the roof had begun to leak.   *(The appositive now modifies* corner.*)*

Sentence

Tami entertained the crowd by singing, a talent she usually kept hidden.   *(The appositive now modifies* singing.*)*

Exploration 4a   Identifying and Correcting Appositive Fragments

The following passage contains several appositive fragments. Underline these fragments. Then, on a separate piece of paper, turn those fragments into complete sentences. Study the example first.

Example   A task that frustrates him.

> *Tim had to balance his checkbook, a task that frustrates him.*

(1) Last year, I worked during the summer as a nanny. (2) The best temporary job I ever had. (3) My duties included dressing, feeding, and enter-

taining two children. (4) The nicest, most well-behaved kids I have ever known. (5) They enjoyed the zoo, the beach, and the park. (6) Only a few of the places I took them. (7) They were always excited, no matter what we did. (8) They especially liked the school playground. (9) A place that was always nearly deserted in the summer. (10) I was sorry to see that summer end.

Exploration 4b Rewriting Appositives Correctly as Sentences

On a separate sheet of paper, turn each of the following appositives into a sentence by adding a main clause containing a word for the appositive to rename or explain. Use the example to guide you.

> **Example** a park on the outskirts of the city
>
> *Evergreen Acres, a park on the outskirts of the city, is the best place to view the comet.*

1. the quietest person in the office
2. the minister who led the protest
3. an inexpensive, plastic toy
4. the most influential musician of the decade
5. a dangerous intersection for pedestrians
6. the welcoming smell of fresh-brewed coffee
7. the person who always cheers me up
8. a color that I love
9. the best seat in the auditorium
10. a required course in my major

Challenge 4 Working with Subordinate Clauses and Appositives

Working with a partner or writing group, read one or more of the essays in Part Seven. Find at least three subordinate clauses and at least two appositives. On a separate piece of paper, write the sentences that contain these elements, and discuss with your partner or group how they contribute to the ideas in the sentences that contain them.

DISCOVERING CONNECTIONS B

1. In Discovering Connections A on page 247, you completed a prewriting on one of three suggested topics. Now work your way through the rest of the writing process, using this prewriting material as your foundation, and complete a draft essay of about 500 words on this subject.
2. Exchange your draft with a partner. Using the material in this chapter to guide you, check the draft you receive for fragments. Underline any fragments, and then return the draft to your partner.
3. Revise your essay, correcting any fragments discovered by your reader.

➤ SUMMARY EXERCISE

Underline the fragments in the following essay. Then, on a separate piece of paper, revise the essay by correcting the fragments, using the techniques you practiced in this chapter. Remember that fragments can be corrected in several ways.

(1) Continues to inspire many people. (2) Helen Keller lived a full, rich life in spite of the many physical challenges she faced. (3) Was left blind and deaf. (4) After an illness before she was two years old. (5) However, Helen did not live a lonely, dark life. (6) Because of her own will to learn and the efforts of Anne Sullivan. (7) Her gifted teacher.

(8) The story of Miss Sullivan, who helped Helen to learn language, is told in the play and the movie, *The Miracle Worker.* (9) Dramatizes the anger, frustration, and finally joy the young pupil and new teacher felt as they both learned a new way of communicating. (10) In her autobiography, *The Story of My Life.* (11) Helen writes about learning her first word, *water.* (12) "That living word awakened my soul, gave it light, hope, joy, set it free! (13) There were barriers still, it is true, but barriers that could in time be swept away."

(14) Helen graduating from Radcliffe College, (15) With the assistance of her teacher, grew to become an accomplished author. (16) She toured the country, (17) Lecturing about women's suffrage and the rights of the blind. (18) Her public life was dedicated to working on behalf of others.

(19) Even after her death, Helen Keller continues to help people. (20) Through the example that she set of the human spirit at its best.

RECAP
FRAGMENTS

New terms in this chapter	Definitions
➤ sentence fragment	➤ a group of words that fails to express a complete thought because it lacks a subject, a verb, or other needed words *Example* Although they tried not to laugh [not a complete thought]
➤ verbal	➤ a verb form that is used as another part of speech and therefore doesn't communicate a complete action or meaning ➤ A verbal cannot substitute for a verb in a sentence. *Example* *Running* down the stairs
➤ phrase fragment	➤ a group of two or more related words that lacks a subject–verb combination, used incorrectly as a sentence *Verb phrase* Are looking *Prepositional phrase* About time
➤ subordinate clause fragment	➤ a group of words that contains a subject and a verb but does not express a complete thought ➤ A subordinate clause must be joined to a main clause to express a complete thought. *Example* That had struck the coast
➤ appositive	➤ a word or group of words that renames or explains a noun or pronoun next to it ➤ An appositive must be connected to a main clause to express a complete thought. *Example* A retired police officer

Continued

To Identify a Fragment   **To Correct a Fragment**

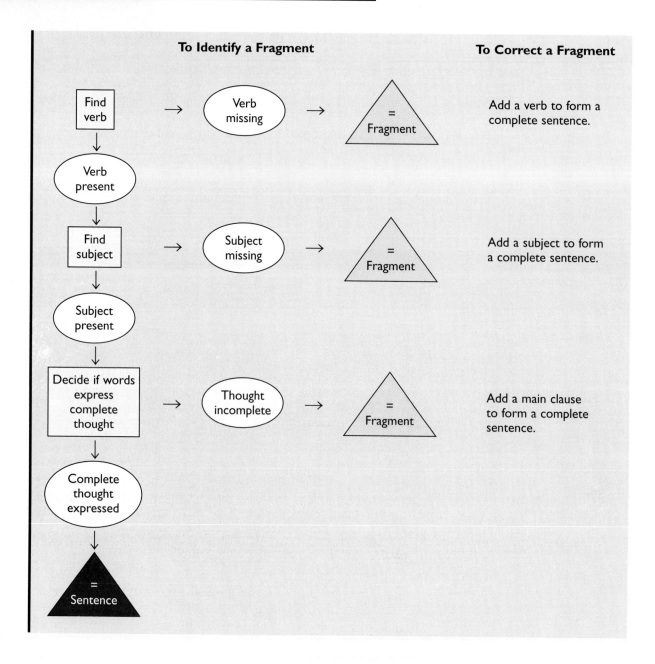

Subordination and Coordination

OVERVIEW: COMBINING CLAUSES FOR SENTENCE COMPLEXITY

Your writing must express complete thoughts in sentence form. However, your communication style would be pretty boring if you used only simple sentences—sentences with a single subject–verb unit. These subject–verb units, called *clauses,* can be joined in various ways to make your sentences more interesting and complex. You can emphasize some ideas by using **subordination,** which means combining an idea in a main clause with an idea in a **subordinate clause.** The subordinate clause depends on the main clause to make sense. Alternatively, you can join ideas through **coordination,** in which two main clauses (or simple sentences) are linked by a semicolon or by a coordinating conjunction and comma.

In this chapter, you will learn to

➤ identify and use simple and complex sentences to express your ideas with variety

➤ use subordinating conjunctions to connect and show relationships between clauses

➤ use relative pronouns to introduce subordinate clauses that describe a noun or pronoun

➤ use a coordinating conjunction and a comma, a semicolon, or a semicolon and a conjunctive adverb to create a compound sentence

DISCOVERING CONNECTIONS A

Using one of the techniques you practiced in Chapter 2, prewrite on one of the following topics: justice, a private or family joke, advertising. Save your work for later use.

➤ **U**SING SUBORDINATION

To use subordination effectively, you need to understand the difference between a simple sentence and a complex sentence. A **simple sentence** consists of only one *clause* or subject–verb unit, as this example shows:

Simple sentence

subject   **verb**
The *owner* of the restaurant *greets* all the patrons.

As a writer, you will also rely on **complex sentences,** which combine a main, or independent, clause and a subordinate, or dependent, clause. Subordinate clauses are introduced by either **subordinating conjunctions** or **relative pronouns:**

■ *Common Subordinating Conjunctions*

after	even though	than	whenever
although	if	though	where
as	in order that	unless	wherever
as if	rather than	until	whether
because	since	when	while
before	so that		

■ *Relative Pronouns*

that	who
what	whom
which	whose

If you join a simple sentence and a subordinate clause in a complex sentence, the simple sentence becomes the **main clause,** as this example shows:

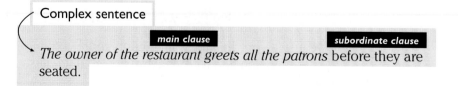

Complex sentence

main clause   **subordinate clause**
The owner of the restaurant greets all the patrons before they are seated.

In a complex sentence, you may also place the subordinate clause before the main clause. In this case, a comma is needed before the conjunction. No matter where it is placed, the main clause of a complex sentence contains the most important idea.

Subordinating conjunctions do more than connect clauses. They also indicate the *relationship* between the two clauses in terms of time, purpose, result, condition, or cause. Study the following complex sentences:

Example

My car insurance increased $500 this year *because* I received a speeding ticket.

Example

If Sherman watches his diet, he'll keep his weight down.

In the first sentence, *because* indicates that the first occurrence—the increase in insurance rates—is the result of the second occurrence. In the second, *if* suggests under what condition Sherman will control his weight.

Relative pronouns are used to introduce subordinate clauses that either *describe* a noun or *specify* a noun or pronoun in the sentence. Look at the following sentences, with the subordinate clauses italicized:

Example

Any person *who provides encouragement and emotional support* is a true friend.

Example

Food *that is low in fat* is better for a healthy heart.

In the first sentence, the relative pronoun *who* introduces the subordinate clause specifying what kind of person qualifies as a true friend. In the second, the relative pronoun *that* indicates which type of food is heart healthy.

Exploration 1a Identifying Subordinate Clauses

The following sentences are complex because they contain both a main clause and a subordinate clause. Underline the subordinate clause in each sentence, and circle the subordinating conjunction or relative pronoun that introduces it. Study the example first.

Example   Caring for a young child (who) is sick can be a stressful job for

any parent.

(1) Newspapers are a bargain because they give so much information in a convenient way. (2) I read the local newspaper every day before I leave my apartment to go to work in the morning. (3) Although I read for only ten minutes or so, I can easily keep up with local events, learn about national issues, find the scores for different sports, read about the newest movie, and even get my horoscope. (4) I can take the newspaper with me wherever I go. (5) Best of all, the local paper, which costs less than two dollars a week, is delivered to my door.

Exploration 1b   Combining Simple Sentences to Create Complex Sentences

The following paragraph is composed of simple sentences. On a separate piece of paper, rewrite it, joining ideas to create complex sentences. Use subordinating conjunctions and relative pronouns to introduce subordinate clauses. (Refer to the lists on page 262.) Be sure that the ideas you want to emphasize are in the main clauses of your new sentences. You may decide to leave some simple sentences just as they are for variety. Be sure you use punctuation and capitals correctly.

(1) Taking a walk has become a top priority in my daily routine. (2) I walk two miles in the park. (3) The park is near my apartment. (4) I have a job, an elderly father to care for, and homework to do every day. (5) I make sure to start each day with my walk. (6) My walk is important to me for many reasons. (7) First, the exercise helps me deal with stressful situations. (8) These may come up at work. (9) I have decisions to make. (10) My walk gives me quiet time to make them. (11) Finally, I enjoy the quiet, relaxing time during my morning walk. (12) My days are very busy. (13) Some mornings it is cold or raining. (14) I refuse to give up the most important hour of my day. (15) Taking a walk is the most positive way I know to begin each day.

Challenge 1   Evaluating Your Use of Subordination

Exchange the paragraph you revised in Exploration 1b with a partner. Compare your versions, and discuss why you made the changes that you did. Did you leave any sentences as simple sentences? Did you emphasize the important ideas by making them the main clauses of the complex sentences? Pick and choose the sentences in each version that you both agree are most effective. Then write a final version of the paragraph, and read it to your class.

USING COORDINATION

Another way to join ideas that are related is to use *coordination.* This is a technique for connecting two or more sentences to give each one equal emphasis. The resulting sentence is called a **compound sentence.**

Achieving Coordination by Using Coordinating Conjunctions

The most common way to create a compound sentence is to connect simple sentences with a **coordinating conjunction** and a comma. Writers may also use coordination to join complex sentences to simple ones or to join complex sentences to one another. The parts of a compound sentence are called **independent clauses** because each part is essentially a simple sentence and can stand on its own. Coordination cannot be used to join clauses that could not function on their own as complete sentences.

The coordinating conjunction in a complex sentence shows the relationship between the equally important ideas that it joins. Here is a list of the coordinating conjunctions.

■ *Coordinating Conjunctions*

and	nor	so
but	or	yet
for		

Using coordination can help you eliminate choppiness from your writing. Read the following sets of simple sentences out loud:

Choppy

The main road was closed for construction. The detour was blocked by an accident.

Choppy

The model tripped on the top step of the runway. A photographer stopped her from falling.

As they are now, these sets of sentences sound choppy. Notice the difference when a conjunction and comma are used to join each set of sentences:

Combined

The main road was closed for construction, *and* the detour was blocked by an accident.

Combined

The model tripped on the top step of the runway, *but* a photographer stopped her from falling down the stairs.

These compound sentences are more fluid and easier to understand than the sets of simple sentences. The coordinating conjunctions clearly show how the two ideas within each sentence are related.

Exploration 2a Using Coordination

Join each pair of simple sentences in the paragraph below with a comma and a coordinating conjunction to create one compound sentence. Insert the new material in the space above, as the example shows.

Example The doors opened*, and the* ~~The~~ line inched slowly ahead.

(1) Maria walked into the coffee shop*, and* ~~S~~he began to look for her friend. (2) Outwardly, she seemed confident*, but* ~~I~~nside, she was nervous. (3) She scanned the room, looking for her friend*, and* A disturbing thought occurred to her. (4) Perhaps Aaron had misunderstood her*, or* Perhaps she had mentioned a different time. (5) Then she heard a familiar voice calling her name*, and* She saw Aaron waving to her.

Exploration 2b More Practice Using Coordination

Fill in the blanks, adding a clause before or after the coordinating conjunction.

Example The basketball game was tied, **so** _the coach left the starting_ _five on the court._

1. The restaurant that I wanted to go to was closed, **so** _I dicided to go to another restaurant, wich I liked too._

2. _The restaurant was not open_, **nor** was the coffee shop open down the street.

3. Our stomachs were growling, **so** _we were looking for place to eat something._

4. The wait at the bus stop was long, **but** _at least there wasn't traffic on the way to the home._

5. _I should buy something to eat_, **or** I would have fainted from hunger.

Challenge 2 Analyzing the Clauses in Compound Sentences

Each of the clauses in a compound sentence must be *independent,* or able to stand on its own as a complete sentence. Underline the subjects and verbs in the clauses you wrote for Exploration 2b. Could each clause stand on its own as a sentence? If not, make any changes necessary to make each one an independent clause.

Achieving Coordination by Using Semicolons

Another way to achieve coordination is to use a *semicolon* (**;**) to connect independent clauses. A semicolon, which has the same power to connect as a coordinating conjunction with a comma, makes the connection more direct. You will learn more about the use of semicolons in Chapter 31.

Consider the two versions of the following sentences:

> **Example**
>
> The day had been long and hot, *and* all I wanted to do was take a shower.

> **Example**
>
> The day had been long and hot**;** all I wanted to do was take a shower.

In the first version, the coordinating conjunction *and* joins the two clauses, *adding* the second thought. In the second version, the semicolon joins the two ideas directly, emphasizing the close relationship between them. Semicolons are used to join sentences that have such a clear, obvious connection.

In addition to using a semicolon alone, you can add a twist to this technique by including a **conjunctive adverb** after the semicolon. Study the following list of conjunctive adverbs:

Common Conjunctive Adverbs

also	however	similarly
besides	instead	still
consequently	meanwhile	then
finally	moreover	therefore
furthermore	nevertheless	thus

Conjunctive adverbs *suggest a relationship* between two thoughts, as the following compound sentences show:

> **Example**
>
> In-line skating is great exercise**;** *furthermore,* it's great fun.

> Example
> The major networks refused to televise the terrorists' news conference; *however,* CNN covered the entire presentation.

Neither *furthermore* nor *however* is actually used to connect the sentences. The semicolon does that. Note that this technique requires two punctuation marks: a semicolon *before* the conjunctive adverb and a comma *after* it.

Exploration 3a Achieving Coordination by Using Semicolons

As you read the sentences in the paragraph below, decide which ones are closely related in meaning. Then join those closely related sentences by using a semicolon. Write your new version of the paragraph on another sheet of paper.

(1) Sometimes I have difficulty sleeping. (2) I have had to learn how to avoid insomnia. (3) Caffeine keeps me awake. (4) I don't drink coffee, tea, or soda after dinner. (5) A warm bath relaxes me. (6) I try to soak in the bathtub for fifteen minutes right before bed. (7) Reading can put me to sleep, too. (8) I keep a novel or a magazine near my bed. (9) One thing that doesn't help is exercise. (10) That just keeps me awake.

Exploration 3b Combining Sentences Using Conjunctive Adverbs and Semicolons

Complete each sentence by adding a conjunctive adverb and an independent clause after the semicolon. Use the list of conjunctive adverbs on page 267. Don't forget a comma after the conjunctive adverb. Study the example first.

Example   The waiting room at the clinic was crowded; ___*however, I*___

___*decided to stay until the doctor was available.*___

1. Washington, D.C.'s Metro system is clean and efficient; _____

_____

_____

2. The wheels on the cars are made of special material that reduces noise;

nevertheless, those wheels still don't

reduce risk of accidents.

3. Last year a record number of visitors used the system; _besides, the number of new visits continues to increse in this year._

4. The New York subway system is quite different; _therefore, the visitors of New York might be confused about that._

5. New Yorkers often choose the bus over the subway; _also, many of them prefer to take a taxi_

Exploration 3c   Using Coordination and Subordination

The paragraph below contains simple sentences. Decide where it can be improved through coordination and subordination. Then rewrite the new version on a separate piece of paper. Use all of the methods you have practiced in this chapter to create compound and complex sentences. You may decide to leave some sentences as they are.

> *Example*   Many people try to avoid taking statistics. It is a difficult course.
>
> *Many people try to avoid taking statistics because it is a difficult course.*

(1) Asthma is a chronic, dangerous lung condition. (2) It can be treated. (3) The causes of asthma are increasing. (4) More and more people suffer from asthma every year. (5) Asthma attacks can be triggered by air pollution, dust, a cold, and even exercise. (6) During an asthma attack, bronchial tubes in the lungs get irritated and constrict. (7) Patients cough, wheeze, and struggle to breathe as a result. (8) Asthma sufferers can lead normal lives. (9) They need proper medication and medical supervision. (10) They also need to understand and avoid the conditions that trigger their asthma attacks.

Challenge 3   Evaluating Your Sentence Combining Techniques

Share the paragraph you revised in Exploration 3c with a partner, and compare the choices you each made to combine ideas. In your discussion, answer the following questions: What options did you use for achieving coordination? Where did you use subordination? Why did you make the changes that you did? Where is your revision different from your partner's? Which ideas did you leave expressed as simple sentences? Why?

DISCOVERING CONNECTIONS **B**

1. In Discovering Connections A on page 262, you prewrote on one of three suggested subjects. Now use this prewriting material as the basis, and work your way through the rest of the writing process to complete a draft essay of about 500 words on this topic.

2. Exchange your draft with a partner. Using the material in this chapter to guide you, check the sentences in the draft to see whether subordination and coordination have been used effectively. Put a ✓ next to any pairs or groups of sentences that could benefit from either of these techniques; then return the draft to the writer.

3. Revise your essay, using subordination or coordination where it is appropriate.

SUMMARY EXERCISE

The writing below is composed of simple sentences. On a separate piece of paper, revise it by combining sentences to emphasize ideas, to show connections among ideas, and to make the writing smooth. Use the methods you have practiced in this chapter to create complex or compound sentences. You may decide to leave some sentences as they are.

(1) Important documents in our nation's history are housed in the National Archives in Washington, D.C. (2) Many are available for the public to view. (3) The documents are old and fragile. (4) They are carefully protected from further deterioration. (5) Many people see these documents. (6) They are impressed both by their importance and by the care taken to preserve them for the future.

(7) The Constitution is housed in the Archives. (8) It is only four pages long. (9) The Constitution contains the foundation of our democratic system. (10) Representatives of twelve of the original states signed it in 1787. (11) Visitors can see two pages of this famous document. (12) They are housed in bronze and glass cases. (13) The cases are filled with helium gas to preserve the old parchment.

(14) The Archives also displays the Declaration of Independence and the Bill of Rights. (15) The Declaration of Independence was adopted on July 4, 1776. (16) It was written primarily by Thomas Jefferson. (17) The Bill of Rights was ratified more than two hundred years ago. (18) Citizens, judges, and

scholars still discuss it today. (19) This document speaks about freedom of the press, freedom of religion, freedom of speech, and the right to bear arms. (20) These are still controversial issues today.

    (21) All of these documents are stored every night in a special vault. (22) The bronze and glass cases are lowered electronically to the bottom of a vault. (23) It is twenty-two feet below the ground.

RECAP
SUBORDINATION AND COORDINATION

New terms in this chapter	Definitions
➤ **subordination**	➤ a way to combine unequal ideas, giving emphasis to one and making the other dependent upon the former
➤ **subordinate clause**	➤ a subject–verb unit that doesn't express a complete thought; also called a *dependent clause* ➤ Some subordinate clauses are introduced by *subordinating conjunctions* or *relative pronouns*.
➤ **coordination**	➤ the combining of independent clauses of equal importance into *compound* sentences to eliminate choppiness and repetition
➤ **simple sentence**	➤ a sentence consisting of a subject and a verb and their modifiers *Example* A mouse had eaten a hole in the bag of popcorn.
➤ **complex sentence**	➤ a sentence consisting of a main clause and a subordinate clause
➤ **subordinating conjunction**	➤ one of a group of connecting words used at the beginning of a subordinate clause to join it to an independent clause: *after, although, as, as if, because, before, even though, if, in order that, rather than, since, so that, than, though, unless, until, when, whenever, wherever, whether, while* ➤ The subordinating conjunction expresses the relationship between the two clauses. *Example* The downtown flooded *because* we had torrential rains.
➤ **relative pronoun**	➤ one of a group of words used to introduce subordinate clauses that describe or specify a noun or pronoun in a main clause: *that, what, which, who, whom, whose* *Example* An author *whose* work I admire is Jamaica Kincaid.

Continued

New terms in this chapter	Definitions
➤ **main clause**	➤ a subject–verb unit that can stand on its own but that is combined with another subject–verb unit ➤ A main clause is an *independent clause.*
➤ **compound sentence**	➤ a sentence containing two or more independent clauses joined by a connector: (1) a *coordinating conjunction* and a comma, (2) a *semicolon,* or (3) a semicolon plus a *conjunctive adverb*
➤ **coordinating conjunction**	➤ one of a set of joining words used to connect words or ideas of equal rank: *and, but, for, nor, or, so,* and *yet*
➤ **independent clause**	➤ a clause with a subject and a verb that can stand alone as a sentence ➤ A compound sentence consists of two or more independent clauses joined by a connector. *Example* *Spring is on the way,* and *the temperature is rising.*
➤ **conjunctive adverb**	➤ one of a group of words used with a connector to link ideas by showing how they are related: *also, besides, consequently, finally, furthermore, however, instead, meanwhile, moreover, nevertheless, similarly, still, then, therefore,* and *thus* ➤ A conjunctive adverb cannot connect simple sentences itself but does emphasize the connection provided by semicolons. ➤ A conjunctive adverb requires a comma after it when used with a semicolon connecting simple sentences. *Example* Cheetahs are an endangered species; *however,* many cheetahs were born at zoos last year.

Structure of the Complex Sentence

Main clause + Subordinate clause

subordinating conjunction + subject–verb unit

or

relative pronoun + subject–verb unit*

*Relative pronoun may serve as subject of the subordinate clause.

Structure of the Compound Sentence

Independent clause + ⎡ comma and coordinating conjunction
⎢ *or*
⎢ semicolon
⎢ *or*
⎣ semicolon, conjunctive adverb, and comma ⎤ + Independent clause

Comma Splices and Run-On Sentences

OVERVIEW: UNDERSTANDING SENTENCE-COMBINING ERRORS

Two of the most common sentence-combining errors are the comma splice and the run-on sentence. A **comma splice** is an error in which sentences are incorrectly connected by a comma. A **run-on sentence** is an error in which two sentences are run together with no punctuation or connectors. Both errors distract readers from the point you are making, so you must recognize and correct these problems in your writing.

In this chapter, you will learn how to recognize and avoid comma splices and run-on sentences. You will practice correcting these errors by using

➤ a coordinating conjunction and a comma
➤ a subordinating conjunction
➤ a semicolon (or a semicolon and a conjunctive adverb)
➤ a period

DISCOVERING CONNECTIONS A

Using one of the techniques you practiced in Chapter 2, prewrite on one of the following topics: credit cards, healthful foods, body piercing, tattooing. Save your work for later use.

➤ IDENTIFYING COMMA SPLICES AND RUN-ON SENTENCES

ESL Note
See "Sentence Basics" on pages 521–523 and "Punctuation and Capitalization" on pages 536–538.

The first step in correcting comma splices and run-on sentences is to identify them. Start by locating the subjects and verbs in your sentences. Have you joined two subject–verb units with only a comma? If so, you have a comma splice. *Commas cannot connect.* They indicate a pause, or they separate elements within a sentence.

Look at the example below:

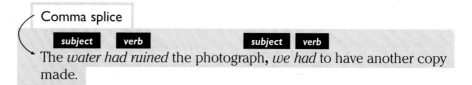

Comma splice

| subject | verb | | subject | verb |

The *water had ruined* the photograph, *we had* to have another copy made.

Each unit contains a subject and verb, and each could stand alone as a simple sentence. A comma alone cannot be used to connect these two units. Therefore, this is a comma splice.

To check for run-on sentences, follow the same method. First, locate the subjects and verbs in your sentences. Then check to see whether you have joined two subject–verb units without any *connector* or *separator.* If so, you have created a run-on sentence.

Read out loud the following example, which has a **/** where one unit ends and the next begins:

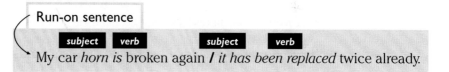

Run-on sentence

| subject | verb | | subject | verb |

My car *horn is* broken again **/** *it has been replaced* twice already.

As you can see, this example consists of two subject–verb units, each of which could stand on its own. Nothing either connects or separates these units. Instead, the first unit just *runs into* the second, which is why this type of error is called a run-on sentence, or simply a run-on.

Exploration 1a   Recognizing Comma Splices and Run-Ons

In the paragraph below, find the comma splices and run-on sentences. First, underline every subject and verb. Then determine whether any two subject–verb units are joined with only a comma or without any connector or separator. Put a / between these units. Study the example first.

> **Example**   The city should lower the speed limit on Plymouth
>
> Avenue / the area is very congested.

(1) Some critics complain about the loyalty of American workers / according to these people, American workers care more about themselves than about their employers. (2) In their view, union workers are interested only in a fat paycheck *and* they will never pitch in to help out their company. (3) Greed has destroyed the work ethic / workers are lazy clock-watchers. (4) These critics are all wrong to me the employers are not loyal to their workers. (5) The CEOs of these companies make enormous salaries, in the meantime, they continue to downsize their staffs.

Exploration 1b   More Practice Recognizing Comma Splices and Run-Ons

The following paragraph contains several commas splices and run-on sentences. Put an * in front of any comma splice or run-on, and insert a / where one sentence should end and the next should begin. Use the example to guide you.

> **Example**   *Jennifer didn't show up for class again today, / this is the fifth
>
> time she has been absent this month.

(1) *In national politics, money talks today / a candidate can't expect to win without enormous financial backing. (2) It isn't unusual for a congressional campaign to cost each candidate a million dollars or more. *(3) Ordinary people simply can't afford to run a campaign alone / they must count on donations. (4) Incumbents have a great advantage over challengers in terms of fundraising. (5) *Incumbents already have contacts / businesses are therefore more

willing to donate to them. (6) With a little luck, the donations will pay off the incumbents will act on behalf of those businesses once they are re-elected. (7) Challengers have no power and no influence, they have difficulty getting corporate support. (8) Of course, there are exceptions, misconduct or criminal charges against an incumbent will often shift popular and financial support to a challenger. (9) Our campaign finance system is not productive or fair, we need to reform the laws that govern it. (10) We should have a system that enables us to elect the best candidate, not the one with the biggest campaign chest.

Challenge 1   Identifying Comma Splices and Run-Ons in Your Writing

Take a recent assignment that you are working on, and exchange it with a partner. Underline the subjects and verbs in each sentence of the paper you receive. Then put a / between any clauses you see that can stand alone. If you discover any comma splices or run-ons, mark these errors. Return the draft to your partner. Save your own draft for later use.

CORRECTING COMMA SPLICES AND RUN-ONS BY USING COORDINATING CONJUNCTIONS

Coordinating conjunctions such as *and, but,* and *or* link independent thoughts and help you to eliminate choppiness and repetition. (See page 265 for a complete list of coordinating conjunctions.) One way to correct comma splices and run-on sentences is to use one of these conjunctions between the independent clauses. Look at these examples, with corrections added:

> **Comma splice**
>
> Science fiction movies don't seem as popular anymore, *yet* two new ones opened this week.

> **Run-on**
>
> Karen does volunteer work at an extended-care facility *, and* she also has a weekend job.

In the first sentence, *yet* provides the connection and shows opposition between ideas. In the second, a comma plus *and* now links the two clauses; *and* suggests addition of ideas. The sentences now flow better, and, more important, they are now correct. By the way, as the examples above show, always include a comma *before* a conjunction used to connect simple sentences.

Exploration 2a   Using a Coordinating Conjunction to Connect Clauses

Each numbered item in the following paragraph is either a run-on sentence or a comma splice. If the item is a run-on, put a / between the independent clauses. Then above the /, add a comma and the coordinating conjunction (*and, or, but, for, nor, so,* or *yet*) that best connects the thoughts in the independent clauses. If the item is a comma splice, simply insert a / and the correct coordinating conjunction between the clauses. Use the examples to guide you.

> *Example*   I had completed my art project on time /I forgot to bring it.   *, but*

> *Example*   Gerald has black hair, /it curls naturally.   *and*

(1) Finally, Martin Luther King Day is celebrated in all 50 states, it certainly   *and*
took a while. (2) For a time, it was a federal holiday most states celebrated it.
(3) A few states, however, did not observe it schools, businesses, and govern-   *so*
ment offices in those states remained open. (4) Many individuals in these
states were outraged about this they stayed home from work and kept their   *so*
children out of school in protest. (5) A special day in Dr. King's honor is well
deserved, he gave his life to improve civil rights for all of us.   *and*

Exploration 2b   More Practice Using a Coordinating Conjunction to Connect Clauses

The following paragraph contains several comma splices and run-on sentences. Put an * in front any comma splice or run-on sentence. Then put a / between independent clauses. Choose an appropriate coordinating conjunction from the list below and insert it above where one sentence should end and the next should begin. Don't forget to add a comma if it is needed. Study the example first.

and	nor
but	so
for	yet
or	

> *Example*   *The officer was clearly lying/the judge allowed his testimony.   *, yet*

(1) Today, the Olympic Games have become little more than another big
business. (2) They are a short-term money maker for the host city they also pro-   *, and*

vide another big-budget spectacle for television. (3) The Olympics are sup-

posed to be about competition among the world's best amateur athletes, *but* they

seem much more about money. (4) All the countries involved talk about the

ideal of the amateur athlete, *and* all of them, including the United States, allow

professional athletes to compete. (5) Of course, these athletes aren't always

identified as professionals. (6) Instead, they are called amateurs, they accept

"expense money" from sporting goods manufacturers or major corporations.

(7) In the last few summer Olympics, a team of NBA players represented the

United States in Olympic basketball. (8) These players make millions of dol-

lars a year playing basketball, they can hardly be considered amateurs. (9) In

the winter Olympics, the star skiers and skaters are also professional, many of

the lesser known athletes receive support as well. (10) All these people are the

big winners in the Olympics, the big losers are the rest of us.

Challenge 2 Working with Coordinating Conjunctions

Take the list of coordinating conjunctions in Exploration 2b, and, working with
a partner, write two sentences for each conjunction in which you use the conjunction to connect the simple sentences. When you are done, explain in a
few sentences which of the conjunctions you found most useful and why.

CORRECTING COMMA SPLICES AND RUN-ONS BY USING SUBORDINATING CONJUNCTIONS

Adding a subordinating conjunction such as *after, because, if,* and *unless* to
connect clauses is another way to eliminate comma splices and run-ons. (See
page 262 for a complete listing of subordinating conjunctions.) As Chapter 19
showed, subordinating conjunctions indicate a relationship between the ideas
they connect. Consider the following examples:

Comma splice

Because oil
~~Oil~~ from the leaking barge fouled the water for over 20 square
miles, more than 1,000 birds were killed.

> **Run-on**
>
> , *although*
> The insurance company never received our payment we mailed the
> check out a week ahead of the due date.
> ^

In the first example, *because* joins two ideas related by cause and effect: The death of the birds *resulted from* an oil spill. In the second example, *although* links the ideas and also indicates the relationship between them: Payment was never received, *despite the fact that* the check was mailed in time.

Exploration 3a   Using a Subordinating Conjunction to Connect Clauses

Each numbered item in the following paragraph is either a run-on sentence or a comma splice. First, put a **/** between the independent clauses. Then add one of the subordinating conjunctions listed below to show a relationship between the clauses. In some cases, more than one correct answer is possible. With a comma splice, you'll need to add only the subordinating conjunction, but with a run-on sentence, you'll need to add a comma as well as the conjunctive adverb. Study the example first.

after	before
although	since
because	when

Before the
Example   ~~The~~ police arrived, / traffic was backed up for three miles.
^

(1) I started work I never saw / the importance of knowing a second language. (2) Having bilingual workers is important, / the needs of all customers can be met. (3) I thought about it / learning a second language seemed like a great idea for me. (4) I am training to be a paralegal, / I will have to deal with people from a wide variety of backgrounds. (5) I know more than one language / a law office will be more interested in hiring me.

Exploration 3b   More Practice Using a Subordinating Conjunction to Connect Clauses

In the following paragraph, find the comma splices and run-ons, and put an ***** in front of each one. Then choose an appropriate subordinating conjunction (*because, since, even though, when, although,* or *so that*), and insert it in the proper place above the line to make the sentence correct. Make sure to add a comma if it is needed. Study the example first.

Example   *because*
They were late leaving the campground they had to wait for Gil
and Sheila.

(1) Some people are counted as unemployed or underemployed by the government they actually have an income. (2) They are part of the "underground economy." (3) Most people in this situation work for cash only *so that* they can hide their income from government agencies. (4) In most cases, they charge substantially less *because* their salary is tax free. (5) Sometimes these workers are amateurs just picking up a little extra cash on the weekends or nights. (6) They don't want to declare their earnings *because* the extra income might raise their overall tax burden. (7) Sometimes trained specialists and union artisans join the underground economy they are between jobs or laid off. (8) Many of the members of the underground economy have no other means of support. (9) They work below the minimum wage they would have no employment otherwise. (10) *Since* The underground economy continues to thrive, the government has tried to control it.

Challenge 3   Using Subordinating Conjunctions

For Exploration 3a, you corrected comma splices and run-on sentences by using subordinating conjunctions to connect the subject–verb units. Working with a partner, explain on a separate sheet of paper the relationships the subordinating conjunctions suggest in the corrected paragraph.

CORRECTING COMMA SPLICES AND RUN-ONS BY USING SEMICOLONS

A semicolon (;) has the same power to connect simple sentences that conjunctions have. Using a semicolon to provide the link between sentences enables you also to emphasize the connection between the units, adding another dimension to your meaning, as these examples, with corrections, show:

Comma splice

Peter injured his shoulder during the game; he tore his rotator cuff.

> **Run-on**
>
> The guest speaker waited for questions from the class $\overset{;}{\underset{\wedge}{}}$ nobody said a word.

In the first example, the clause stating that an injury occurred is now properly joined to the clause describing that injury. In the second example, the clause explaining the speaker's expectation is connected by a semicolon to the clause describing the class's lack of response.

To clarify the relationship between the clauses, you can use a conjunctive adverb (*also, furthermore, instead, however, moreover, then, therefore,* etc.) with a semicolon. (See page 267 for a complete list of conjunctive adverbs.) Consider these examples:

> **Example**
>
> The suit was expensive; *however,* it was very well made.

> **Example**
>
> After playing for five minutes, the band suddenly left the stage; *meanwhile,* two technicians began to check the sound system.

In each example, the semicolon joins the ideas, and the conjunctive adverb clarifies why the ideas are linked. Notice that a comma is needed after each of these conjunctive adverbs.

Exploration 4a   Using a Semicolon to Connect Clauses

Each numbered item in the following paragraph is either a comma splice or a run-on sentence. First, put a / between the independent clauses. Then insert a semicolon, alone or with a conjunctive adverb, to connect the clauses. If you add a conjunctive adverb, write it above the point where the first clause ends and the second clause begins. If you use a conjunctive adverb, remember to place a comma after it. A complete list of conjunctive adverbs appears on page 267. Use the examples to guide you.

> *Example*   At first, the puppy wouldn't come out from behind the chair/$^;$
>
> Michelle eventually coaxed it out with a doggie biscuit.

or

> *Example*   At first, the puppy wouldn't come out from behind the chair/ *; however,*
>
> Michelle eventually coaxed it out with a doggie biscuit.

(1) Television talk shows often exploit their guests; there seems to be no lack of people willing to be exploited. (2) Last week, one show featured a

woman, her mother, her husband, and her ex-husband, all fighting for custody of the woman's children; the woman's lawyer was there, along with the ex-husband's sister and the current husband's mother. (3) The woman accused the ex-husband of abusing the children; the woman's mother sided with the ex-husband against the woman. (4) During the show, the people on stage accused each other of various crimes and offenses the audience was yelling and booing. (5) All of these people seemed seriously disturbed the talk show host should be arrested for taking advantage of them.

Exploration 4b More Practice Using a Semicolon to Connect Clauses

The following paragraph contains several comma splices and run-on sentences. Put an * in front of any comma splice or run-on sentence. Then insert a semicolon, with or without a conjunctive adverb. If you use a conjunctive adverb, insert it above where one sentence should end and the next should begin, and put a comma after it. Study the examples first.

> *Example* * The injury to her ankle was severe; she was in great pain.

or

> *Example* * The injury to her ankle was severe; consequently, she was in great pain.

(1) Jasmine earns money for college by delivering the morning newspaper. (2) An adult can make a pretty good paycheck this way; the person just has to be willing to get out of bed at 5 a.m every day. (3) Her route covers ten miles outside the city, she delivers a total of 200 papers on weekdays and 100 on Sundays. (4) Jasmine never complains, her job is far from easy. (5) She spends the first hour folding papers and putting them in plastic bags, these steps are vital in order to keep the papers dry. (6) She then piles the papers into the passenger's seat in her car and begins driving. (7) The process of delivering the papers is a little dangerous she puts her emergency blinkers on and drives slowly along her route. (8) Her delivery method is interesting she grabs a paper from the seat and throws it completely over the car and into the

subscriber's yard. (9) By 6:30, she has finished her entire route. (10) She then stops at the bakery at the end of her route for coffee she is too tired to read the paper, though.

Exploration 4c   Connecting Sentences with Conjunctive Adverbs and Semicolons

The following passage contains a number of comma splices and run-on sentences. Correct them by using a semicolon and one of the conjunctive adverbs listed below. Study the example first.

nevertheless	however	meanwhile
finally	therefore	consequently
still		

Example   The heavy rains destroyed the old earthen dam *; therefore,* the mayor was

forced to declare a state of emergency.

(1) Ray Martini is a popular man because it is hard to find a good cobbler anymore. (2) He has been repairing shoes for almost 40 years; *therefore* he has developed a long list of satisfied customers. (3) He learned the craft from his father, a cobbler his whole life, first in Italy and then here in the United States. (4) Ray worked with his father for 25 years; *finally,* his father retired and Ray took over. (5) Ray has never made a great deal of money *; however,* he has enjoyed a comfortable life. (6) He has never had a phone in his shop *; nevertheless* new customers find him. (7) He has relocated three times; *meanwhile,* old customers manage to track him down. (8) They say the inconvenience is worth the effort because he does quality work. (9) Ray will retire eventually the customers just keep pouring in. (10) None of his children followed him into the business; *consequently,* his retirement will mean the end of the store.

Challenge 4   Working with Semicolons and Conjunctive Adverbs

For Exploration 4a, you made some choices about how to connect clauses in a paragraph by using either a semicolon or a semicolon and a conjunctive adverb. Now, working with a partner, compare the two different versions of the passage. Discuss why you made your choices. If, after your discussion, you prefer another way of joining some of your sentences, make those changes.

CORRECTING COMMA SPLICES AND RUN-ONS BY USING PERIODS

Another way to correct comma splices and run-on sentences is to use a period between the subject–verb units to create separate sentences. This option isn't a good idea if the simple sentences are short because it may make your writing seem choppy. If the sentences are longer, however, separating them may be a good choice, as these examples show:

> **Comma splice**
>
> Dani's ambition is to start her own obedience and pet-grooming
> _. she_
> business, she hopes that she'll be able to open her shop next year.

> **Run-on**
>
> "Good Health through Moderation" is the theme of this year's health
> _. Last_
> fair last year's theme was "Smoking Cessation—Good Riddance to a
> Bad Habit."

You could certainly eliminate these errors by using a conjunction and a comma or a semicolon. The sentences that would result would be fairly long, however, and long sentences can be difficult to follow. Therefore, using a period to create separate simple sentences is a better choice. When you use this option to correct run-on sentences and comma splices, remember to capitalize the first word of the second sentence.

Exploration 5a   Using a Period to Separate the Units

In this paragraph, using a period to separate the independent clauses is probably the best option because the clauses are long. Put a / between the clauses, and then insert a period to eliminate the run-on sentence or comma splice. Start the first word of a new sentence with a capital letter. Use the example to guide you.

> _Example_   By noontime on opening day, the line leading into the stadium
> _. Inside,_
> was already a quarter of a mile long / inside, 10,000 people
> had already taken their seats, waiting for the first ball to be
> thrown out.

(1) The recent hurricane changed the entire landscape at Horseneck Beach, fortunately, only a few of the houses along the edge of the beach

suffered from the effects of severe erosion. (2) The most severely damaged house was owned by Mr. Lionel Partridge, one of the oldest residents of the community. the storm ripped off the front of the house, sending all his belongings into the churning ocean. (3) The contour of the beach itself was the most dramatic change of all. the dunes separating the beach from the road were completely flattened. (4) Foundations of several homes destroyed by earlier hurricanes were visible again. they had been buried for over 25 years. (5) Even with the changes, Horseneck Beach is still beautiful. the whole experience should remind everyone of the tremendous power of nature.

Exploration 5b   More Practice Using a Period to Separate the Units

The following paragraph contains several comma splices and run-on sentences. Put an * in front of any comma splice or run-on sentence. Then put a / between the independent clauses. Insert a period where the first sentence should end, and then start the word that begins the second sentence with a capital letter. Study the example first.

> *Example*   * The landscapers spent the afternoon digging up the dead
>   . *The*
>   sod/the grass had been completely destroyed by grubs.

*(1) Max's first experience with a credit card was not a good one, even at age twenty-one, he wasn't ready for the responsibility. (2) Five years ago, he filled out an application for a credit card at his favorite clothing store. (3) A week later, the card came in the mail. his troubles began at that point. (4) His original plan was to buy one item a week. he would then pay off the entire bill at the end of the month. (5) For the first two months, he had no trouble keeping up with the payments. as a result, Max decided to buy more things. (6) However, his bill for the third month was over $800, and he had put aside only $200. (7) Max panicked and didn't pay the bill. for the next two months he received the same bill, plus a finance charge. (8) A few weeks later, Max received a letter from the credit department of the store. it instructed him to

call the department. (9) He was scared and ashamed, so he also ignored that letter. (10) Shortly after that, Max received a letter threatening him with legal action after that warning, he began to make payments again, and he cut up his credit card.

 Challenge 5 Correcting Comma Splices and Run-Ons in Your Writing

Return to the work you completed for Challenge 1 (page 277). Using the methods you have learned in this chapter, correct any comma splices and run-ons that your partner marked. Then reassess your writing. Do your ideas flow more smoothly? Are the relationships among the ideas clear?

DISCOVERING CONNECTIONS B

1. In Discovering Connections A on page 275, you prewrote on one of four suggested subjects. Now, using this prewriting material as the foundation, work your way through the rest of the writing process, and complete a draft essay of about 500 words on this topic.
2. Exchange your draft with a partner. Using the material in this chapter to guide you, check the draft you receive for any comma splices and run-ons. Mark these errors with a *cs* or an *ro,* and then return the draft to the writer.
3. Revise your essay, correcting any comma splices or run-ons identified by your reader.

SUMMARY EXERCISE

The following passage contains a number of comma splices and run-ons. First, identify these errors by putting an * in front of each one. Then, using the various techniques discussed in this chapter, correct the comma splices and run-ons. In some cases, more than one solution is possible. Check to make sure you have used punctuation and capital letters correctly.

(1) In the neighborhood where I grew up, there was an old, abandoned house. (2) According to all the kids in the neighborhood, it was haunted, but I didn't believe them. (3) At age eleven, I finally explored that house with

my two best friends. I became convinced that there was something weird about it.

(4) The house was located across the street from our school. *and* it seemed to call to us every time we passed it. (5) Jack and Nickie wanted to break *but* in, I kept talking them out of it. (6) Finally, we could resist no longer, *so* we made our plans to enter the haunted house on the following Saturday night.

(7) At eight o'clock that evening, we met in my backyard. *and* I had told my mother we were going to play basketball under the lights at nearby Pulaski Park. (8) We often played at night, so she wasn't suspicious. (9) We left my yard quickly and headed off to the house. We were all set for the big break-in.

(10) We had spent a few days planning our caper, so we had come well prepared. (11) Nickie had brought a hammer and a crowbar, *and* Jack had taken his father's big flashlight. (12) I had brought a screwdriver and a pair of pliers, We wanted to be prepared for every possibility.

(13) Twenty minutes later, we reached the house, *and* it was pitch dark and very quiet. (14) We went around back and snuck in through the cellar door. The lock was badly rusted, so we only had to pry a little with the crowbar. (15) Once inside, we crept down the stairs to the dirt cellar, *also,* it was dark and clammy. (16) Jack shined his light around the cellar, everything was covered with dust and cobwebs. (17) We never made it upstairs. The floorboards squeaked, and we ran out at lightning speed.

(18) We ran two blocks before stopping. None of us had ever been so scared in our whole lives. (19) We all headed home and agreed not to tell anyone else. (20) I've kept the secret, I don't know if Nickie or Jack ever told.

RECAP

COMMA SPLICES AND RUN-ON SENTENCES

New terms in this chapter	Definitions
➤ comma splice	➤ an error in which sentences are incorrectly connected by a comma
	Example The storm dumped four inches of rain across the region, / several cities and towns suffered heavy flooding.
➤ run-on sentence	➤ an error in which two sentences are run together with no punctuation or connectors
	Example James forgot his wallet at home / he didn't realize until he arrived at the register.

To Identify Comma Splices and Run-On Sentences

1. Identify all subject–verb units.

2. Establish that the clauses can stand alone.

Four Ways to Correct Comma Splices and Run-On Sentences

1. subject–verb unit   +   *comma and coordinating conjunction*   +   subject–verb unit

2. subject–verb unit   +   *subordinating conjunction*   +   subject–verb unit
   or
   subordinating conjunction   +   subject–verb unit and *comma*   +   subject–verb unit

3. subject–verb unit   +   *semicolon*   +   subject–verb unit
   or
   subject–verb unit   +   *semicolon, conjunctive adverb, and comma*   +   subject–verb unit

4. subject–verb unit   +   *period*   +   subject–verb unit (*begin with capital*)

Understanding Subjects and Verbs

21	Subject–Verb Agreement
22	Basic Tenses for Regular Verbs
23	Irregular Verbs and Frequently Confused Verbs
24	Passive Voice, Additional Tenses, and Maintaining Consistency in Tense

21

Subject–Verb Agreement

OVERVIEW: UNDERSTANDING SUBJECT–VERB AGREEMENT

When two parties, either companies or individuals, plan to do something jointly, they sit down and draw up an agreement. Essentially, an agreement is a document outlining what role each party will play in the relationship so that everything will run smoothly. Agreement is part of writing, too, and the general definition of agreement fits the grammatical meaning of the word. For your sentences to run smoothly, you must make each subject agree with its verb in terms of number. In other words, a *singular* subject calls for a *singular* verb form, and a *plural* subject calls for a *plural* verb form. Ensuring that each subject agrees with its verb is important because subjects and verbs communicate the basic meaning of your sentences.

In this chapter, you will learn how to recognize and avoid the following difficulties with subject–verb agreement:

➤ problems when the subject follows the verb

➤ problems when words come between subjects and verbs

➤ problems with indefinite pronouns

➤ problems from other causes, including compound subjects; collective nouns; singular nouns ending in *-s*; and words referring to measurements, money, time, and weight

DISCOVERING CONNECTIONS **A**

Using one of the techniques you practiced in Chapter 2, prewrite on one of the following topics: sexism, computer games, gossip. Save your work for later use.

➤ **A** VOIDING AGREEMENT ERRORS WHEN THE SUBJECT FOLLOWS THE VERB

ESL Note
See "Sentence Basics" on pages 521–523 and "Agreement" on pages 526–529.

The secret to avoiding errors in **subject–verb agreement** is to identify the subject: the person or thing that is performing the action or that is being discussed. To do this, as Chapter 17 shows (page 239), ask yourself *who or what is doing the action or being discussed?* The answer to that question is the subject.

In the majority of the sentences you write, the subject comes before the verb, as these examples show:

> **Example**
>
> The *Executive Committee meets* every other week.
> [subject] [verb]

> **Example**
>
> The *Internet puts* the world at a person's fingertips.
> [subject] [verb]

But not all sentences follow this pattern. In some sentences, the subject appears after the verb. One type of sentence in which the subject follows the verb is a question:

> **Example**
>
> *Has* the *staff completed* the CPR course?
> [verb] [subject] [verb]

> **Example**
>
> *Is ESPN planning* to broadcast the X-Games again?
> [verb] [subject] [verb]

In the first sentence, *staff* is the subject; in the second, *ESPN* is the subject. Note, however, that in each case part of the verb precedes the subject: *has* in the first sentence and *is* in the second.

Sentences beginning with *there* or *here* also feature subjects that follow the verb. *There* and *here* are adverbs, and only a noun or pronoun can be the subject of a sentence. So in sentences beginning with *there* or *here,* the actual subject follows the verb, as these examples show:

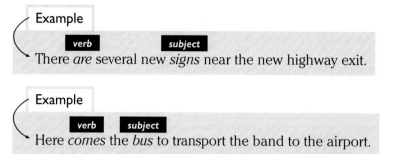

Example

verb   subject

There *are* several new *signs* near the new highway exit.

Example

verb   subject

Here *comes* the *bus* to transport the band to the airport.

In the first sentence, *signs* is the subject, even though it follows the verb *are.* In the second sentence, the subject is *bus,* even though it follows the verb *comes.*

Exploration 1a Identifying Subjects That Follow the Verb

For each sentence in the following passage, identify the verbs and subjects, circling the verbs and underlining the subjects. Use the following example as a guide.

> *Example*   Here (is) the missing notebook.

(1) Decades after their introduction, there are still many game shows on television. (2) There is nothing challenging about some of them, for instance *Wheel of Fortune.* (3) Then there is *Jeopardy.* (4) Is there a harder game show anywhere? (5) Don't the producers of *Jeopardy* have any mercy for the poor contestants?

Exploration 1b Maintaining Agreement When Subjects Follow the Verb

Each of the sentences in the following paragraph contains a pair of verbs in parentheses. First, find and underline the subject with which the verb must agree. Then circle the verb that agrees with that subject. Study the example first.

> *Example*   (Has/(Have)) Louie and Lee rented their apartment yet?

(1) (Doesn't/Don't) people know how easy it is to register as a bone marrow donor? (2) According to recent news articles, there (is/are) a shortage of bone marrow donors. (3) It's too bad, because here (is/are) a wonderful

opportunity to help save someone's life, and people are missing out on it because of misconceptions about the procedure itself. (4) First, there (is/are) a blood test. (5) (Is/Are) there a simpler form of testing available? (6) Once a blood sample is taken, there (is/are) some sophisticated tests done at a special lab, and the results are entered into a special bone-marrow-donor registry. (7) Here (is/are) the point at which everyone waits for a match between someone in need of a transplant and a potential donor. (8) Once a match is identified and the donor is notified, there (is/are) a few simple steps during which marrow is extracted from the donor's hip. (9) For the donor, the good news is that there (is/are) very little discomfort. (10) (Does/Do) people have to know any more than this to get involved?

Challenge 1   Identifying Subjects and Verbs to Achieve Subject–Verb Agreement

Working with a partner, choose one of the readings from Part Seven, and select three paragraphs from it. Working together, identify the subjects and verbs, crossing out all prepositional phrases, subordinate clauses, and other words between the subjects and verbs. Then, on a separate sheet of paper, identify which subjects and verbs you found most difficult to identify, and explain why.

➤ **A**VOIDING AGREEMENT ERRORS WHEN WORDS COME BETWEEN THE SUBJECT AND VERB

Often, problems with subject–verb agreement occur because of the words you use *between* subjects and verbs. Don't be fooled by the noun closest to the verb, which may not actually be the subject. Instead, be sure that you identify the person or thing that is performing the action or that is being discussed.

In some cases, what comes between a subject and verb is a *prepositional phrase*. As Chapter 17 explains (page 240), a prepositional phrase begins with a preposition and ends with a noun or pronoun. Common prepositions include *about, against, around, behind, beneath, by, down, during, inside, out, through, to, up, within,* and *without.* Here is an example of a sentence with a prepositional phrase coming between the subject and the verb:

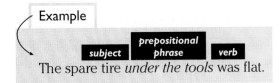

Example

| | prepositional | |
| subject | phrase | verb |

The spare tire *under the tools* was flat.

In this sentence, the verb *was* agrees with the singular subject *tire*, not with the noun closest to it, the plural object of the preposition, *tools*.

Other times, a subject and a verb are separated by a *subordinate clause*. As Chapter 19 explains (pages 262–263), a subordinate clause is a subject and verb unit introduced by a subordinating conjunction or relative pronoun. Common subordinating conjunctions include *after, although, because, if, since, unless, until, when, whether,* and *while*. Common relative pronouns include *that, which, who,* and *whose*. Here is a sentence in which the subject and verb are separated by a subordinate clause:

> ### Example
>
> **subject**   **subordinate clause**   **verb**
> Students *who have computer network experience* enjoy great job prospects.

In this sentence, the verb agrees in number with the actual subject, *students*, not with the word closest to the verb, *experience*.

Exploration 2a   Identifying Subjects Separated from Verbs by Other Words

For each sentence in the following passage, identify the verbs and subjects, circling the verbs and underlining the subjects. This task will be easier if you cross out any words that come between subject and verb, as the example shows.

> *Example*   On some days, the <u>crowd</u> in the cafeteria lining up for lunch
>
> (reaches) the back of the building.

(1) Advertisements on the Internet, especially on Web pages and search engines, continue to generate controversy. (2) For one thing, some people using the Web, especially those using it for work, find the advertisements annoying. (3) The most distracting ones, according to these users, feature words or characters "crawling" across the top of the screen. (4) Other critics of the practice dislike the lack of government regulation over the advertisements. (5) Yet many other people using the 'Net for pleasure or work simply pay little attention to the ads.

Exploration 2b   Maintaining Agreement with Subjects Separated from Verbs by Other Words

Each of the sentences in the following passage contains a pair of verbs in parentheses. First, find and underline the subject with which the verb must agree. Then circle the verb that agrees with the subject you have underlined. Study the example first.

Example The burners on the stove, which are now covered with drips of

paint from the ceiling, (needs/need) to be replaced soon.

(1) A good mechanic who has worked on a variety of cars and who knows how to do a variety of repairs (is/are) difficult to find. (2) Yet consumer surveys have found that many people, especially those who own low- to medium-priced cars, (reports/report) good experiences with certified service centers in their area. (3) The comments that these car owners have made on these surveys (emphasizes/emphasize) the important role customer service plays in consumer satisfaction. (4) The surveys, which are completed as customers are leaving a service center, generally (reports/report) satisfaction with the cleanliness of the waiting area and courtesy of the staff. (5) Successful certified service centers, especially those connected with new car dealerships, (recognizes/recognize) that customers who are satisfied with service are also more likely to purchase a new car from that same dealership. (6) In addition, the surveys report that customers, while never happy about paying for repairs, (understands/understand) the need for a reasonable hourly charge. (7) Charges at certified service centers (tends/tend) to run between $45 and $50 per hour. (8) Of course, customers, when faced with such fees, (expects/expect) service centers to guarantee their work. (9) The most trusted service centers, according to these surveys, (provides/provide) a written guarantee along with a breakdown of all work completed. (10) Obviously, the good old days when most people could find a good mechanic in their neighborhoods (has/have) disappeared for good.

Challenge 2 Examining Subjects and Verbs in Your Writing

1. Sentence 3 in Exploration 2b suggests that customer service is vital to the success of a business. Now write a paragraph of 100–150 words on the

subject of the importance of customer service, using present tense verbs only.

2. Exchange your paragraph with a partner. On the paper you receive, identify the subjects and verbs by underlining the subjects and circling the verbs. Put a ✓ next to any sentence that contains an error in subject–verb agreement. When you are finished, return the paragraph to your partner, and check the work your partner did on your paragraph.

➤ **A**VOIDING AGREEMENT ERRORS WITH INDEFINITE PRONOUNS

Another potential difficulty with subject–verb agreement involves indefinite pronouns. *Indefinite pronouns* are used to refer to general rather than specific people and things, for instance, the indefinite *somebody* rather than the specific *Bill*, the indefinite *anything* rather than the specific *a burrito*. See page 361 in Chapter 25 for a further discussion and a complete list of indefinite pronouns.

Some indefinite pronouns are singular, some are plural, and some are singular or plural depending on how you use them. Of these words, *another, anybody, anyone, anything, each, either, everybody, everyone, everything, much, neither, nobody, no one, nothing, one, somebody, someone,* and *something* are singular and call for singular verb forms:

> Example
>
> | singular | singular verb form |
> |---|---|
>
> *Everybody leaves* that movie smiling.

> Example
>
> | singular | singular verb form |
> |---|---|
>
> *Someone has* to find the owner of that puppy.

Both, few, many, and *several* are always plural and call for plural verb forms:

> Example
>
> | plural | plural verb form |
> |---|---|
>
> *Both* of the apartments *look* well maintained.

> Example
>
> | plural |
> |---|
>
> *Many* of the over one hundred people attending the presentation
>
> | plural verb form |
> |---|
>
> now *want* to participate in the training program.

All, any, more, most, none, and *some* are either singular or plural depending on the word they refer to in the sentence. With one of these pronouns, check the word it refers to. If that word is singular, choose a singular form of the verb; if it is plural, choose a plural form of the verb, as these examples show:

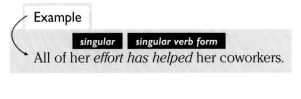

Example

singular **singular verb form**

All of her *effort has helped* her coworkers.

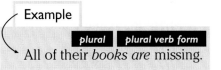

Example

plural **plural verb form**

All of their *books are* missing.

Exploration 3a Maintaining Agreement with Indefinite Pronouns

Underline the verbs in the following sentences. Then fill in the blank in each sentence with an appropriate indefinite pronoun from the list below. In some cases, you may use the same pronoun more than once.

anyone   everyone   no one   none   some

Example Of the new medications available to combat asthma,

_____*some*_____ have proven to be especially effective.

(1) _____ likes to save money. (2) Now, _____*noone*_____ has to pay high long-distance fees, thanks to the Internet. (3) With the right Internet service provider and computer hardware, _____ can route long-distance calling through the Internet. (4) Because of occasional problems in sound quality, _____ view this innovation as a waste of time. (5) But according to a recent article on the subject, _____*none*_____ of the small business owners currently paying $500 or more a month in standard long-distance fees seem to agree.

Exploration 3b   More Practice Maintaining Agreement with Indefinite Pronouns

For each sentence in the following passage, identify the subject by underlining it. Then circle the verb that agrees with that subject from the pair of verbs in parentheses. Study the example first.

> *Example*   Nobody in the office (has/have) a personal parking space.

(1) Springfield, like most medium-sized cities, (has/have) several major neighborhoods. (2) The east end of the city is called "the Flint," and nobody (seems/seem) to know where the name came from. (3) Many of the people living in the Flint (traces/trace) their heritage to Canada. (4) Everyone who lives in the south end of the city (refer/refers) to this neighborhood as "Maplewood." (5) Some of the larger homes in this part of the city (displays/display) the elegance of the Victorian Age. (6) The neighborhood in the center of the city is called "Below the Hill," and many of the young professionals working in the city (lives/live) here. (7) This part of the city is undergoing a rejuvenation, and everyone (has/have) been rushing to buy and restore the brownstone buildings that line the streets. (8) "The Highlands" and "the Lowlands" in the hilly north end of the city are the other two neighborhoods, and everybody in the city (enjoys/enjoy) the beauty of these two areas. (9) Both (has/have) similar characteristics, with tree-lined streets and large homes with big yards. (10) Each also (features/feature) a clear view of the Springfield River.

Challenge 3   Writing Sentences Using Indefinite Pronouns That Can Be Either Singular or Plural

Here again is the list of indefinite pronouns that are either singular or plural depending on what they are referring to:

all	any	more
most	none	some

Working with a partner, write two sentences for each, one in which the word refers to a singular word and one in which the word refers to a plural word.

➤ **A** VOIDING AGREEMENT ERRORS FROM OTHER CAUSES

The following situations can also create confusion as you make decisions about subject–verb agreement.

When the Subject Is Compound

As Chapter 17 (page 241) indicates, not all subjects are individual words. Many are *compound subjects:* more than one noun or pronoun connected in most cases by *and* or *or.* Compound subjects connected by *and* are almost always plural. The exceptions are subjects that are commonly thought of as one, such as *pork and beans, peanut butter and jelly, peace and quiet, ham and eggs,* and *rock and roll.*

> **Example**
>
>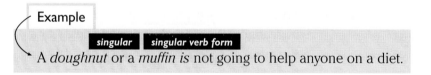
> A *headache* and a *bruise* on her arm *were* the only indications that Margarita had been in an accident.

If the two subjects are singular and connected by *or,* use a singular form of the verb:

> **Example**
>
> A *doughnut* or a *muffin is* not going to help anyone on a diet.

But if the subjects are both plural, use a plural form of the verb:

> **Example**
>
> *Doughnuts* or *muffins are* not going to help anyone on a diet.

When the compound subject consists of one singular word and one plural word connected by *or,* use the form of the verb that agrees with the subject closest to it:

> **Example**
>
>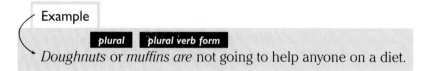
> The *supervisor* or the *workers are* responsible for the decreased level of production.

Workers is closer to the verb, so the correct choice is the form that agrees with *workers.*

When the Subject Is a Collective Noun

Collective nouns are words that name *groups* of items or people. Common collective nouns include *audience, class, committee, faculty, flock, herd, jury, swarm,* and *team.* (See Chapter 25, page 353, for more on collective nouns.) Collective nouns are singular, so they call for singular verb forms:

Example

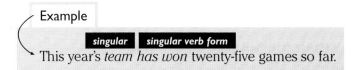

This year's *team has won* twenty-five games so far.

In some cases, certain words, called *cue words,* help you to identify whether a subject is singular or plural. Common singular cue words include *a, an, another, each, either, every, neither,* and *one.* A subject introduced by one of these words will be singular and call for a singular verb form:

Example

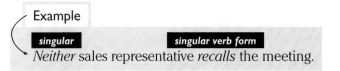

Neither sales representative *recalls* the meeting.

Common plural cue words include *all, both, few, many, several,* and *some.* Subjects introduced by these words call for a plural verb form:

Example

Few great novels ever *make* good movies.

When the Subject Is a Singular Word Ending in *-s,* a Word Referring to an Amount, or a Word That Has the Same Singular and Plural Form

Certain words that end in *-s* may look plural, but they are actually singular and call for singular verb forms. Common words in this category include *economics, ethics, mathematics, measles, mumps, news, physics,* and *politics.*

Example

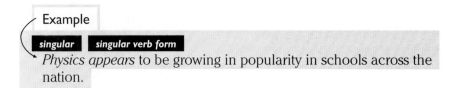

Physics appears to be growing in popularity in schools across the nation.

Nouns used to refer to measurements, money, time, and weight can also cause some confusion in terms of subject–verb agreement. These words may seem plural, but because they are used to refer to the entire amount as one unit, they are actually singular and call for singular verb forms:

Example

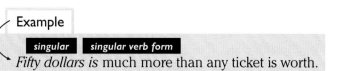

singular	singular verb form

Fifty dollars is much more than any ticket is worth.

Finally, with certain words such as *antelope, deer, fish,* and *species,* use either a singular or plural form of the verb depending on whether you mean one or more than one:

Example

singular	singular verb form

That *moose has broken* out of its holding area.

Example

plural	plural verb form

Those *moose look* so peaceful as they stand together.

Exploration 4a   Maintaining Agreement with Compound Subjects

Each of the sentences in the following passage includes a pair of verbs in parentheses. First underline the compound subject, and then circle the verb that agrees with that subject. Study the example first.

Example   Even after working all afternoon, <u>David and Bobbie</u> still

(has/(have)) not been able to start the car.

(1) In today's modern world, eye specialists and patients looking to improve their eyesight (has/<u>have</u>) a number of alternatives available. (2) For those still interested in glasses, ultra-thin lenses and smaller shapes (has/<u>have</u>) replaced coke-bottle lenses and clunky frames. (3) Today, <u>style and comfort</u> (<u>do</u>/does) not have to be sacrificed, thanks to the advent of low-cost designer frames. (4) In addition, <u>bifocals</u> or <u>trifocals</u> (has/<u>have</u>) been replaced in many cases with an innovative type of lens that allows the wearer to see clearly regardless of the distance. (5) For those wanting to do without glasses altogether,

daily-wear contact lenses or extended-care contact lenses (remains/<u>remain</u>) the most common options. (6) Colored lenses and patterned lenses (is/<u>are</u>) among the variations of contacts available to the daring and style-conscious wearer. (7) Bifocal contacts and contacts that reshape the lens (is/<u>are</u>) recent innovations in this field. (8) Also, conventional surgery or laser surgery (enables/enable) people with vision problems to go without glasses or contacts. (9) Of course, any surgery has risks, so with this type of procedure, either the eye specialist or a specially trained technician thoroughly (<u>explains/</u>explain) to the patient what will occur. (10) The improved vision and freedom from vision aids of any type (makes/<u>make</u>) these surgical alternatives an increasingly popular choice among the young and physically active.

Exploration 4b   Maintaining Agreement with Collective Nouns, with Singular Words Ending in -s, and with Words Referring to Amounts

Each of the following sentences contains the infinitive of a verb (to + a simple form of the verb—*to speak*) in parentheses. Identify the subject of the verb by underlining it, and then write the proper *present tense* form of the verb on the line provided. Remember—the story is told in the present, so use present tense forms only. Study the example first.

> *Example*   The <u>audience</u> (to be) ___*is*___ clearly enjoying the concert.

(1) The <u>committee</u> in charge of selecting the Youth Center's Volunteer of the Year (to have) ___*has*___ an important job. (2) A nominating team of five committee members first (to select) ___*selects*___ five semi-finalists from the many nominations. (3) In most years, 50 to 100 nominations (to be) _____ not unusual. (4) The ethics of the situation (to require) _____ careful, objective scrutiny of the nominations. (5) That's because politics often (to play) _____ a part in the nom-

inating process, with companies and organizations lobbying for the opportunity to highlight the activities of one of their employees to thousands of people across the state. (6) Economics (to do) _____ not come into play, however, because no monetary reward is attached to the award. (7) After the initial selections are made, two hours (to be) _____ set aside so that the team can rank the candidates in 10 categories on a 1–5 scale. (8) Ultimately, simple mathematics (to determine) _____ the winner, with the nominee holding the highest composite score being unanimously named Volunteer of the Year. (9) Despite efforts to keep the results secret until the annual recognition banquet, news often (to spread) _____ among the rest of the committee. (10) On the night of the recognition banquet, as the audience (to applaud) _____ for the winner, the committee sits back and enjoys what their hard work has brought about.

Challenge 4 Revising to Achieve Subject–Verb Agreement

Help the writer of the following letter to the editor revise her writing so that readers will clearly understand her points. Working with a partner, rewrite the letter on a separate piece of paper, making any changes in subject–verb agreement that you think are needed. Some sentences are correct as written.

Dear Editor:

(1) No one who lives in our community seems concerned about the budget problems we are facing. (2) Two million dollars are too big of a deficit. (3) Something has to be done soon. (4) The general population are unwilling to cut the budget or raise taxes. (5) Either politics or economics have to win, however. (6) After all, few solutions is acceptable to all of us. (7) Someone needs to make the tough decisions. (8) Each of the elected officials are responsible for part of the problem, and all of them should works together to resolve it. (9) One thing is certain. (10) If we don't succeed, every one of the town officials face rejection at the polls during the next election.

DISCOVERING CONNECTIONS B

1. In Discovering Connections A on page 293, you did some prewriting on one of three suggested subjects. Now, using that material as your foundation, work your way through the rest of the writing process, and complete a draft essay of about 500 words.
2. Exchange your draft with a partner. Using the material in this chapter to guide you, check the draft you receive for any mistakes in subject–verb agreement. Circle any incorrect verbs, and then return the draft to the writer.
3. Revise your essay, correcting any errors in subject–verb agreement identified by your reader.

➤ SUMMARY EXERCISE

The following passage contains the various kinds of errors in subject–verb agreement discussed in this chapter. Using the examples in the chapter to guide you, identify the errors in agreement. Then correct each error by crossing it out and writing the correct verb form above the incorrect one.

(1) There is many choices available for the person looking for a laptop computer. (2) Thanks to price cuts by most major manufacturers, anybody wanting the option of a portable computer now have that possibility. (3) This new class of laptops appear to consist of the first portables to have broad consumer appeal.

(4) Attractive laptop computers with huge amounts of memory now costs far less than ever before. (5) Only a few years ago, $3,000 were considered a bargain basement price for a basic portable computer. (6) Right now, a laptop with 10 times as much memory and many more built-in features run under $2,000.

(7) In the last two years alone, there has been improvements almost beyond belief. (8) Today, for example, five pounds are considered heavy for these powerhouse portables. (9) Tiny keyboards and awkward pointers were negative features of many of the older portable computers. (10) Today, however, everybody trying these new laptops consistently give positive marks to these features in the new generation of laptop computers.

(11) Either a brighter active matrix color screen or the many built-in features is also cited by consumers as factors causing them to consider purchasing one of these laptops. (12) In addition, there have been great interest in the compact CD-ROM drives, extended-life batteries, and fast modems available as accessories. (13) All of these features has been applauded by prospective buyers.

(14) According to consumer responses, here are the most popular improvement: speed. (15) Everyone trying these new laptops remark on this improvement, especially with complex tasks. (16) Many of these new laptops features the newest generation of Pentium chips. (17) Now some of the most complex functions takes only a few seconds.

(18) Does manufacturers expect these innovations in laptops to lead most people to abandon their desktop computers? (19) Nobody seem to know for sure. (20) But with prices for portable computers so low, a real choice between desktop computers and this new generation of laptops exist for the first time.

RECAP
SUBJECT–VERB AGREEMENT

New terms in this chapter	Definitions
➤ **subject–verb agreement**	➤ a state in which the subject and verb agree in number ➤ Use a singular form of a verb with a singular subject. ➤ Use a plural form of a verb with a plural subject.

Ways to Maintain Agreement

➤ When the **subject follows the verb**

in a question ——————————➤ *Does* she *know* the directions to the party?

in a sentence beginning with *there* or *here* ——➤ There *are* six days left in the term.

Identify the verb and ask "who or what?" to find the subject.

➤ When the **subject and verb are separated** by other words

prepositional phrases ——————➤ The *baby* across the hall *cries* all night.

subordinate clauses ——————➤ The substitute *teacher,* because she is strict, *controls* the class.

Identify the verb and ask "who or what?" to find the subject.

➤ When the **subject is compound**

with *and* the subject is usually plural ——➤ *Marcus and Simon are* friends.

unless the compound is considered one ——➤ *Rock and roll is* here to stay.

with *or* the subject can be singular ——➤ *Red or blue is* my favorite color.

with *or* the subject can be plural ——➤ *Pancakes or waffles are* good for breakfast.

Find the conjunction and determine what is being connected.

➤ When the **subject is an indefinite pronoun**

singular ——————————➤ *Everyone is* late today.

plural ——————————➤ *Both* of my grandparents *are* immigrants.

Use singular verbs with singular pronouns and plural verbs with plural pronouns.

➤ When the **subject is a collective noun or singular noun ending in -s**

collective noun ——————➤ The *jury returns* today.

singular noun ending in -s ——➤ The *news follows* my favorite comedy.

If the subject is a unit, use a singular verb.

Singular Indefinite Pronouns

another	each	everything	nobody	somebody
anybody	either	neither	nothing	someone
anyone	everybody	no one	one	something
anything	everyone			

Plural Indefinite Pronouns

both	many
few	several

Indefinite Pronouns Affected by the Words That Follow Them

all	more	none
any	most	some

22

Basic Tenses
for **Regular Verbs**

OVERVIEW: UNDERSTANDING TENSE

ESL Note
See "Agreement"
on pages 526–529.

No words are more important to you as a writer than verbs. As Chapter 17 showed, verbs convey action or link elements in a statement. Verbs enable you to communicate about events that occur and about ideas or possibilities. Verbs also signify *when* the action or situation occurs, in either the *present, future,* or *past.* The aspect of a verb that indicates time is called **verb tense,** and it is indicated by changing the verb in some way. Most verbs are *regular,* meaning they form their *simple* or basic tenses in consistent ways.

In this chapter, you will discover how to use the following for regular verbs:

➤ the present tense to describe a fact or an action or situation that is happening now or that happens habitually

➤ the future tense to describe an action or situation that hasn't occurred yet

➤ the past tense to describe an action or situation that has already occurred

➤ the past participle and perfect tenses to describe an action or situation that was either completed in the past or will be completed in the future

DISCOVERING CONNECTIONS **A**

Using one of the techniques you practiced in Chapter 2, prewrite on one of the following topics: entertainment, the environment, personal responsibility. Save your work for later use.

USING THE SIMPLE PRESENT, SIMPLE FUTURE, AND SIMPLE PAST TENSES

The **present tense** signifies a fact or an action or situation that is happening *at the moment* or that happens habitually. For regular verbs, the simple present tense is the basic form of the verb, the one you would use in the simplest "I" statement: I laugh, I jump.

What makes the present tense a little confusing sometimes is that its form changes depending on the subject. If the subject is *singular,* meaning *one* person or thing, then the verb ends in -*s* or -*es.* If the subject is plural (or *I*), the verb has no -*s.*

> Example
> All day long, that dog *digs* holes in the yard.

> Example
> Most children *enjoy* a magic show.

The subject in the first example is singular (*dog*), so the verb ends in -*s: digs.* In the second example, the plural subject *children* calls for a verb without an -*s* ending: *enjoy.* The exceptions to this guideline are the pronouns *I* and *you.* Even though *I* is singular, you don't add an -*s* to the present tense verb when *I* is the subject:

> Example
> I *play* basketball every weekend.

You also don't add an -*s* to a present tense verb when *you* is the subject, even when it is singular:

> Example
> You always *clean* your apartment on Saturday.

The simple **future tense** conveys an action or relationship *that hasn't occurred yet.* For regular verbs, the future tense for both singular and plural subjects is formed by adding *will* to the basic form of the verb. No -*s* or -*es* is necessary.

Example

The actors *will prepare* for the play. The director *will coach* them.

The simple **past tense** indicates an action or situation *that has already oc-curred.* For regular verbs, the simple past tense is formed by adding *-ed* to the basic verb form. If the verb ends in *-e,* only a *-d* is added. For some regular verbs that end in *-y,* or with a single consonant preceded by a single vowel, forming the past tense requires a little more work. You must either change the last letter or add a letter before you add the *-d* or *-ed* ending. Chapter 29, "Spelling," discusses ways to treat these verbs. Again, the simple past tense is the same for both singular and plural subjects.

Example

Osvaldo *answered* many questions in botany class.

Example

Several dozen applicants *responded* to our ad for an assistant manager.

How to Form Simple Tenses for Regular Verbs
(Example verb—call)

	Simple Present Tense (Use the basic form of the verb, adding -s or -es for singular subjects except I and you.)	Simple Past Tense (Use the basic form of the verb plus -d or -ed.)	Simple Future Tense (Use the basic form of the verb plus will.)
Basic or "I" Form	I *call* friends in the evening.	I *called* friends last night.	I *will call* friends tomorrow evening.
Singular	Ami *calls* friends in the evening.	Ami *called* friends last night.	Ami *will call* friends tomorrow evening.
Plural	Joe and Estella *call* friends in the evening.	Joe and Estella *called* friends last night.	Joe and Estella *will call* friends tomorrow evening.

Exploration 1a   Practice Working with Future Tense Verbs

Complete the following sentences by adding a completing thought containing a future tense verb. Study the example first.

Example   When the warm weather arrives,   *the campus will look*

     beautiful   .

1. At the end of this century, _____

   _____ .

2. When the election results are finally tabulated, _____

   _____ .

3. After Albert shaves off his moustache and cuts his hair, _____

   _____ .

4. As soon as the semester is over, _____

   _____ .

5. The proposed increase in property taxes _____

   _____ .

6. Once the jury reaches a verdict, _____

   _____ .

7. A new manufacturing plant is opening up in town, so _____

   _____ .

8. If you learn to speak a second language, _____

   _____ .

9. Soon, high-speed trains _____

   _____ .

10. When the parade is over, the city's public works department _____

    _____ .

Exploration 1b   Practice Working with Past Tense Verbs

The italicized verbs in the sentences below are in the present tense. Change them to the past tense by adding -d or -ed. Cross out the present tense verb, and write the revised verb in the space above. Review the table on simple tenses (page 312) to use the -s or -es ending correctly. Study the example first.

> *tried*
> **Example**   During the first few classes, the instructor ~~tries~~ to make the
>
> class comfortable with the subject matter.

(1) My friend Andrea *works* with stained glass. (2) She *constructs* small items such as holiday ornaments. (3) She also *creates* larger items. (4) For

example, she *designs* wall displays. (5) My favorite *shows* an open door lead-ing into a cozy room, as a way to say "Welcome."

Exploration 1c   More Practice Working with Past Tense Verbs

Use the following list of basic verbs to complete the paragraph below. Make all verbs past tense by adding *-d* or *-ed*.

purchase	line	wash	measure	redecorate
brush	fold	pick	start	place

(1) Last weekend, my friend Kathy _____ the living room in her apartment by wallpapering. (2) First, she _____ the walls to find out how much wallpaper to buy. (3) Then she _____ the paper, along with a kit containing several wallpapering tools. (4) She also _____ up two containers of premixed wallpaper paste. (5) She then _____ the walls down to make sure the surface was clean. (6) Once the walls dried, she _____ to hang the wallpaper. (7) After cutting a strip of paper to the correct length, she _____ paste onto the back of the paper. (8) Next, she _____ the strip of paper in half and carried it from the table to the wall. (9) She unfolded the paper and _____ its top edge against the ceiling. (10) She then _____ up the right side of the paper against the guideline she had drawn to ensure that the paper was straight.

Challenge 1   Analyzing the Formation of Past Tense Verbs

Select a reading in Part Seven, and review it to find ten sentences that include past tense verbs. Write these sentences on a separate piece of paper, and ex-change sentences with a writing partner. Underline the past tense verb in each sentence, and write the basic form of the verb above it. Are all the past tense verbs formed the same way? Discuss your conclusions with the rest of the class.

USING THE PERFECT TENSES

Writers use another verb form called the **past participle** to form additional tenses: past perfect, present perfect, and future perfect. All of the **perfect**

tenses are formed by adding a helping verb to the past participle of a verb. For regular verbs, the past participle is the same as the simple past tense: the basic verb form plus -*d* or -*ed*.

This chapter discusses perfect tense verbs that use *has, have,* or *had* as helping verbs. Chapter 24 will discuss progressive tense verbs that use *am, is, was,* and *were* as helping verbs.

To form the perfect tenses for regular verbs, use the helping verbs shown below:

Perfect Tense	=	*Helping Verb*	+	*Past Participle*	*Example*
Past perfect		had		walked	I *had walked.*
Present perfect		has, have		walked	I *have walked.*
Future perfect		will have		walked	I *will have walked.*

Perfect tense verbs cover time in a slightly different way than simple past, present, and future tenses do.

➤ The *past perfect tense* expresses action completed in the past before some other past action or event. (Jim *had bought* Nikki's birthday gift before they broke up.)

➤ The *present perfect tense* expresses action completed at some indefinite period in the past, or action that began in the past and is still going on. (Jim *has bought* me a birthday gift every year since 1988.)

➤ The *future perfect tense* refers to actions that will be completed in the future before some other future event or action. Note that this tense requires the word *will* before the helping verb. (By August, Jim *will have bought* all his Christmas gifts.)

Study the timeline below, which shows the relationship of all the tenses discussed in this chapter.

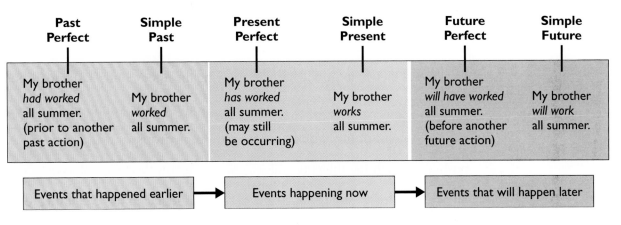

Exploration 2a   Practice Working with the Perfect Tenses

On another sheet of paper, rewrite the following sentences, changing the present tense verb to either the present perfect, past perfect, or future perfect form. Study the example first.

> *Example*   Josh earns all of his tuition money.
>
> *Josh will have earned all of his tuition money.*   *[Future perfect]*

1. The blue jay eats the blueberries on the ground below the bush.
2. The pie chills in the refrigerator at least two hours before dinner.
3. Bryan asks his friend for help with algebra.
4. The meteorologist forecasts a stormy weekend.
5. Dan states his preferences for vacation before anyone else.
6. The class turns in a teacher evaluation.
7. The secretary sorts the papers on the manager's desk.
8. I revise my essay one more time before submitting it.
9. The artist sketches the scene for an oil painting.
10. The baseball team practices every day for six weeks.

Exploration 2b   More Practice Working with the Perfect Tenses

Each of the sentences in the following paragraph contains a past participle that is missing a helping verb. Write the correct helping verb in the space provided to form a complete verb in the perfect tense. Then, label these verbs in the space above the line. Use *PaP* for past perfect tense, *PP* for present perfect tense, and *FP* for future perfect tense. Remember that the future perfect tense requires the word *will* along with the helping verb. Study the example first.

> *Example*   My daughter was delighted that the groundhog ___*had*___ *[PaP]*
>
> failed to see his shadow this year.

(1) When March comes to New England, usually the worst days of winter _____ passed. (2) The trees that _____ appeared barren and lifeless for months begin showing tiny green buds. (3) Squadrons of geese that _____ headed south for the winter fill the skies. (4) By the end of the month, a few early snowdrops _____ pushed through the thawing soil. (5) Moreover, on the faces of people you meet in the streets, smiles _____ replaced the chattering teeth and grimaces.

Challenge 2   Writing with the Perfect Tenses

1. Using the paragraph in Exploration 2b as a model, write a five-sentence paragraph about the signs of spring in your part of the country. Use at least one perfect tense verb in each sentence.

2. Exchange your writing with a partner. On the paper you receive, underline the perfect tense verbs and label them, using the abbreviations you used in Exploration 2b. Then return the paragraph to the writer. Check to see whether all of the labels are accurate. Which perfect tense did you choose most often? Which perfect tense did your partner choose most often? With the class, discuss how the topic affected your choices.

DISCOVERING CONNECTIONS B

1. In Discovering Connections A on page 311, you completed a prewriting on one of the subjects suggested. Now work your way through the rest of the writing process, and create a draft essay of about 500 words on this topic.
2. Exchange your draft with a partner. Using the material in this chapter to guide you, check the essay you receive for any problems with simple tenses. Underline any errors, and then return the essay to the writer.
3. Revise your draft, correcting any errors in tense identified by your reader.

SUMMARY EXERCISE

For each italicized verb in the following passage, identify the tense, using the labels listed below.

Pr = present tense	*PaP* = past perfect tense
Pa = past tense	*PP* = present perfect tense
F = future tense	*FP* = future perfect tense

(1) Recent research on the human brain *offers* us a number of interesting findings about the "wiring" of the human brain. (2) Scientists are now theorizing that, before your birth, your brain *programmed* itself. (3) It *dedicated* large numbers of nerve cells to performing basic functions. (4) However, it *reserved* even more nerve cells for specialized functions that help you learn about the world. (5) These findings *add* great significance to the way that we *treat* children. (6) We now believe that a child's neurons *will thrive* with appropriate stimulation. (7) Without direct stimulation and use, however, these nerve cells *will wither* away.

(8) This research *will encourage* parents and teachers to change some of our old views about learning. (9) For one thing, the findings *suggest* that there

are certain peak periods of opportunity for learning. (10) They *indicate* that children will make the greatest strides in learning mathematics between birth and four years. (11) The same thing *appears* to be true for learning music. (12) Parents who *had played* simple number games and *had introduced* their children to music during this period *saw* impressive results.

(13) The findings also *urge* us to examine how we *have treated* language. (14) Children *learn* language most easily from birth to age ten. (15) The first few years of life *matter* most. (16) It now *appears* likely that those infants and toddlers who master language quickly *have heard* more words than other children. (17) In addition, children who *have listened* to many words before they reach age two *will have developed* large vocabularies by the time they reach adulthood.

(18) If these preliminary findings *prove* to be true, parents and schools *will want* to make some serious adjustments. (19) For one thing, teachers *will expect* parents to be much more involved at home, since a great deal of valuable learning time occurs before children attend public school. (20) In addition, schools *will arrange* to offer instruction in a second language much earlier, perhaps as early as the first few grades.

RECAP

BASIC TENSES FOR REGULAR VERBS

New terms in this chapter	Definitions
➤ verb tense	➤ the form of a verb which tells when the action or situation occurs, either in the present, future, or past
➤ present tense	➤ the basic form of the verb signifying a fact or an action or situation that is occurring now or habitually ➤ Many singular present tense verbs end in -s or -es. *Example* My son *cleans* our apartment on the weekend. *Example* We *ignore* the dust during the week.
➤ future tense	➤ the form of the verb signifying a future action or state of being; the basic verb plus *will* *Example* This weekend he *will wash* the kitchen floor.

New terms in this chapter	Definitions
➤ past tense	➤ the form of the verb signifying an action or state of being that has already occurred; the basic form of the verb plus *-ed* or *-d* *Example* He *shopped* for groceries on Saturday.
➤ past participle	➤ for regular verbs, a form created by adding *-d* or *-ed* to the basic form ➤ Use the past participle with a helping verb to form the perfect tenses. *Example* Martha *had ended* the relationship months ago.
➤ perfect tenses	➤ verb tenses formed by adding some form of *to have* to the past participle of another verb ➤ Perfect tenses express actions that are complete with reference to another indicated time. *Example* We *have shared* the work this way for a few months. *Example* I *had finished* the rest of the chores earlier. *Example* We *will have succeeded* in sharing responsibilities.

Forming the Basic Tenses for Regular Verbs

Basic verb
"I" form
(arrange)

+ -d or -ed *(arranged)*	**+ -s or -es** *(arranges)*	**(same form)** *(arrange)*	**+ will** *(will arrange)*
Past singular and plural	**Present** singular	**Present** plural	**Future** singular and plural

Forming the Perfect Tenses for Regular Verbs

Past Participle
(called)

+ had been *(had been called)*	**+ has been** *(has been called)*	**+ have been** *(have been called)*	**+ will have been** *(will have been called)*
Past perfect singular and plural	**Present perfect** singular	**Present perfect** plural	**Future perfect** singular and plural

Irregular Verbs and Frequently Confused Verbs

OVERVIEW: UNDERSTANDING IRREGULAR VERBS AND OTHER VERB PROBLEMS

Chapter 22 illustrated how to form the basic tenses for regular verbs. However, many **irregular verbs** don't conform to these rules. As they change tense, they also change form in unpredictable ways. The irregular verb that causes the greatest confusion to writers is the verb *to be*. As a writer, you will need to memorize the forms of this and other irregular verbs. In addition, you will need to know how to choose correctly between such confusing pairs of verbs as *can* and *could* and *will* and *would*.

In this chapter, you will learn how to

➤ form the present, past, and past participle forms of common irregular verbs

➤ work effectively with forms of *to be*

➤ choose correctly between *can* and *could* and between *will* and *would*

DISCOVERING CONNECTIONS A

Using one of the techniques you practiced in Chapter 2, prewrite on one of the following topics: heroism, a real success story, religion. Save your work for later use.

IDENTIFYING IRREGULAR VERBS

The verbs in the following list are all irregular. As you learned in Chapter 22, the past participle form (column three below) is used with a helping verb to form a perfect or progressive tense verb.

Irregular Verb Forms

Present Tense	Past Tense	Past Participle (+ a helping verb)
am/is/are	was/were	been
arise	arose	arisen
awaken	awoke, awaked	awoke, awaked
become	became	become
begin	began	begun
bend	bent	bent
bind	bound	bound
bite	bit	bitten, bit
bleed	bled	bled
blow	blew	blown
break	broke	broken
bring	brought	brought
build	built	built
burn	burned, burnt	burned, burnt
burst	burst	burst
buy	bought	bought
catch	caught	caught
choose	chose	chosen
cling	clung	clung
come	came	come
cost	cost	cost
creep	crept	crept
cut	cut	cut
deal	dealt	dealt

(continued)

Irregular Verb Forms (continued)

Present Tense	*Past Tense*	*Past Participle* (*+ a helping verb*)
dig	dug	dug
dive	dived, dove	dived
do/does	did	done
draw	drew	drawn
dream	dreamed, dreamt	dreamed, dreamt
drink	drank	drunk
drive	drove	driven
eat	ate	eaten
fall	fell	fallen
feed	fed	fed
feel	felt	felt
fight	fought	fought
find	found	found
flee	fled	fled
fling	flung	flung
fly	flew	flown
forbid	forbade, forbad	forbidden
forget	forgot	forgotten, forgot
freeze	froze	frozen
get	got	got, gotten
give	gave	given
go/goes	went	gone
grind	ground	ground
grow	grew	grown
hang	hung	hung
hang (execute)	hanged	hanged
have/has	had	had
hear	heard	heard
hide	hid	hidden, hid
hold	held	held
hurt	hurt	hurt
keep	kept	kept
kneel	knelt, kneeled	knelt, kneeled
knit	knit, knitted	knit, knitted
know	knew	known
lay	laid	laid
lead	led	led
leap	leaped, leapt	leaped, leapt
leave	left	left
lend	lent	lent
let	let	let
lie	lay	lain
light	lighted, lit	lighted, lit
lose	lost	lost

Irregular Verb Forms (continued)

Present Tense	Past Tense	Past Participle (+ a helping verb)
make	made	made
mean	meant	meant
meet	met	met
mistake	mistook	mistaken
pay	paid	paid
plead	pleaded, pled	pleaded, pled
prove	proved	proved, proven
put	put	put
quit	quit	quit
raise	raised	raised
read	read	read
ride	rode	ridden
ring	rang	rung
rise	rose	risen
run	ran	run
say	said	said
see	saw	seen
seek	sought	sought
sell	sold	sold
send	sent	sent
set	set	set
sew	sewed	sewn, sewed
shake	shook	shaken
shine	shone, shined	shone, shined
shine (polish)	shined	shined
shoot	shot	shot
show	showed	shown, showed
shrink	shrank, shrunk	shrunk, shrunken
shut	shut	shut
sing	sang, sung	sung
sit	sat	sat
sleep	slept	slept
slide	slid	slid
sling	slung	slung
slink	slunk, slinked	slunk, slinked
sow	sowed	sown, sowed
speak	spoke	spoken
speed	sped, speeded	sped, speeded
spend	spent	spent
spit	spit, spat	spit, spat
spring	sprang, sprung	sprung
stand	stood	stood
steal	stole	stolen

(continued)

Irregular Verb Forms (continued)

Present Tense	Past Tense	Past Participle (+ a helping verb)
stick	stuck	stuck
sting	stung	stung
stink	stank, stunk	stunk
stride	strode	stridden
strike	struck	struck, stricken
string	strung	strung
strive	strived, strove	striven, strived
swear	swore	sworn
sweat	sweat, sweated	sweat, sweated
swell	swelled	swelled, swollen
swim	swam	swum
swing	swung	swung
take	took	taken
teach	taught	taught
tear	tore	torn
tell	told	told
throw	threw	thrown
understand	understood	understood
wake	woke, waked	woken, waked, woke
wear	wore	worn
weave (make cloth)	wove, weaved	woven, weaved
weep	wept	wept
win	won	won
wind	wound	wound
wring	wrung	wrung
write	wrote	written

As the list shows, the past and past participle forms of irregular verbs are often different. Consider these examples:

> **Example**
> The man sleeping on the bar *drank* four beers in half an hour.

> **Example**
> The fifteen-year-old driver *had drunk* an entire six-pack before he stole my car and crashed it.

Because of their unpredictability, irregular verbs in all their forms must be memorized. As you learn the irregular verb forms, keep two things in mind: (1) You *don't* use a helping verb with the past tense, and (2) You *must* use a helping verb with the past participle.

Exploration 1a   Forming Perfect Tenses for Irregular Verbs

In the following paragraph, fill in the blanks with the past participle form of the verb in parentheses to form a perfect tense verb. Remember to provide the appropriate helping verb (*have, has,* or *had*) for each past participle. Then label these verbs in the space above the line. Use *PaP* for past perfect tense, *PP* for present perfect tense, and *FP* for future perfect tense. Study the example first.

> **Example**   It looks as though Caryl's eye (swell) *has swollen* shut.   [PP]

(1) When I asked my friend Jarod how he (cut) _____ his forehead, he began to laugh. (2) Then Jerod told me that he (fall) _____ while roller blading, but he hadn't hurt himself. (3) Feeling very proud of himself for having avoided any injury, he stood up, but he (forget) _____ to tighten the binding on his skate boot. (4) He fell again, and when he wiped his forehead and saw red on his fingers, he realized he (hurt) _____ himself. (5) He said that his friends (make) _____ him captain of the Olympic klutz team, but he vows he (prove) _____ them wrong by the end of the roller blading season.

Exploration 1b   Using Irregular Verbs in Your Writing

On a separate sheet of paper, write three related sentences for each of the irregular verbs listed below: one each for the present tense, the past tense, and the past participle forms. Remember—the past participle requires a helping verb to form a perfect tense verb. Study the example first.

> **Example**   *Joe and Mary Beth always <u>hear</u> the noise from the Fourth of July fireworks.*
>
> *Last night, they also <u>heard</u> the oohs and ahhs of the crowd.*
>
> *On previous years, Joe and Mary Beth <u>have heard</u> the band as well as the fireworks.*

1. keep	3. sleep	5. freeze	7. write	9. raise
2. bite	4. shake	6. speak	8. become	10. stand

Exploration 1c   Using Irregular Verbs Correctly

The following narrative takes place in the past. Each sentence contains a present tense verb in parentheses. Write the correct form of this verb on the line that follows. Use the form that the context calls for; include a helping verb if necessary. In some cases, more than one correct answer is possible. Study the example first.

> **Example**   When I was growing up, I always (do) _____*did*_____ my
>
> assigned chores as quickly as I could.

(1) I went to a local flea market for the first time last week and (spend) _____ a fascinating day there. (2) Dozens of dealers had set up tables to sell goods, and some (go) _____ so far as to put up big signs advertising exactly what was for sale. (3) I (see) _____ everything from handmade Christmas ornaments to paintings of cowboys on black velvet. (4) The artist was there, and he explained that his partner had drawn the pictures in charcoal but that he himself (do) _____ the actual painting. (5) At one table, a young girl (buy) _____ and (sell) _____ comic books. (6) She said that last month she (buy) _____ a number of valuable comic books at flea markets around the area. (7) Next to her, an older man (set) _____ up a table to sell secondhand clothes. (8) He claimed that most of the items (wear) _____ only once or twice. (9) For me, the best part of the flea market (be) _____ the food. (10) With all the different kinds of food available, I (eat) _____ practically all afternoon.

Challenge 1   Revising the Tense of a Paragraph

Ten verbs are listed below. On a separate sheet of paper, use at least five of these verbs in the present tense to write a paragraph. Exchange your work with a partner, and rewrite the paragraph you receive, changing the tense of each verb to either the past or past perfect form. Consult the list of irregular verbs (pages 321–324) as necessary.

feed	eat
give	sit
make	grind
see	bring
break	forget

▶ WORKING WITH FORMS OF TO BE

The most irregular of the irregular verbs is the verb **to be.** For example, it is the only verb that uses different forms for different persons in the past tense. However, memorizing the various forms of *to be* is not that difficult because many do *not* change when the subject changes.

Look at the table below, which shows the most common forms of the verb *to be*:

Common Forms of the Verb to Be				
When the subject is ...	the present tense is ...	the past tense is ...	the future tense is ...	the past participle is ...
I	am	was	will be	been
he, she, or it	is	was	will be	been
we, you, or they	are	were	will be	been

As you can see, *will be* and *been* are used with *all* subjects, although different helping verbs are needed for *been.*

To simplify your understanding of *to be*, concentrate on those forms that *do* change, as this version of the same table shows:

When the subject is ...	the present tense is ...	the past tense is ...	Examples
I	am	was	I *am* tired tonight. I *was* more energetic yesterday.
he, she, or it	is	was	He *is* late for his dental appointment. She *was* early for her guitar lesson.
we, you, or they	are	were	You *are* the best friend I've ever had. They *were* childhood sweethearts before they married.

If you keep these forms straight, you'll experience far fewer problems using *to be.*

In addition, keep in mind two rules when you are using forms of *to be.*

1. Never use *been* without *has, have,* or *had:*

> *have been*
> For some time, we ~~been~~-looking for a house.

> *had been*
> Just a year earlier, that superstar comedian ~~been~~ a complete unknown.

2. Never use *be* by itself as the verb in a sentence:

> *are*
> We ~~be~~ proud of your achievement.

> *are*
> You ~~be~~ the reason for this celebration.

Although you may hear violations of these rules in informal speech, such usages are not acceptable for the writing you will do in college and the workplace.

Exploration 2a   Working with Forms of *to Be*

In the following paragraph, complete each sentence by writing the correct form of the verb *to be* in the space provided. Use the tables on page 327 for help with the most irregular forms of *to be.* Study the example first.

> **Example**   Annette _____*will be*_____ thirty on her next birthday.

(1) Today, one way to get a brighter smile _____ to use a chemical whitener. (2) Some observers of trends in business believe that these whiteners _____ among the fastest growing personal care products in this decade. (3) These analysts note that many people _____ embarrassed by stains on their teeth but don't want to pay $300 to have a dentist bleach them. (4) Unfortunately, until now, there _____ no alternative. (5) Now, however, an over-the-counter product _____ finally available for the general public.

Exploration 2b   Correcting Errors in the Forms of *to Be*

In the following paragraph, correct the errors in the use of *be* and *been*. Cross out the error, and write the verb correctly above it. Study the example first.

is
> **Example**   Mary ~~be~~ the most experienced worker in the office.

(1) With all the injuries suffered in professional boxing each year, it be hard to understand why we allow the sport to continue. (2) Nevertheless, boxing is still legal, and it been causing permanent damage to hundreds of people every year. (3) The brutality of boxing been no longer reserved for men only, either. (4) A few years ago, the first professional bouts between female boxers been broadcast. (5) Regardless of the sex of the combatants, the impact of a punch be unbelievably damaging. (6) Fighters be often lifted off their feet when they been hit. (7) The physical state of former heavyweight champion Muhammad Ali was the greatest evidence for the argument that boxing should be banned. (8) At the beginning of his career, Ali been among the most articulate people in the world of sports. (9) Now he be barely able to speak. (10) Ours are a civilized society, so why do we allow this brutality to continue?

Exploration 2c   Additional Practice Working with Forms of *to Be*

Change the verbs in the following paragraph to the past tense. Cross out the present tense verb, and write the past tense form above it. Study the example first.

was
> **Example**   Marcy ~~is~~ the right person to run the business.

(1) In the city, a group of volunteers is organized to clean up the waterfront area. (2) These workers are organized by the local chapter of the Sierra Club. (3) The hope of the organizing committee is to attract fifty volunteers. (4) Many spots are in terrible shape. (5) After years of neglect, the three-mile stretch of beach near Reflecting Lake is full of litter like old tires and beer cans. (6) The worst area is the spot near the abandoned Kerr Mill. (7) This

section is the hardest to reach because of a city barrier to keep people out.

(8) Nevertheless, the area is a frequent party spot for teenagers in the city.

(9) Glass slivers from hundreds of windows broken by vandals are every-

where on the pavement around the old mill building. (10) However, the vol-

unteers are so dedicated that the area is soon clean and attractive enough

for family picnics.

Challenge 2   Explaining Problem Verbs

Identify the form of *to be* that you think is most difficult to use, and write a paragraph in which you explain why you find this form confusing. Include brief sentences illustrating how you use the form incorrectly, and then show what you must do to use it correctly. Share your paragraph and example sentences with a partner. Did you both choose the same form of *to be* to write about?

➤ CHOOSING BETWEEN CAN AND COULD AND BETWEEN WILL AND WOULD

Beginning writers often have trouble choosing between *can* and *could* as helping verbs. These two verbs both mean *to be able to*. *Can* is used to indicate the present tense, and *could* is used to indicate the past tense:

> **Example**
> At this moment, no one in the conference *can beat* our relay team.

> **Example**
> Last season, no one in the conference *could beat* our relay team.

Sometimes *could* is also used to indicate a *possibility* or *hope* of doing something:

> **Example**
> Our competitors wish they *could beat* our relay team.

Beginning writers also have trouble deciding between the helping verbs *will* and *would*. Although both verbs are used to indicate the future, each links the future with a different period of time.

Look at the following versions of the same sentence, with the verbs italicized:

> **Example**
>
> **present tense**
>
> Carlos *thinks* that he *will major* in computer programming.

> **Example**
>
> **past tense**
>
> Carlos *thought* that he *would major* in computer programming.

The first sentence says that *right now* Carlos intends to focus on computer programming in the future. The second sentence indicates that *at an earlier time,* he had intended to study computer programming.

In some instances, *would* is also used to indicate a *hope* or *possibility* rather than a certainty, as this sentence shows:

> **Example**
>
> Many people *would* be able to save if they budgeted carefully.

Exploration 3a   Choosing between *Can* and *Could* and between *Will* and *Would*

In each sentence in the following paragraph, circle the correct verb in parentheses. Study the example first.

> *Example*   If he didn't work, Arnie (will, (would)) take an evening class.

(1) From personal experience, I can tell you that counseling (can, could) make a real difference. (2) If you are suffering from depression, you (will, would) benefit from working with a counselor. (3) Before I made the decision to seek help, I didn't think there was any way I (can, could) break out of my depression. (4) I (will, would) sit in my bedroom for hours at a time, doing nothing but staring. (5) Thanks to counseling, however, I (can, could) now function like a real person and enjoy life most of the time.

Exploration 3b   Correcting Errors in the Use of *Can* and *Could* and *Will* and *Would*

The following passage contains a number of errors in the use of *can* and *could* and *will* and *would*. Correct the errors by crossing out the incorrect word and writing the correct word above it. If a sentence is correct as written, write *OK* above it. Study the example first.

will

Example   I don't know if I ~~would~~ be available to begin work on Monday.

(1) Soon, physicians would have a new weapon in their battle to help burn victims. (2) The Food and Drug Administration (FDA) recently approved an artificial skin that can be used in grafting procedures. (3) Up until now, patients can expect attempts at skin grafting to fail more often than not. (4) When a person is severely burned, in many cases only the outer layer of skin would grow back. (5) If the skin graft cannot attach itself to healthy tissue, the procedure would fail. (6) So the best that burn patients can hope for was to minimize the number of failures. (7) Each time a graft failed, the surgeon will harvest a new graft and begin the procedure again. (8) Now, however, it appears that the new artificial skin would dramatically improve the success rate for grafting. (9) The new material, which eventually breaks down to be absorbed by the body, will provide an anchor for the skin graft. (10) Now that the FDA has approved the use of this artificial skin, doctors would soon begin using it in their surgical procedures.

Challenge 3   Analyzing Correct *Can/Could* and *Will/Would* Choices

1. Working with a partner, write a brief paragraph that explains the differences between *can* and *could* and between *will* and *would*. Provide examples of correct and incorrect usage for each word.

2. Now look again at the work you did for Explorations 3a and 3b. Examine the choices you made between *can* and *could* and between *will* and *would* to see whether they match the explanation you wrote for step 1 above. If they don't match, then revise your explanation to clarify why you made those choices. Exchange your paragraph with a partner. In the paragraph you receive, put a ✓ next to any part of the explanation that is still unclear. Return the paragraph to your partner, and revise any part of your own paragraph that needs clarification.

DISCOVERING CONNECTIONS **B**

1. In Discovering Connections A on page 321, you completed a prewriting on one of three suggested subjects. Now work your way through the rest

of the writing process, drawing from this prewriting material, and complete a draft essay of about 500 words on this topic.

2. Exchange your draft with a partner. Using the material in this chapter to guide you, check the draft you receive for any errors in the use of irregular verbs, *can* and *could,* or *will* and *would.* Circle any errors, and then return the draft to the writer.

3. Revise your essay, correcting any errors that your reader identified.

➤ **S**UMMARY EXERCISE

Proofread the following sentences, and revise any errors you find in the use of irregular verbs, *can* and *could,* or *will* and *would.* Cross out the incorrect word or words, and write a correct version above it. If a sentence is correct as written, write *OK* above it.

(1) Today, you could buy a greeting card for just about any occasion or person. (2) As might be expected, there be plenty of cards for standard events such as birthdays, weddings, and so on. (3) What is surprising is the range of holidays, occasions, and special needs and concerns addressed through greeting cards.

(4) If you have had no luck in buying the perfect birthday present for someone, you can find a card that apologizes for your failure. (5) You can also bought birthday cards for every variety of relative you can imagine. (6) For example, if you want to get a card created specifically for great-grandmothers or stepsons, you could find one.

(7) In addition to the cards commemorating traditional events, such as Thanksgiving, Christmas, Hanukkah, and Valentine's Day, you would find cards for special occasions, such as St. Patrick's Day and Halloween. (8) The list continues to grow, too. (9) For example, cards celebrating Kwanzaa recently been added to stores across the nation.

(10) If your boss just gave birth, you don't need to worry. (11) There be cards to mark the occasion. (12) You can chosen between pink ones for girls

and blue ones for boys. (13) Do you need a card to apologize to your old friend for not writing sooner? (14) Just check the racks, and you could find one.

(15) These cards isn't just for family and close friends, either. (16) They came in different levels of familiarity. (17) For example, if you need a sympathy card for someone you barely known, one is available. (18) There even been greeting cards for ex-spouses and ex–in-laws.

(19) Finally, whether you like humor, sentimentality, or inspirational messages, you would discover a greeting card that suits you. (20) Just head to the nearest card store, and plan to spend some enjoyable time reading over the possibilities.

RECAP
IRREGULAR VERBS AND FREQUENTLY CONFUSED VERBS

New terms in this chapter	Definitions
➤ irregular verbs	➤ verbs that do not form their past tense and past participle in typical ways

Strategies for Learning Irregular Verb Forms: Grouping by Pattern

	Present	Past	Past Participle
All tenses use the same form	let burst	let burst	let burst
Past tense and past participle use the same form	feel mean	felt meant	felt meant
In each tense, one letter changes	ring drink	rang drank	rung drunk
In past tense, one letter changes; in past participle, one letter is added	throw blow	threw blew	thrown blown

New terms in this chapter	Definitions
➤ to be	➤ the most challenging irregular verb for writers ➤ Always use *has, have,* or *had* with *been.* ➤ Never use *be* alone as a verb. ➤ Follow the chart below for tenses of *to be.*

Common Forms of the Verb *to Be*

When the subject is . . .	the present tense is . . .	the past tense is . . .	the future tense is . . .	the past participle is . . .
I	am	was	will be	been
he, she, or it	is	was	will be	been
we, you, or they	are	were	will be	been

Verb Pairs Often Confused	
➤ can/could	➤ helping verbs that mean *to be able to* ➤ Use *can* to show present tense. *Example* Jose *can* win the contest. ➤ Use *could* to show past tense, or the possibility or hope of being able to do something. *Example* If I *could* sing, I'd join the chorus immediately.
➤ will/would	➤ helping verbs that indicate the future ➤ Use *will* to point to the future from the *present.* *Example* Howard promises he *will* return before midnight. ➤ Use *would* to point to the future from the *past.* *Example* Howard promised he *would* return before midnight.

24

Passive Voice, Additional Tenses, and Maintaining Consistency in Tense

OVERVIEW: UNDERSTANDING ADDITIONAL ELEMENTS OF VERB USE

In the last two chapters, you learned some essentials about verb use that will help you as a writer. So far, you've worked with basic and perfect tenses for regular and irregular verbs, and you've learned how to choose between confusing pairs of verbs.

However, there's still more to verb use. As a writer, you need to consider the differences between *active* and *passive voice*. You also need to master the *progressive* and the *perfect progressive tenses*. And finally, you need to understand the importance of keeping verb tenses *consistent* within a piece of writing.

In this chapter, you will learn how to

➤ form the passive and active voices and when each is appropriate

➤ form and use the progressive and perfect progressive tenses correctly

➤ maintain consistency in verb tense

DISCOVERING CONNECTIONS A

Using one of the techniques you practiced in Chapter 2, prewrite on one of the following topics: fate, hypocrisy, the behavior of a crowd. Save your work for later use.

FORMING THE PASSIVE AND ACTIVE VOICE

When you combine the past participle form of a verb with a form of *to be*, such as *am, is, was,* or *were,* you are using the **passive voice.** In a sentence with a passive voice verb, the subject *receives* the action:

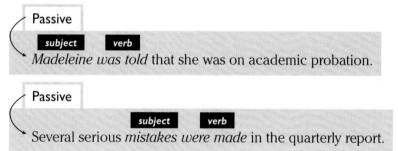

Passive

subject   **verb**
Madeleine was told that she was on academic probation.

Passive

subject   **verb**
Several serious *mistakes were made* in the quarterly report.

In general, the passive voice is considered less forceful than the active voice; it can sound awkward (The game *was won* by us.). With a verb in the **active voice,** the subject *performs* the action and is the *focus* of the sentence.

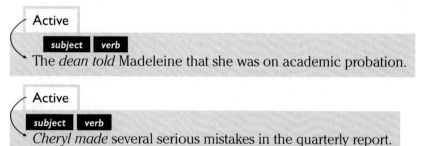

Active

subject **verb**
The *dean told* Madeleine that she was on academic probation.

Active

subject   **verb**
Cheryl made several serious mistakes in the quarterly report.

Using a string of passive verbs in your writing tends to weaken it. The active voice generally makes your language sound more direct, powerful, and concise. In addition, because it indicates the doer of the action, the active voice also establishes responsibility for that action. Therefore, the passive voice should be used sparingly. However, it is useful for expressing actions in which the actor is unknown or for emphasizing the receiver of an action.

Effective passive voice

subject   **verb**
The stolen *necklace was returned*; no questions were asked.

Exploration 1a   Identifying Passive and Active Voice

Underline the simple subjects and verbs in the following sentences. Watch for compound subjects and verbs and compound sentences. Label active voice verbs with an *A* and passive voice verbs with a *P.* Remember—if the subject receives the action, the sentence is in the passive voice. Study the example first.

> *Example*   During the police chase, several <u>shots</u> <u>were fired</u>.
> <small>P</small>

(1) Last month, my roommate and I held a yard sale to get rid of our unwanted things. (2) By 9 A.M., our treasures were piled on tables in front of the apartment house. (3) For the next two hours, every item was handled, but not one thing was bought. (4) By 2 P.M., Carol and I called off our sale. (5) We carried everything back upstairs and laughed about our short careers as entrepreneurs.

Exploration 1b   Using Passive Voice

In the paragraph below, fill in the blanks with the passive forms of the verbs in parentheses. Study the example first.

> *Example*   The championship game (to televise) _____*was televised*_____ .

(1) Recently, a bicycle path (to complete) _____ along the edge of the Allen River, right near downtown. (2) The path (to intend) _____ to beautify the old abandoned railroad route. (3) The tracks (to tear) _____ up and smooth asphalt (to lay) _____ over the track bed. (4) The path (to design) _____ to be wide enough for six bicyclists. (5) In addition, all the lighting along the path (to repair) _____ so that the path could be used late at night. (6) On the first weekend, a local television camera crew (to send) _____ to film the opening day crowd.

(7) The officials who attended were delighted when they noted that helmets (to wear) _____ by most of the cyclists. (8) The first weekly amateur bike race (to conduct) _____ at 5 P.M. (9) Prizes (to supply) _____ by several local businesses. (10) When the day ended, police estimated that the new path (to enjoy) _____ by more than 150 bicyclists.

Challenge 1   Analyzing the Effect of Active and Passive Voice

With a partner, rewrite the paragraph in Exploration 1a on page 338 two ways. In one version, use every verb in the active voice; in the other, make every verb passive. Use a separate sheet of paper for your paragraphs. Evaluate both versions of the paragraph, and then answer the following questions. Discuss your answers with the rest of the class.

1. Who or what is the subject in each sentence?
2. Who or what should be emphasized in each sentence?
3. Which version of each sentence do you think is most effective? Why?

USING THE PROGRESSIVE AND PERFECT PROGRESSIVE TENSES

In addition to using the basic tenses, you also need to master the progressive and perfect progressive tenses.

The Progressive Tenses

The simple and perfect tenses that you learned about in Chapters 22 and 23 also have progressive forms to indicate ongoing action. For the simple past, present, and future, **progressive tenses** are formed by adding a form of *to be* to the **present participle** (the *-ing* form) of a verb.

Progressive Tense =	*Form of* to Be +	*Present Participle*	*Example*
Present progressive	am, are, is	going	I *am going.*
Past progressive	was, were	going	I *was going.*
Future progressive	will be	going	I *will be going.*

➤ The *present progressive tense* indicates something that is currently ongoing. (I *am taking* piano lessons.)
➤ The *past progressive tense* indicates something that was ongoing in the past. (She *was serving* an internship while she attended the university.)

➤ The *future progressive tense* indicates something that will be ongoing in the future. (They *will be showing* slides continuously throughout the open house.)

The Perfect Progressive Tenses

You form the **perfect progressive tenses** by using the *-ing* form of a verb with *have been, has been, had been,* or *will have been.*

Perfect Progressive Tense	=	Helping Verb	+	Present Participle	Example
Present perfect progressive		has been, have been		studying	She *has been studying.*
Past perfect progressive		had been		studying	She *had been studying.*
Future perfect progressive		will have been		studying	She *will have been studying.*

➤ The *present perfect progressive tense* indicates an action that began in the past but that is still ongoing. (Our membership *has been growing* steadily for five years.)

➤ The *past perfect progressive tense* indicates an action that had been happening in the past but that stopped before the present. (Until 1996, our membership *had been growing.*)

➤ The *future perfect progressive tense* indicates an action that will be on-going in the future but that will end before something else begins. (By 2001, our membership *will have been growing* for six straight years.)

Remember—all of these tenses allow you to express actions in time with great precision. It is much more important to learn how to use them than it is to be able to name them or even identify them. When you do the Exploration and Challenge exercises below, refer back to this section if you get confused about the correct tense.

Exploration 2a   Recognizing the Progressive Tenses

In the sentences below, circle the progressive and perfect progressive tense verbs. Then, in the space above the line, label those verbs as either progressive *(P)*, perfect progressive *(PP)*, or future progressive *(FP)*. Study the example first.

Example   Lately, I have been spending all of my spare time surfing the

Internet.

(1) I am becoming a cyberfreak. (2) Last week, my family bought a computer with a modem, and I have been doing some very foolish things with this

new equipment. (3) I discovered a chat room for chihuahua owners, so I am wasting a lot of time in foolish conversation about my pet. (4) In addition, my daughter and I have been visiting a new sitcom homepage almost every night. (5) I am thinking that, if I don't set limits for myself, soon I will be struggling to keep the rest of my life in balance.

Exploration 2b   Using the Progressive Tenses

For each sentence below, change the present tense verb in parentheses to a progressive tense verb by adding a helping verb (a form of *to be*) to the present participle. Write the correct verb form in the blank space. Study the example first.

> **Example**   My sister (watches) _____*is watching*_____ *Nightline* now.

(1) Right now I (learns) _____ to use a new word processing program. (2) With the help of this new software program, I (discovers) _____ my mistakes before I hand in a paper. (3) As a result, I find I (earns) _____ better grades. (4) I also (enjoys) _____ my work more. (5) In the future, I (recommends) _____ this program to my friends.

Exploration 2c   Using the Perfect Progressive Tense

Choose at least five verbs from the following list. Then, on a separate sheet of paper, write a paragraph in which you use perfect progressive tense forms (a form of *to have* plus the present participle) of the verbs you have selected. Study the example first.

to ask	to answer
to complain	to reassure
to think	to observe
to speak	to laugh
to look	to find

> **Example**   to think
>
> *I had been thinking about dropping out before I spoke to Dennis.*

Challenge 2   Working with Verb Tenses in Your Writing

1. Choose two verbs from the list of irregular verbs on pages 321–324 and two regular verbs. Write three sentences for each, using verbs in the progressive and perfect progressive tenses.

2. Exchange your writing with a partner. On the paper you receive, underline the verbs and label them either progressive *(P)* or perfect progressive *(PP)*. Then return the sentences to the writer.

➤ M AINTAINING CONSISTENCY IN TENSE

ESL Note
See "Agreement"
on pages 526–529.

In addition to choosing the correct tense for your sentence context, you must also use that tense *consistently.* To maintain **consistency in tense,** use a logical pattern for your verb choices, and avoid switching carelessly from one tense to another. Actions or situations occurring now call for the present tense. If they happened earlier, the past tense is needed, and if they have not yet happened, then the future tense is called for.

It's important to use a consistent time frame within a paragraph and especially within a sentence. To write about past events, use the past tense; don't switch, without good reason, to the present or the future. Use present tense verbs to write about events occurring now.

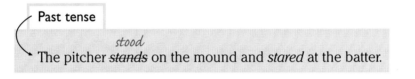

Past tense

stood
The pitcher *stands* on the mound and *stared* at the batter.

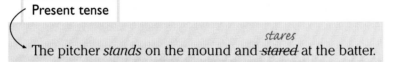

Present tense

stares
The pitcher *stands* on the mound and ~~stared~~ at the batter.

The tense you choose will depend upon the context of your writing. You must make the choice that is most logical to help readers understand the thoughts or events you are writing about.

Exploration 3a   Practice Maintaining Consistency in Tense

Fill in the blanks in the following sentences with the correct form of the verb in parentheses to maintain consistency in verb tense. Study the example first.

Example   Once the police arrived, a crowd (to start) ____*started*____

to gather.

(1) When I first started doing my work in college, the main thing that (to hold) _____ me back was my lack of self-esteem. (2) When it came to studying, I was so sure I couldn't do the work that I (to do) _____ not even bother. (3) For the first few weeks, I (to fail) _____ every quiz and examination I took. (4) As a result, I (to become) _____ more convinced that I had no ability. (5) My lack of confidence (to begin) _____ to influence other aspects of my life. (6) I (to think) _____ that nobody liked me. (7) Of course, because I didn't bother with anybody, nobody (to bother) _____ with me either, so I became more convinced that I had no worth. (8) I was just about ready to drop out when my business instructor (to talk) _____ to me and said that I could do the work. (9) Her words (to shock) _____me. (10) I (to decide) _____ that if she thought I could do it, I would give college one more try.

Exploration 3b Additional Practice Maintaining Consistency in Tense

Several sentences in the following passage suffer from inconsistency in verb tense. Cross out each error, and write the correct verb form above it. Study the example first.

> *Example* As I walked along Main Street, suddenly I ~~see~~ *saw* my friend Kelly
>
> with somebody I didn't recognize.

(1) One of the most unusual places that I've seen is Clarkin Caverns. (2) Even though we go there almost nine years ago, I still remember what a strange and wonderful place it is. (3) The last time I am there, I first have to go into a small ticket center. (4) Once there were enough people to make up a group, a guide walks us to an extra large elevator, which quickly lowers us about sixty feet beneath the surface of the earth. (5) When I stepped out of the

elevator, I am amazed at what I saw. (6) All around me were beautiful rock for-

mations, and as the group walks around, the guide talked about the cavern.

(7) She explains the differences between *stalactites,* which "grow" down from

the roof of the cavern, and *stalagmites,* which "grow" up from the ground.

(8) As we walked, I keep looking all around, because I was afraid a bat was

going to fly down and get caught in my hair. (9) At the end of the tour, our

guide puts out the lights for a minute so we can experience total darkness.

(10) It is so dark that I can't even see my hands in front of me; never had a

place felt peaceful and spooky at the same time.

Exploration 3c   Evaluating Tenses for Effectiveness

In each sentence below, fill in the blanks with a form of the verb in parentheses, using a consistent tense. Then, on a separate sheet of paper, copy the paragraph over, using verbs in a different tense to fill in the blanks. Reread both
versions, and write a brief paragraph in which you explain which tense you feel
is most effective and why. Study the example first.

Example   The young boy (to kick) _____*kicked*_____ an empty can into

the vacant lot.

or

The young boy (to kick) _____*kicks*_____ an empty can into

the vacant lot.

(1) My car (to be) _____ such a piece of junk. (2) Every time

I (to drive) _____ it for more than twenty minutes, it

(to stall) _____ . (3) When I (to stop) _____ at a

stop sign or traffic light, I always (to feel) _____ the telltale shak-

ing. (4) Then the red lights on the dashboard (to come) _____

on. (5) It (to do) _____ not always start up again right away,

either.

Challenge 3   Analyzing the Effect of Inconsistent Tense

Reread the paragraph in Exploration 3b in its original (uncorrected) form. Then, working with a partner, write a brief paragraph in which you explain what effect inconsistent verb tense has on the reader's ability to understand the point of the writing.

DISCOVERING CONNECTIONS B

1. In Discovering Connections A on page 337, you prewrote on one of three suggested subjects. Now, using this prewriting material as the foundation, work your way through the rest of the writing process, and complete a draft essay of about 500 words on this topic.
2. Exchange your draft with a partner. Using the material in this chapter to guide you, check the draft you receive for any errors in voice, progressive tenses, or consistency in tense. Underline any errors, and then return the draft to the writer.
3. Revise your essay, correcting any errors identified by your reader.

SUMMARY EXERCISE

The following passage contains a number of the errors in verb use outlined in this chapter. Using the various examples throughout the chapter to guide you, identify errors in voice, tense, and consistency. Cross out the incorrect form, and write the correct form above it. In some cases, more than one correct answer is possible.

(1) I often wish I spend more time reading as a child. (2) If more reading has been done by me, I wouldn't feel so embarrassed and frustrated now every time I sat down to read.

(3) When I start elementary school, I missed almost half of first grade because of illness. (4) While all my classmates are learning the basics of reading, I was at home in bed. (5) In spite of this, at the end of the year, I am promoted anyway, and my difficulties began.

(6) I never misbehaved in class, so breaks were always given to me by my teachers. (7) When I read aloud, if I hesitate over a word, my teacher would say it for me. (8) As a result, I become very good at pretending to be able to read.

(9) Although I was fall further behind each year, I keep getting promoted. (10) When courses were failed by me, I went to summer school. (11) Even though I attended summer classes, I am still not learning anything.

(12) In my senior year of high school, I have earned straight D's for the first term, except for English, which I will be failing. (13) Because she is concerned about me, my English teacher arranged for me to take a reading test. (14) When the test was finished by me, I discovered that I am not even reading on the sixth grade level. (15) My teacher gets me a special reading tutor, and after working hard the rest of the year, I am able to read well enough to graduate with my class.

(16) However, when I am thinking about college, all my shame and frustration returned. (17) I failed the college's reading placement test, and a remedial reading course had to be taken by me. (18) I will be determined not to lose this chance to make something of myself, so I work as hard as I could.

(19) I'm proud to say that by the end of that course, I am reading better than any of the other students in the class. (20) However, I still felt insecure about my ability, and I was planning to keep working to change my attitude.

RECAP
PASSIVE VOICE, ADDITIONAL TENSES, AND MAINTAINING CONSISTENCY IN TENSE

New terms in this chapter	Definitions
➤ passive voice	➤ a characteristic of sentences in which the subject receives the action of the verb *Example* Her bicycle was stolen.

New terms in this chapter	Definitions
➤ **active voice**	➤ a characteristic of sentences in which the subject does or is responsible for the action *Example* A photographer took a picture of the scene.
➤ **progressive tenses**	➤ forms of a verb created by combining some form of *to be* with the present participle of another verb ➤ Progressive forms express ongoing actions or situations. *Example* Eddie and Karen *are talking* about buying a house. *Example* Louis *was reading* in the library. *Example* Laura *will be wallpapering* her room soon.
➤ **present participle**	➤ formed by adding *-ing* to the basic form of regular and irregular verbs *Examples* play*ing*; ris*ing*
➤ **perfect progressive tenses**	➤ forms of a verb created by combining some form of *to have* with the present participle of another verb ➤ Perfect progressive forms express actions or situations that occur over a period of time. *Example* Eddie and Karen *have been talking* about buying a house. *Example* Louis *had been reading* in the library. *Example* By 8 P.M., Laura *will have been wallpapering* her room for five hours.
➤ **consistency in tense**	➤ refers to a logical pattern for the verbs within a sentence, paragraph, or essay ➤ Consistency requires avoiding careless mixing of verb tenses and maintaining a unified time frame within a piece of writing. *Inconsistent* I *answer* all the questions that were asked. *Consistent* I *answered* all the questions that were asked.

Continued

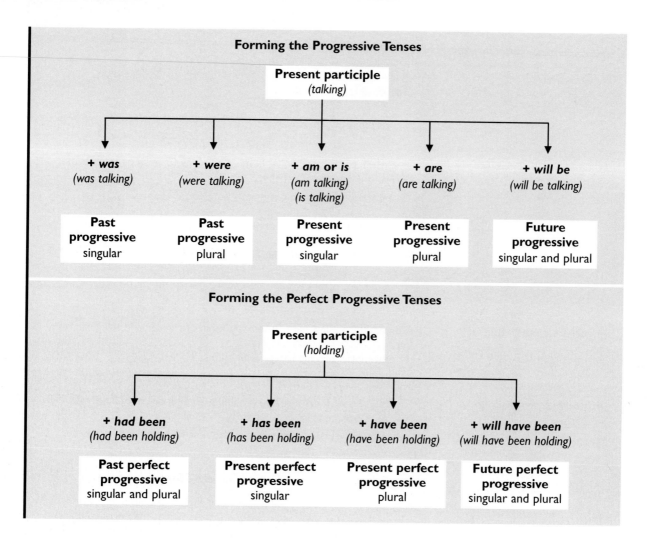

Keeping Your Writing Correct

25	Nouns and Pronouns
26	Adjectives, Adverbs, and Other Modifiers
27	Ensuring Pronoun–Antecedent Agreement
28	Maintaining Parallelism
29	Spelling
30	Commas
31	Other Punctuation and Capitalization

25

Nouns and Pronouns

OVERVIEW: UNDERSTANDING WORDS THAT NAME

Among the words you use most often as a writer are nouns and pronouns. **Nouns** are words that name people, places, things, and ideas, and **pronouns** are the words that we use as substitutes for these nouns. Because nouns and pronouns are so essential, it's important to master several aspects of their use.

In this chapter, you will learn how to

➤ turn a singular noun into a plural one
➤ use collective nouns effectively
➤ choose the right case, or form, of a pronoun
➤ use indefinite pronouns correctly

DISCOVERING CONNECTIONS A

Using one of the techniques you practiced in Chapter 2, prewrite on one of the following topics: greeting cards, reunions, tradition. Save your work for later use.

MAKING SINGULAR NOUNS PLURAL

A singular noun names one person, place, or thing; a plural noun names two or more. To change most nouns from singular to plural, simply add -s:

Singular	Plural
cup	cups
decision	decisions
flower	flowers

Some nouns form their plurals in other ways. For example, most words that end in -ch, -sh, -x, and -s form their plurals by adding -es:

Singular	Plural
brush	brushes
mix	mixes
pass	passes
watch	watches

For words that end in a -y preceded by a consonant, form the plural by changing the -y to -i and adding -es:

Singular	Plural
candy	candies
enemy	enemies
eulogy	eulogies
mystery	mysteries

Certain words that end in -f or -fe form their plurals by changing the ending to -ves:

Singular	Plural
half	halves
leaf	leaves
shelf	shelves
wife	wives

Combined or *hyphenated* words form their plurals by adding -s to the main word:

Singular	Plural
attorney-at-law	attorneys-at-law
brother-in-law	brothers-in-law
maid of honor	maids of honor
runner-up	runners-up

Some common words form their plurals by *changing letters within the word*:

Singular	*Plural*
foot	**fee**t
man	m**e**n
mouse	m**ice**
tooth	t**ee**th

Some words have the same singular and plural forms:

Singular	*Plural*
deer	**deer**
rice	**rice**
sheep	**sheep**
species	**species**

In addition, some words that end in *-o* form their plural by adding *-s*: *sopranos* and *pros.* Other words that end in *-o* form their plural by adding *-es*: *tomatoes* and *heroes.* Some words from foreign languages form their plurals in keeping with their original language: *analysis/analyses* and *crisis/crises.*

If you have a question about the plural form of a noun, a dictionary should be your first stop. It gives the plural ending after the singular form if the noun forms its plural in an irregular way.

Exploration 1a   Making Nouns Plural

In the paragraph below, change the italicized singular nouns to their plural forms. Cross out each singular noun, and write the plural noun above it. Review the rules above, and study the example first.

> **Example**   As we drove through the city, we saw the ~~church~~ *churches* and the ~~museum~~ *museums*.

(1) The bus tour I took last spring introduced me to Midwestern architecture, from *skyscraper* and *cathedral* to *university* and *barn.* (2) After *year* of reading *magazine* and *book* about architecture, I finally decided to take a first-hand look at some *treasure* of Americana. (3) Our group, which filled two *bus,* was a chatty, friendly group of *individual* from a variety of *country.* (4) Our first stop was Chicago, where we toured famous *building*: the Sears Tower, the Hancock Observatory, and Water Tower Place. (5) The view from the Observatory was breathtaking: sparkling *roof,* swimming *pool* like gems atop *skyscraper,* bustling *street,* and a vast expanse of Lake Michigan spread out before us.

(6) After several brief walking *tour* in the city, we were off for the country, munching *sandwich* and swapping *story* about the history we had learned. (7) Our *guide* pointed out interesting *style* of *barn* and *silo* and explained the *influence* that produced them as we glided past big, prosperous *farm*. (8) In *community* along the Mississippi River, quaint little *church* and *house* on *stilt* enchanted us. (9) We even toured several Victorian *mansion* and the *home* of two former U.S. *president*. (10) Inspired by my adventure, I am preparing slide *show* and *article* about the *structure* I saw and the *theory* and *history* behind them.

Challenge I   Evaluating the Correctness of Plural Forms

Choose three paragraphs from one of the reading selections in Part Seven. On a separate sheet of paper, list all the singular nouns you find, and then write the plural forms next to them. Use the guidelines on pages 351–352 or a dictionary if you need help. Exchange your list with a partner, and correct each other's work.

WORKING WITH COLLECTIVE NOUNS AND CUE WORDS

ESL Note
See "Articles" on
pages 532–533.

Collective nouns are words that stand for *groups* of items or individuals. Here is a list of common collective nouns:

Common Collective Nouns

audience	faculty	group	populace
class	family	herd	school
committee	flock	jury	team
congregation	government	office	tribe

Even though they represent a number of people or things, collective nouns are singular in form. In most cases, a collective noun used as a subject requires a singular form of the verb, as the following sentences illustrate:

Example
The *jury wants* to see a copy of the trial transcript.

Example
The *faculty looks* forward to meeting the incoming students.

You should also become familiar with the following words. When they precede the subject, they alert you that it is singular and therefore calls for a singular verb.

■ *Common Singular Cue Words*

a, an	every
another	neither
each	one
either	

Example

Every student *needs* a notebook to use as a journal.

Example

Either book *is* a good choice as a gift.

Also be aware of the following words. When they precede the subject, they cue you that it is plural and therefore calls for a plural verb.

■ *Common Plural Cue Words*

all	many
both	several
few	some

Example

Many children *are* actually afraid of clowns.

Example

Several stray cats *live* in my neighborhood.

Exploration 2a Working with Collective Nouns and Cue Words

Underline the collective noun or cue word in each sentence below. Decide whether the subject is singular or plural. Then circle the correct verb. Study the example first.

Example   Each class (has, have) its unique demands on my time and

energy.

(1) A group that (seems, seem) to be diminishing day by day is people

who read newspapers. (2) From all appearances, the average family today (is, are) far less interested in print journalism than the family of thirty years ago. (3) As a result, the audience that a reporter reaches with a story today (has, have) lessened—in some cases by more than 25 percent. (4) The jury (is, are) still out as to why readership has dropped off so drastically. (5) Several recent studies (has, have) indicated that people prefer to get their news from television. (6) Some critics (maintains, maintain) that newspapers' continuing emphasis on sensationalism has turned many people away. (7) The government (has, have) recently funded a major study, but the results won't be available for several months. (8) Meanwhile, a blue ribbon committee of editors and publishers (has, have) decided to conduct a separate study. (9) At this point, each member of the committee (feels, feel) that if action isn't taken, the number of newspapers published will continue to plummet. (10) One concern shared by both the industry and the government (is, are) the indication that the populace overall (is, are) reading less than it did a decade ago.

Exploration 2b   Using Collective Nouns and Verbs Correctly

Complete the following sentences by adding a present tense verb with modifiers. Underline the collective noun or cue word in the first part of the sentence to help you choose the correct present tense verb. Study the example first.

Example   The <u>herd</u> of cows ___*heads for the barn like clockwork at 5 P.M.*___

1. Every time we try to eat outdoors, a swarm of wasps _____

   _____

2. Each month, the congregation at that church _____

   _____

3. Few chairs in the waiting room _____

   _____

4. Neither winner of the tri-state lottery _____

_____

5. Many students enrolled in this college _____

_____

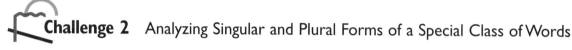

Challenge 2   Analyzing Singular and Plural Forms of a Special Class of Words

Working with a partner, for each of the words below, write a sentence on a separate sheet of paper.

mumps	mathematics	statistics
economics	three centimeters	news
ethics	physics	politics

What did you notice about each of these nouns' singular and plural forms? Write a guideline for maintaining subject–verb agreement for this category of nouns.

➤ **U**NDERSTANDING PRONOUN CASE

Among the pronouns that you use most often as a writer are the **personal pronouns,** which point out *particular* people, places, things, and ideas. As the table shows, personal pronouns have three separate forms, or *cases: subjective, objective,* and *possessive.*

Personal Pronouns			
	Subjective	*Objective*	*Possessive*
First person	I, we	me, us	my, mine, our, ours
Second person	you	you	your, yours
Third person	she, he, it, they	her, him, it, them	her, hers, his, its, their, theirs

Use the *subjective* case pronouns as *subjects* of sentences.

Example
➤ *We* were stuck in traffic for over an hour.

Example
➤ *They* sat in front of the fireplace.

Use the objective case pronouns as *objects;* objects receive the action of the verb (as *direct objects*) or are governed by a preposition (as *objects of prepositions*). See pages 240–241 for a discussion of prepositional phrases.

Example

`direct object`

In the final inning, the pitcher threw four straight *balls.*

Example

`preposition` `object of the preposition`

All the trees *around them* looked the same to the lost children.

Use possessive pronouns to show ownership.

Example

Your class has been canceled for today.

Example

Her friends were planning a surprise birthday party.

Exploration 3a Identifying Pronoun Case

In the following paragraph, underline all personal pronouns. Write an *S* above subjective pronouns, an *O* above objective pronouns, and a *P* above possessive pronouns. Use the table of personal pronouns on page 356 for reference. Study the example first.

>   S   O   S   P
> *Example* I wanted to show him how important he was in my life.

(1) Every Monday when we were in elementary school, my sister and I used to take our library cards and go to the municipal library. (2) It was about two miles from our apartment, so we would take the bus downtown. (3) To us, riding the bus was an adventure, and we were always a little nervous until the driver gave us back our bus passes with the new holes punched in them. (4) When we finally reached the library, she and I would look through a number of books to see which of them we wanted to check out. (5) It was a challenge to see who could find books that would impress the head librarian more. (6) As we were leaving, he would always say, in his formal, bass tone, "Be

careful going home, girls, and take care of the books because they belong to all of us."

Exploration 3b   Using Personal Pronouns and Identifying Pronoun Case

Fill in each blank in the following paragraph with an appropriate personal pronoun. Then label the pronoun you have supplied with an *S* for subjective, an *O* for objective, or a *P* for possessive case. Study the example first.

> *P*
> **Example**   Children need to learn a great deal more about ____our____ world than children did twenty-five years ago.

(1) After a decline in _____ numbers stemming back thirty years or more, bald eagles are making a major comeback throughout North America. (2) During the 1960s, _____ were affected by both industrial pollution and toxic pesticides like DDT. (3) At that time, _____ didn't have a full understanding of the effect of these compounds on the environment. (4) However, as we later learned, these poisons worked _____ way through the food chain, becoming more concentrated in each species. (5) Eagles were especially hard hit; the concentrated chemicals made it impossible for _____ to produce the calcium needed for eggshells. (6) In essence, _____ industrial society was making reproduction impossible for eagles. (7) In the 1970s, _____ government acted to preserve the bald eagle by declaring _____ an endangered species and banning DDT. (8) _____ decisions proved to be the correct ones. (9) Across the United States today, the number of nesting pairs of bald eagles is somewhere between 4,000 and 5,000, and _____ species designation has been changed from endangered to threatened. (10) Now it appears that _____ won't bear responsibility for the extinction of one of nature's most majestic creatures.

Challenge 3 Analyzing Your Use of Personal Pronouns

Take a look at some paragraphs that you have written for other assignments. Find and copy several sentences in which you have used personal pronouns. Make sure your sentences include at least one subjective pronoun, one objective pronoun, and one possessive pronoun. If necessary, write new sentences. Save these sentences for Challenge 4.

USING PERSONAL PRONOUNS CORRECTLY

You need to keep a few points in mind when using personal pronouns.

➤ *An objective pronoun can never serve as a subject.*

The exceptions are *you* and *it*, which can serve as either subjects or objects. *Her, him, me, us,* and *them* are never subjects. Be careful when you are writing sentences with compound subjects linked by *and* or *or*. Make sure that each word in the compound subject could be used alone with the verb in the sentence.

> **Example**
>
> *she*
> *Muriel, Billy, and ~~her~~ are taking a drawing course together.*

> **Example**
>
> *I*
> *Either the hostess or ~~me~~ will seat the guests at the reception.*

➤ *A subjective pronoun can never serve as an object.*

Errors in the use of objective case also tend to occur in compound objects. Again, try using each element in the compound object alone to see if it can serve as an object.

> **Example**
>
> *him.*
> The boss had to make a choice between *Joe and ~~he~~.*

> **Example**
>
> My mother could not remember whether Grandpa taught *my uncle or*
> *her*
> ~~she~~ to drive first.

Finally, do not confuse the possessive pronoun *its* with the contraction for *it is* (*it's*). *Its* needs no apostrophe because the word is already possessive. To avoid this error, try inserting *it is* whenever you want to use *its*. If *it is* fits, use *it is* or the contraction *it's*. If *it is* doesn't fit, use the possessive form, *its*.

> **Example**
>
> *It's*
> ~~Its~~ too late to go to the movies now.

> **Example**
>
> *its*
> The owl flew to ~~it's~~ nest.

Exploration 4a   Avoiding Usage Errors with Personal Pronouns

Circle the correct pronoun from the choices in parentheses in each of the sentences below. Use the discussion about personal pronouns above to guide you. Remember—objective pronouns can't serve as subjects, subjective pronouns can't serve as objects, and the possessive pronoun *its* does not have an apostrophe. Study the example first.

Example   Maureen, Kaisa, and (Ⓘ, me) study in the library every

Wednesday morning.

(1) Most people who meet us think that Donna and (I, me) are not well suited to be best friends. (2) (Its, It's) true that we are very different, but I think our friendship derives (its, it's) strength from our differences. (3) Neither of (we, us) is bothered by the other person's likes or dislikes. (4) Sometimes we do the kinds of things that appeal to (she, her), such as riding around or going out to a club. (5) Other times we do the kinds of things that (I, me) enjoy, such as going to a movie or shopping at the mall.

Exploration 4b   More Practice Avoiding Usage Errors with Personal Pronouns

Each sentence in the following paragraph contains an error in personal pronoun use. Cross out the incorrect pronoun, and write the correct form above it. Study the example first.

she
Example   Traci and ~~her~~ were able to settle their differences.

(1) Between you and I, computer dating services are not the best way to meet other single people. (2) My friend Brendan said that his cousins Greg and Mike and him all tried different services and were all disappointed. (3) For one thing, them had to pay $50 just to register for the services. (4) In addition, Greg explained that the questionnaire he filled out was too general to give an accurate picture of he. (5) Also, the dating services didn't provide he and Mike enough information about prospective dates. (6) For they, the dates they went on felt more like blind dates than arranged meetings between compatible people. (7) Brendan agreed, because the woman that the dating consultant and him picked wasn't his type. (8) On the night of their date, it was obvious right away that him and his date had nothing in common. (9) After about an hour, the woman asked Brendan to take she home. (10) Before he dropped her off, however, her and him agreed that computer dating services are not for them.

Challenge 4 Evaluating Pronoun Usage and Correcting Errors in Your Writing

Exchange the sentences you copied for Challenge 3 (page 359) with a partner, and check for any pronoun errors. When you get your sentences back, revise any of them in which your reader found an error.

▶ *U*SING INDEFINITE PRONOUNS

Indefinite pronouns refer to someone or something general. For instance, the pronoun *somebody* could refer to one of any number of people, and the indefinite pronoun *anything* could refer to one of any number of items or events. The following indefinite pronouns are always singular:

▪ *Singular Indefinite Pronouns*

another	each	everything	nobody	other
anybody	either	little	no one	somebody
anyone	everybody	much	nothing	someone
anything	everyone	neither	one	something

Singular indefinite pronouns call for singular verbs. In addition, they must be referred to by singular pronouns (*he, him, his, she, her, hers, it, its*).

> **Example**
>
> *Everyone* standing in line to pay a fine *looks* unhappy.

> **Example**
>
> *Anyone* who wants to compete in the drama festival must memorize *his or her* lines by Friday.

The following indefinite pronouns are always plural:

Plural Indefinite Pronouns

both	others
few	several
many	

> **Example**
>
> *Several* of the students *have* started up a rowing club.

> **Example**
>
> The officials gave high scores to *both* dancers for *their* originality.

Some indefinite pronouns are either singular or plural, depending on the word to which they refer:

Indefinite Pronouns Affected by the Words That Follow Them

all	more	none
any	most	some

When you encounter one of these pronouns, check the word to which it refers. If that word is singular, choose a singular form of the verb, and if it is plural, choose a plural form of the verb.

> **Example**
>
> `plural antecedent` `plural verb`
>
> *Some* of the *shirts* on sale *were* seconds.

> **Example**
>
> `singular antecedent` `singular verb`
>
> *All* of the *soil* at that construction site *is* contaminated with chemicals.

Exploration 5a   Using Indefinite Pronouns and Verbs Correctly

Underline the indefinite pronouns in the sentences below. Underline each pronoun and label it as *singular* or *plural*. Circle the correct verb in parentheses. Refer to the material about indefinite pronouns on pages 361–362 if you need help. Study the example first.

> *singular*
> **Example**   <u>Everyone</u> enrolled in the liberal arts curriculum (**is**, are)
>
> expected to take at least one course in mathematics.

(1) For the last few weeks, something (has, have) been troubling my grandmother. (2) Both of my parents (feels, feel) that I am overreacting, but I'm sure that my grandmother is upset about something. (3) I'll admit that some of her behavior (is, are) just as it has always been. (4) For instance, everybody who has ever visited her (has, have) remarked that she seemed quiet and shy. (5) Lately, however, everyone (has, have) noticed that she smiles a lot less, so I guess I'll just ask her what's wrong.

Exploration 5b   Selecting Indefinite Pronouns for Correct Agreement

In each of the following sentences, underline the verb that must match the missing word. Then fill in the blank in each sentence with an appropriate indefinite pronoun from the list below. You may use the same pronoun more than once. Study the example first.

few	everyone	some
somebody	all	many
nobody	no one	none

> **Example**   _____*Many*_____ of the delegates <u>have</u> never before <u>attended</u> a
>
> political convention.

(1) _____ hopes that he or she will do the right thing when faced with a crisis. (2) For example, _____ of us like to believe we would rush into a burning building to save the people inside. (3) _____ wants to think she or he would stand there,

paralyzed with fear. (4) But the truth is that _____ knows

for certain how he or she would react. (5) It is true that, faced with such a sit-

uation, _____ are able to run right through the flames.

(6) Not _____ is able to play the role of a hero, however.

(7) _____ of us experience a kind of paralysis in crisis sit-

uations. (8) A _____ even become sick or pass out.

(9) Faced with the same crisis, _____ of us is likely to react

in exactly the same way. (10) Even _____ who is a leader

in everyday situations may not be able to take charge in a crisis.

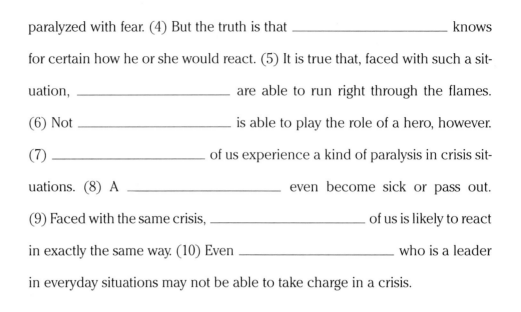

DISCOVERING CONNECTIONS **B**

1. In Discovering Connections A on page 350, you prewrote on one of three suggested topics. Working from this prewriting material, work through the rest of the steps in the writing process, and complete a draft essay of about 500 words on your topic.
2. Exchange your draft with a partner. Using the material in this chapter to guide you, check the draft you receive for any errors in the use of nouns or pronouns. After checking the paper, return it to the writer.
3. Revise your essay, correcting any errors your reader has identified in the use of nouns or pronouns.

➤ **S**UMMARY EXERCISE

The following sentences contain errors in the use of nouns and pronouns, in-cluding lack of subject–verb agreement. Correct the errors by crossing out the incorrect word and writing the correct word above it. Check the spelling of plural nouns. Make sure subject nouns or pronouns agree with their verbs. Finally, make sure the pronoun case is correct.

(1) Because of advances in technology, some educators feels that cursive

writing is fast becoming a thing of the past. (2) At one time, good penmanship was considered one of the most important signes of professionalism. (3) Even today, many still views handwriting as a measure of individuality and maturity. (4) Now, because so many people is using computers for writing, the art of handwriting is losing it's status.

(5) At one time, every student were taught handwriting as a separate subject in school. (6) In many cases, the handwriting teacher was chosen because him or her writing was considered excellent. (7) Students learned cursive by first practicing different strokes and ovales that they copied from handwriting books. (8) Once the students had mastered the various shapes, the teacher and them would begin work on actual letters and numbers, with particular emphasis on precision and accuracy.

(9) In many schools today, however, nobody seem concerned about handwriting instruction. (10) According to a recent article, typical elementary classies spend very little time on handwriting. (11) Apparently, the various other educational crisies that must be handled in the classroom take priority over handwriting.

(12) Not everyone are concerned about this apparent change in attitude toward cursive writing. (13) In fact, many sees this change as a part of the natural transition to the electronic age. (14) In some elementary schools today, as soon as children learn the alphabet, a team of teachers show them how to use a word processor. (15) They quickly learn to write all their storys electronically, using a keyboard. (16) Some proponents of the change say that the only scenarioes that will call for handwriting in the future will be taking notes in class, completing written tests, or writing signatures.

(17) Everybody recognize that the world is a different place than it was 100 years ago. (18) No one seriously expect handwriting to disappear completely. (19) But it does seem clear that it's importance will continue to diminish.

RECAP
NOUNS AND PRONOUNS

New terms in this chapter	Definitions
➤ **noun**	➤ a word that names a person, place, thing, or idea ➤ Form plural nouns by adding -s or following spelling guidelines.
➤ **pronoun**	➤ a word used in place of a noun named earlier *Example* Georgie picked up a *rock* and threw *it* at the abandoned house.
➤ **collective noun**	➤ a noun that stands for a group of items or individuals ➤ Collective nouns are singular in form, and generally call for the singular form of the verb. *Example* The *team is* about to win the tournament.
➤ **personal pronoun**	➤ a pronoun that specifies a particular person, place, thing, or idea ➤ Personal pronouns have three separate forms, or cases, to show person.

Personal Pronouns

	Subjective	Objective	Possessive
First person	I, we	me, us	my, mine, our, ours
Second person	you	you	your, yours
Third person	she, he, it, they	her, him, it, them	her, hers, his, its, their, theirs

➤ **indefinite pronoun**	➤ a pronoun used to refer to someone or something in general

Singular Indefinite Pronouns

another	each	everything	nobody	other
anybody	either	little	no one	somebody
anyone	everybody	much	nothing	someone
anything	everyone	neither	one	something

Plural Indefinite Pronouns

both	others
few	several
many	

Indefinite Pronouns Affected by the Words That Follow Them

all	more	none
any	most	some

Adjectives, Adverbs, and Other Modifiers

OVERVIEW: UNDERSTANDING THE ROLES OF ADJECTIVES AND ADVERBS

Adjectives and adverbs are words or groups of words that describe or limit other words in a sentence. Writers use them to make their writing precise and colorful. **Adjectives** describe nouns or pronouns, and **adverbs** describe verbs, adjectives, and other adverbs. Adjectives and adverbs are also useful for making comparisons and expressing negation.

In this chapter, you will learn to

➤ use the positive, comparative, and superlative forms for adjectives and adverbs correctly

➤ distinguish between commonly confused adjectives and adverbs

➤ avoid dangling and misplaced modifiers

➤ avoid double negatives

DISCOVERING CONNECTIONS A

Using one of the techniques you practiced in Chapter 2, prewrite on one of the following topics: the Internet, welfare reform, nostalgia. Save your work for later use.

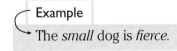NDERSTANDING ADJECTIVES AND ADVERBS

Adjectives and adverbs have three forms: positive, comparative, and superlative. The **positive form** of an adjective describes a noun or pronoun without making a comparison. It tells the reader *how many, what kind,* or *which one.*

> **Example**
>
> The *small* dog is *fierce.*

In this sentence, the adjective *small* tells *which dog* and the adjective *fierce* describes *what kind* of dog.

The positive form of an adverb describes a verb, an adjective, or another adverb without making a comparison. It tells the reader *how, when,* or *to what extent.*

> **Example**
>
> *Finally,* the child spoke *quietly* to the nurse.

In this sentence, the adverb *finally* tells *when,* and the adverb *quietly* describes *how* the child spoke.

Exploration 1a   Identifying Adjectives and Adverbs

Circle the positive adjectives, and underline the positive adverbs in the sentences below. Study the example first.

> *Example*   On Sundays, I frequently enjoy peaceful outings with my
>
> friends.

(1) Last Sunday, my friends and I went to the park near the river for an old-fashioned picnic. (2) Sunlight sparkled on the calm water, and the wind blew gently across the tall grass. (3) Terry, Shannon, and I first spread old blankets and then unpacked the feast. (4) We greedily devoured tasty chicken, fresh salad, and greasy chips. (5) After we ate, we sat peacefully and listened to our favorite CDs.

CREATING COMPARATIVE AND SUPERLATIVE FORMS OF ADJECTIVES AND ADVERBS

The **comparative form** of an adjective or an adverb is used to compare *two* things.

> Adjective
>
> This new word processing program is *more complex* than the one I used last year.

> Adverb
>
> The nursery school students play *longer* than the first graders.

In the first sentence, the adjective *more complex* compares one computer program with another. In the second sentence, the adverb *longer* compares the extent to which two groups of children play.

The **superlative form** of an adjective or an adverb is used to compare *more than two* things.

> Adjective
>
> This store has the *lowest* prices for name brand clothes as well as household appliances.

> Adverb
>
> Of all the young women in the chorus, Eleanor was the one who danced *most gracefully.*

In the first sentence, the adjective *lowest* compares the prices of many stores. In the second sentence, the adverb *most gracefully* compares the style of many dancers.

For adjectives and adverbs of one syllable, create the comparative by adding *-er,* and create the superlative by adding *-est* to the end of the positive form of the word.

Positive	*Comparative*	*Superlative*
dark	dark**er**	dark**est**
high	high**er**	high**est**
far	far**ther**	far**thest**
hard	hard**er**	hard**est**

For adjectives and adverbs of more than two syllables, place *more* in front of the word for the comparative or *most* in front of the word for the superlative.

Positive	Comparative	Superlative
ridiculous	**more** ridiculous	**most** ridiculous
intelligent	**more** intelligent	**most** intelligent
remarkably	**more** remarkably	**most** remarkably
unfortunately	**more** unfortunately	**most** unfortunately

If the adjective or adverb is *two* syllables, which of these two methods should you use? The answer depends on the word. Some two-syllable words take an *-er* or *-est* ending:

Positive	Comparative	Superlative
early	earli**er**	earli**est**
angry	angri**er**	angri**est**
lazy	lazi**er**	lazi**est**
funny	funni**er**	funni**est**

Other two-syllable words require that you use *more* or *most* before them:

Positive	Comparative	Superlative
private	**more** private	**most** private
slowly	**more** slowly	**most** slowly
careful	**more** careful	**most** careful
safely	**more** safely	**most** safely

To avoid errors, look up two-syllable adjectives or adverbs in the dictionary. In addition to definitions, a dictionary gives the correct spelling for adjectives and adverbs that form their comparative and superlative forms by adding *-er* or *-est*. If no *-er* or *-est* forms are listed, then use *more* and *most*.

Regardless of the number of syllables, never use both *more* and *-er* or *most* and *-est* with the same adjective or adverb. Expressions like *more faster* and *most completest* are always wrong.

Some adjectives and adverbs form their comparative and superlative forms in irregular ways:

Positive	Comparative	Superlative
bad (adjective)	worse	worst
badly (adverb)	worse	worst
good (adjective)	better	best
well (adverb)	better	best
little	less	least
much	more	most

As you can see, two pairs of words on this list share the same comparative and superlative forms. However, these similar words have different functions. *Bad* and *good* are adjectives used to identify *what kind* of people, places, ideas, or things a writer is discussing. *Well* and *badly* are adverbs used to explain *how* something was done.

Exploration 2a   Using Comparative and Superlative Forms Correctly

Each sentence in the following paragraph contains an incorrect positive, comparative, or superlative adjective or adverb. Cross out the incorrect form, and write the correct form above it, as the example shows.

fastest

Example   Secretariat was the ~~most fast~~ racehorse I had ever seen.

(1) My friend Laura wants to be a singer, and she already sings more well than most professionals. (2) She has the most sweet voice I've ever heard. (3) She even does a great job with the national anthem, which most singers claim is the more difficult song around. (4) Her sound is like Whitney Houston's, except Laura's voice is more deep. (5) Laura is so talented that she tried out for a local talent show when she had the flu, had the worse audition of her life, and still won a place in the show. (6) A local agent who manages Laura says that her abilities are improving quicklier than those of his other singers. (7) Even though it's most difficult now than it was ten years ago for an unknown singer to get a record contract, Laura has been sending "demo" tapes all over the country. (8) She figures that at worse, all the record companies will turn her down, and she will have wasted a few dollars. (9) Meanwhile, she is attending college, which has made her parents more happy than they were when she announced that she wanted to be a professional singer. (10) Right now the more frustrating thing of all for Laura is finding time both to study and to rehearse.

➤ WORKING WITH CONFUSING PAIRS OF ADJECTIVES AND ADVERBS

ESL Note
See "Word Order" on pages 524–526.

Some words have both adjective and adverb forms. Choosing the right form can be confusing for writers. The list on page 372 contains the most commonly confused pairs of adjectives and adverbs.

Adjective	Adverb
awful	awfully
bad	badly
good	well
poor	poorly
quick	quickly
quiet	quietly
real	really

Deciding between *good* and *well* and between *bad* and *badly* probably causes the most headaches for writers. *Good* and *bad* describe a person or thing, whereas *well* and *badly* describe how something is done. In other words, you can say that a person is a *good* singer or a *bad* singer, but you must say that this individual sings *well* or sings *badly.*

Consider the following examples:

Example

Kathryn is a *good* chef.

Example

Elie cooks *well.*

In the first sentence, the adjective *good* tells *what kind* of chef Kathryn is. In the second, *well* acts as an adverb, describing *how* Elie cooks.

Exploration 3a Working with Confusing Adjective and Adverb Pairs

In the sentences below, underline the correct adjective or adverb from the choices given in parentheses. Study the example first.

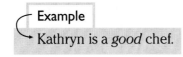

Example   The Bulls played (awful, <u>awfully</u>) last night.

(1) To do my best writing, I need a (quiet, quietly) place. (2) When I'm around other people, I find it (real, really) difficult to concentrate. (3) I've always written (poor, poorly) when I try to do my work with anybody else around. (4) I have found that I write better and more (quick, quickly) when I work in the library. (5) To make sure I write as (good, well) as possible, I carefully plan my time so that I'm able to complete my drafts in the library's computer room.

Exploration 3b Correcting Errors in the Use of Confusing Adjectives and Adverbs

The following sentences contain some errors in the use of adjectives and adverbs. Cross out the incorrect form, and then write the correct one above it. If a sentence is correct as written, write *OK* above it. Study the example first.

Example   The dog ran out from between the two cars so ~~quick~~ *quickly* that the driver couldn't avoid hitting it.

(1) For years, I needed eyeglasses bad, but I didn't know it. (2) In grade school, I performed poor on any test that required me to read the blackboard. (3) At first, my teachers thought I was being lazy and that I could do good if I paid more attention in class. (4) Then my third grade teacher sent me for a vision test, and the doctor said I was awful near-sighted. (5) I was real afraid I'd have to wear glasses like my grandfather's, with ugly frames. (6) As it turned out, my glasses didn't look so badly, and the difference they made in my life was unbelievable. (7) Until I got glasses, I was used to sitting quiet in the back of the room, participating only when forced to. (8) After I got my glasses, all that changed quick. (9) When I could see every word on the board well, all I wanted to do was make up for lost time. (10) Although I still received a few poorly test scores, school became a more happy experience for me.

Challenge 3 Using Confusing Pairs of Adjectives and Adverbs in Your Writing

Write topic sentences for three paragraphs. Include in each sentence an adjective or adverb from the list of confusing pairs on page 372. Then, working with a partner, develop one of the sentences into a paragraph. Include adjectives and adverbs to make your writing colorful and precise.

➤ *A*VOIDING DANGLING AND MISPLACED MODIFIERS

ESL Note
See "Word Order"
on pages 524–526.

As you saw in Chapter 24, the present participle, or *-ing* form of a verb, can be combined with a helping verb to form a verb in the progressive tense. Without a helping verb, this *-ing* form can't act as the verb in a sentence, but it can act as a **modifier** describing another word or phrase, as these examples show:

Example

Yelling angrily, Dion left the room.

Example

The teacher tried to quiet the *laughing* children.

In the first sentence, the *-ing* modifier *Yelling* is describing the proper noun *Dion.* In the second sentence, the *-ing* modifier *laughing* is describing the noun *children.*

Using *-ing* modifiers can help you combine ideas and eliminate choppiness in your writing. Consider these sentences:

Example

The telephone service workers were having coffee in the small restaurant. They were taking a break from work.

Example

The teenaged girl behind the counter polished the glass pastry cabinets. She was whistling softly.

Although the sentences in each example are correct, they are choppy. By changing one of the sentences to a dependent clause beginning with an *-ing* modifier and making a few other changes in wording, you can combine these sentences:

Example

Taking a break from work, the telephone service *workers* were having coffee in the small restaurant.

Example

Whistling softly, the teenaged *girl* behind the counter polished the glass pastry cabinets.

In the first example, the *-ing* modifier and the words that follow it, *Taking a break from work,* now describe *workers.* In the second example, the *-ing* modifier and the words that follow it, *Whistling softly,* now describe *girl.*

When you use an *-ing* modifier, be sure to place it near the word it describes in a sentence. Otherwise, your readers may not understand what word it is describing. Consider these examples:

Faulty

Hanging from the ceiling, Jacob saw the new lamp.

Faulty

Looking for her dress, the cat suddenly jumped onto Janet's back.

The *-ing* modifier in the first sentence is *Looking*. At this point, the sentence indicates that *Janet's cat* was *looking* for a dress. This type of error, which occurs when a modifier has no word that it can logically modify, is called a **dangling modifier.** The *-ing* modifier in the second sentence is *Hanging*. Right now, however, the sentence suggests that it is *Jacob* and not the new lamp that is *hanging* from the ceiling. This type of error, which occurs when a modifier is placed near a word that it does not modify rather than near the word it does, is called a **misplaced modifier.**

Avoiding these types of errors is simple. Always check any sentence in which you have included an *-ing* modifier to make sure the modifier is describing the correct word. If there is an error, you can correct it by putting the *-ing* modifier next to the word it modifies or by changing the wording of the sentence:

> Corrected
>
> *Looking for her dress,* Janet suddenly felt her cat jump onto her back.

or

> Corrected
>
> *As Janet was looking for her dress,* her cat suddenly jumped onto her back.

> Corrected
>
> *Hanging* from the ceiling, the new lamp caught Jacob's eye.

or

> Corrected
>
> Jacob stared at the new lamp *hanging* from the ceiling.

Not all misplaced modifiers involve *-ing* words. Any modifier, whether it is an individual word or a group of words, is a misplaced modifier if it suggests a relationship between words when no such relationship does or could exist. Consider these examples:

> Misplaced
>
> *As a young child,* my great-grandfather often took my sister to the park.

> Misplaced
>
> The new sales representative sold the portable stereo to the woman *with the built-in compact disc player.*

The modifiers in these two sentences are obviously misplaced because the resulting sentences just don't make sense. A person can't be a young child and

a great-grandfather at the same time. And people don't have stereo components in their bodies.

Avoid these kinds of misplaced modifiers by restating parts of the sentence
or rearranging the order of the sentence so that the modifiers are next to the
words they modify, as these corrected versions show:

> **Corrected**
>
> As a young child, my sister often went to the park with my
> great-grandfather.

> **Corrected**
>
> The new sales representative sold the portable stereo with the built-in
> compact disc player to the woman.

Exploration 4a   Identifying -ing Modifiers

Each of the sentences in the following paragraph contains an -ing modifier.
Underline the -ing modifier and the word it is describing. Then draw a line to
connect these two elements. Study the example first.

> *Example*   Staring at the map, Gracie tried to determine where she was.

(1) Entering a convenience store downtown last week, my brother Joe
knew something was wrong. (2) Standing behind the counter, the clerk
seemed very nervous. (3) Looking around the store, Joe noticed a figure at the
back of the store, dressed all in black, with sunglasses and a baseball hat.
(4) Pretending he couldn't find what he needed, Joe left the store, went to a
pay phone, and called the police. (5) Running from the store with a bag of
stolen cash, the man in black ran into two undercover police officers who had
responded to Joe's phone call.

Exploration 4b   More Practice Identifying -ing Modifiers

Each sentence below contains an underlined -ing word that acts either as a
verb or a modifier. Label the word with a *V* or an *M* to indicate its function. For
words labeled *V*, find and underline the helping verb. For words labeled *M*,
find and underline the word being described. Study the examples first.

Example   By the time Henry reached the finish line, he was gasping.

Example   Swirling around the room, the dancer was dressed in red.

1. Laughing uncontrollably, Janine finally had to sit down.

2. A group protesting capital punishment demonstrated outside the prison.

3. The bus is leaving right now.

4. The pipe had been leaking for several weeks before anyone noticed.

5. Staring straight into the camera, the reporter smiled and began her report.

6. Smiling, the President accepted the gift and sat down.

7. The man walking on the treadmill was at least seventy-five years old.

8. Renee was cooking a gourmet dinner.

9. The woman changing the tire was covered with grease.

10. Waving happily, the child stepped out of the bus.

Exploration 4c   Identifying and Correcting Dangling and Misplaced Modifiers

Each of the following sentences contains a dangling or misplaced modifier. First, underline the dangling or misplaced modifier. Then, on a separate piece of paper, restate or rearrange each sentence so that the modifiers are describing the correct words. More than one correct answer is possible. Study the example first.

Example   Flying around the lamp, the child was fascinated by the moth.

Corrected   Flying around the lamp, the moth fascinated the child.
            or
            The child was fascinated by the moth flying around the lamp.

(1) Lying under her refrigerator, Jennifer found a letter that she had dropped the previous day. (2) When she read the letter, she broke into a smile, informing her that she had gotten the summer job she was hoping for. (3) Shaking, the phone seemed to move as she called to accept the job. (4) As a prospective employee, her supervisor, Mr. Tally, told Jennifer about

the various duties involved. (5) Hanging up the phone, her smile of happiness grew even broader.

Challenge 4   Using *-ing* Modifiers to Combine Sentences

Working with a partner, combine the following simple sentences to eliminate choppiness by changing one of the sentences into an *-ing* modifier. All of these modifiers should be phrases rather than single words. Study the example first.

Example   The puppy was waiting for its supper. It was wagging its tail.

Wagging its tail, the puppy was waiting for its supper.

1. Caroline was walking around the park. She was trying to get some exercise.

   _____

   _____

2. Reggie was reading a novel. He was sitting on the couch.

   _____

   _____

3. The strikers were marching in front of the factory. They were carrying signs.

   _____

   _____

4. The truck was fleeing from two police cars. It was traveling the wrong way on the highway.

   _____

   _____

5. The little boy was playing hide and seek. He was hiding from his friends.

   _____

   _____

➤ AVOIDING DOUBLE NEGATIVES

Expressing negation can also cause problems for writers. *No, never, nowhere, nobody, nothing, no one,* and *none* are all used to express the idea of *no.* Adverbs like *scarcely, hardly,* and *barely,* as well as *not,* the adverb used to create *contractions* (such as *did + not = didn't*), also express negation.

When two of these negative words are used in the same sentence, they form what is called a **double negative.** Double negatives are never acceptable in college or professional writing. To avoid double negatives in your writing, check your sentences to make sure you have only one negative in each.

Correcting a double negative is easy: Simply eliminate one of the negative words or change it to a positive form. Note the negatives in the examples below as well as the methods used to correct the errors.

Example

Although my feet are very narrow, I have ~~not~~ had no trouble finding reasonable work shoes.

or

Although my feet are very narrow, I have not had ~~no~~ *any* trouble finding reasonable work shoes.

Example

The firefighters could~~n't~~ do nothing to stop the forest fire.

or

The firefighters couldn't do ~~nothing~~ *anything* to stop the forest fire.

As corrected, each of these sentences expresses the point originally intended, but now each does so with a single negative.

Exploration 5a   Avoiding Double Negatives

In the following paragraph, circle the correct words in parentheses, avoiding double negatives. Use the material above and the example as a guide.

Example   Madeleine and David don't plan to travel ((anywhere,)

nowhere) special this summer.

(1) Even though I don't know (anything, nothing) about professional sports, I enjoy going to see a professional baseball game once in a while. (2) In

fact, I never turn down (any, no) invitation to see the Mud Hens, the minor league team in my city. (3) When my cousin can't get (anybody, nobody) from work to drive her to the park, I drive and she buys me a ticket. (4) The small stadium means you can't find a bad seat (anywhere, nowhere). (5) Unfortunately, it seems as if every time I go to a game, the team doesn't have (any, no) luck and ends up losing.

Exploration 5b   Identifying and Correcting Double Negatives

Some of the sentences in the paragraph below contain double negatives. Put an * in front of any sentence containing a double negative, and then rewrite the sentence on a separate sheet of paper. More than one correct version is possible. Study the example first.

> **Example**   *She wouldn't never leave town without contacting me first.
>
> *She would never leave town without contacting me first.*
> or
> *She wouldn't leave town without contacting me first.*

(1) Bad habits are a plague not only for the offenders but also for the victims of the offending behavior. (2) For instance, many people who swear in public probably don't intend to offend nobody. (3) However, even if these people don't mean nothing by it, their bad habit can frighten, anger, or depress listeners. (4) Another bad habit many people share is not listening fully to those who are talking to them. (5) These offenders engage you in conversation, ask you a question, and then do not pay no attention as you try to answer. (6) There is not hardly anything more frustrating than trying to communicate with someone whose mind has moved on to other things. (7) The worst habit of all is gossiping about others. (8) Gossiping is particularly unfair because the people being discussed are not around to say nothing to defend themselves. (9) They never have no chance to confront the people talking about them. (10) Unfor-

tunately, I am guilty of all these bad habits myself, so I don't have the right to lecture nobody else.

Challenge 5 Building an Argument for Using Standard English

Although some people use double negatives in casual speech, these errors aren't acceptable in college or professional writing. Imagine you have been asked to address a class of sixth graders on the subject of using proper language in writing and speaking. Working with a partner, list on a separate sheet of paper at least four reasons you would give to explain why double negatives and other nonstandard forms (*ain't, we be,* and so on) are unacceptable. Still working together, turn your list into a paragraph that could be handed out to the sixth grade students as a guide.

DISCOVERING CONNECTIONS B

1. In Discovering Connections A on page 367, you completed a prewriting on one of three suggested subjects. Now work your way through the rest of the writing process, using your prewriting material as a basis, and complete a draft essay of about 500 words on this topic.
2. Exchange your draft with a partner. Using the material in this chapter to guide you, check the draft you receive for any errors in the use of adjectives or adverbs. Then return the draft to the writer.
3. Revise your essay, correcting any errors that your reader identified.

SUMMARY EXERCISE

The following passage contains errors involving double negatives, incorrect forms of adjectives and adverbs, and misplaced *-ing* modifiers. Cross out each error, and write the correct form above it. For misplaced modifiers, you may need to insert new words or cross out an entire clause and rewrite it. Also, there may be more than one way to correct the double negatives. If a sentence is correct as written, write *OK* above it.

(1) I didn't never think my life would improve when a 24-hour supermarket opened in my neighborhood, but I was in for a pleasant surprise. (2) I have never been no believer that bigger always means more better. (3) Also, the

idea of grocery shopping at midnight seemed awful strange to me, but I decided to give it a try.

(4) I was real surprised to see how few people had the same idea. (5) When I drove into the parking lot at midnight, I saw a smallest number of cars. (6) When I entered it, I saw that the store itself was the most enormousest I'd seen. (7) Cluttering the aisles, the produce section had a small crowd. (8) They were thumping melons, inspecting heads of lettuce, and picking apples just as they would if the sun were shining its most bright.

(9) I quick discovered the appeal of shopping at night. (10) First of all, there weren't hardly any customers at midnight, so it was more simple to maneuver in the aisles. (11) Also, I didn't have to fight no crowds, so I felt more freer to examine the selection of items at my leisure. (12) In addition, the shelves seemed weller stocked than they are during the day.

(13) The store seemed calmest, too. (14) Speaking more quiet than they do during the day, I found the workers more pleasanter. (15) Even the checkout area was awful still. (16) The most loud sound was the beep of the computer scanners.

(17) Best of all, there wasn't no long wait in line to check out and pay for my groceries. (18) Normally, I am squeezed in between people who apparently don't have no limits on their grocery budgets. (19) Imagine my delight when I found I could check out quick, without the normal ten-minute wait in line. (20) The checkout clerk was more relaxed and carefuller than usual, too.

(21) Leaving the parking lot, this shopping trip was a positive experience. (22) I liked going about my shopping quiet and calm, without being bothered by other shoppers. (23) The only problem was that the next day I was more sleepier than usual.

RECAP

ADJECTIVES, ADVERBS, AND OTHER MODIFIERS

New terms in this chapter	Definitions
➤ **adjective**	➤ a word that describes a noun or pronoun ➤ An adjective answers the question *which one, how many,* or *what kind?*
➤ **adverb**	➤ a word that describes a verb, adjective, or another adverb ➤ An adverb tells *how, when, where, to what extent,* or *how much.*
➤ **positive form**	➤ the form of an adjective or adverb that describes a noun or pronoun without making a comparison *Example* tall, poorly
➤ **comparative form**	➤ the form of an adjective or adverb used to compare two things *Example* **more** handsome, lovel**ier**
➤ **superlative form**	➤ the form of an adjective or adverb used to compare more than two things *Example* **most** remarkably, slow**est**
➤ **modifier**	➤ a word or phrase that functions like an adjective or adverb to describe another word or phrase in a sentence ➤ An *-ing* modifier functions as an adjective in a sentence. *Example* *Singing* sweetly, the nightingale darted from tree to tree. ➤ Use *-ing* modifiers to combine sentences and eliminate choppiness.
➤ **dangling modifier**	➤ a modifier with no word that it can logically modify
➤ **misplaced modifier**	➤ a modifier placed near a word that it does not modify ➤ Place an *-ing* modifier near the word or words it describes in a sentence.
➤ **double negative**	➤ an incorrect construction using two negative words in the same unit of ideas *Example* *Nobody* should bring *nothing* flammable. ➤ Negative words include *no, not, never, nowhere, nobody, nothing, no one, none, scarcely, hardly, barely.*

Continued

Guidelines for Adjective and Adverb Forms

Type of word	Positive	Comparative	Superlative
One-syllable word	brave	positive form + *-er* *braver*	positive form + *-est* *bravest*
Words of three or more syllables	enjoyable	*more* + positive form **more** *enjoyable*	*most* + positive form **most** *enjoyable*
Some two-syllable words	funny	change *-y* to *-i* + *-er* *funnier*	change *-y* to *-i* + *-est* *funniest*
Other two-syllable words	famous	*more* + positive form **more** *famous*	*most* + positive form **most** *famous*

Commonly Confused Adjectives and Adverbs

Positive	Comparative	Superlative
bad (adjective)	worse	worst
badly (adverb)	worse	worst
good (adjective)	better	best
well (adverb)	better	best
little	less	least
much	more	most

Ensuring Pronoun–Antecedent Agreement

27

OVERVIEW: CHOOSING THE CORRECT PRONOUN

ESL Note
See "Agreement"
on pages 526–529.

Pronouns are words writers use in place of nouns. They allow writers to avoid repetition and give their sentences variety. The words that pronouns take the place of or refer to are called **antecedents.** When you write, you must make sure that the pronouns and antecedents in your sentences *agree,* or match. Otherwise, your readers will be confused about which people, ideas, or things you are referring to. To ensure pronoun–antecedent agreement, you need to attend to several concerns.

In this chapter, you will learn how to

➤ ensure that pronouns and antecedents agree in number
➤ keep the relationship between pronouns and antecedents clear for your reader
➤ make sure that pronouns and antecedents agree in gender
➤ avoid sexist language

DISCOVERING CONNECTIONS **A**

Using one of the techniques you practiced in Chapter 2, prewrite on one of the following topics: a vacation destination, universal health care, fame. Save your work for later use.

➤ **M**AINTAINING AGREEMENT IN NUMBER

A pronoun must agree with its antecedent in *number:* Both must be singular, or both must be plural. Use singular pronouns to refer to singular antecedents and plural pronouns to refer to plural antecedents.

> **Examples**
>
> **singular antecedent**   **singular pronoun**
> *Rachael* dropped *her* book bag to the floor with a crash.
>
> **plural antecedent**   **plural pronoun**
> The *students* in health class volunteered *their* time to run the blood drive.

The use of *collective nouns* such as *class, herd, jury,* and *team* can cause confusion in pronoun–antecedent agreement. Remember that collective nouns represent groups of people or things but are generally considered singular, so they call for singular pronouns (see pages 353–354).

> **Example**
>
> **singular antecedent**   **singular pronoun**
> Last night, the Ordinance *Committee* closed *its* meeting, in violation of the Open Meetings Act.

Exploration 1a   Maintaining Pronoun–Antecedent Agreement

Each of the following sentences contains a pair of pronouns in parentheses. For each sentence, underline the antecedent, and circle the correct pronoun. Study the example first.

   Example   Five <u>children</u> had misplaced (his or her, (their)) books.

(1) Last week, several employees of P. A. Cummings International Airport were hospitalized after experiencing nausea and tingling in (his or her, (their)) arms. (2) When an airport official was first contacted by the media, ((she), they) refused to comment. (3) Instead, the official scheduled a news conference for the next morning, saying ((she), they) would respond to questions at that time.

(4) In the meantime, state environmental officials studied the airline terminal to see if (he, they) could discover the cause of the illness. (5) The officials first tested the air to see if (it, they) contained carbon monoxide. (6) After that test proved negative, the chemicals used to clean the carpet were checked to see if (it, they) could have caused the illness. (7) The officials discovered that maintenance workers had used too much cleaning solution when (he, they) cleaned one portion of carpeting on the previous evening. (8) The excess solvent dried to a powder behind the ticket counter, and when the employees walked across that area, (his, their) shoes released the chemical. (9) The employees then breathed in the powder, and (it, they) made them ill. (10) At the news conference, the director of the airport announced that (she, they) would have the carpet in that terminal replaced immediately.

Exploration 1b   Maintaining Agreement with Collective Nouns

Below is a list of collective nouns. Working with a partner, write a sentence using each collective noun as an antecedent with an appropriate pronoun. Write your sentences on a separate sheet of paper. Underline both the collective noun and its replacement pronoun.

association	committee	crowd	gang	mob
club	company	family	group	union

Example   *The union has ordered a strike if it can't get management to authorize a wage increase.*

Challenge 1   Revising a Paragraph and Maintaining Pronoun–Antecedent Agreement

1. In each of the sentences in Exploration 1a above, you chose the pronoun that agrees with the antecedent. Now, working with a partner, rewrite the paragraph, using the *other* pronoun in parentheses and then changing its antecedent. Keep in mind that you may also have to change some of the verbs to maintain subject–verb agreement.

2. Still working together, write a brief paragraph in which you explain which version is better and why.

MAINTAINING AGREEMENT WITH INDEFINITE PRONOUNS

Writers often use indefinite pronouns as subjects in sentences. When an indefinite pronoun is the antecedent for another pronoun, maintaining agreement can be tricky. That's because, as you saw in Chapter 25 (pages 361–362), and as you can see in the list below, some indefinite pronouns are always singular and some are always plural. Still others are sometimes singular and sometimes plural, depending on the context.

Number of Indefinite Pronouns

Always Singular	*Always Plural*	*Singular or Plural*
another, anything, each, everyone, everybody, everything, much, no one, nothing, someone, nobody	both, few, many, several, some	all, any, more, most, none

To avoid agreement errors with indefinite pronouns, first identify the subject and the pronoun that refers to it. Check to see whether they agree in number. If they don't agree, change the sentence so that the pronoun and its antecedent match, as these examples show:

> Singular antecedent
>
> *Anyone* needing more information about financial aid should bring
> *his or her*
> ~~their~~ questions to the Financial Aid Office.

or

> Plural antecedent
>
> *Students*
> ~~Anyone~~ needing more information about financial aid should bring
> *their* questions to the Financial Aid Office.

> Plural antecedent
>
>   *their*
> *Few* of the parents understood the relief that ~~his or her~~ children felt
> when the test was postponed.

or

> Singular antecedent
>
> *Each*
> ~~Few~~ of the parents understood the relief that *his or her* children felt
> when the test was postponed.

Exploration 2a   Maintaining Agreement with Indefinite Pronouns

Circle the indefinite pronoun in each of the following sentences, and then fill in the blanks with a pronoun that agrees with this antecedent. Study the example first.

> **Example** (Few) of the people sitting in the waiting room had already
>
> filled out _____*their*_____ applications.

(1) The newspaper and the news give us the impression that nobody wants to get involved in helping _*his or her*_ neighbors. (2) However, a restaurant in my city has proved that not everyone is apathetic about what happens in _*his or her*_ community. (3) The restaurant owner serves holiday dinners for free to any and all in the surrounding neighborhood who otherwise couldn't afford to pay for _*their*_ meals. (4) Many of the restaurant employees volunteer _*their*_ time to serve the dinners. (5) Several of the city's most prominent citizens also sacrifice time with _*their*_ families to serve people who are less fortunate.

Exploration 2b   Correcting Errors in Agreement with Indefinite Pronouns

Most of the sentences in the following passage contain errors in agreement with indefinite pronouns. Cross out each error, and then write the correct pronoun above it. Change the verb if necessary. More than one answer may be possible, as the example shows.

> **Example**   Anybody could improve ~~their~~ *his or her* grades by working harder.
>
> *or*
>
> *Most students* ~~Anybody~~ could improve their grades by working harder.

(1) A job interview is uncomfortable enough for someone in search of employment without the interviewers trying to give them a hard time. (2) On my last two interviews for administrative positions, it seemed as if everybody in the office did their best to put me on edge. (3) For example, at the firm that

was looking for a receptionist, the office manager asked if I knew how to use desktop publishing software. (4) Some of my friends work as receptionists, and *they do* ~~she does~~ not even do any writing, let alone desktop publishing. (5) I later learned that many of the managers at this company ask questions like that merely to test the poise of the people *they are* ~~he is~~ interviewing. (6) At the other office, somebody asked me whether I would mind serving *his* ~~their~~ coffee and then asked whether I'd be willing to give them a backrub. (7) Any questions of this sort are a form of sexual harassment, so I refused to answer it. (8) I wish that someone who works at a decent office would just offer me a job in *his* ~~their~~ firm so that I don't have to do any more interviewing.

Challenge 2   Maintaining Agreement with Indefinite Pronouns in Your Writing

As the section above indicates, the indefinite pronouns *all, any, more, most,* and *none* are either singular or plural depending on the word following them. Working with a partner, write two sentences for each of these indefinite pronouns, using each one first as a singular antecedent and then as a plural antecedent.

MAINTAINING AGREEMENT WITH DEMONSTRATIVE AND REFLEXIVE OR INTENSIVE PRONOUNS

You may also occasionally experience difficulties in maintaining pronoun–antecedent agreement with **demonstrative pronouns,** which point out a particular person or thing.

Demonstrative Pronouns

Singular	Plural
this	these
that	those

As the list indicates, two demonstrative pronouns are singular (*this* and *that*), and two are plural (*these* and *those*). *This* and *these* point out things that are near or point to things in the future. *That* and *those* point out things that are farther away or point to things in the past.

When you use a demonstrative pronoun to begin a sentence in a paragraph or essay, you may be referring to the antecedent in the previous sentence. In these cases, check for any errors in pronoun–antecedent agreement by identifying that antecedent. If the antecedent is singular, use *this* or *that;* if it is plural, use *these* or *those*.

> **Example**
>
> **antecedent**
>
> There have been *four major accidents* near the park entrance.
> *Those have*
> ~~That has~~ caused the city to install warning signs.

> **Example**
>
> The Civic Improvement League is donating $15,000 to establish an
>
> **antecedent**   *This*
> *urban entrepreneur's scholarship* at the college. ~~These~~ will be given to
>
> students majoring in marketing or accounting.

Often writers add a clarifying word to the demonstrative pronoun to make the reference more precise. In this case, the demonstrative pronoun then becomes a *demonstrative adjective,* as in the following versions of the sentences that appear above:

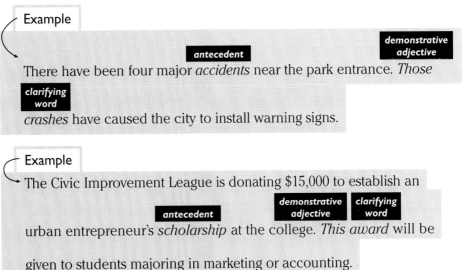

> **Example**
>
> **antecedent**   **demonstrative adjective**
>
> There have been four major *accidents* near the park entrance. *Those*
>
> **clarifying word**
>
> *crashes* have caused the city to install warning signs.

> **Example**
>
> The Civic Improvement League is donating $15,000 to establish an
>
> **demonstrative adjective** **clarifying word**
> **antecedent**
> urban entrepreneur's *scholarship* at the college. *This award* will be
>
> given to students majoring in marketing or accounting.

Another potential problem in maintaining pronoun–antecedent agreement involves the use of **reflexive** or **intensive pronouns,** which are used to emphasize the words to which they refer.

■ *Reflexive or Intensive Pronoun Forms*

myself	oneself
yourself	ourselves
himself, herself	yourselves
itself	themselves

You should never use reflexive or intensive pronouns in a sentence unless you have included the word to which the pronoun refers. These pronouns may not be used as subjects.

Reflexive

The capsized sailboat righted *itself.*   *[To direct verb's action back to subject]*

Intensive

The president *himself* will testify.   *[To emphasize]*

If these pronouns are used incorrectly as subjects, replace the reflexive or intensive form with a personal pronoun that suits the situation.

Example

I
Connie and ~~myself~~ did most of the work on that presentation.

Exploration 3a   Maintaining Agreement with Demonstrative Pronouns

The sentences in the passage below contain errors in pronoun–antecedent agreement. In each sentence, cross out the incorrect demonstrative pronoun or demonstrative adjective, and above it write one that matches the antecedent. Also, add a clarifying word or change the noun following the demonstrative adjective if necessary. Study the example first.

Example   During the storm, a huge tree fell across the power lines, and
this tree
~~these~~ caused a major power outage.

(1) The Red Cross held a blood drive on campus yesterday, and ~~those~~ events proved to be a big success. (2) More than a hundred donors showed up; many
those them
of ~~that~~ participants were first-time donors. (3) Some of the newcomers seemed
this
nervous, and for ~~those~~ reasons, the Red Cross workers tried hard to reassure everyone that giving blood is simple and painless. (4) The workers explained
those steps
the steps involved while pointing out the safety of ~~that~~. (5) After the first few
those
newcomers successfully donated, ~~that~~ people made the others who were wait-

ing feel relaxed. (6) All of the donors agreed that the blood drive made them feel good about themselves; next year, they will support these event again.

Exploration 3b Using Reflexive and Intensive Pronoun Forms Correctly

Fill in the blanks in the following sentences with an appropriate reflexive or intensive pronoun form from the list on page 391. Study the example first.

> *Example*   After waiting at the register for five minutes, the woman finally decided to check the price _____ *herself* _____ .

1. I will be picking you up at the airport _____ *myself* _____ .

2. The participants _____ *themselves* _____ criticized the organizers of the natural healing seminar most harshly.

3. At the end of this semester, perhaps you will decide to major in business _____ *yourself* _____ .

4. After several hours, the storm finally blew _____ *itself* _____ out.

5. Rather than wait for the city crew to arrive, we cleaned up the field _____ *ourselves* _____ .

KEEPING THE RELATIONSHIP BETWEEN PRONOUN AND ANTECEDENT CLEAR

To help your reader understand your meaning, you must also make the relationship between the pronoun and the antecedent clear. Look at this sentence:

> Ambiguous
> *Ed* and *Bill* had a fight, and *he* broke *his* nose.

The problem with this sentence is obvious. It does not make clear who did what to whom. The simplest way to correct this type of error is to restate the sentence completely to eliminate the ambiguity, as this version shows:

> Revised
> During their fight, *Ed* broke *Bill's* nose.

You often face this same potential problem when you use the pronoun *it:*

> **Ambiguous**
>
> Stephanie made a mess when she poured coffee from the pot into the cup because *it* was cracked.

The problem here is that the pronoun *it* has *two* potential antecedents: *pot* and *cup.* To correct the error, specify which of the two objects was cracked:

> **Revised**
>
> Stephanie made a mess when she poured coffee from the pot into the cup because *the cup* was cracked.

or

> Stephanie made a mess when she poured coffee from the pot into the cracked cup.

Exploration 4a   Identifying the Pronoun–Antecedent Relationship

In each of the following sentences, a pronoun is italicized. Circle the antecedent for each of these pronouns, and draw an arrow from the pronoun to the antecedent, as the example shows.

> *Example*   The (lock) on the suitcase was broken, so I asked my uncle to
>
> fix *it.*

(1) Although voice mail has become very popular over the last few years, many people don't like *it.* (2) For one thing, people don't like having to follow a lengthy series of commands when all *they* want to do is talk to an actual person. (3) For another thing, voice mail systems are often quite complicated, and *they* cause people to become lost or confused. (4) Even when a caller pushes the button for an operator, *he or she* is often put on hold. (5) For the average person, such a system often increases the frustration *it* is meant to eliminate.

Exploration 4b   Correcting Unclear or Ambiguous Pronoun References

Each sentence below contains an unclear or ambiguous relationship between a pronoun and an antecedent. Circle the unclear or ambiguous pronoun. On another sheet of paper, revise the sentence to clarify the relationship. There may be more than one way to correct each sentence. Study the example first.

> **Example**   When the vase she threw hit the window, (it) shattered.
>
> *The window shattered when the vase she threw hit it.*
>
> *or*
>
> *When the vase she threw hit the window, the window shattered.*

1. When the bus collided with the tanker, it burst into flames.

2. The bus had hit a curb and the driver lost control of it.

3. Paramedics arrived on the scene immediately after the firefighters, and they began helping the victims of the accident.

4. The bus had also hit a street sign; it was badly damaged.

5. Traffic was snarled, a crowd gathered on the sidewalk, and that created problems at rush hour.

Challenge 4 Writing with Clear Pronoun–Antecedent Agreement

Working with a partner, write a sentence to precede each of the sentences provided below. Make sure to include an antecedent that matches the pronoun that begins the second sentence. If necessary, add a clarifying word to those pronouns. Study the example first.

> **Example**   *Yesterday, Diane reminded me of the time the two of us*
>
> *locked ourselves out of the office.* That still makes me laugh.
>   ^story

1. _____

   She left the scene of the accident before the police arrived.

2. _____

   It caused the restaurant to be closed for an entire week.

3. _____

   These should be modified to make access easier for disabled people.

4. _____

   They finally decided to rent a movie.

5. _____

That means I won't have to take out a loan to attend classes next semester.

MAINTAINING AGREEMENT WITH THAT, WHO, AND WHICH CLAUSES

Clauses introduced by a **relative pronoun,** *that, who,* or *which,* may also create problems with pronoun–antecedent agreement. If the antecedent that the clause describes is singular, then the verb in the clause must be singular. If the antecedent of the clause is plural, then the verb must also be plural.

> ### Examples
>
> **singular antecedent**   *sells*
> The *store that sell* baked goods at half price is always crowded.
>
> **plural antecedent**   *allow*
> The *special parking stickers, which allows* a student to park in the campus garage, may be purchased in the bookstore.

Exploration 5a   Maintaining Agreement with *That, Who,* and *Which* Clauses

The italicized clauses in the following paragraph contain errors in agreement. Circle the antecedent, and then correct the error by crossing out the incorrect verb and writing the correct one above it. Study the example first.

was
Example   The (firefighter) *who were involved in the rescue* received a

citation for bravery.

were
(1) Most people *who was questioned in a recent survey* felt that their mem-

were
ories aren't as strong as they'd like. (2) These respondents, *who was between*

the ages of forty-five and sixty-five, felt that their memories were not as good as

they had been five years earlier. (3) According to several experts surveyed, the

were
memory losses *that was reported* are a normal part of the aging process.

(4) Nonetheless, anyone *who experiences sudden memory loss* should see a

is
doctor immediately. (5) That condition, *which fortunately are not common,*

could be a symptom of a serious neurological problem.

Exploration 5b   More Practice Maintaining Agreement with *That, Who,* and *Which* Clauses

The following passage contains several errors in agreement with *that, who,* and *which* clauses. Cross out any incorrect verb, and write the correct verb above it. If a sentence does not contain an error, write *OK* above it. Study the example first.

> *ride*
> **Example**   Because of the crowd, many people who usually ~~rides~~
>
> the 8 A.M. crosstown bus had to wait for the 8:30 bus.

(1) I attended a great workshop that ~~were~~ *was* held at school the other day.
(2) A counselor who work in the counseling center on campus presented the workshop. (3) The program, which was called "How to Build an Effective Personal Relationship," attracted about twenty participants, both male and female. (4) She first discussed several common misconceptions that people has about love. (5) For example, "love conquers all," a concept which are believed by many people, isn't always true. (6) In some cases, a person can have so many problems that love alone isn't enough to maintain a relationship. (7) She also disproved the naive idea that there is only one right person in the world for each of us. (8) Then she showed how people who thinks the right partner will be the salvation for all their problems in life are setting themselves up for disappointment. (9) All of us who ~~was~~ *were* participating in the session were impressed, because we had all had fantasies like those she described. (10) I'm looking forward to the follow-up session, which ~~are~~ scheduled for next Friday.

AVOIDING PROBLEMS WITH GENDER IN PRONOUN–ANTECEDENT AGREEMENT

Gender refers to whether a word is masculine or feminine. Making sure that pronouns agree in gender is usually much easier than making them agree in number. In English, inanimate objects and ideas don't have masculine or feminine forms as they do in languages such as Spanish and French.

With personal pronouns, identifying gender is easy. *I, me, we, you,* and *your* can be either feminine or masculine. Likewise, the plural pronouns *they, them, their,* and *themselves* apply to both genders. The personal pronoun *it* refers to objects only. In fact, you need to worry about gender only with third-person pronouns: *she, her, hers, he, him,* and *his.* To correct errors in agreement with any of these words, change the pronoun so that it matches the gender of the word to which it refers:

> **Example**
>
> *her*
> Mother Teresa devoted ~~his~~ life to helping the poor in India.

> **Example**
>
> *his*
> As the man turned to leave, a ticket fell out of ~~her~~ coat.

When you use pronouns, you should also eliminate any accidental *sexism* in your writing. **Sexist language,** as the National Organization for Women (NOW) and the National Council of Teachers of English (NCTE) have been pointing out since the 1970s, is language that inappropriately designates gender. The word *foreman,* for instance, suggests that only a man can direct a group of workers.

Words have tremendous power. When you use words like *chairman, salesman,* or *mailman,* you send out the message that only males should conduct meetings, sell things, or deliver mail. The proper way to deal with these words is to make them gender-neutral, that is, with references to neither sex: *supervisor, chairperson, salesperson,* and *mail carrier.*

You must also be concerned with sexism when you use singular indefinite pronouns such as *anybody, someone,* or *everybody.* These words can be either masculine or feminine. It was once acceptable to use *he, him, himself,* and *his* to represent both sexes when referring to a singular indefinite pronoun. Today, however, this usage is considered sexist, so you should either use pronouns of both genders or rewrite the sentence to make both your pronoun and your antecedent plural.

If you choose the first option, you can connect a feminine and a masculine pronoun with *or* to refer to the indefinite pronoun: *he or she, him or her,* and *his or her,* rather than *he, him,* and *his.* Reverse the pairs if you prefer: *she or he, her or him, her or his.*

> **Example**
>
> *Everybody* should always be prepared to do *her or his* best.

The other option is to make both pronoun and antecedent plural. This method is generally a better choice. It eliminates sexism and eliminates the possibility of making an error in gender agreement, as this version shows:

> **Example**
>
> *People* should always be prepared to do *their* best.

Exploration 6a   Avoiding Problems with Gender in Pronoun–Antecedent Agreement

In the following passage, identify errors in pronoun gender and uses of sexist language. Cross out each error you find, and write the correction above it in the space provided between the lines. More than one correct answer may be possible. Study the example first.

People who ride motorcycles   *their helmets*

Example   ~~Anyone who rides a motorcycle~~ should wear ~~his helmet~~, even

on short trips.

or

her or his

Anyone who rides a motorcycle should wear ~~his~~ helmet, even

on short trips.

(1) My ambition is to finish school and begin a career in the business world. (2) My first step will be sales because a good salesman can earn a great salary and help her company at the same time. (3) Of course, to be effective, a salesman has to develop contacts in the firms with which he deals. (4) To do this, a salesman has to make regular rounds and get to know as many people as possible in the companies she visits. (5) For example, when a salesman visits a company, he should first visit the foreman to find out what ~~her~~ needs are. (6) Succeeding as part of the sales force is just the first step in my career plans. (7) Eventually, I hope to work my way up to chief executive officer, or even chairman of the board of directors. (8) An effective chairman can make money for ~~herself~~ and ~~his~~ corporation by ensuring that the managers are doing a good job. (9) Everybody has her own management strategies, but I feel the best strategy is to make sure that people are treated fairly and paid according to their efforts. (10) With these kinds of simple ideas, anybody should be able to make his mark in the business world.

Exploration 6b   Avoiding Sexist Language

Below is a list of sexist words. In the spaces provided, write a neutral, nonsexist alternative for each one. Make sure you don't substitute another equally sexist word in its place. For instance, don't replace *stewardess* with *steward*. Instead, use *flight attendant.* Then, on a separate sheet of paper, compose a sentence using each of your substitutions.

fireman _____   actor _____

congressman _____   anchor woman _____

mankind _____   businessman _____

weatherman _____   policewoman _____

Challenge 6   Evaluating Sexist Language and Nonsexist Alternatives

Make a list of the sexist words you have read or used in your own writing. Working with a partner, discuss your lists. Develop a nonsexist version for each word on your list. Then, still working with a partner, compose a brief paragraph in which you discuss the ways that sexist language may affect people.

DISCOVERING CONNECTIONS B

1. In Discovering Connections A on page 385, you completed a prewriting on one of three suggested subjects. With this prewriting material as a basis, work through the rest of the writing process to complete a draft essay of about 500 words on this topic.
2. Exchange your draft with a partner. Using the material in this chapter to guide you, check the draft you receive for errors in pronoun–antecedent agreement and sexist language. Then return the draft to the writer.
3. Revise your essay, correcting the errors identified by your reader.

SUMMARY EXERCISE

Proofread the following essay for problems with pronoun–antecedent agreement, agreement in *who, that,* and *which* clauses, and sexist language. Make any necessary changes by crossing out the incorrect word and writing a more effective choice above it. If a sentence is correct as written, write *OK* above it.

(1) I am godmother to five-year-old twins, a boy and a girl, and I recently went to the toy store to buy him or her birthday presents. (2) Unfortunately, the expedition turned out to be a depressing experience. (3) I discovered that a person can find plenty of toys, but they will find that most of them are unbelievably expensive or inappropriate for young children.

(4) First, I went to the game aisle. (5) With the exception of Candyland, Cootie, and a few other simple games, which they already owned, all of the board games were too complicated or too expensive. (6) There were plenty of video game cartridges, but I couldn't afford to buy the game unit themselves. (7) Also, the one game cartridge that seemed as if it would be suitable for children their age was almost $40. (8) One of the salesmen said that she had just reordered that cartridge because they were so popular.

(9) My niece and nephew also wanted some action figures. (10) Anybody who has their own children or has ever babysat knows how much kids enjoy pretending. (11) James and Jenna are no different. (12) Both of them enjoy playing his or her own special roles and pretending to have super powers. (13) However, their favorite characters, which changes colors when dunked in water, cost over $15 each. (14) That amazed me.

(15) Even more amazing and sickening was the number of realistic-looking guns and war toys in the store. (16) Why would anyone want to spend a lot of money so their children could pretend to kill each other? (17) The huge arsenal I observed, however, made it seem as if almost everybody wants to buy their children a toy machine gun.

(18) By the time I finished shopping, I was much sadder and poorer than I had been on the way in. (19) My godchildren loved his or her cards and toys; that helped me feel better. (20) However, after spending an afternoon seeing

what kinds of toys are out there, I'm glad I don't have to make that choices for my own children yet.

ENSURING PRONOUN–ANTECEDENT AGREEMENT

New terms in this chapter	Definitions
➤ **antecedent**	➤ the word or words to which a pronoun refers ➤ Singular antecedents call for singular pronouns; plural antecedents call for plural pronouns. *Example* The little *girl* dropped *her* hat. ➤ Indefinite pronoun antecedents must agree with their pronouns. *Example* *Everyone* who has a coupon will receive 25 percent off *her or his* purchase.
➤ **demonstrative pronoun**	➤ singular: *this, that* ➤ plural: *these, those* ➤ If a demonstrative pronoun begins a sentence, find the antecedent in the preceding sentence. ➤ A demonstrative pronoun placed next to a noun is then called a *demonstrative adjective*. *Example* Some clothes in *that* box are damaged. *Those* should be mended.
➤ **reflexive/intensive pronoun**	➤ a combination of a personal pronoun with *-self* or *-selves: myself, yourself, himself, herself, itself, ourselves, yourselves, themselves.* ➤ Reflexive or intensive pronouns are used for emphasis (Ginny *herself* paid for the repair.) or to direct the action of the verb back to the subject (Peter threw *himself* across the saddle.).
➤ **relative pronoun**	➤ *that, who, which* ➤ A relative pronoun introduces a clause that describes an antecedent; the verb in the clause must agree with the antecedent. *Example* The *attorney* who *is* addressing my class this morning graduated from this college.
➤ **gender**	➤ refers to whether a word is masculine or feminine ➤ Pronouns must match the gender of their antecedents.

New terms in this chapter	Definitions
➤ **sexist language**	➤ language that inappropriately excludes one gender
	➤ Try using plural antecedents and pronouns instead.
	Example *All bicyclists* using the municipal bike path must wear *their* helmets.

Maintaining Parallelism

28

OVERVIEW: BALANCING IDEAS IN YOUR WRITING

Chances are you've seen pictures of triplets or quadruplets all dressed in identical clothes. You should keep this kind of picture in mind to understand **parallelism.** In writing, maintaining parallelism means presenting a series of similar or related items all in the same form. Whenever you connect like words or phrases, check to make sure you have kept those connected ideas parallel.

In this chapter, you will discover how to maintain parallelism

➤ with words in a series
➤ with phrases
➤ with words linked by correlative conjunctions such as *either/or*

DISCOVERING CONNECTIONS A

Using one of the techniques you practiced in Chapter 2, prewrite on one of the following topics: the ideal home, pollution, physical fitness. Save your work for later use.

MAINTAINING PARALLELISM WITH WORDS IN A SERIES

When you use words in a series, all of the words should have the same grammatical structure. Generally, coordinating conjunctions (*and, but, for, nor, or, so,* and *yet*) are used to join the words. To maintain parallelism, keep two things in mind:

1. *Connect only similar parts of speech.* Join nouns with nouns, verbs with verbs, adjectives with adjectives, and so forth. Do not connect a verb with an adjective, a noun with an adverb, and so forth.
2. *Do not connect individual words in a series to phrases or clauses.* Keep the structure of the series, as well as the number of words in it, parallel.

Example

Steve Martin is an actor, a comedian, and ~~he writes plays~~. *a playwright*

Example

The weather this summer has been hot, rainy, and ~~a steam bath~~. *steamy*

Exploration 1a   Using Parallel Words in a Series

Complete each statement with a word that maintains the parallel structure of the sentence. Study the example first.

Example The antique painting was dusty, scratched, and ____*faded*____ .

(1) Is beauty a blessing or a _____ ? (2) Some people appear to believe that beautiful people cannot be intelligent, talented, or _____ . (3) In their minds, beautiful people can only have careers as models or _____ . (4) Ironically, these same critics are also convinced that good looks guarantee an enviable and _____ life. (5) In truth, however, dating isn't always easy for beautiful people because many potential partners become shy or _____ when they see a stunning person.

Exploration 1b   Maintaining Parallel Structure with Words in a Series

Several sentences in the following passage contain errors in parallelism. Cross out the errors, and write the correct version above the faulty one if necessary. In some cases, you can correct the sentence simply by eliminating words. More than one correct answer may be possible. Study the example first.

> *Example*   Every time I try to stop smoking, I gain weight, get headaches,
> *become irritable*
> or ~~irritability takes over.~~

(1) You need a good education and to be ambitious to get a decent job today. (2) A high school diploma or having a G.E.D. doesn't land you a job with a future. (3) After my military service, I applied and actually got an interview for dozens of jobs, but I was always passed over. (4) After a year of looking for a desirable job, I became discouraged, angry, and I was depressed. (5) Now that I'm studying computer science and working in the computer lab, I know I'll have some knowledge, confidence, and I will also have experience to offer an employer.

*M*AINTAINING PARALLELISM WITH PHRASES

Phrases connected by *and* and *or* must also follow parallel structure. A phrase is a group of words that acts as a single word. Common types of phrases include prepositional phrases, *-ing* phrases, and *to + verb* phrases. It's correct to connect prepositional phrases with other prepositional phrases or *to + verb* phrases with other *to + verb* phrases. To correct errors that join nonparallel phrases, all you have to do is change the incorrect phrase to match the others, as these examples show:

> Example
> The explosion affected people living *near the house, around the*
> *throughout the entire city*
> *neighborhood, and ~~the entire city was involved~~.*

> **Example**
>
> When she's not in art class, she is busy *sketching animals, painting* *drawing portraits* nature scenes, or ~~to draw portraits~~.

> **Example**
>
> *to decorate* My grandmother always loved *to knit sweaters and ~~decorating~~ handkerchiefs.*

Exploration 2a   Using Parallel Structure with Phrases

Circle the conjunctions in each of the sentences below. Then underline the phrases that the conjunctions connect. If the connected phrases are not expressed in parallel form, change one so that it matches those to which it is connected. More than one correct answer may be possible. Study the example first.

> *Example*   The car crashed <u>through the fence</u>, <u>across the yard</u>, (and)
>
> <u>~~it went~~ into the pool.</u>

(1) Until I was ten years old, I was frequently in trouble for breaking windows, beating up little kids, and hassle the old people in my neighborhood. (2) Then I became involved with the Agnes Kidd Memorial Boys and Girls Club, where the staff taught me to respect others, to leave the property of others alone, and helping those less able than I was. (3) Within a month, I became a different person at home, in school, and to be around the neighborhood. (4) I am determined to repay the staff for their help by studying hard and to get my degree in physical education. (5) Then I can begin working with children in a community center or maybe get a job in an elementary school.

Exploration 2b   More Practice Keeping Phrases Parallel

The sentences in the following passage contain errors in parallelism. Cross out these errors, and then provide correct versions above the faulty ones if necessary. In some cases, you can correct the sentence simply by eliminating words. More than one correct answer may be possible. Study the example first.

Example   Stretching and ~~to take~~ *taking* a brief walk are simple ways to exercise every day.

(1) Yesterday, a guest speaker in my American history class gave an outstanding lecture on racist attitudes, unfair stereotypes, and on race relations. (2) When my professor first announced that Dr. George Henry from City University would be showing a film, giving a speech, and he would then answer questions, I wished that I had cut class. (3) However, when the class began, I quickly discovered that whether he was discussing attitudes, asking questions, or he related a personal experience, Dr. Henry had my complete attention. (4) For example, he handed out a questionnaire delving into our deepest racial fears and to expose our hidden racist outlooks. (5) As I read the questions, I began to see that many educators, people in the business world, and politics hold racist feelings without even being aware of them. (6) After his lecture, Dr. Henry led a discussion on ways to improve race relations, eliminate stereotypes, and overcoming our unconscious racist feelings.

Challenge 2   Analyzing Effective Use of Parallel Structure

Here is a brief passage from *Night*, Elie Weisel's powerful memoir of his experiences in Nazi death camps. Working with a partner, underline any parallel words or phrases. Circle the conjunctions. Find the most effective use of parallel structure, and explain to the class why it is effective.

All around me death was moving in, silently, without violence. It would seize upon some sleeping being, enter into him, and consume him bit by bit. Next to me, there was someone trying to wake up his neighbor, his brother, perhaps, or a friend. In vain. Discouraged in the attempt, the man lay down in his turn, next to the corpse, and slept too. Who was there to wake him up?

MAINTAINING PARALLELISM WHEN USING CORRELATIVE CONJUNCTIONS

You must also be careful to maintain parallelism when you use the following word pairs, called *correlative conjunctions,* to connect items:

both/and	not only/but also
either/or	whether/or
neither/nor	

These pairs indicate two possibilities, alternatives, conditions, and so on. The words or phrases that these pairs connect must be parallel. To eliminate faulty parallelism in this kind of construction, make the second item match the first, as these examples show:

Example

I tried to sneak into the club *both by trying the back door* and ~~*I showed*~~ *by showing the guard a fake ID.*

Example

The salesclerk was *neither polite nor* ~~*did she work efficiently.*~~ *efficient.*

Exploration 3a Maintaining Parallelism with Units Connected by Correlative Conjunctions

Complete the following sentences by filling in the blanks with words or phrases that complete the thought and maintain sentence parallelism. Study the example first.

Example By the time I get to the shower in the morning, either all the hot water is used up or _all the towels are missing_ .

(1) The fire at my neighbor's house last Christmas was terrifying not only for my friend but also _____.

(2) The fire started when one of his houseguests either dropped a cigarette on a chair or couch or _____.

(3) When I looked out the window, not only was the roof smoking, but also

_____. (4) By the time the fire

department arrived, both the front door and _____

were engulfed in flames. (5) Whether he was suffering from smoke inhalation

or _____, my neighbor was hospitalized for three days.

(6) Neither I nor _____ could sleep until we knew that he

and his guests were all right. (7) Fortunately, my neighbor was able to collect

insurance money and _____.

Exploration 3b   Using Parallelism Correctly in Your Writing

One element in each of the following groups is not parallel. Cross out the non-parallel element, and revise it to make it parallel. Then, on a separate sheet of paper, write a sentence using each item.

1. both a midterm and we must write three papers

2. either a situation comedy or to watch a talk show

3. near the cafeteria, the gym, and beside the administration building

4. dribbling, pass, and shoot

5. not only interesting but it was funny, too

Challenge 3   Analyzing Parallelism in Literature

1. Read the following excerpt from John Steinbeck's *The Grapes of Wrath*. This powerful epic novel details the struggle of the Joads, a family who traveled west during the Great Depression in a vain search for work, security, and dignity. In this passage, Steinbeck describes one source of anguish for starving families like the Joads. They were forced to stand idly by while agribusinesses bent on controlling prices destroyed surplus food.

   The people come with nets to fish for potatoes in the river, and the guards

hold them back; they come in rattling cars to get the dumped oranges, but the

kerosene is sprayed. And they stand still and watch the potatoes float by, listen

to the screaming pigs being killed in a ditch and covered with quick-lime,

watch the mountains of oranges slop down to a putrefying ooze; and in the eyes of the people there is failure; and in the eyes of the hungry there is a growing wrath. In the souls of the people the grapes of wrath are filling and growing heavy, growing heavy for the vintage.

2. Working with a partner, identify and underline the parallel elements you find in this passage.
3. Discuss ways in which the parallel structure helps you understand the point Steinbeck is making.

DISCOVERING CONNECTIONS **B**

1. In Discovering Connections A on page 404, you completed a prewriting on one of three suggested topics. Now take this prewriting material and work through the rest of the steps in the writing process to create an essay of about 500 words on this subject.
2. Exchange your draft with a partner. Using the material in this chapter to guide you, check the essay you receive for any problems with parallelism. Mark any errors in parallel structure, and return the draft to the writer.
3. Revise your draft, correcting the errors in parallelism identified by your reader.

SUMMARY EXERCISE

Check the sentences in the following passage for the types of errors in parallelism described in this chapter. Cross out each incorrect form, and write your correction in the space above. In some cases, more than one correct answer is possible. If a sentence is correct as written, write *OK* above it.

(1) Alcohol abuse is one of the most misunderstood problems in the world. (2) Even though researchers have shown that alcoholism is a disease, many people still think that it's a sign of a defect, weakness, or the person is lazy. (3) As a result, many individuals suffering from this disease are more likely to hide the problem than seeking treatment.

(4) One thing that makes alcohol abuse such a problem is the attitude about drinking in this country. (5) In the United States, drinking is treated as sexy, glamorous, and you can look macho. (6) For example, television commercials for alcohol show beautiful bars filled with attractive models, sports stars, or some are celebrities, all having fun. (7) People are encouraged to think that they can be like those glamorous, famous people if they drink.

(8) However, for many, drinking is neither glamorous nor it is not special; instead, their genetic makeup means that drinking is as dangerous for them as to play Russian roulette. (9) For those people, drinking is neither entertaining nor is it a pleasure; instead, it is an instant addiction. (10) Without even being aware of it, they become dependent on alcohol, and their patterns of living can change, too. (11) As time passes, they need to drink more and more alcohol to function. (12) Without alcohol, both their bodies and their mental state of being go through excruciating symptoms of withdrawal.

(13) Alcoholism is a disease of denial, and many individuals suffering from it are unable to admit they have a problem. (14) In some cases, they lose their families, their jobs, their friends, and finally their self-respect is gone before they finally admit that they are addicted. (15) Unfortunately, some alcoholics choose to die rather than acknowledging that they have a problem.

(16) Those who do accept that they are addicted can begin recovery with a treatment program. (17) They can go into a detoxification center, they might go to a public treatment center, or a private substance abuse clinic. (18) With professional care, they undergo withdrawal from alcohol and also receiving counseling to understand why they feel the need to drink. (19) For recovering alcoholics, Alcoholics Anonymous provides a support group; they can draw strength from others who have admitted they are alcoholics, are taking steps to overcome their addiction, and put their lives back together.

(20) Most of us think of addiction as a problem with drugs such as cocaine, heroin, or amphetamines are making a comeback. (21) However, the most common addicts do not stick needles in their arms or are swallowing pills; they abuse alcohol. (22) If more of us were aware that alcohol abuse affects people without regard for age, race, people of both sexes, or religion, then perhaps fewer would start down that road to alcohol addiction.

RECAP
MAINTAINING PARALLELISM

New term in this chapter	Definition
➤ parallelism	➤ a way of creating structural balance in writing by expressing similar or related ideas in similar form ➤ Individual words that are connected by a conjunction should be parallel. *Example* That car is *old* and *rusty*. ➤ Phrases that are connected by a conjunction should be parallel. *Example* She looked *in the closet* and *under the bed*. ➤ Words that follow pairs of correlative conjunctions should be parallel. *Example* *Neither* the police *nor* the insurance adjuster could identify the cause of the accident.
➤ Parallelism means balancing words.	pens pencils and, or
➤ Parallelism means balancing phrases.	a package of pens / was purchasing pens / to use a pen a box of pencils / was selling pencils / to break a pencil and, or

Continued

➤ **Parallelism means balancing items with connecting pairs.**

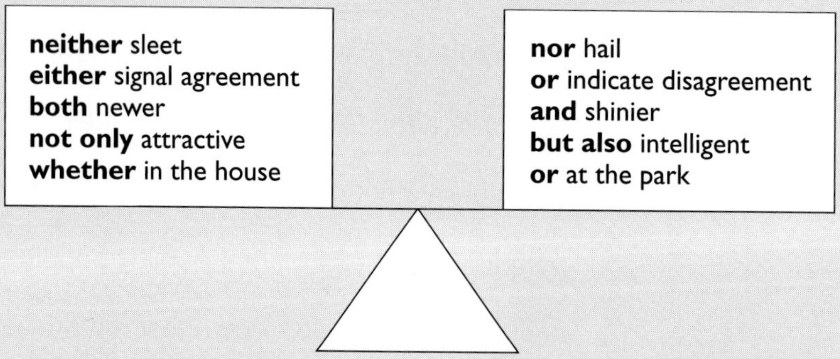

neither sleet
either signal agreement
both newer
not only attractive
whether in the house

nor hail
or indicate disagreement
and shinier
but also intelligent
or at the park

 # Spelling

OVERVIEW: UNDERSTANDING THE IMPORTANCE OF CORRECT SPELLING

ESL Note
See "Spelling" on pages 533–534.

Ask any experienced writer. Spelling *always* counts. Misspelled words can spoil the effect of an otherwise excellent paper. However, avoiding these errors is no easy task. Many words are not spelled the way they sound. Some pairs of words sound the same but are spelled differently and have different meanings. In addition, many common words break the rules that govern the spelling of other words.

The good news is that there are a number of techniques you can use to become a better speller. Besides learning basic spelling rules, you can review commonly confused words and maintain a personal dictionary of words that you have trouble spelling.

In this chapter, you will learn how to

➤ spell plural forms correctly

➤ add prefixes and suffixes

➤ decide whether to double the final consonant of a word before adding *-ing* or *-ed*

➤ spell words with *-ei* or *-ie* combinations

➤ choose correctly among *-sede*, *-ceed*, and *-cede*, and other endings that sound alike

➤ deal with commonly confused words

➤ master the most commonly misspelled words

DISCOVERING CONNECTIONS **A**

Using one of the techniques you practiced in Chapter 2, prewrite on one of the following topics: vigilante justice, parenthood, organ donation. Save your work for later use.

BASIC RULES FOR FORMING PLURALS

As Chapter 25 illustrated, the most basic rule for forming plurals is to add -s to the singular forms:

book book**s**   computer computer**s**   banana banana**s**

However, there are numerous exceptions to this basic rule, as the following guidelines show.

Nouns that end in -ch, -sh, -x, and -s   For nouns that end in -ch, -sh, -x, -s, form the plural by adding an -es:

porch porch**es**   fox fox**es**   lash lash**es**

Nouns that end in -y   The plural for most nouns ending in -y depends on the letter preceding the -y. If that letter is a vowel (a, e, i, o, u), simply add -s:

delay delay**s**   key key**s**   tray tray**s**

If the letter before the -y is a consonant, change the -y to -i and add -es:

worry worr**ies**   duty dut**ies**   sky sk**ies**

Nouns that end in -o   For nouns that end in -o, look at the preceding letter to decide whether to add -s or -es. If the letter preceding the final -o is a *vowel,* simply add -s:

radio radio**s**   stereo stereo**s**   trio trio**s**

If the letter before the -o is a *consonant,* you usually add an -es:

potato potato**es**   echo echo**es**   veto veto**es**

Exceptions   Nouns referring to music, such as alto**s,** falsetto**s,** solo**s,** and soprano**s,** do not obey this rule. In addition, with a few nouns ending in -o preceded by a consonant, you may add either -s or -es:

cargo cargo**s** *or* cargo**es**   motto motto**s** *or* motto**es**
zero zero**s** *or* zero**es**

Words that end in *-f* or *-fe* Learn which plurals end in *-fs* or *-fes* and which ones must change to *-ves*. Some nouns that end in *-f* or *-fe* form plurals with a simple *-s:*

safe   safe**s**   belief   belief**s**   chief   chief**s**

For others, however, you must change the *-f* to *-ves:*

thief   thie**ves**   knife   kni**ves**   wife   wi**ves**

For some nouns, two forms are acceptable:

scarf   scarf**s** *or* scar**ves**   hoof   hoof**s** *or* hoo**ves**
dwarf   dwarf**s** *or* dwar**ves**

If you are in doubt about how to form the plural for one of these words, use the dictionary to find the proper spelling.

Nouns with Latin endings   Make nouns with Latin endings plural in keeping with the original language:

alumnus   alumn**i**   appendix   append**ices**
crisis   cris**es**   memorandum   memorand**a**
index   ind**ices**

For some of these nouns, however, it is also acceptable to add *-s* or *-es* to form the plural:

appendix   append**ices** *or* appendi**xes**
memorandum   memorand**a** *or* memorand**ums**
index   ind**ices** *or* inde**xes**

Hyphenated or combined nouns   For hyphenated and combined words, form the plural by adding *-s* to the main word:

sister**s**-in-law   leftover**s**   attorney**s** general

Irregular plurals   With some common words, form the plural by *changing letters within the word* or *adding letters to the end:*

man   m**en**   foot   f**ee**t   louse   l**ice**   child   child**ren**

Nouns with the same singular and plural forms   A few common words have the same form whether they are singular or plural:

one deer   several deer   one sheep   many sheep
one species   five species

Nonword plurals and words discussed as words   For abbreviations, figures, numbers, letters, words discussed as words, and acronyms, form the plural by adding either an -s or -'s (apostrophe + -s). Use the -'s with all lower-case letters, with the capital letters *A, I, U,* or any other time when adding the -s alone might confuse the reader:

| one A   four A**'s**   one i   several i**'s**   one the   many the**'s**

Exploration 1a Providing the Correct Plural Form of Words

In each blank, write the plural form of the word in parentheses. Use the guide-lines above for help. Study the example first.

> *Example*   Oak (leaf) _____*leaves*_____ remain on the trees through the fall
>
> and into the winter.

(1) We love to ride our bikes along the bike (path) _____

that run alongside the (highway) _____ in surrounding

(county) _____ . (2) We all wake up very early, pack our

(lunch) _____ and (bottle) _____ of

water, and hit the trail. (3) After a few miles, we are in the countryside where

(farm) _____ line the (roadside) _____ .

(4) All the (quality) _____ of these calm places begin to work

their magic, draining away (stress) _____ that have built up

all week. (5) We love the leisurely way that (field) _____ ,

rustic barns and shiny (silo) _____ , household gardens

with their rows of staked-up (tomato) _____ , and little rural

(church) _____ rise up to meet us and then slip past. (6) We

often spot (deer) _____ , (fox) _____ ,

(rabbit) _____ , and assorted other wildlife. (7) Occasionally,

wild (turkey) _____ break from the long grass beside the

path and fly helter-skelter into the dazzling sunlight. (8) In the distance, the

(roof) _____ of townhouses and office buildings glint.

(9) This kind of peace, far from office (memorandum) _____ ,

and all the (stimulus) _____ that add stress to our lives, is good for the soul. (10) We return home in the evening tired but happy and ready

to face our (responsibility) ——————————— .

Exploration 1b   More Practice Providing the Correct Plural Form of Words

Following the guidelines on pages 416–418, provide the plural of each italicized word in the following passage. Cross out the singular form, and write
the plural above it.

> Example   *heroes*   *men*
> The ~~hero~~ were two ~~man~~ who tackled the purse snatcher.

(1) Winter seems to bring with it a variety of *illness,* and this last winter

was one of the worst *season* in a long time for *family* with young *child.* (2) I am

a single parent of two *son,* both under five *year* old and both with *allergy.*

(3) Last month, both *boy* had *bout* with *cold* or *infection.* (4) It was hard for me

to see my two *baby* suffer. (5) There were many *night* when I was still counting

sheep at 2 or 3 A.M. (6) One morning, after staying up with them most of the

night, I awoke with *pain* in my chest. (7) It felt as though ten *knife* were cutting

into my *lung.* (8) "Why us?" I thought. "How many *crisis* do we have to endure?"

(9) Finally, I called one of my *sister-in-law* and asked her to take me to the

clinic. (10) The doctor diagnosed double pneumonia, which kept me out of

class for two *week.* (11) I've never been one to fantasize about *superhero,* but

there were certainly *time* last winter when I dreamed of being rescued.

B ASIC RULES FOR PREFIXES AND SUFFIXES

You can change the form and meaning of many words by adding *prefixes* and
suffixes to them. A **prefix** is a unit such as *un-, dis-, mis-,* or *semi-* added to the
beginning of a word. A **suffix** is a unit such as *-ness, -ing,* or *-ous* added to the
end of a word.

Prefixes   When you add a prefix to a word, do not change the spelling of
the word:

believable   **un**believable   obey   **dis**obey
understand   **mis**understand

Suffixes -ly and -ness   In most cases, simply add -*ly* and -*ness* without changing the spelling of the original word:

| real real**ly**   faithful faithful**ness**   usual usual**ly**

For words with more than one syllable that end in -*y*, you change the -*y* to -*i* before you add -*ly* or -*ness*:

| lonely lonel**iness**   easy eas**ily**   silly sill**iness**

Exception   When you add -*ly* to *true*, you drop the final -*e*: *truly*.

Suffixes for words ending in -e   For words ending in -*e*, drop the final -*e* when adding a suffix beginning with a vowel:

| cope cop**ing**   disapprove disapprov**al**   fame fam**ous**

Keep the final -*e* if the suffix begins with a consonant:

| care care**ful**   arrange arrange**ment**   safe safe**ty**

Exceptions   With words such as *mile*, *peace*, and *notice*, you keep the final -*e* when you add suffixes beginning with a vowel: mile*age*, peace*able*, notice*able*.

   Drop the final -*e* on such words as *whole*, *argue*, and *judge* when you add a suffix beginning with a consonant: whol*ly*, argu*ment*, judg*ment*.

Suffixes for words ending in -y   For words ending in -*y* preceded by a consonant, change the -*y* to -*i* before you add the suffix, unless the suffix itself begins with -*i*, as with -*ing*:

| bury bur**ied**   simplify simplif**ied**   *but*   hurry hurry**ing**

Doubling the final consonant when adding a suffix   For one-syllable words that end in a *single* consonant preceded by a *single* vowel, *double the final consonant* before adding a suffix beginning with a vowel:

| plan plan**ned**   slip slip**ping**   flat flat**ten**

However, if the final consonant is preceded by *another consonant* or by *more than one vowel*, do not double the final consonant. Just add the suffix beginning with a vowel:

| brash brash**ness**   room room**ing**   fail fail**ure**

   Multi-syllable words ending with a vowel–consonant pattern must be pronounced to identify which syllable is emphasized or *accented*. If the accent is on the *final syllable*, double the final consonant before adding the suffix:

| begin begin**ning**   commit commit**ted**   control control**lable**

If the accent is *not* on the last syllable, just add the suffix:

| benefit benefit**ed**   profit profit**able**   suffer suffer**ing**

Exploration 2a   Adding Suffixes to Words

Complete each sentence in the following passage by combining the word and suffix in parentheses. Refer to the guidelines on page 420 for help. Study the example first.

   Example   When it comes to (happy + ness) _____*happiness*_____,

   Jerome has more than his share.

(1) When I was growing up, I wanted to take piano lessons, but my parents could never afford to make the (arrange + ments) _____ . (2) Year after year, I would listen wistfully to my favorite songs, (hope + ing) _____ they could work out a way to pay for lessons. (3) I knew we didn't have much money to spare, so I never questioned their (judge + ment) _____ . (4) If they (true + ly) _____ felt we couldn't afford it, I understood. (5) I didn't want to cause any (argue + ments) _____ between them. (6) At the same time, I was (whole + ly) _____ convinced that I could be a good pianist if I got the chance. (7) When it came to my schoolwork, I learned (easy + ly) _____ , and I was sure that music would be no different. (8) It wasn't that I wanted to become (fame + ous) _____ or anything; I just wanted a chance to learn to play the piano. (9) (Final + ly) _____ , last year, I was able to put aside enough money from my own job to start piano lessons. (10) Now, one afternoon a week, I travel to a small office downtown, and I (happy + ly) _____ indulge in my long-awaited lesson.

Exploration 2b   Deciding Whether to Double the Final Letter

Each sentence in the following passage contains a word and a suffix in parentheses. Decide whether to double the final letter of the word before adding the suffix. Write the correct spelling of each word on the line provided. Study the example first.

Example   On my Caribbean vacation, I went (snorkel + ing) _snorkeling_

among brilliantly colored reefs and tropical fish.

(1) I'll never forget the day when I finally (stop + ed) _____

smoking. (2) For years, my mother had been (beg + ing) _____

me to quit. (3) Even though I was only thirty, I found activities like

(run + ing) _____ almost impossible. (4) Nonetheless, it

wasn't until I visited my grandfather in the hospital that I finally

(realize + ed) _____ the damage I was doing to myself. (5) My

grandfather had been a heavy smoker for forty years, and now he was

(suffer + ing) _____ from emphysema and lung cancer. (6) He

and my grandmother had looked forward to his retirement so they could

spend their time (travel + ing) _____ . (7) His sickness meant

that they had done all that hoping and (plan + ing) _____ for

nothing. (8) As I walked out of the hospital, I threw my pack of cigarettes in

the trash, and I haven't (pick + ed) _____ up a cigarette since.

(9) (Occasional + ly) _____ , I think of Grandfather. (10) I re-

member my (mortal + ity) _____ and am no longer tempted.

➤ *T*HE BASIC RULE FOR IE OR EI

The basic rule for words with *-ie* or *-ei* combinations is this:

> *I* before *e*
> Except after *c*
> And when sounded like *a*
> As in *neighbor* or *weigh*

These common words feature *-ie* combinations:

| grief   believe   field   achieve   hygiene

And these common words need an *-ei* combination:

| receive   perceive   ceiling   beige   freight

Receive, perceive, and *ceiling* call for *-ei* because these letters follow *c*. *Beige* and *freight* call for *-ei* because the combination sounds like *a*.

Exceptions   There are a number of exceptions to this rule. For instance, even though the combination doesn't follow *c*, *e* comes before *i* in the words *either, neither, leisure, seize, their,* and *weird*. And in *species, science,* and *ancient, i* comes before *e* even though the letters follow *c*. Whenever you come across these exceptions in your reading, make a note of them. Later in this chapter, you will learn how to make your own spelling dictionary.

➤ **B**ASIC RULES FOR -SEDE, -CEED, AND -CEDE, AND OTHER ENDINGS THAT SOUND ALIKE

Words that end in -sede, -ceed, and -cede   Only one word in English ends in *-sede:*

super**sede**

Only three words in English end in *-ceed:*

pro**ceed**   ex**ceed**   suc**ceed**

All other words with this sound end in *-cede:*

pre**cede**   se**cede**   inter**cede**

Have versus of   The correct forms *could've, should've,* and *would've* sound like the incorrect forms *could of, should of,* and *would of.* When it comes to these three verbs, don't trust your ear; always write *could have, should have,* and *would have.* Then, if you still want to use the contraction, change the words in your final draft.

Used to and supposed to   In speaking, we often fail to sound the final *-d* in the expressions *used to* and *supposed to.* As a result, these two expressions are frequently misspelled as *use to* and *suppose to.* Always add the final *-d* to *used* or *supposed.*

Exploration 3a   Choosing the Correctly Spelled Word

Circle the correctly spelled word in parentheses to complete each of the following sentences. Study the example first.

Example   I didn't (receive, recieve) my paycheck this week.

(1) I (beleive, believe) that metaphors and cliches have more possibilities than most people realize. (2) Most of my (neighbors, nieghbors) don't agree. (3) I'm willing to (conceed, concede) that not all metaphors are created equal, but (niether, neither) are all ideas. (4) My (niece, neice), for instance,

thinks that a "mood swing" should be standard playground equipment. (5) Playground architects (should of, should've) considered putting career ladders on playgrounds, too, especially if there is a way to put a glass ceiling at the top. (6) And imagine what a boost secretaries would (receive, recieve) if every office had a secretarial pool for the recreational pleasure of secretaries alone.

(7) Of course, a slippery slope wouldn't work well for recreation in the office, but it's easy to (conceive, concieve) of places where it would be valuable. (8) Soldiers being trained for rain forest assault teams could learn how difficult it is to (besiege, beseige) a hilltop fortress. (9) And civilians could learn how to press their luck or push the envelope, especially if they want to learn to (succeed, succede) in life.

(10) If you're not (use to, used to) thinking this way, a metaphorical playground is too rich for your system. (11) Those who are (supposed to, suppose to) avoid all playfulness with language should never ask for gender rolls at the local bakery.

Exploration 3b Identifying and Correcting Misspelled and Misused Words

Each of the sentences in the following passage contains at least one misspelled or misused word. Cross out each incorrect form, and write the correct version above it. Study the example first.

> *proceeded*   *leisurely*
>
> **Example** The caravan ~~proceded~~ at a ~~liesurely~~ pace.

(1) Although many people have trouble beleiving it, thousands and thousands of adults in the United States cannot read. (2) It's wierd to think of adults being unable to do what schoolchildren can, but many are well behind second-graders in reading ability. (3) In my sociology class, a guest speaker from the Adult Literacy Program explained that these people should of been given special help in school but somehow "fell through the cracks." (4) As a result,

they never recieved the attention they needed. (5) The speaker explained that some of our friends and nieghbors might fall into this category. (6) In many cases, niether parents nor teachers noticed that these people were having difficulty during the course of growing up, so they did nothing to help. (7) It's amazing that many individuals manage to succede at various jobs despite their lack of literacy. (8) Somehow, they get use to bluffing their way through life. (9) The guest speaker explained that the greatest fear these people have is that someone will percieve that they cannot read. (10) Fortunately, the Adult Literacy Program has a 90 percent success rate, so these people can hope to acheive literacy if they are willing to try.

➤ **D**EALING WITH COMMONLY CONFUSED WORDS

Sometimes, rather than misspelling a word, you wind up using a word that sounds like or reminds you of the one you intended to use. Such mistakes are common for *homonyms*, words that sound the same but have different spellings and meanings. They also occur with words that, for a number of reasons, people tend to confuse. On the following pages is a list of the most commonly confused words.

Commonly Confused Words

Words	*Definitions*	*Examples*
accept	to take or receive	The family refused to *accept* any financial support.
except	other than, excluding, but	They refused all donations *except* food.
advice	opinions, suggestions	The counselor tried to provide sound *advice.*
advise	to give suggestions, guide	To *advise* the man any further, she would need to know more about his finances.
affect	(*verb*) to influence, stir the emotions	Exercising definitely *affects* me.
effect	(*noun*) a result, something brought about by a cause	One welcome *effect* is an increased energy level.

(continued)

Words	Definitions	Examples
among	used to refer to a group—more than two	Kerry stood *among* the crowd of students protesting the newly imposed dress code.
between	used to refer to two items or to compare items in a group	The principal, standing *between* the superintendent and the mayor, glared at her.
brake	(*noun*) a device to stop; (*verb*) to come to a halt	The driver's foot slipped off the *brake.* He could not *brake* in time to stop for the light.
break	to shatter, pause	He was lucky he didn't *break* his nose when he hit the windshield.
can	to be physically able to	I *can* usually get the new clothes priced and hung up on the display racks in about three hours.
may	to have permission to	*May* I leave once I've completed my work?
choose	to decide or select [present tense]	This semester, Terence will *choose* his own classes for the first time.
chose	decided or selected [past tense]	Last semester, he wasn't sure what classes to take, so his adviser *chose* all his courses.
conscience	inner sense of right and wrong	To live with a guilty *conscience* is a terrible ordeal.
conscious	aware, awake	All day long, you are *conscious* that you've done something wrong.
council	a group formally working together	The city *council* reacted angrily to the charge that the real estate agent had bribed them.
counsel	(*verb*) to give advice; (*noun*) a legal representative	The mayor tried to *counsel* the members to be quiet, but she was unsuccessful.
desert	(*noun*) a dry, arid, sandy place; (*verb*) to abandon	The park was as hot and dry as a *desert.* One by one, the picnickers began to *desert* us and headed straight for the beach.
dessert	the final part of a meal	None of them even bothered with the *dessert* Kathy had made, a delicious blueberry pie.

Words	Definitions	Examples
fewer	refers to items that can be counted	During the last month, I've had *fewer* quizzes in accounting.
less	refers to amounts or quantities that can't be counted	Unfortunately, I've had *less* time to study.
good	used to describe persons, places, things, and ideas	My brother has had *good* results with his used computer.
well	used to specify how something is, was, or would be done	He told me that it has run *well* from the moment he plugged it in.
hear	to listen	I could barely *hear* the music.
here	refers to direction or location	Sit *here*, where the sound is better.
its	possessive form of *it*	The kitten kept dunking *its* nose in the milk.
it's	contraction for *it is* and *it has*	*It's* funny to see the kitten with a milk mask.
knew	understood [past tense]	The senator *knew* her constituents well.
new	recent, unused, fresh	She felt that it was time for someone *new* to take a turn.
know	to understand [present tense]	You *know* what the problem is.
no	negative, the opposite of yes	The problem is that we get *no* direction from Jerry.
now	at this point	The question *now* is what are we going to do about it?
lay	to put down, spread out	Once you *lay* the chair on its side, disconnect the arms.
lie	to rest or recline	Then *lie* down on the floor and find the seam running up the back of the chair.
lead	to go first, direct [present tense]	Parents should always *lead* their children by example.
led	went first, directed [past tense]	When they are grown, you'll be glad you *led* them well.
lead	soft metal; graphite [rhymes with *bed*]	The responsibilities of parenthood sometimes feel like a *lead* weight.
loose	not tight, unfastened	*Loose* clothing is better for exercise.
lose	to misplace, fail, not win	If you *lose* the game, don't *lose* your sense of humor.

(continued)

Words	Definitions	Examples
of	stemming from, connected with or to	Peter is fond *of* late night TV.
off	away from, no longer on	On his day *off,* he sleeps late.
passed	went by [past tense of *pass*]	An ambulance suddenly appeared and *passed* us.
past	time gone by, former time	From *past* experience, I knew that it was heading to Parklane Hospital.
personal	individual, private	The shoplifter had a history of *personal* problems.
personnel	employees, staff	When the security *personnel* took her to the manager's office, she began cursing and kicking.
precede	to come before	One goal of this intervention program is to identify what *precedes* an incident of child abuse.
proceed	to go on	After they study the causes, they *proceed* through the formal process of filing an official complaint.
principal	(*noun*) the head of a school; (*adjective*) primary, chief	In high school, Giselle wanted to get back at the *principal* by ordering ten pizzas in his name. My *principal* objection to this plan was that it was dishonest.
principle	a rule of conduct; a basic truth	One of my *principles* is to be honest.
quiet	still; silent	After Joanie finished yelling, the room was completely *quiet.*
quite	very; completely	Her friends were *quite* surprised that their party had disturbed her.
than	conjunction, used in comparisons	From a distance, people think John is older *than* his older brother Billy.
then	next, at that time	*Then* they take a closer look and see that Billy has wrinkles and gray hair.
their	the possessive form of *they*	The reporters were ordered to reveal the names of *their* sources to the judge.
there	refers to direction or location	Immediately, the lawyers who were *there* objected.
they're	contraction for *they are*	The reporters will be going to jail because *they're* not going to follow the judge's orders.

Words	Definitions	Examples
threw	tossed, hurled [past tense]	The supervisor accidentally *threw* out the envelope containing the day's receipts for the store.
through	in one side and out the other, from beginning to end	We had to go *through* twenty bags of trash before we found the envelope.
to	in the direction of, toward	Joe and Marlene stopped at a gas station for directions *to* the hotel.
	also used to form an infinitive	They needed *to* fill the tank anyway.
too	also, excessively	They bought some snacks for the evening, *too.*
two	more than one, less than three	They had stopped just *two* blocks away from the hotel.
weather	atmospheric conditions	The *weather* has been unusually mild.
whether	indicating an alternative or question	Scientists are now trying to determine *whether* these warmer temperatures are due to global warming.
were	past tense plural of *are*	My mother and I *were* hoping to drive to Washington, D.C., in April.
we're	contraction for *we are* or *we were*	*We're* going to go in September instead.
where	indicates or raises a question about direction or location	The neighborhood *where* my uncle lives is near the National Zoo.
who	used as subject	It took us several minutes to discover *who* had started the fight on the floor.
whom	used as object	Once we cleared the room, we decided which shoes belonged to *whom.*
who's	contraction for *who is* or *who has*	I'm not sure *who's* supposed to drive.
whose	possessive form for *who*	I don't know *whose* car we will use, either.
your	possessive form of *you*	Sometimes knowing all the rules governing *your* job is not enough.
you're	contraction for *you are*	Once *you're* on the job by yourself, rules don't help much.

Exploration 4a   Identifying the Correct Word from Pairs of Commonly Confused Words

In each sentence in the following passage, circle the correct word from the pair in parentheses. Study the example first.

> *Example*   A job can have a profound (affect, (effect)) on your whole life.

(1) If I had to (choose, chose) the strangest experience in my (passed, past), it would be the summer I worked third shift at the aluminum barrel factory. (2) When the interviewer asked me if I was willing to work from 11 P.M. (to, too) 7 A.M., I thought it was a great idea. (3) I figured I could (lead, led) a beachcomber's life by day and (than, then) go nightclubbing with my friends before my shift started. (4) My brother tried to tell me that the job would be (know, no) picnic, but I ignored him and took it. (5) After the first two days, I realized that I had planned on everything (accept, except) sleep. (6) Instead of going to the beach when I came home from work, I'd wash up and (than, then) crawl into bed. (7) I always had a tough time drifting (of, off) to sleep because there was no (quiet, quite) around my house during the day. (8) I could (hear, here) every laugh and conversation and was aware of the beautiful summer (weather, whether) slipping by. (9) (Their, There) were few days when I could wake up in time to go to the beach. (10) My (principal, principle) goal became making it through each week. (11) (Its, It's) no exaggeration to say that was the worst summer I ever suffered (threw, through).

Challenge 4   Using Commonly Confused Words in Your Writing

1. Write a paragraph in which you use at least five of the following groups of commonly confused words correctly.

there, their, they're	your, you're	who, whom
whose, who's	its, it's	lay, lie
to, too, two	good, well	can, may

2. Exchange your paper with a partner. Mark any incorrectly used words and return the paper to its writer. Revise your paper to correct any errors your partner identified.

LEARNING THE MOST COMMONLY MISSPELLED WORDS

In addition to remembering the various spelling rules and their exceptions, you should also keep your own personal spelling dictionary. Make a list, *in alphabetical order,* of words you misspell in your day-to-day writing. Keep this list with your dictionary for handy reference when you write.

A computer file is the best place to maintain your list. You can easily insert new words in alphabetical order and print out a new copy. If you handwrite your list, leave two or three lines between words. When you discover a misspelled word in one of your papers, add it on an extra line.

Look through the list of commonly misspelled words below and mark the ones that you misspell. Use these words to start your personal spelling dictionary.

A
absence
accurate
acquaintance
address
amateur
analyze
anonymous
answer
apologize
approval
argument
athlete

B
balance
bargain
beginning
believe
benefit
breathe
business

C
calendar
catastrophe

cemetery
certain
characteristic
column
comfortable
committee
comparative
convenience
courteous
criticize

D
decision
definitely
dependent
describe
different
disappointment
discipline
disease

E
efficient
eligible
embarrass
emphasize

environment
exaggerated
excellent
existence

F
fallacy
familiar
fascinate
February
foreign

G
generally
government
grammar
guarantee

H
height
hoping
humorous

I
immediately
important

inevitable
intelligence
interest
interfere
interpret

J
jewelry
judgment

K
knowledge

L
language
laugh
leisure
license

M
maintain
marriage
mathematics
medicine
minimum
(continued)

mischievous	permanent	reference	thorough
mortgage	persuade	referring	tomorrow
	possess	repetition	tragedy
N	possibility	rhythm	transferring
necessary	preferred	ridiculous	
negotiate	prejudice		**U**
noticeable	privilege	**S**	unanimous
	probably	schedule	
O	procedure	separate	**V**
occasion	psychology	similar	valuable
occurred	pursuing	souvenir	vegetable
opinion		strategy	
opportunity	**Q**	strength	**W**
optimism	questionnaire	subtle	Wednesday
original		summarize	written
	R	surprise	
P	realize		
parallel	receive	**T**	
particularly	recognize	technique	
perform	recommendation	temperature	

Challenge 5   Correcting Spelling in Your Writing

Review two or three assignments that you have recently written in this or other classes. Proofread for spelling errors, following the spelling guidelines in this chapter. Add any misspelled words to your own personal spelling dictionary.

DISCOVERING CONNECTIONS **B**

1. In Discovering Connections A on page 416, you completed a prewriting on one of three suggested topics. Now, using this prewriting material as your basis, work your way through the rest of the writing process, and create a draft essay of about 500 words on this subject.
2. Exchange your draft with a partner. Using the material in this chapter to guide you, check the essay you receive for any problems with spelling. Circle any spelling errors, and return the draft to the writer.
3. Revise your essay, correcting the misspelled words your reader has identified.

➤ **SUMMARY EXERCISE**

The following passage contains numerous misspelled words. Using the various rules and examples in the chapter to guide you, find and cross out errors. Write the correct version above.

(1) Throughout our marraige, my husband and I have been pushovers for the forlorn, homless animal who secretly plots to invade our home and create chaos. (2) Over the years, a parade of dogs and cats—real caracters—seems to have had our adress, probablely past on quitely along the stray underground until it has become legend. (3) However it came to us, each of these animals has quickly made itself comfortible and established it's place in the family. (4) What's more, each has left us shakeing our heads over the crazyness of its antics.

(5) First their was Pogo Pete, a midsized collie-shepherd mix who adored chasing birds and insectes for hours. (6) On one vacation, his principle amusement was chasing dragonflys up and down the dock outside our cabin. (7) One paticular dragonfly seemed to enjoy it, two, leading the dog a little farther with each pass until, in one final leap, Pogo flew gracefuly up into the air and down into the lake. (8) We didn't see how he could top this preformance until, as we floated along in a little fishing boat, he lunged at another dragonfly and almost capsized the boat.

(9) Another pet who established himself as a first-class eccentric and a certifyed character was Hoboken, fondly called Sir HB. (10) This Hershey-colored cat came to us as a thin, defiant stray and threwout his long life remained feircely independent and reserved. (11) Self-reliant as well, this young cat quickly learnned how to pull the old-fashioned latch and open the door of our rented farmhouse. (12) When we went for a walk threw the fields

and woods, Sir HB insisted on coming along, and despite getting overheated and tired, made it clear he had no intention of excepting a lift.

(13) O.B., a roly-poly beagle mix from the pound, adoptted us somewhat later, after we had to childs to entertain him. (14) Beleiving himself to be a hunting dog, he loved nothing better than to spy an open gate or door and make a brake for it. (15) What a rediculous picture our family made chaseing after him as he raced happyly in the long grass. (16) The rabbits, of course, watched in amusment as he tried to sniff them out but inevitabley ran in the wrong direction. (17) The orignal chow hound, O.B. generaly did his best hunting from our table. (18) Once, he even stole and consumd a whole pack of gum from the babysitter, who's expression of horror were unable to forget.

(19) Ragamuffin, the latest feline addition to the family, has taken the least time to perswade us that she is insane. (20) Long, lean, and snakelike, she loves wraping herself around bannisters and squeezeing into tight places. (21) Not long ago, I heard the stranggest rustling in the kitchen. (22) "Now suprise," I thought, "Ragamuffin is in the pots and pans." (23) A through cupboard search proved fruittless, and the worrysome noise continued. (24) Finally I found her, flatened out and wedged tightly in a full drawer of kitchen knifes and utensils.

(25) Your asking yourselves, I no, "Why do these people chose to share they're home with these excedingly strange creatures?" (26) Its true they take a lot of time and trouble and sometimes even medecine and veterinary care. (27) We can only anser: We do it for the laughs, for the priveledge of knowing these unforgetable creatures, and for the love that flowes both ways.

RECAP
SPELLING

New terms in this chapter	Definitions
➤ prefix	➤ letter or letters added to the beginning of a word that changes its meaning: *un-, dis-, semi-, re-, il-* *Examples* **un**able, **il**legible
➤ suffix	➤ letter or letters added to the end of a word that changes its meaning: *-ness, -able, -ous, -ly, -er, -ed, -ing* *Examples* sad**ness**, slow**ly**

Spelling Guidelines for Adding Prefixes and Suffixes
(Check the dictionary for exceptions to these general guidelines.)

To add a prefix

prefix + word (no spelling change)

dis + approve = **dis**approve

To add -ly or -ness

word + -ly or -ness (usually no spelling change)

clear + ly = clear**ly**

Change -y to -i before adding -ly or -ness

silly + ness = sill**iness**

To add -ed

Change -y to -i before adding -ed

carry + ed = carr**ied**

To add a suffix that begins with a vowel

Drop -e at the end of a word before adding suffix

cope + ing = co**ping**

Double the final consonant if
➤ the word has one syllable

stop + ed = stop**ped**

➤ the final consonant is preceded by a single vowel

hot + est = hot**test**

➤ the accent is on the last syllable of a word with two or more syllables

admit + ing = admit**ting**

To add a suffix that begins with a consonant

Keep -e at the end of a word

hope + ful = hope**ful**

30

Commas

OVERVIEW: UNDERSTANDING COMMA USAGE

ESL Note
See "Punctuation and
Capitalization" on
pages 536–538.

When you speak, you include pauses within your sentences to clarify or emphasize ideas. When you write, the mark of punctuation you will use most often to signify these interior pauses is the **comma.**

In this chapter, you will learn how to use a comma to

➤ indicate a pause between two clauses connected by a conjunction

➤ separate items in a series

➤ indicate a brief break between introductory material and the main part of the sentence

➤ set off words, phrases, and clauses that interrupt the flow of a sentence

➤ set off a direct quotation from the rest of a sentence

➤ set off elements in certain letter parts, dates, addresses, and numerals

➤ set off nouns of direct address

DISCOVERING CONNECTIONS A

Using one of the techniques you practiced in Chapter 2, prewrite on one of the following topics: communications, true beauty, creativity. Save your work for later use.

USING A COMMA BETWEEN CLAUSES CONNECTED BY CONJUNCTIONS

A comma is used to indicate a pause between clauses connected by a conjunction or a pair of conjunctions.

Compound sentence

coordinating conjunction

The movie was good, *but* the book was better.

Compound sentence

correlative conjunction   correlative conjunction

Either the wind blew the campfire out, *or* the ranger put it out.

Complex sentence

subordinating conjunction

Even though the office was warm, everyone put in a full day's work.

[Use a comma when the subordinate clause comes first.]

Exploration 1a   Practice Working with Commas and Conjunctions

Add a comma, a conjunction, and another clause to complete the following sentences. Review Chapter 19 to remember rules for creating complex and compound sentences and to find lists of subordinating and coordinating conjunctions. Study the example first.

Example   *When Jerry misplaced his calculator,* he had to buy a new one.

1. _____

jury duty is part of every citizen's responsibility.

2. Serving on a jury can disrupt a person's life _____

_____

3. _____

   prospective jurors are often able to delay serving for a variety of reasons.

4. Being part of the judicial system is interesting _____

   _____

5. The juror's day at court starts at 8:30 A.M. _____

   _____

6. _____

   all the jurors are sworn in.

7. Then, the presentations by the lawyers begin _____

   _____

   _____

8. In my state, most jurors serve for only a day _____

   _____

   _____

9. Jurors may serve for up to a month for trials of capital crimes _____

   _____

   _____   _____

10. _____

    sometimes jurors are sequestered.

U SING COMMAS TO SEPARATE ITEMS IN A SERIES

Commas are used to separate three or more items in a series. When only two items are connected by *and, or,* or *but*, no comma is needed.

Words in series

Jacqueline spends her summer days *swimming, sailing, sunbathing,* or *sleeping.*

> **Phrases in series**
>
> ➤ *In the fall,* *in the winter,* and *in the spring,* however, her schoolwork leaves her little time for these activities.

Exploration 2a Using Commas in a Series

Fill in the blanks in the following sentences, supplying the items to complete each series. Place commas where necessary. Study the example first.

> **Example** The _____*city*_____ and _____*county*_____ cooperate on
>
> a recycling program that requires people to separate
>
> _____*plastic,*_____ _____*paper,*_____ and _____*glass*_____
>
> from the rest of their trash.

(1) I work full-time on the third shift, so my workday begins at 11 P.M., when other people are _____ or _____. (2) The plant where I work makes plastic items such as _____ _____ and _____. (3) The machines I work with generate a great deal of _____ and _____, so I dress lightly and wear ear plugs. (4) In addition to running my machines, I supervise two other workers to make sure they _____ and _____. (5) The factory has a series of small windows near the ceiling, and if I look up from my machine, I can see _____ _____ and _____. (6) After three hours, I take my first break, during which I _____ or _____. (7) When my break is over, I _____ and _____. (8) Before I know it, it's supper time, so I _____ or _____. (9) During the rest of the shift, I have time to complete my paperwork, including _____ and _____. (10) At 7 A.M., I head home to

bed while everybody else is _____⌒_____⌒or

_____ .

➤ **U**SING A COMMA TO SET OFF INTRODUCTORY MATERIAL

Often the main portion of a sentence is introduced by a word, phrase, or clause that indicates a time, place, or condition. If this introductory material consists of *four or more words* or contains a *verbal,* separate it from the rest of the sentence by a comma. (See page 247 for a discussion of verbals.)

> **Example**
>
> *Within the pile of shredded paper,* the mouse nursed three babies.

> **Example**
>
> *Yelling and splashing frantically,* Courtney drifted away from shore.

Occasionally, you will use a word or brief phrase to introduce a sentence. Use a comma to set off such an introductory element if it helps to emphasize or clarify the main point of the sentence.

> **Example**
>
> *In fact,* the substitute teacher had never even been in the school before.

> **Example**
>
> *Soon after,* the meeting was interrupted by strange noises.

Exploration 3a   Using Commas after Introductory Phrases and Clauses

If the introductory phrase in each of the sentences in the following paragraph needs a comma, insert it. If a comma appears where it is not necessary, cross it out.

> *Example*   At the major intersection near the entrance of the school‸ an
>
> accident was slowing‚ down traffic.

(1) On my area's cable television system‚ there is a television station that shows nothing except old movies. (2) Today, it showed three Marx brothers movies. (3) Before the start of each movie‚ a commentator gives a brief intro-

duction about the film. (4) Because it is part of the public broadcasting system, the station doesn't show any commercials. (5) Therefore, people are able to see the movies without interruption. (6) From watching this station for the past year, I've developed a real appreciation for older movies—especially those about rebels. (7) Of all the movies I've seen, my favorite is *Cool Hand Luke*, starring Paul Newman as a small-time convict. (8) When he is in prison, Luke refuses to conform to the system, and he must endure vicious treatment. (9) For even minor infractions, Luke is forced to spend twenty-four hours in "the box," a windowless wooden booth in the hot sun. (10) As a fan of movies about rebels, I've also enjoyed seeing *One Flew Over the Cuckoo's Nest Rebel Without a Cause* and *The Wild Ones*, all shown on my favorite station.

USING COMMAS TO SET OFF ELEMENTS THAT INTERRUPT SENTENCE FLOW

Sometimes you use commas within a sentence to surround a word, phrase, or clause that interrupts the flow of the sentence. For instance, when a word adds emphasis, provides transition, or renames or illustrates another word in the sentence, use commas to set it off:

> **Example**
> Our next car, *however*, ran like a top.

> **Example**
> The crow, *for example*, is a highly intelligent bird.

> **Example**
> We had skybox seats, *the best in the stadium*, for the game.

Also use commas to set off *nonrestrictive elements,* clauses or phrases that could be left out of the sentence without changing its basic meaning. Nonrestrictive clauses and phrases add extra but nonessential information:

> **Example**
>
> **nonrestrictive clause**
>
> This year's spring weather on Cape Cod, *which is usually calm and warm*, was cool and blustery.

If you were to leave *which is usually calm and warm* out of the sentence, the reader would still understand the main point. The clause is *nonrestrictive*.

Some clauses and phrases are *restrictive*, meaning that your reader needs them to identify or restrict the meaning of the word they modify. Therefore, you don't set them off with commas, as this example shows:

> **Example**
>
> **restrictive phrase**
>
> All students *driving vehicles with handicapped plates* may park in the first row of Parking Lot C.

Leave the italicized phrase out of this sentence, and you send the wrong message. Without these words, the sentence says that *all* students may park in a lot that is actually reserved for disabled students only. Therefore, *driving vehicles with handicapped plates* is restrictive, and no commas are used.

Exploration 4a   Using Commas around Elements That Interrupt Sentence Flow

Read the sentences in the following paragraph. If a comma is needed in a sentence, write it in the blanks provided. If no comma is needed, put an × in the blank. Study the example first.

Example   My asthma __,__ which usually doesn't cause me much

trouble __,__ has been flaring up recently.

(1) Sometimes parents __,__ who want to protect their children __,__ can go overboard. (2) A newspaper article about two children __,__ which I read in the dentist's office __,__ tells an incredible story about parental overprotection. (3) The mother of a three-year-old daughter __×__ according to the story __×__ obtained a restraining order to keep a three-year-old boy away from her child. (4) She said that her daughter __,__ who attends preschool with the boy __,__ is afraid to play in the park because of the boy's aggression. (5) Why didn't the judge __,__ who should temper justice with common sense __,__ tell the parents to straighten out the difficulties between their children by themselves? (6) I wonder whether that little girl __×__ with a mother like hers __×__ will ever learn to solve problems on her own.

Exploration 4b More Practice Using Commas around Elements That Interrupt Sentence Flow

In the following sentences, insert commas where you think they are needed to set off words from the rest of the sentence. Put *OK* above any sentence that doesn't require additional commas. Study the example first.

> **Example** She began singing lessons with her neighbor, a former
>
> professional, only to discover that she really didn't enjoy
>
> studying voice.

(1) If I won the lottery, I'd buy a plane ticket and head for Tahiti a beautiful island in the South Pacific right now. (2) As soon as I arrived at my hotel, which would overlook the island's best beach, I'd drop my bags in the room and put on my swimsuit. (3) I'd swim for a while and then take a nap, in a comfortable net hammock strung, between two palm trees at the edge of the beach. (4) Rested and refreshed, I'd head back to my room to change for a little shopping. (5) Before going out, however, I'd call room service and order a late lunch. (6) I'd wander around the little shops, the best places to find handmade souvenirs for a couple of hours, before heading out for my night on the town. (7) I'd go to the best restaurant, which would also have the highest prices, and I'd order whatever looked good. (8) After I finished my meal, I'd go to a bar with live music. (9) I'd dance to every song, no matter how foolish I looked, and stay out until dawn. (10) Finally, the rising sun would remind me to head for my room, for a few hours of sleep.

➤ **U**SING COMMAS TO SET OFF DIRECT QUOTATIONS

As a writer, you will sometimes want to *quote*, to write down word for word what other people say. When you do so, you let your reader know that the words are a *direct quote* by enclosing the passage in quotation marks (" ").

You then use a comma to set the direct quote off from the *attribution,* the part that identifies the speaker.

Note the placement of the comma in these three formats incorporating a direct quotation.

1. When the quote is at the beginning of a sentence, insert a comma within the closing quotation mark:

Example

"My wallet—it's not in my pocketbook," Katlyn said, with an edge of panic in her voice.

2. When the quote is at the end of a sentence, place a comma before the opening quotation mark:

Example

She said quietly, *"I can't find it anywhere."*

3. When the quote is interrupted in the middle by the attribution, insert a comma within the closing quotation mark of the first portion and a second before the opening quotation mark of the second portion:

Example

"And I'm sure I had it," she cried, *"when we left the mall."*

➤ RECOGNIZING OTHER SITUATIONS IN WHICH COMMAS ARE NEEDED

In addition to these uses of commas, remember to use a comma

➤ to set off the salutation of a personal letter (not a business letter): *Dear Monique,*

➤ to set off the parts of dates from the rest of the sentence: *August 25, 1990,* was a crucial day for my family.

➤ to set off parts of addresses in a sentence: His last permanent address was *756 Craft Street, Tampa, FL 34268.*

➤ to indicate thousands within numbers: *9,870* or *9,000,000*

➤ to set off a name when you address someone directly: I'm telling you, *John,* that you need to save for retirement.

Exploration 5a   Using Commas with Quotation Marks

In the following paragraph, underline each attribution, and insert commas and quotation marks where needed to separate the attribution from the exact words of the speaker.

> *Example*   Then the announcer said," I'm afraid I have some bad news
>
> to report."

(1) "Things aren't the way they used to be," my Aunt Mil complained the other day. (2) She then said," I don't mean to complain, but you young people haven't done much to make this world any better." (3) I winked at her and said with a smile," For one thing, my generation *is* trying to help improve the world."

(4) "And you should remember another thing," I added," I'm forty-three, so I'm not young anymore, either."

(5) "Well, my goodness, Jack," she said as she laughed," I guess you are just an old optimist."

Exploration 5b   Using Commas

Help this job applicant make a positive impression with this cover letter. Proofread and insert commas where they are needed. If a numbered item needs no commas, write *OK* above it.

325 Whipple Street,
East Franklin, MA 02652,
June 6, 1997

Ms. Mary Hayes
Director of Personnel,
East Franklin, Y.M.C.A.,
49 Richmond Street,
East Franklin, MA 02650

Dear Ms. Hayes:

(1) I am writing to apply for the part-time position as Assistant to the Director of Youth Services, which you have advertised in the *East Franklin Gazette*. (2) Having spent the last three summers, as a youth counselor in the

"Kids at Work" summer job program, here in Taunton, I have the experience enthusiasm and qualifications your position requires.

(3) I have just completed my first year at Bristol Community College, where I am majoring in criminal justice. (4) After I receive my degree, I plan to work full time with young people, either through a social agency or the State Police Outreach Center.

(5) As a counselor for "Kids at Work", I was in charge of twenty teenagers between the ages of fourteen and eighteen. (6) In fact, this position called for both responsibility and leadership. (7) During my first two summers on the job, for example, I arranged work schedules supervised work activities and taught a job skills seminar. *OK* (8) The seminar was so successful that my director made it a permanent part of the summer program. (9) For the past two summers, I've also served as senior counselor, which means I was in charge of training all new counselors.

(10) All in all, I think my experiences have prepared me well for the position of Assistant to the Director of Youth Services, and I look forward to meeting with you to discuss my qualifications in greater detail. (11) Please schedule me for an interview at your convenience. (12) Thank you.

(13) Sincerely

Cosette J. Valjean

Cosette J. Valjean

Challenge 5   Analyzing Comma Functions in Literature

Read the following passage from Harper Lee's Pulitzer prize–winning novel, *To Kill a Mockingbird*. In this passage, narrator Jean Louise Finch discusses the town's Halloween celebration.

Notice the various ways Lee has used commas in the passage. After you have finished reading the paragraph, discuss with a partner what function each of the commas serves. In the first sentence, for instance, the two commas set off a word that interrupts the flow of the sentence.

I soon learned, however, that my services would be required on stage that evening. Mrs. Grace Merriweather had composed an original pageant entitled *Maycomb County: Ad Astra Per Aspera,* and I was to be a ham. She thought it would be adorable if some of the children were costumed to represent the county's agricultural products: . . . Agnes Boone would make a lovely butterbean, another child would be a peanut, and on down the line, until Mrs. Merriweather's imagination and the supply of children were exhausted.

Our only duties, as far as I could gather from our two rehearsals, were to enter from stage left as Mrs. Merriweather (not only the author, but the narrator) identified us. When she called out, "Pork," that was my cue. Then the assembled company would sing, "Maycomb County, Maycomb County, we will aye be true to thee," as the grand finale, and Mrs. Merriweather would mount the stage with the state flag.

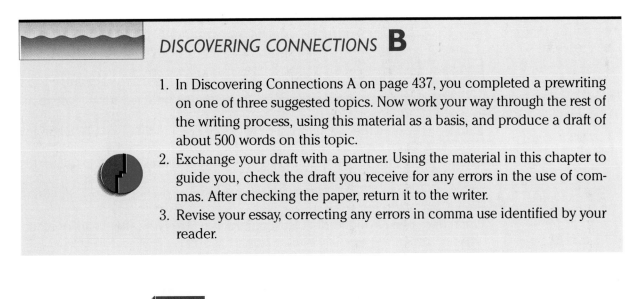

DISCOVERING CONNECTIONS B

1. In Discovering Connections A on page 437, you completed a prewriting on one of three suggested topics. Now work your way through the rest of the writing process, using this material as a basis, and produce a draft of about 500 words on this topic.
2. Exchange your draft with a partner. Using the material in this chapter to guide you, check the draft you receive for any errors in the use of commas. After checking the paper, return it to the writer.
3. Revise your essay, correcting any errors in comma use identified by your reader.

➤ SUMMARY EXERCISE

Add commas where they are needed in the sentences below. If a sentence is correct as written, write *OK* above it. Review the functions of commas to help you as you proofread.

(1) From what I have observed, most people spend too much time chasing after the wrong things in life. (2) The things that are truly valuable, such as good health, love, friendship, family, and spirituality, are right there in front of us. (3) Unfortunately, most of us don't see the obvious.

(4) Instead of noticing these marvelous things, we tend to concentrate on other aspects of life. (5) Some of us focus on such pursuits as making money, buying fancy cars or clothes, and gaining status. (6) In so many cases, people spend their whole lives driving themselves toward these goals.

(7) However, when they near the end of their lives, people sometimes begin to realize that material things are not fulfilling. (8) They've had the fancy cars, for instance, or the beautiful homes. (9) What they discover, though, is that these things still leave them feeling empty. (10) When they realize how unfulfilled they are, they begin to focus on the truly important things. (11) After years of ignoring their families, for example, they may desperately try to make up for lost time. (12) If they are lucky, they still have time to rebuild those bridges.

(13) In many cases, however, there isn't enough time left for people to attend to everything they've ignored. (14) If they don't maintain their health, for instance, they may be saddled in old age with problems like ulcers, diabetes, heart disease, or cancer. (15) If they had acted earlier perhaps these conditions could have been avoided or at least controlled. (16) Now, after years of ignoring warning signs, they often must face permanent consequences.

(17) The answer, of course, is to reassess what we value most right now. (18) After all at the end of life nobody says, "I wish I had devoted more time to work." (19) The truly important things the ones on which we should focus, are in front of us at all times. (20) Whenever I hear someone say, "The best things in life are free," I just nod my head and smile.

RECAP
COMMAS

New term in this chapter	Definition
➤ comma	➤ a punctuation mark that indicates a pause within a sentence

Comma Functions

➤ To indicate a pause between two clauses connected by a conjunction

> *Example*   She picked up the pen, but then she put it down again.

➤ To separate items in a series

> *Example*   Accounting, marketing, and management are all areas that interest me.

➤ To separate an introductory phrase of four or more words from the rest of the sentence

> *Example*   Until the end of the race, I'll keep my fingers crossed.

➤ To set off words, phrases, or clauses that interrupt the flow of a sentence

> *Example*   The people in the front of the line, those who had camped out all night on the sidewalk, bought the first tickets.

➤ To set a direct quotation off from the rest of a sentence

> *Example*   "This course has been wonderful," said Lee-Ann.

➤ To set off the salutation in a personal letter

> *Example*   Dear Latisha,

➤ To set off parts of dates and addresses and names of direct address

> *Example*   Will you join us, Tim, on July 14, 1999, at Flying Y Ranch, Casper, Wyoming?

➤ To indicate thousands within numbers

> *Example*   6,950 or 1,000,000

31

Other Punctuation and Capitalization

OVERVIEW: USING PUNCTUATION AND CAPITALIZATION TO CLARIFY MEANING

ESL Note
See "Punctuation and Capitalization" on pages 536–538.

Punctuation and capitalization are the nuts and bolts that hold your writing together. **Punctuation** involves the use of the various symbols that help you to group words and clarify their meaning. **Capitalization** involves the use of an uppercase letter at the beginning of a word to distinguish it or clarify its meaning.

In this chapter, you will learn how to use

➤ periods, question marks, and exclamation points to indicate the end of a sentence

➤ quotation marks to indicate a person's exact words

➤ apostrophes to indicate ownership or to take the place of letters left out when contractions are formed

➤ colons to signal important information

➤ semicolons to emphasize a connection between independent clauses

➤ parentheses and dashes to signal additional information

➤ capitalization to emphasize words

DISCOVERING CONNECTIONS A

Using one of the techniques you practiced in Chapter 2, prewrite on one of the following topics: endurance, terrorism, the elements of a great movie. Save your work for later use.

USING PERIODS, QUESTION MARKS, AND EXCLAMATION POINTS

To indicate the end of a sentence, use one of three marks of end punctuation. Use a **period** to indicate a stop at the end of a sentence that makes a statement:

Example
The old man sitting under the tree is my uncle**.**

Use a **question mark** when a sentence expresses a question directly:

Example
Where did you park the car**?**

Use an **exclamation point** when a sentence expresses strong excitement or emotion:

Example
Watch out for that hot pipe**!**

Be careful not to overuse exclamation points. Use them only when you need to demonstrate profound excitement or emotion, not merely to spice up your writing.

Exploration 1a Practice Using End Punctuation

The sentences in the following passage all lack end punctuation. In the space provided, write the correct mark of end punctuation for each sentence. Study the example first.

Example   The telephone company indicated that the phones wouldn't

be repaired for a month __.__

(1) When I was eight years old, my family and I moved into an apartment where no pets were allowed . (2) My parents knew that my sister and I were disappointed, but what choice did they have ? (3) After a few weeks, my father discovered that the people next door had a cat and that the people upstairs had a poodle . (4) Then he found out that the lady who lived on the top floor had a rabbit, a Gila monster, and a monkey . (5) What a zoo ! (6) We finally ended up getting a parakeet . (7) After all, we reasoned, if all these people could conceal pets in their apartments, why couldn't we ?

➤ USING QUOTATION MARKS

When you record a person's words exactly as they were said, the resulting material is called a **direct quotation.** Direct quotations must be enclosed in **quotation marks:**

Example

The smiling clerk said, "Thank you. Come again."

Notice that the first word of a direct quotation is capitalized and that the end punctuation is placed within the closing quotation mark. Notice also that a comma sets the direct quotation off from the *attribution,* the words that identify the speaker.

You can also place the direct quotation before the attribution:

Example

"Thank you. Come again," the smiling clerk said.

Notice that a comma is still needed to separate the direct quotation from the attribution. In this case, the comma is placed *within* the closing quotation mark. Punctuation of direct quotations is discussed further in Chapter 30 (pages 443–444). In writing, an exchange of direct quotations between two speakers is called a **dialogue.** Start a new paragraph each time you switch speakers so that readers can keep track of who is talking.

Example

"Marguerite, you know I can't stand the smell of tuna fish," said Brian.

"But you know it's my favorite food. How could I give it up?" she replied.

When you restate or explain what someone has said, the resulting expression is called an **indirect quotation.** No quotation marks are needed because indirect quotations do not represent a person's exact words.

> **Example**
> Then the clerk behind the counter thanked us and said that she hoped we'd come again.

> **Example**
> The company president said that profits for the third quarter were far lower than she had anticipated.

Quotation marks are also used to set off titles of short documents such as magazine or newspaper articles, book chapters, songs, short stories, and poems:

> **Example**
> Leon read the fourth chapter, "Your Child's Brain," aloud to Joyce.

> **Example**
> Listening to "Unchained Melody" always makes me cry.

Exploration 2a Practice with Direct and Indirect Quotations

Some of the sentences below contain indirect quotations, and others contain direct quotations. Insert quotation marks in the space above the direct quotations. Study the example first.

> *Example* "Please check to make sure that you've locked the door," my
> ∧   ∧
> grandmother said as we left her apartment.

(1) "I think the secret to success in life is self-confidence," said the speaker at the motivational seminar I attended recently. (2) As I sat in the audience, I asked myself if I had the kind of self-confidence she described. (3) "It's all a matter of recognizing your strengths and weaknesses," she went on. (4) She added, "Once you can do that, you can overcome your fears." (5) I know she is correct, and from now on, I'm going to remind myself that I am just as capable as the next person.

Exploration 2b   Converting and Punctuating Direct and Indirect Quotations

Some of the sentences below contain indirect quotations, and others contain direct quotations. On a separate sheet of paper, rewrite each indirect quotation as a direct quotation, and rewrite each direct quotation as an indirect quotation. Study the examples first.

Example   Lauren explained that she found the hours too long and the work too confusing.

"I just find the hours too long and the work too confusing," Lauren explained.   [Indirect to direct]

Example   "I don't know why, but I love broccoli," said Peter.

Peter said that he doesn't know why, but he loves broccoli.   [Direct to indirect]

(1) When I walked into the emergency room on the day I cut my head while running, the attendant behind the counter asked me to explain what had happened. (2) I felt myself blush as I said, "I ran into the side of a building." (3) He looked up from the desk and asked me to repeat what I had said. (4) I told him again that I had run into a building. (5) "How could that happen?" he asked. (6) "A piece of the building was jutting out, and I didn't see it," I explained. (7) "Are you kidding me?" he asked, beginning to laugh. (8) I told him that I was serious and that I'd appreciate it if he would lower his voice. (9) "I'm sorry," he said, as he tried to stop laughing. (10) When he finally asked a doctor to examine me, he graciously refrained from laughing as he told her why I needed help.

Challenge 2   Writing Dialogue

After you have completed Exploration 2b, use a separate sheet of paper to rewrite the exchange between the runner and the hospital attendant in dialogue form. Make all sentences direct quotations, and remember to begin a new paragraph every time the speaker changes. Exchange your work with a partner. On the paper you receive, circle any errors you find in the use of end punctuation or quotation marks. Return the paper to the writer. Correct any errors that your partner circled in your paper.

USING APOSTROPHES

Writers use **apostrophes** (') to show possession and form contractions. Make singular nouns possessive by adding an apostrophe and -s, even if the noun ends in -s:

> **Examples**
> artist**'s** easel; girl**'s** wallet; business**'s** assets

If the possessive form sounds awkward to you, change it to a prepositional phrase. Rather than writing *Jonas's response,* write *the response of Jonas.*
Make most plural nouns possessive by adding an apostrophe:

> **Examples**
> artist**s'** easels; girl**s'** wallets; leopard**s'** spots

For plural words that *don't* end in *-s,* form the plural by adding an apostrophe and *-s:*

> **Examples**
> men**'s** shirts; people**'s** attitudes; children**'s** toys

Pronouns such as *your* and *its* are already possessive, so they don't require an apostrophe. To make indefinite pronouns—such as *anybody, everybody, anyone, everyone,* and *nobody*—possessive, add an apostrophe and an *-s:*

> **Examples**
> everyone**'s** fault; anybody**'s** attention

To make compound subjects possessive, determine whether you are discussing one item that is possessed jointly or separate items owned by each subject. If the subjects jointly possess something, put an apostrophe and an *-s* after the last subject. If each subject possesses his or her own item, then add an apostrophe and an *-s* to each subject:

> **Example**
> Lenny and Lila**'s** house   *[One item jointly owned]*

> **Example**
> Lenny**'s** and Lila**'s** paychecks   *[Two items separately owned]*

For compound words like *maid of honor* and *father-in-law,* form the possessive by adding an apostrophe and an *-s* to the end of the word. Do the same for names of businesses and corporations that are compound:

> **Examples**
> brother-in-law**'s** car; Lord & Taylor**'s** sale

Apostrophes are also used to form contractions, words that you create by combining two words. The apostrophe takes the place of the letters left out when the words are combined.

Here is a list of common contractions:

▨ Common Contractions

are**n't** are not	he**'s** he is, he has	should**n't** should not
ca**n't** cannot	I**'d** I would	should**'ve** should have
could**n't** could not	I**'ll** I will	that**'s** that is
did**n't** did not	I**'m** I am	they**'ll** they will
does**n't** does not	is**n't** is not	they**'re** they are
do**n't** do not	it**'ll** it will	who**'s** who is, who has
had**n't** had not	it**'s** it is, it has	wo**n't** will not
has**n't** has not	she**'d** she would	you**'d** you would
have**n't** have not	she**'ll** she will	you**'ll** you will
he**'d** he would	she**'s** she is, she has	you**'re** you are
he**'ll** he will		

Notice that the letters in a contraction follow the same order as they do in the original two words. The exception is *won't*, the contraction for *will not*.

When you write, be sure to distinguish between *it's*, the contraction for *it is* and *it has*, and *its*, the possessive pronoun, which requires no apostrophe.

Exploration 3a   Using Apostrophes

Each of the sentences below contains a number of italicized words. Some need an apostrophe to show possession; others can be combined into contractions. Write the appropriate contraction or possessive form above each italicized section. Study the example first.

Example   We will reach Frannys house in about twenty-five minutes.
(handwritten: We'll   Franny's)

(1) *It is* hard to believe that the local train station *has not* been replaced *(handwritten: It's   hasn't)* yet. (2) *Did not* the *mayors* task force recommend five years ago that the station be knocked down and rebuilt? *(handwritten: Didn't)* (3) *I am* surprised that the public safety *(handwritten: I'm)* commissioners office *has not* condemned the structure. (4) I *do not* think I am *(handwritten: hasn't   don't)* overreacting when I say that city officials *are not* considering the safety of local *(handwritten: aren't)* residents. (5) *Is not* our well-being the *citys* first responsibility? *(handwritten: Isn't)*

Exploration 3b   Correcting Errors in the Use of Apostrophes

The following passage contains errors resulting from missing or misused apostrophes. Rewrite incorrect words, inserting an apostrophe wherever one is needed, and eliminating unnecessary apostrophes. Study the example first.

Example   After he smashed up his ~~brothers~~ car, Matt knew it's resale

value would take a dive.

(correction above: brother's ... its)

(1) You can't beat the companionship a dog gives, but you must be willing to invest a little time. (2) First of all, you've got to make sure that it gets all it's shots. (3) You must also make sure that the dog's other needs are met. (4) For example, don't buy just any dog food. (5) You'll find that your dog is healthier and has more energy if you buy food that contains the right mix of vitamins and minerals. (6) In addition, whether it's you, a friend, or another family member, somebody has to make sure that your pet gets exercise every day. (7) Also, unless the dog is a purebred that you're planning to mate, you should have it spayed or neutered so that nobody ends up with a bunch of unwanted puppies. (8) If you're patient, you can train your dog to follow your commands very quickly. (9) That way, you won't have to worry that your dog will misbehave. (10) If you follow these steps, you'll be able to count on a number of years of companionship from a loving animal.

Exploration 3c   Using Apostrophes in Your Writing

Use apostrophes to create contractions or phrases with possessive nouns from each of the following items. Then, on a separate sheet of paper, write a sentence that includes each word you create. Study the example first.

Example   the notebook of Bernard _____ *Bernard's notebook* _____

After a long search, I found Bernard's notebook under the couch.

1. do not _____ *don't* _____

2. the house of that family _____ *family's house* _____

3. I would _____ *I'd* _____

4. the answer of the professor _____ *professor's answer* _____

5. it is _____ *It's* _____

6. the sweater of Ray ___ *Ray's sweater* ___

7. should have ___ *should've* ___

8. the schedule of Nick ___ *Nick's schedule* ___

9. she will ___ *she'll* ___

10. the music of today ___ *today's music* ___

Challenge 3   Using *Its* and *It's* in Your Writing

As you can see from the list of common contractions on page 456, contractions of *it has* and *it is* are written as *it's*. For this Challenge, write ten sentences, five in which you use *its* and five in which you use *it's*. Then recopy the sentences, eliminating all apostrophes, and exchange your sentences with a partner. On the paper you receive, insert apostrophes where they are needed, and return the paper to the writer. Check to see whether you and your partner agree on the changes made to each of your papers.

➤ USING OTHER MARKS OF PUNCTUATION

Colons

A **colon** calls attention to what comes next. It is used to introduce a formal statement such as an explanation or announcement or a long or formal quotation. It is also used to introduce a list, often in combination with the words *as follows* or *the following*. Study the following examples:

> **Example**
> Now it was clear why grandfather had been behaving so strangely: He had suffered a small stroke.

> **Example**
> So far, I've test driven four cars: a Geo Metro, a Dodge Neon, a Nissan Sentra, and a Ford Escort.

In the first example, the colon introduces an explanation. If the explanation is a full sentence, it should begin with a capital letter. In the second example, the colon introduces a list.

Do not use a colon for a list that follows a verb or a preposition.

> **Example**
> You must bring two pencils, a calculator, and a good eraser.

Colons have other functions, too:

➤ Use a colon after the salutation of a formal letter (*Dear Ms. Newman:*).
➤ Use a colon to separate hours and minutes (*10:45*), biblical chapter and verse (*John 4:11*), and the city of publication and the publishing company in bibliographic citations and footnotes (*Boston: Allyn & Bacon*).

Exploration 4a   Using Colons

Insert colons where they are needed in the space above the following sentences. If a sentence is correct, write *OK* above it. Study the example first.

Example   My goal was simple : write a play, sell it to Broadway and

Hollywood, and become filthy rich.

1. I had a 330 P.M. appointment with Dr. Smits to petition to take her popular

   playwriting seminar.

2. I had not completed the course prerequisites : English 312, Oral Interpreta-

   tion 250, and Communications 225.

3. My plan was simple : I would demonstrate my ambition and talent and then

   throw myself on her mercy.

4. I did not anticipate her degree of concern, experience, and insight into the

   limitations of college freshmen.

5. Her parting words were wise ones "Talent and ambition are desirable, but

   preparation and perseverance are essential."

Semicolons

A **semicolon,** as you saw in Chapter 19 (pages 267–268), has the same power to connect as *and* preceded by a comma. When you use a semicolon to connect clauses, the semicolon calls attention to the connection:

Example

By ten o'clock, Elaine's car had already been stuck in the snow three times; she just wanted to turn around and head for home.

The semicolon connects the two thoughts and emphasizes the connection between Elaine's experience and her wish to quit.

As Chapter 19 also showed, using a conjunctive adverb with a semicolon is another way to connect clauses. Conjunctive adverbs, which include words such as *however, finally,* and *therefore,* can suggest a relationship between sentences. However, a conjunctive adverb alone can't connect, so you must use a semicolon *before* the conjunctive adverb to connect the sentences:

Example

David has had plenty of experience as a pipe fitter; *however,* he hasn't done much welding.

The semicolon connects the two sentences and the conjunctive adverb *however* stresses that David's experience as a pipe fitter doesn't include welding.

Exploration 5a   Practice Using Semicolons

Many of the sentences in the following paragraph are missing semicolons. In the space above these sentences, insert semicolons where they are needed. Some sentences are correct. Just mark these sentences *OK.* Study the example first.

Example   My friend couldn't have been involved in the incident ; he was

out of town on that day.

(1) Last year, my friend's life was thrown into turmoil; she discovered that she had been adopted. (2) The knowledge that she actually had other biological parents upset her greatly; she wondered why her adoptive parents never told her. (3) Furthermore, her discovery affected her relationship with her brother. (4) It had always been obvious to her that she and her brother were different; now she wondered if her parents loved her brother more than they loved her. (5) After a year of counseling, she finally adjusted; now she accepts the fact that she was adopted.

Parentheses and Dashes

Parentheses enclose information added to a sentence but not vital to it. Added dates, asides, and explanations may be enclosed in parentheses.

Example

The people in the car **(all wearing seatbelts)** escaped injury.

> **Example**
>
> Hypothermia (dangerously low body temperature) threatens the elderly during these cold stretches.

In the first example, the parentheses enclose added information that the reader doesn't actually need to understand the sentence. In the second example, the parentheses enclose the definition of a specialized term.

Dashes are used to set off information that deserves special attention.

> **Example**
>
> The murderer turns out to be—but I don't want to spoil the ending for you.

> **Example**
>
> As the winners were announced—the crowd had been waiting more than an hour for this moment—a loud cheer filled the auditorium.

In the first example, the dash indicates an abrupt change in thought and sentence structure. In the second, the dashes set off information that emphasizes the importance of the main idea. Dashes and parentheses are sometimes interchangeable; however, dashes indicate a stronger interruption. Neither mark should be used frequently, or it will lose its effectiveness.

Exploration 6a   Using Parentheses and Dashes

Some sentences in the following passage need either parentheses or dashes. Correct the sentences by inserting the proper marks of punctuation. In some cases, more than one correct answer is possible. Write *OK* above any sentence that is correctly punctuated. Study the example first.

> *Example*   In the back of the arcade (the one on Main Street, not the one ^
>
> on Plymouth Avenue) police found the missing boy. ^

(1) Working as an aide in two hospitals St. Jude's and United has proven to me that I want to become a nurse. (2) In the two years that I've worked at these hospitals, I have gotten to know some of the most dedicated people I've ever met. (3) These are people who put their patients before everything even themselves. (4) I've seen some of them stay an hour beyond their shift because a patient took a sudden turn for the worse. (5) In the cardiac intensive care

units at St. Jude's there is one for adults and another for infants I've seen nurses going out of their way to reassure patients and their families. (6) The nurses don't mind because they feel comforting people is an important part of their job. (7) I've even seen them trying to calm the emergency medical technicians EMTs who have had to transport a badly injured person. (8) When you consider the hours and the stress, the pay isn't great around $25,000 a year, but there are other things to be gained. (9) When you can see that you've made someone feel better, you can walk away with a good feeling. (10) Sometimes not as often as you might think you can even help to save lives.

➤ UNDERSTANDING CAPITALIZATION

Capitalization, the practice of using initial capital letters to distinguish words, is governed by basic guidelines for standard use.

➤ Always capitalize the first word of any sentence:

Example

The bike was the first thing the thieves took.

➤ Always capitalize the personal pronoun *I:*

Example

As far as **I** am concerned, Eileen is the only one of my childhood friends who ever understood me.

➤ Capitalize *proper names* of individuals or things, including holidays, countries, states, historical periods or events, buildings or monuments, months (but not seasons), days of the week, planets, races, religions, and nationalities:

Marge **H**ill	**A**rgentina	**L**incoln **M**emorial	**V**alentine's **D**ay
Renaissance	**M**ay (but **s**pring)	**C**ivil **W**ar	**M**onday
Venus	**I**slam	**C**hinese	**B**aptist
Maine (**ME**)			

➤ Capitalize words designating family relationships when these words are part of, or a substitute for, a specific name:

Example

When I was in elementary school, **A**unt Mary always went with my parents to parent/teacher night.

➤ Capitalize the first letter of a formal title such as *Doctor, Senator,* or *Mayor* when the title is used with a name:

Example

We expect **M**ayor Cummings to call a news conference soon.

➤ Capitalize words like *Street, Avenue,* and *Boulevard* when these words are part of a specific address:

Example

50 Earle **S**treet

➤ Capitalize geographical regions in the United States and other parts of the world, but not directions:

Example

After being stationed in the **F**ar **E**ast for three years, I settled in the **M**idwest on the **e**ast side of the **M**ississippi.

➤ Capitalize languages and the main words of *specifically* named courses:

Examples

Introduction to **P**hysics; **E**cology of **N**orth **A**merica; **W**riting 101; **S**panish; **S**wahili

➤ Capitalize the names of languages, whether or not they refer to specific academic subjects:

Examples

Chinese; **K**hmer; **P**ortuguese

➤ Capitalize the main words in the titles of books, magazines, newspapers, television shows, songs, articles, poems, movies, and so on. Do not capitalize a preposition or conjunction of fewer than five letters or *a, an,* or *the* unless it is the first word in the title.

Examples

The Invisible Man; Rolling Stone; Of Mice and Men; "**A** **R**ose for **E**mily"

➤ Capitalize the names of specific brands, companies, clubs, associations, and so on:

Examples

Mazda **P**rotege; **G**eneral **E**lectric; **N**ational **O**rganization for **W**omen

➤ Capitalize *acronyms,* words formed from the first letters of several words:

Example

MADD (**M**others **A**gainst **D**runk **D**riving)

Example

AIDS (**A**cquired **I**mmune **D**eficiency **S**yndrome)

➤ Capitalize the first words at the beginning of a letter, known as the *salutation,* and the first word of the ending, called the *complimentary close:*

Common Salutations	Common Complimentary Closes
Dear **D**r. **L**annon:	**S**incerely,
Dear **K**urtis,	**V**ery truly yours,
Dear **S**ir or **M**adam:	**R**espectfully,

Exploration 7a   Practice with Capitalization

Circle the correct letter—capital or lowercase—from each set in parentheses. Refer to the guidelines above if you are in doubt. Study the example first.

Example   (F/f)or any florist, the busiest days of the (Y/y)ear are

(V/v)alentine's (D/d)ay and (M/m)other's (D/d)ay.

(1) (P/p)rofessor (G/g)odwin, my instructor for (I/i)ntroduction to (B/b)usiness, always stresses the importance of making a good appearance on the job. (2) (O/o)n the first day of (C/c)lass, (P/p)rofessor (G/g)odwin said, "(I/i)f you want (P/p)eople to take you seriously, you must dress as if you belong on the cover of (*B/b)usinessweek.*" (3) (H/h)e urged us to go down to (S/s)outh (M/m)ain (S/s)treet and (W/w)est 53rd (S/s)treet, where (R/r)etail stores like (E/e)ddie (B/b)auer and (M/m)arshall (F/f)ield's and the (C/c)orporate offices for (T/t)imex and (J/j)ohn (H/h)ancock are located. (4) (T/t)here, he said, we

would see (M/m)anagers and (E/e)xecutives dressed in (C/c)onservative (B/b)usiness suits. (5) (N/n)one of these (B/b)usinesspeople is dressed in (L/l)evi's (J/j)eans or (N/n)ike (S/s)neakers because all of them know the importance of dressing well on the job.

Exploration 7b   More Practice with Capitalization

Decide which words in the following letter should be capitalized. Cross out the incorrect lowercase letter, and write the capital above it. Each line or sentence is numbered for you.

(1) 49 buena vista way

(2) st. charles, il 60174

(3) march 31, 2000

(4) director, consumer complaint division

(5) megahertz computer company

(6) 25 blythe street

(7) springfield, ak 67583

(8) dear director:

(9) a month ago, i purchased one of your megahertz 5000 personal computers, model number 328. (10) since that time, i have taken it to your authorized st. charles service center, microcomputers and more, five times for repairs. (11) although the costs were covered by my warranty, i feel that the number of repairs required has been excessive. (12) i have therefore decided that i want to return the computer for a full refund.

(13) when i returned to mr. electronics, the store from which i had originally purchased my megahertz 5000, ms. tamara lacey, electronics department manager, told me that your company will not authorize a refund because the case

of the computer had been opened. (14) i explained to ms. lacey that the case had been opened by a service technician authorized by megahertz. (15) she insisted that since the computer was no longer in its original condition, your company would not give me a full refund.

(16) i sincerely hope that ms. lacey is mistaken and that you will authorize my refund. (17) i originally decided to purchase a megahertz 5000 because i had read that the megahertz computer company was particularly sensitive to the needs of its customers. (18) as the enclosed copy of my original sales slip shows, my total purchase price, including tax, was $1,453.55. (19) please contact me if you need additional information.

(20) sincerely,

(21) steven h. amster

Challenge 7   Revising for Correct Capitalization

1. As you revise your writing, check to be sure you have capitalized correctly. To practice focusing on this aspect of revising, select two paragraphs that you have drafted, and exchange them with a partner.
2. Using the guidelines on pages 462–464, check the paragraphs you receive to make sure the words are correctly capitalized. Circle any problems you notice, and return the paragraphs to the writer.
3. Correct any errors your reader has identified.

DISCOVERING CONNECTIONS   B

1. In Discovering Connections A on page 451, you completed a prewriting on one of three suggested topics. Using this prewriting material as a basis, work your way through the rest of the writing process, and create a draft essay of about 500 words on the subject you've chosen.
2. Exchange your draft with a partner. Using the material in this chapter to guide you, check the draft you receive for any errors in punctuation and capitalization. After checking the paper, return it to the writer.
3. Revise your essay, correcting any errors your reader has identified in punctuation and capitalization.

SUMMARY EXERCISE

The following passage contains numerous errors in the use of end punctuation, quotation marks, apostrophes, colons, semicolons, dashes, parentheses, and lowercase and capital letters. Using the examples throughout the chapter to guide you, correct all errors by inserting needed punctuation or by writing corrected words in the space above.

(1) For almost forty years 1905–1945 franklin and eleanor roosevelt forged one of the most remarkable partnerships in the History of the united states. (2) It began with marriage, moved on to public service, and ended with contributions to political life and social reform that transformed our nations indeed the worlds history.

(3) The marriage of the wealthy, outgoing roosevelt to his shy fifth Cousin, eleanor, led first to the creation of their children elliot, james, john, fdr, jr., and anna. (4) eleanor put her ambition for Public Service on hold to raise the children, meanwhile, the young roosevelt proved himself an able and progressive leader to the new york democrats.

(5) In 1921, the family suffered a staggering blow while they were vacationing at their summer home on campobello island in new brunswick, canada, roosevelt was stricken with polio. (6) This was a terrible shock roosevelt had always been strong, active, and very able physically but the couple neither bent nor broke. (7) Eleanor who later encouraged her husband to return to Politics now became both a physical and psychological support. (8) Although confined to a wheelchair for the rest of his life, F.D.R. went on to become a master politician and one of the worlds most revered leaders.

(9) Roosevelt was elected governor of new york in 1929 he became President of the united states in 1932. (10) For three consecutive terms 1932–1945, he would lead the Country through two of the most traumatic upheavals of the century the great depression and world war ii. (11) the Roosevelt team proved

equal to the challenge of these catastrophic events they conceived and implemented inventive programs and projects such as the new deal, the works progress administration, the tennessee valley authority, and the civilian conservation corps.

(12) When the japanese attacked pearl harbor, Roosevelt responded for an outraged nation when he called december 7, 1941, a day that will live in infamy. (13) Through the war years, he worked closely with prime minister winston churchill of great britain. (14) these two men personally determined military strategy for the allies in the west.

(15) During all these years, Eleanor was a tireless worker for social causes, such as Civil Rights for african-americans and women. (16) As first lady, she set a standard for public involvement and accomplishment that is still unmatched. (17) Her workday began at 600 A.M. and ended after midnight. (18) She not only conducted press conferences and had her own Radio Program, but she also wrote the daily newspaper column, my day. (19) Friends and enemies alike had to wonder, is there no end to this woman's energy (20) Eleanors tireless work and travel, public speaking and leadership, and selfless advocacy of the underdog made her well known to the world and beloved to millions.

(21) F.D.R., exhausted and in terrible health, died in 1945, months before the War ended. (22) Eleanor went on to serve as a u.s. delegate to the united nations and helped draft the u.n. declaration of human rights. (23) in addition, she wrote two books *this I remember* and *the autobiography of eleanor roosevelt.* (24) When she died in 1962, eleanor roosevelt was, as one Biographer has said, the most admired person in the world. (25) The lives of these two remarkable people had ended, but this verse is an appropriate epitaph They are not dead who live in lives they leave behind. In those whom they have blessed, they live a life again.

RECAP
OTHER PUNCTUATION AND CAPITALIZATION

New terms in this chapter	Definitions
➤ **punctuation**	➤ a system of symbols that signal starts, stops, and pauses in writing
➤ **capitalization**	➤ the practice of emphasizing words by beginning them with capital letters
➤ **period (.)**	➤ an end mark used to indicate the end of a statement *Example* I have a dream**.**
➤ **question mark (?)**	➤ an end mark used to indicate the end of a question *Example* Have we met before**?**
➤ **exclamation point (!)**	➤ an end mark used to indicate the end of an exclamation and to show great feeling *Example* Stop**!** That area is mined**!**
➤ **direct quotation**	➤ a record of someone's exact words *Example* Peter said, "If you'll wait, I'll go with you."
➤ **quotation marks (" ")**	➤ marks used to set off someone's exact words

➤ **dialogue**	➤ an exchange of direct quotations between two or more people
	➤ Mark shifts in speakers with new paragraphs.
	
	Example "I said I wanted to go home at ten," said Joe.
	         "Yes, but you didn't specify A.M. or P.M.,"
	      said Dianne.

➤ **indirect quotation**	➤ a restatement of someone else's words *Example* Peter asked me to wait and said he'd go with me.

➤ **apostrophe (')**	➤ a mark used in a noun to show ownership or possession or in a contraction to signify letters left out
	➤ To show possession:
	    add **'s** to singular nouns a child's book
	    add **'** to plural nouns the students' answers
	    add **'s** to plural nouns that don't end in *-s* women's concerns
	➤ To form contractions:
	    add **'s** to show letters omitted in the contraction haven't

Continued

New terms in this chapter	Definitions
➤ colon (:)	➤ a mark that indicates a pause in a sentence and that introduces a quotation, formal statement, or list ➤ Begin full sentences following colons with a capital letter. *Example* The news was good: The test results were negative.
➤ semicolon (;)	➤ a connecting mark that separates related independent clauses but emphasizes the connection between them *Example* Shelley is dramatic; her twin sister is quite shy.
➤ parentheses	➤ marks that enclose non-vital information within a sentence *Example* The movie (*Shine*) made Mavis cry.
➤ dashes	➤ marks that set off information to create emphasis *Example* Vincent Van Gogh—who cut off his ear—was insane.

Guidelines for Capitalization

The first word in a sentence

Example   **A** light bulb burned out in the kitchen.

The personal pronoun *I* and the proper names of people, things, and places

Example   **S**ean and **I** are going to **T**ulsa on **F**riday.

Words that designate family relationships when they are part of, or a substitute for, a specific name

Example   **U**ncle Rod always calls to check on **G**randma.

Formal titles used with a person's name

Example   **D**r. Warner has been selected for the award.

Words that are part of a specific address or specific section of a country

Example   Our plant in the **S**outhwest is located at 1411 **L**incoln **W**ay in **T**ucson.

Main words in specific academic subjects, languages, and titles

Example   In my **I**ntroduction to **E**nvironment class, we are reading Rachel Carson's *Silent Spring*.

Brand names, company and association names, and letters of acronyms

Example   My sister works for **AT&T.**

First letters of the salutation and complimentary close of a letter

Example   **D**ear Paul,   **Y**ours truly,

part

seven

Connecting: Responding to Reading

Teaching as an Amusing Activity   Neil Postman   475

Fish Cheeks   Amy Tan   477

Intimacy and Independence   Deborah Tannen   479

Nightwatch   Paul Fletcher   481

Caesar   Therese C. MacKinnon   484

How Boys Become Men   Jon Katz   487

"Growing Up" Is Cumulative, Evolutionary
      and Never-Ending   Brian Dickinson   490

Thanksgiving Is the Greatest Holiday   Robert C. Maynard   493

Go and Conquer the World   Michaela Otway   496

The Importance of Wearing a Safety Belt   Larissa R. Houk   499

Exposed Toes   Diane Riva   501

A Religion?   Henry Bousquet   504

A Bully Who Wore Bobby Pins   Amanda Beaulieu   506

Fear Not   Greg Andree   508

To Smoke or Not to Smoke   Charlotte Medeiros   510

Thoughts about Writing   Charlotte Medeiros   512

➤ **O**VERVIEW: RESPONDING TO READING

Reading and responding to what other authors have written is another way to ensure your success as a writer. To read actively is to respond to the ideas other authors have developed and to discover the strategies they have used to express those ideas. This part of the text includes writings by both professional authors and students. After each selection, you will find questions to help you think about and respond to the ideas in the readings. Additional assignments will help you explore the connections between those ideas and your own experiences. The questions will also encourage you to use the modes in your own writing.

In this section of the text, you can explore

➤ a variety of modes that writers use to fulfill their purpose

➤ additional subjects for writing

➤ strategies writers use to express their ideas and experiences

➤ **T**AKING NOTES

You have already learned that writing effectively has many benefits. In the same way, the more you practice reading actively, the more you will profit from what you read. As a way to improve your reading skills, your instructor may ask you to record in a journal your responses, questions, and comments about what you read. Some readers *annotate* or make notes in the margins of the pages they are reading or highlight sections for later reference. Still others collect responses in a computer file or on an audiocassette tape. Whatever method or methods you use, cultivate the habit of taking notes. Your notes will help you prepare for discussions with your classmates and explore ideas for your own writing assignments.

➤ **A**CTIVE READING STRATEGIES

Sometimes it is difficult to know what questions to ask and what notes to take. The five guidelines below apply to any reading assignment. They will provide direction and help you focus your responses to the readings.

Review them before you begin to read each selection, and be sure to record your responses as you read.

1. **Establish the context**

   What's going on? Who is involved? When did it happen? Where? How? Why? These are the questions that news stories generally answer in their opening sentences to establish the *context* for readers. As you read, use these kinds of questions to identify details and examples that establish the context of the reading.

2. **Explore the modes**

   As you learned in Chapters 5 through 15, writers use techniques, or modes, to communicate their ideas to readers. These are narration, description, example, process, definition, comparison and contrast, cause and effect, and division and classification. To construct an argument, writers use a combination of these modes. As you read, first determine the author's purpose for writing. Is it to inform, to entertain, or to persuade? What is the dominant mode the author uses to fulfill this purpose? What other modes does the author use, and how are they combined?

3. **Explore the main ideas**

   As you read, highlight or record in your journal parts of the reading that state the author's thesis. Do the same for evidence that supports that idea. Finally, highlight or record the author's conclusions about the subject.

   Try to identify the main ideas or topic sentences of the paragraphs. Can you trace a common thread, the element that all the paragraphs have in common? Are there sentences or paragraphs that confuse you or sections that you don't understand? Make note of these to discuss with your classmates. Next, take note of supporting information that helps you understand the writer's points. What details catch your eye? Why are these effective?

4. **Respond to the ideas**

   What do you think of the essay? Why do you think the way you do? Do you agree with the ideas the author has expressed? Are you familiar with the context or the ideas in the reading? Does the author present an experience or view of the world that is new to you? Your answers to these questions will help you greatly in understanding the writing. As you talk or write about the piece, you will also be making sense of it. Remember as you read that a good piece of writing touches the reader. When you read, explore what the writer has done to make this happen.

5. **Read again**

   Active reading can be challenging and rewarding. Effective readers usually read a piece of writing more than once. You'll no doubt discover some elements or aspects in a second reading that you missed in the first. Regardless of what they are, these elements helped to make that writing successful. It is worth your effort to analyze them so that you will be able to use a similar approach in your own writing.

➤ **A**CTIVE READING ILLUSTRATED

Here is a brief excerpt from "The Future of TV Sports Is Glowing," by Ted Rose. This article explores and explains how technological innovations are changing the way televised sports are presented. The annotations illustrate the way active reading can help you uncover the writer's meaning and the various techniques that enabled the writer to communicate that meaning:

Modes: Main purpose — to inform

Main Ideas: Topic sentence

Context: Who

Context: What

The task presented many technical challenges, but [Stan] Honey was most concerned about how computers would locate the puck on the ice. Under normal conditions, baseballs and golf balls travel pre-

Modes: Process

Supporting ideas

Modes: Comparison and contrast

Modes: Cause and effect

Context: Why

dictable—thus, mathematical—trajectories. Not so a hockey puck. Instead, surrounded by dozens of wooden sticks and metal skates wielded by aggressive hockey players, a puck can carom in any direction.

Main ideas: Topic sentence

Modes: Process and cause and effect

Context: Who

Context: What

Context: How

Working with a team of 12 engineers, Honey designed a special puck that emitted bursts of infrared energy, and a system of sensors to be placed around an arena to detect those emissions. With this sensor data, a computer could identify the puck's location. That, along with

Supporting ideas

information from broadcast cameras themselves, produced the desired result: the TV-viewing fan could find the puck on the ice because a blue glow would illuminate it. When a player fired a puck at a high speed (usually more than 50 miles per hour), a red tail would follow

Context: How

Modes: description

in the wake. (*Brill's Content*, May 1999, 64–65)

Response: *Pretty cool! Just another way computers are changing the world. Lots of people wouldn't watch hockey on TV before because it was too hard to follow the puck. This innovation has changed that for sure.*

As the annotations illustrate, active reading helps you isolate a number of elements of the writing. For instance, it helps you focus on the *context: what* was involved (the development of a hockey puck that would be easier to see on a television screen), *who* was involved (Stan Honey and a team of twelve engineers), and how they did it (they built a puck that emits signals and installed sensors throughout the ice rink).

Active reading also enables you to note the various *modes* (*comparison and contrast, process, cause and effect,* and *description*), as well as the *main ideas* (the *topic sentences* and the *supporting sentences*). And the *response* to the reading helps you focus on the significance or meaning of the passage to a more complete degree. When you understand how a writer communicates ideas to a reader, you are better able to communicate your own ideas to your reader. That's why active reading is so important.

Teaching as an Amusing Activity

Neil Postman

In this excerpt from his 1985 book Amusing Ourselves to Death, *Neil Postman asks readers to question their assumptions about a popular television program. As you read, see if you agree with Postman's line of reasoning and if you find his evidence convincing.*

There could not have been a safer bet when it began in 1969 than that *Sesame Street* would be embraced by children, parents and educators. Children loved it because they were raised on television commercials, which they intuitively knew were the most carefully crafted entertainments on television. To those who had not yet been to school, even to those who had just started, the idea of being *taught* by a series of commercials did not seem peculiar. And that television should entertain them was taken as a matter of course.

Parents embraced *Sesame Street* for several reasons, among them that it assuaged their guilt over the fact that they could not or would not restrict their children's access to television. *Sesame Street* appeared to justify allowing a four- or five-year-old to sit transfixed in front of a television screen for unnatural periods of time. Parents were eager to hope that television could teach their children something other than which breakfast cereal has the most crackle. At the same time, *Sesame Street* relieved them of the responsibility of teaching their preschool children how to read—no small matter in a culture where children are apt to be considered a nuisance. They could also plainly see that in spite of its faults, *Sesame Street* was entirely consonant with the prevailing spirit of America. Its use of cute puppets, celebrities, catchy tunes, and rapid-fire editing was certain to give pleasure to the children and would therefore serve as adequate preparation for their entry into a fun-loving culture.

As for educators, they generally approved of *Sesame Street,* too. Contrary to common opinion, they are apt to find new methods congenial, especially if they are told that education can be accomplished more efficiently by means of the new techniques. (That is why such ideas as "teacher-proof" textbooks, standardized tests, and, now, micro-computers have been welcomed into the classroom.) *Sesame Street* appeared to be an imaginative aid in solving the growing problem of teaching Americans how to read, while, at the same time, encouraging children to love school.

We now know that *Sesame Street* encourages children to love school only if school is like *Sesame Street*. Which is to say, we now know that *Sesame Street* undermines what the traditional idea of schooling represents. Whereas a classroom is a place of social interaction, the space in front of a television set is a private preserve. Whereas in a classroom, one may ask a teacher questions, one can ask nothing of a television screen. Whereas school is centered on the development of language, television demands attention to images. Whereas attending school is a legal requirement, watching television is an act of choice. Whereas in school, one fails to attend to the teacher at the risk of punishment, no penalties exist for failing to attend to the television screen. Whereas to behave oneself in school means to observe rules of public decorum, television watching requires no such observances, has no concept of public decorum. Whereas in a classroom, fun is never more than a means to an end, on television it is the end in itself.

Yet *Sesame Street* and its progeny, *The Electric Company,* are not to be blamed for laughing the traditional classroom out of existence. If the classroom now begins to seem a stale and flat environment for learning, the inventors of television itself are to blame, not the Children's Television Workshop. We can hardly expect those who want to make good television shows to concern themselves with what the classroom is for. They are concerned with what television is for. This does not mean that *Sesame Street* is not educational. It is, in fact, nothing but educational—in the sense that every television show is educational. Just as reading a book—any kind of book—promotes a particular orientation toward learning, watching a television show does the same. *The Little House on the Prairie, Cheers* and *The Tonight Show* are as effective as *Sesame Street* in promoting what might be called the television style of learning. And this style of learning is, by its nature, hostile to what has been called book-learning or its handmaiden, school-learning. If we are to blame *Sesame Street* for anything, it is for the pretense that it is any ally of the classroom. That, after all, has been its chief claim on foundation and public money. As a television show, and a good one, *Sesame Street* does not encourage children to love school or anything about school. It encourages them to love television.

Exploring the Reading through Discussion

1. Did you watch *Sesame Street* when you were growing up, or do children you know watch it now? Why did you enjoy it, or why do children now enjoy it?

2. With your classmates, list the reasons, according to Postman, why parents and educators "embraced" and "generally approved" of children watching *Sesame Street.* Do you think parents and teachers have other reasons? What are they?

3. How does *Sesame Street* "undermine" traditional ideas about learning? What mode does Postman use to present his evidence in the fourth paragraph?

4. Postman asserts that "*Sesame Street* does not encourage children to love school or anything about school. It encourages them to love television." Do you agree? Explain.

5. Explain how Postman uses the techniques of *cause and effect* and *comparison and contrast* writing to help him fulfill his purpose in this essay.

Developing Vocabulary

List at least three words in this selection that are new to you. Write your understanding of each word from the context. Then look up each word in the dictionary, and write the definition that you think best fits the meaning in this writing.

Discovering Connections through Writing

1. Do you agree or disagree with Postman's ideas about *Sesame Street*? Write a paragraph to explain your answer. Provide specific examples from the program to support your opinion about the program's educational value.

2. How would you define effective teaching? How would you describe the ideal classroom? Should school be more or less entertaining? Should students have more or less technology to work with?

3. Many children spend more hours in front of the TV than they spend in school or doing other activities. What do you think are the positive and negative effects of watching so much television? What lessons do children learn from television?

Fish Cheeks

Amy Tan

Amy Tan is an acclaimed writer who has explored the relationships between immigrant Chinese mothers and their daughters. Her first novel, The Joy Luck Club *(1989), is based on some of her own experiences. As you read this essay, first published in* Seventeen *magazine, try to understand the feelings of a little girl living in two cultures.*

I fell in love with the minister's son the winter I turned fourteen. He was not Chinese, but as white as Mary in the manger. For Christmas I prayed for this blond-haired boy, Robert, and a slim new American nose.

When I found out that my parents had invited the minister's family over for Christmas Eve dinner, I cried. What would Robert think of our shabby Chinese Christmas? What would he think of our noisy Chinese relatives who lacked proper American manners? What terrible disappointment would he feel upon seeing not a roasted turkey and sweet potatoes but Chinese food?

On Christmas Eve I saw that my mother had outdone herself in creating a strange menu. She was pulling black veins out of the backs of fleshy prawns. The kitchen was littered with appalling mounds of raw food: A slimy rock cod with bulging eyes that pleaded not be thrown into a pan of hot oil. Tofu, which looked like stacked wedges of rubbery white sponges. A bowl soaking dried fungus back to life. A plate of squid, their backs crisscrossed with knife markings so they resembled bicycle tires.

And then they arrived—the minister's family and all my relatives in a clamor of doorbells and rumpled Christmas packages. Robert grunted hello, and I pretended he was not worthy of existence.

Dinner threw me deeper into despair. My relatives licked the ends of their chopsticks and reached across the table, dipping them into the dozen or so plates of food. Robert and his family waited patiently for platters to be passed to them. My relatives murmured with pleasure when my mother brought out the whole steamed fish. Robert grimaced. Then my father poked his chopsticks just below the fish eye and plucked out the soft meat. "Amy, your favorite," he said, offering me the tender fish cheek. I wanted to disappear.

At the end of the meal my father leaned back and belched loudly, thanking my mother for her fine cooking. "It's a polite Chinese custom to show you are satisfied," explained my father to our astonished guests. Robert was looking down at his plate with a reddened face. The minister managed to muster up a quiet burp. I was stunned into silence for the rest of the night.

After everyone had gone, my mother said to me, "You want to be the same as American girls on the outside." She handed me an early gift. It was a miniskirt in beige tweed. "But inside you must always be Chinese. You must be proud you are different. Your only shame is to have shame."

And even though I didn't agree with her then, I knew that she understood how much I had suffered during the evening's dinner. It wasn't until many years later—long after I had gotten over my crush on Robert—that I was able to fully appreciate her lesson and the true purpose behind our particular menu. For Christmas Eve that year, she had chosen all my favorite foods.

Exploring the Reading through Discussion

1. What is the lesson that the author appreciates after "many years"? Why doesn't she agree with her mother at the time?
2. Compare the responses of the two families to the dinner. How did the narrator feel? Why?
3. What sensory details does Tan use to describe the Christmas Eve menu? Can you find examples of both objective and subjective description in this essay?
4. What transitional expressions are included in the essay?
5. Do you think "Fish Cheeks" is a good title for this story? Explain why.

Developing Vocabulary

List at least three words in this selection that are new to you. Write your understanding of each word from the context. Then look up each word in the dictionary, and write the definition that you think best fits the meaning in this writing.

Discovering Connections through Writing

1. The narrator's mother tells her, "You must be proud you are different. Your only shame is to have shame." Do you agree? Write about a situation you know about or an experience you have had that supports her belief.

2. Have you participated in a traditional event or shared a special occasion with friends of another religion or culture as Robert and his family do? How did you feel? What did you learn? Provide plenty of concrete examples in your essay.

3. Write a narrative about a holiday celebration you remember well. In your essay, be sure to use effective description to put your readers at the scene.

Intimacy and Independence

Deborah Tannen

As you read this excerpt from Deborah Tannen's book You Just Don't Understand, *see if you can discover the reasons why Tannen thinks that spoken communication can be challenging.*

Intimacy is key in a world of connection where individuals negotiate complex networks of friendship, minimize differences, try to reach consensus, and avoid the appearance of superiority, which would highlight differences. In a world of status, *independence* is key, because a primary means of establishing status is to tell others what to do, and taking orders is a marker of low status. Though all humans need both intimacy and independence, women tend to focus on the first and men on the second. It is as if their lifeblood ran in different directions.

These differences can give women and men differing views of the same situation, as they did in the case of a couple I will call Linda and Josh. When Josh's old high-school chum called him at work and announced he'd be in town on business the following month, Josh invited him to stay for the weekend. That evening he informed Linda that they were going to have a houseguest, and that he and his chum would go out together the first night to shoot the breeze like old times. Linda was upset. She was going to be away on business the week before, and the Friday night when Josh would be out with his chum would be her first night home. But what upset her the most was that Josh had made these plans on his own and informed her of them, rather than discussing them with her before extending the invitation.

Linda would never make plans, for a weekend or an evening, without first checking with Josh. She can't understand why he doesn't show her the same courtesy and consideration that she shows him. But when she protests, Josh says, "I can't say to my friend, 'I have to ask my wife for permission'!"

To Josh, checking with his wife means seeking permission, which implies that he is not independent, not free to act on his own. It would make him feel like a child or an underling. To Linda, checking with her husband has nothing to do with permission. She assumes that spouses discuss their plans with each other because their lives are intertwined, so the actions of one have consequences for the other. Not only does Linda not mind telling someone, "I have to check with Josh"; quite the contrary—she likes it. It makes her feel good to know and show that she is involved with someone, that her life is bound up with someone else's.

Linda and Josh both felt more upset by this incident, and others like it, than seemed warranted, because it cut to the core of their primary concerns. Linda was hurt because she sensed a failure of closeness in their relationship: He didn't care about her as much as she cared about him. And he was hurt because he felt she was trying to control him and limit his freedom.

A similar conflict exists between Louise and Howie, another couple, about spending money. Louise would never buy anything costing more than a hundred dollars without discussing it with Howie, but he goes out and buys whatever he wants and feels they can afford, like a table saw or a new power mower. Louise is disturbed, not because she disapproves of the purchases, but because she feels he is acting as if she were not in the picture.

Many women feel it is natural to consult with their partners at every turn, while many men automatically make more decisions without consulting their partners. This may reflect a broad difference in conceptions of decision making. Women expect decisions to be discussed first and made by consensus. They appreciate the discussion itself as evidence of involvement and communication. But many men feel oppressed by lengthy discussions about what they see as minor decisions, and they feel hemmed in if they can't just act without talking first. When women try to initiate a freewheeling discussion by asking, "What do you think?" men often think they are being asked to decide.

Communication is a continual balancing act, juggling the conflicting needs for intimacy and independence. To survive in the world, we have to act in concert with others, but to survive as ourselves, rather than simply as cogs in a wheel, we have to act alone. In some ways, all people are the same: We all eat and sleep and drink and laugh and cough, and often we eat, and laugh at, the same things. But in some ways, each person is different, and individuals' differing wants and preferences may conflict with each other. Offered the same menu, people make different choices. And if there is cake for dessert, there is a chance one person may get a larger piece than another—and an even greater chance that one will *think* the other's piece is larger, whether it is or not.

Exploring the Reading through Discussion

1. Tannen writes that "humans need both intimacy and independence." Do you agree?
2. How are the worlds of "connection" and "status" different? In which world would you rather live?
3. "Communication is a continual balancing act." Explain your understanding of this statement.
4. According to the author, how do men and women differ in the way they make decisions? Do you agree with Tannen?
5. What examples does the author provide to help readers understand the terms *intimacy* and *independence*?

Developing Vocabulary

List at least three words in this selection that are new to you. Write your understanding of each word from the context. Then look up each word in the dictionary, and write the definition that you think best fits the meaning in this writing.

Discovering Connections through Writing

1. Help Josh and Linda or Louise and Howie solve their communication problems. Write your advice, explaining how they can juggle their "conflicting needs for intimacy and independence."
2. Define the terms *masculine* and *feminine*. Provide examples, as Tannen does, to help readers understand what you mean by these terms.
3. Do men and women view the same situations in different ways, as Tannen suggests? Tell a story about a situation that supports this statement or about a situation that contradicts Tannen's opinion.

Nightwatch

Paul Fletcher

In this essay, originally published in 1990, Paul Fletcher writes about a minor car accident which led to more harm than a broken fender. As you read, see if you can discover the facts of what happened one night in a small town.

It is a quiet spring night. In the oak-paneled living room of one of the gussied-up old houses that line Main Street, my daughter, Rosemary, and her boyfriend, Dan, are watching TV. A fire burns in the nicely detailed fireplace.

Crash. Tinkle, tinkle, bang!

Dan leaps up.

"Damn! If that's my car. . . ."

He throws open the front door and runs out, with Rosemary at his heels.

The driver's side of Dan's station wagon is, as they might have said years ago in this old seacoast town, "stove in." Dan and Rosemary are just in time to see a Mustang take off.

Then, unaccountably, the car comes to a halt; it slowly backs into a driveway and stands there, idling. In the moonlight, one can just make out the head and shoulders of the driver, a young woman.

By now, several neighbors are out on the street, under the bare horse-chestnut trees. Against the old Colonial church, the shadows of the trees look like the ghosts of slaves. In the half-light, their bony arms seem to be warding off an overseer's whip.

From the back of the historic house on the corner, a young black man emerges. He is followed by another, and another, and yet another, until there are five young black men standing across the street from the driveway where the young woman sits in the Mustang.

The great tower of the old church, which has watched over the town since the days of the slave trade, chimes one.

A police car, its blue lights flashing, pulls up, and a young officer approaches the young woman in the car. She appears to be dazed. She is blonde, well dressed, in the preppie fashion—apparently a student at the local college.

"I didn't do any damage," she moans, more to herself or her absent parents than to anyone else.

Dan shakes his head as he looks at the large strip of chrome from his station wagon protruding from her front-wheel sprockets.

Under the great church tower, there in the moonlight, everyone seems to be frozen in time: the young woman; the police officer, joined now by a backup; the neighbors; the five young black men—all members, it turns out, of the college's basketball team. One of them seems to know the woman, and he steps toward her, to try to calm her.

"Take it easy," he seems to say, though his voice is muffled by those of the bystanders.

It appears that the young woman is intoxicated. One of the police officers tries to conduct a sobriety test, and she stands there flailing her slender arms as she tries to connect with the tip of her nose.

"Be cool," encourages the young man.

"Get away from her!" barks the officer. His even features turn distorted with rage.

"Get away from her!" he repeats.

"I'm only trying to help."

Now everything speeds up, and it seems that the policeman has struck the youth.

"That'll teach you," he says.

Did he jab the young man in the kidneys? Despite the bright, brittle moonlight, it's too dark to see.

Murmurs of protest emanate from the onlookers. The police officers hustle the young man into one of the patrol cars.

The church clock watches.

Gradually, the distorted mien of the angry policeman reverts to normal. He strides over to Dan.

"You wouldn't mind signing this report, would you, sir?" he says. "Just to witness that this young man was disorderly—don't want any stuff about police brutality."

Dan refuses. "I saw you manhandle that young man. He was only trying to quiet the girl."

The patrol car with the young woman and the young man drives off. Rosemary turns to go back into the house with Dan. She looks up at the church tower, which looms over the peaceful skyline of our old town, as it has always done, since the time when black people here were traded and transported.

Exploring the Reading through Discussion

1. Describe the neighborhood where this story takes place. Do you think the setting is important? Why?

2. Why is the police officer whose face is "distorted with rage" so angry?

3. Do you agree with Dan's decision to refuse to sign the report? Why?

4. Why do you think the author called his story "Nightwatch"? Who or what is watching?

5. What point of view does Fletcher use to write his narrative essay? Do you agree with his choice? Explain.

Developing Vocabulary

List at least three words in this selection that are new to you. Write your understanding of each word from the context. Then look up each word in the dictionary, and write the definition that you think best fits the meaning in this writing.

Discovering Connections through Writing

1. Have you ever seen an incident in which a person was treated unfairly because of his or her race, religion, ethnicity, or sexual orientation? Write about what happened, using effective description to create a vivid sense of the scene. Provide details that will clarify the causes and effects of the behavior.

2. Fletcher writes about the early history of the seacoast town in which his story takes place. Write about the history of your own community. How has it changed? How does the city or town commemorate its roots?

3. Describe an accident that you have witnessed or been involved in. Be sure to include descriptive details to help readers visualize the scene as you saw it.

Caesar

Therese C. MacKinnon

Therese MacKinnon's essay originally was published in 1995, in a book entitled Circles of Compassion: A Collection of Humane Words and Work. *In this selection, you'll read about a unique cat whose life, unfortunately, comes to an all too familiar conclusion. As you read, see if you can discover why the author has such strong feelings for the animal.*

Caesar, a "stray" cat, was euthanized today. I use the word *stray* in the loosest of terms, because, contrary to popular belief, cats very seldom stray from home. They're much too provincial for that sort of thing. More likely, that scraggly looking cat you see wandering through your yard has been abandoned, or it is the offspring of such a cat. Its family may have moved away, having decided that it was inconvenient to pack the cat along and that it would surely "find" another home. Or the cat may have been intentionally discarded when it reached maturity and began marking its territory and fighting, or when it became pregnant. Of course, these problems could easily have been solved with a simple spay or neuter operation.

Seldom does a cat choose to leave its home territory, so when a nameless, yellow, unaltered male cat was brought in to the animal shelter one morning in a wire trap it was no surprise to hear the bearer say that his neighbors had moved away, leaving kitty behind.

The man set the trap down by the counter. Huddled tensely in the steel mesh box, eyes wide with terror, the little animal didn't look like much, just another scared vagabond. I took down what sketchy information the neighbor could offer. The cat was about four years old—not so old—not, that is, until placed in a shelter, surrounded by cuddly, highly adoptable kittens. He had been on his own for several weeks and had been fighting with every cat in the neighborhood. He had the distinct musk odor of an unaltered male feline. Age, behavior and sex, I thought: three strikes, you're out. He was the classically unadoptable cat.

As I brought him into the holding room and set him up in a clean cage, I wondered what his personality would reveal once he settled in with us. Well, Caesar, as he was soon to be dubbed, was trouble from the very start, and it was not long before I was hopelessly in love.

He was a yellow tabby—yellow, not like buttercups or tangerines, but subtle, like cornmeal. He was compact and solid, all muscle, all tomcat, yet his fur was as soft as cotton balls and thicker than lamb's wool. His coat was short and silky along his flanks, and he had a long ruff around his neck that made him look like a handsome young lion. The fur on his belly was thick and downy and, oh, his tail! It was magnificent, dense and bushy so that pieces of litter and food were always getting caught up in it. I was constantly combing it out with my fingers. Diagonally across his nose and cheeks was painted a single white stripe, rather like the make-up of an Indian brave.

Caesar had clear, round eyes, yellow, the color of his fur. They weren't the kind of eyes that you might say, "could see right through you." Not at all. He wasn't a wise sort. But he was dashing and devil-may-care, and when I looked in his eyes and he gazed back at me, I knew that he trusted me and considered me his friend.

As I said, Caesar was trouble from the start. We all knew it the day he began picking the latch on his cage door and taking nightly excursions through the corridors of the shelter. We would come in mornings to find him staring down at us happily from some shelf or curled up on a pile of blankets in a storage cabinet. Murphy-Cat, our wimpy shelter mascot, never turned up with any wounds after these evenings of freedom, so I suppose they either never met or Caesar preferred exploring to ravaging. I like to think the latter. When we finally got wise and put a lock on his cage, Caesar began picking the latch on the door next to him. My little freedom fighter: If he couldn't be foot-loose, he was going to see to it that someone else was.

Although Caesar was a mature adult cat, he still had the heart of a kitten. That which remained still, was sniffed and passed by. But that which moved, or growled, or just looked inviting, was fair game for a pounce. It made perfect cat sense. One day, Carole, my co-worker, was moving a cat with an exceptionally fluffy and inviting tail. She passed too close to Caesar's cage, and he, always the opportunist, grabbed it—and tenaciously refused to let go. The more the poor gray Persian wailed, the more worth keeping hold of her tail. Caesar was finally persuaded, forcibly, to give it up. But the second time he grabbed someone, a sweet little black Angora, I knew his days were numbered. However, being not so wise, and not inclined to change for anyone, Caesar remained full of the mischief that was to be his undoing.

One day a young couple came in, hoping to adopt not one, but two adult cats! They had recently lost their cat to feline leukemia, a deadly disease. After looking at all of the available candidates, they chose Wiggins, a neutered, buff-colored Angora, and Caesar. This was the one chance for adoption that had come Caesar's way in the two months and a day that he had been with us. Knowing his impetuous nature, we feared there might be bloodshed, but wanting dearly for him to find a home, we decided to give it a try. We brought both cats and the couple into a visiting room to see how they would all get along. As we placed the cats on the floor in opposite corners, their eyes met. I held my breath and waited, tensed to intervene, should there be trouble. The cats ran straight at each other, sniffed a greeting and then, began to explore the room! I breathed a heavy sigh of relief—and then it happened. Caesar, with his flare for the unexpected, spied a mama cat nursing her three kittens in a nearby upper cage, and leaped. He leaped six feet in the air and landed vertically on the bars of the cage. The terrified mother cat, determined to defend her brood to the end, hissed and lashed with all her might, but Caesar held fast. As far as he was concerned, this was fun! The horrified couple looked on as we pried him from the bars and carried him back to his cage. They later adopted Wiggins and Whitey, both neutered males, highly adoptable and very lucky animals indeed.

I'd like to say that someone came in that very day, saw something in Caesar and realized that he was just the companion they were looking for. Or maybe I could say that the owner finally came in to claim him, their beloved long-lost pet. I'd love to say that I or one of the other shelter staff members was able to rescue him at the last moment and take him home to be our very own. But the reality is that there are just too many animals and not enough homes for them all. Pet breeding is out of control. It's not the fault of Caesar or any of the animals that come in to the hundreds of shelters across the country. It's something that only we, the pet owners, can do anything about. We must take the responsibility for curbing the thousands of unwanted domestic animal births that occur every day in our own little corners of the world. And we must make a lifelong commitment to the pets we choose to keep.

Caesar's fate was sealed that day, through no fault of his own. The next day he was placed on the list for euthanasia. *Euthanasia* is a Greek word in origin. Literally it means "good death" and is described as the act of killing painlessly for reasons of mercy. I wonder who the Greeks did it to, and how they did it, and was it really painless or did they just prefer to hope or wish it was, as we do at the animal shelter.

We killed several animals that day, two months and two days after Caesar had arrived. There were two dogs, seven cats, three kittens and a rabbit. Two of the animals were old and sickly; the kittens were too young to survive in a shelter environment. The rest of the animals, one puppy, six cats, including Caesar, and the rabbit were killed simply and senselessly because no one wanted them. Too many animals, not enough homes.

That afternoon, I held Caesar in the corridor and waited for the veterinarian to finish with the rabbit. He lay in my arms, squinting up at me peacefully, purring as I scratched his neck and clucked at him. I thought, maybe it will be okay, maybe he won't struggle and it will be quick. But deep inside I knew that Caesar would not give up his life so easily, and I really expected nothing less of him.

It took four hands to restrain him on the table, to stop his thrashing, to silence his objections as the veterinarian pumped what seemed like a horse's dose of sodium pentobarbitol into his veins. He did not die a good death, because death is never good outside of the natural order of things. Caesar was a victim of someone's thoughtlessness or perhaps just the simple ignorance of a society that thinks of other living creatures as objects, to be used for a while and then discarded. But if we would truly look into the eyes of another living being, our souls would be changed. We would realize their incredible worth. Like all living creatures, Caesar was unique, he was one-of-a-kind, I loved him, and he will never be again.

Exploring the Reading through Discussion

1. From what you know about Caesar, would you want to adopt him as a pet? Why?

2. What concrete details does the author include to help readers see what Caesar looked like?
3. Describe Caesar's personality. What specific examples help you understand him?
4. Why does the author tell Caesar's story? What is her purpose for writing?
5. MacKinnon begins her story by giving away the ending. Should she have waited until the conclusion before revealing Caesar's fate? Why?

Developing Vocabulary

List at least three words in this selection that are new to you. Write your understanding of each word from the context. Then look up each word in the dictionary, and write the definition that you think best fits the meaning in this writing.

Discovering Connections through Writing

1. Describe a pet that you have owned or have known so that readers can understand its personality.
2. What are some solutions to the problem of "too many animals, not enough homes"?
3. Do you feel strongly about a controversial issue involving animals, such as protecting endangered species, regulating the use of animals for research, or banning fur clothing? Write to argue your position on one of these issues.

How Boys Become Men

Jon Katz

Jon Katz wrote this essay originally for Glamour, *a women's magazine, in 1993. As you read, see if you discover what experiences of your own support or contradict the statements the author makes.*

Two nine-year-old boys, neighbors and friends, were walking home from school. The one in the bright blue windbreaker was laughing and swinging a heavy-looking book bag toward the head of his friend, who kept ducking and stepping back. "What's the matter?" asked the kid with the bag, whooshing it over his head. "You chicken?"

His friend stopped, stood still and braced himself. The bag slammed into the side of his face, the thump audible all the way across the street where I stood watching. The impact knocked him to the ground, where he lay mildly stunned for a second. Then he struggled up, rubbing the side of his head. "See?" he said proudly. "I'm no chicken."

No. A chicken would probably have had the sense to get out of the way. This boy was already well on the road to becoming a *man*, having learned one of the central ethics of his gender: Experience pain rather than show fear.

Women tend to see men as a giant problem in need of solution. They tell us that we're remote and uncommunicative, that we need to demonstrate less machismo and more commitment, more humanity. But if you don't understand something about boys, you can't understand why men are the way we are, why we find it so difficult to make friends or to acknowledge our fears and problems.

Boys live in a world with its own Code of Conduct, a set of ruthless, unspoken, and unyielding rules:

> Don't be a goody-goody.
> Never rat. If your parents ask about bruises, shrug.
> Never admit fear. Ride the roller coaster, join the fistfight, do what you have to do. Asking for help is for sissies.
> Empathy is for nerds. You can help your best buddy, under certain circumstances. Everyone else is on his own.
> Never discuss anything of substance with anybody. Grunt, shrug, dump on teachers, laugh at wimps, talk about comic books. Anything else is risky.

Boys are rewarded for throwing hard. Most other activities—reading, befriending girls, or just thinking—are considered weird. And if there's one thing boys don't want to be, it's weird.

More than anything else, boys are supposed to learn how to handle themselves. I remember the bitter fifth-grade conflict I touched off by elbowing aside a bigger boy named Barry and seizing the cafeteria's last carton of chocolate milk. Teased for getting aced out by a wimp, he had to reclaim his place in the pack. Our fistfight, at recess, ended with my knees buckling and my lip bleeding while my friends, sympathetic but out of range, watched resignedly.

When I got home, my mother took one look at my swollen face and screamed. I wouldn't tell her anything, but when my father got home I cracked and confessed, pleading with them to do nothing. Instead, they called Barry's parents, who restricted his television for a week.

The following morning, Barry and six of his pals stepped out from behind a stand of trees. "It's the rat," said Barry.

I bled a little more. *Rat* was scrawled in crayon across my desk.

They were waiting for me after school for a number of afternoons to follow. I tried varying my routes and avoiding bushes and hedges. It usually didn't work.

I was as ashamed for telling as I was frightened. "You did ask for it," said my best friend. Frontier Justice has nothing on Boy Justice.

In panic, I appealed to a cousin who was several years older. He followed me home from school, and when Barry's gang surrounded me, he came barreling toward us. "Stay away from my cousin," he shouted, "or I'll kill you."

After they were gone, however, my cousin could barely stop laughing. "You were afraid of *them*?" he howled. "They barely came up to my waist."

Men remember receiving little mercy as boys; maybe that's why it's sometimes difficult for them to show any.

"I know lots of men who had happy childhoods, but none who have happy memories of the way other boys treated them," says a friend. "It's a macho marathon from third grade up, when you start butting each other in the stomach."

"The thing is," adds another friend, "you learn early on to hide what you feel. It's never safe to say, 'I'm scared.' My girlfriend asks me why I don't talk more about what I'm feeling. I've gotten better at it, but it will *never* come naturally."

You don't need to be a shrink to see how the lessons boys learn affect their behavior as men. Men are being asked, more and more, to show sensitivity, but they dread the very word. They struggle to build their increasingly uncertain work lives but will deny they're in trouble. They want love, affection, and support but don't know how to ask for them. They hide their weaknesses and fears from all, even those they care for. They've learned to be wary of intervening when they see others in trouble. They often still balk at being stigmatized as weird.

Some men get shocked into sensitivity—when they lose their jobs, their wives, or their lovers. Others learn it through a strong marriage or through their own children.

It may be a long while, however, before male culture evolves to the point that boys can learn more from one another than how to hit curve balls. Last month, walking my dog past the playground near my house, I saw three boys encircling a fourth, laughing and pushing him. He was skinny and rumpled, and he looked frightened. One boy knelt behind him while another pushed him from the front, a trick familiar to any former boy. He fell backward.

When the others ran off, he brushed the dirt off his elbows and walked toward the swings. His eyes were moist, and he was struggling for control.

"Hi," I said through the chain-link fence. "How ya doing?"

"Fine," he said quickly, kicking his legs out and beginning his swing.

Exploring the Reading through Discussion

1. What is your first reaction to this essay? Do you agree with the author? Do you disagree with some of his statements?
2. Why does the author think it is important to "understand something about boys"?
3. What lessons do boys learn as they are growing up, according to Katz?
4. How do the lessons boys learn affect their behavior as men? Do you agree with what the author says are the results?
5. Katz begins and ends his essay with a narrative. Is using this technique in the introduction and conclusion effective? Why?

Developing Vocabulary

List at least three words in this selection that are new to you. Write your understanding of each word from the context. Then look up each word in the dictionary, and write the definition that you think best fits the meaning in this writing.

Discovering Connections through Writing

1. Do girls have their own "Code of Conduct" when growing up? What are the rules? For what behaviors are girls rewarded?

2. Besides the influence of peers, who or what else defines the sex roles boys and girls learn? Does television play a role? School? Parents?

3. Write about a time when you learned a lesson about what it means to be a man or what it means to be a woman.

"Growing Up" Is Cumulative, Evolutionary and Never-Ending

Brian Dickinson

Brian Dickinson is an editorial columnist for the Providence Journal. *Because of an illness, he is paralyzed and can communicate only with the aid of an adaptive computer that allows him to type his thoughts. As you read, explore your own thoughts about the claim he makes in this 1995 column: "The subject of learning matters less than the resolve to keep on learning."*

A couple of college faculty friends dropped by recently. One teaches English, the other, sociology. They can talk interestingly about almost anything, which is useful since I, because of my illness, can't talk at all. Those two are better company than Jay Leno (which some would argue is not much of a feat).

Both are in their late 50s, as am I. We fell to talking about careers and the curious turns that they sometimes take. One of them said, "I wonder what I'll do when I grow up," and we all laughed. How absurd, really, for a man in his late 50s to be talking about when he "grows up." We of that age group instinctively imagine—nay, we know—that we *are* "grown up."

But are we, really? How would we know? What distinguishes a "grown-up" from a person who is not grown up?

The distinction would scarcely matter, except for the fact that our society places such emphasis on "growing up." Much advertising points its appeal at young people considered to be on their way to growing up (when they presumably will have money to spend on the products being peddled). The status of "grown-up" is a large part of this appeal, whether the pitch is for aftershave lotion, autos, or beer.

The underlying assumptions behind such ads are demonstrably false. The first is that grown-upness is more desirable than kidness. I doubt that this is true and challenge anyone to prove it. The second assumption, equally bogus, is that grown-ups automatically know what they are doing at all times, and why. I feel no need to refute this one, either. The history books are crammed with examples.

Getting to be a "grown-up" is usually thought of in chronological terms. First you're a child, then you bump your way through the Scylla and Charybdis of adolescence. Then you hit 18, and you can enlist in the armed forces, vote and do all sorts of other things. One more hop, and you're 21, and in every way a grown-up in the eyes of the law.

Maybe that's how the law looks at it, but I wonder if the distinction has any other meaning. If there really is such a thing as a grown-up, I doubt that it has much to do with one's chronological age. I have known people in their teens who had a good bit of horse sense and the ability to make sound judgments most of the time. I've also known people well along in years who were barely functional and should not have been trusted with a driver's license.

What accounts for the difference? Maybe most of us get goofy and frequently flummoxed after we've put on a goodly number of years. We may put on a brave front, and we may do our jobs passably well or better. But even so, there may be times when our insides feel all strange, and we'd just as soon retreat from things until they settle down. It's then that even the most stalwart don't feel much like grown-ups at all.

Stress will sniff you out, wherever you are. You don't have to be Woody Allen to feel that modern life is overwhelming much of the time. Being a grown-up about it all is tough, maybe impossible. I know a man who, when a young boy, banged his knee or sustained some other injury. When his father urged him to be big and brave, the boy replied, through his sniffles, "I'm not very big. And I'm not very brave." Not a grown-up response, perhaps, but a true one.

At times, for many of us, stress threatens to be overwhelming.

Coping and adapting to change is a big part of what "growing up" entails. The thing is—and they don't tell you this when you're a kid—that adapting to change is going to occupy center stage for as long as you live. Growing up is never-ending. There is no magic threshold that you cross, heave a sigh of satisfaction and say, "Wow! Now I'm grown up!"

This is just as well. How stultifying it would be if one were to pass abruptly into grown-up status. It would be like having a teacher stamp your hand with indelible ink when you arrived at a high school dance: You could stay until the end, but once you left, there could be no returning. If you were officially designated a grown-up at the age of, say, 30, you would gaze out on a bleak vista of sameness for all of your remaining days. There would be no challenge, no novelty, no refreshment or diversion.

The term *grown-up* implies all kinds of growth, and I suppose one of the most important is learning, and not just from books, although the printed word, allowing ideas, chronicles, and tales to be passed down the generations, may be humankind's greatest achievement. Learning is how we grow, and keep on growing, for a lifetime. The subject of learning matters less than the resolve to keep on learning, hence "growing up." We're never entirely grown up. The process is evolutionary, continuous, cumulative—and it's the process (of growth) that really matters.

Exploring the Reading through Discussion

1. Does Dickinson define what it means to be grown up?

2. The author doubts that "grown-upness is more desirable than kidness." What evidence does he provide to support his opinion? Would you rather be a kid or a grown-up? Why?

3. Chronologically, what are the ages that signal we're growing up? Can you think of other ages, besides the ones mentioned in the essay, that signal important stages in life?

4. "Growing up is never-ending." Do you agree? Why?

5. Does Dickinson consider both the denotative and the connotative meanings of the term *grown up*? Explain.

Developing Vocabulary

List at least three words in this selection that are new to you. Write your understanding of each word from the context. Then look up each word in the dictionary, and write the definition that you think best fits the meaning in this writing.

Discovering Connections through Writing

1. Dickinson asks in his essay, "What distinguishes a 'grown-up' from a person who is not grown up?" What do you think the differences are?

2. "Learning is how we grow, and keep on growing, for a lifetime," writes Dickinson at the end of his essay. Do you agree? In your answer, present some examples to support your answer.

3. "Never trust anyone over thirty" was a favorite expression of teens and twenty-somethings in the 1960s and 1970s. Are there barriers today that separate generations? What are they?

Thanksgiving Is the Greatest Holiday

Robert C. Maynard

Journalist, editor, and publisher Robert C. Maynard was the first African American to own a major metropolitan daily, the Oakland Tribune. *In this column, collected in* Letters to My Children *(1995), Maynard explores his memories of a family celebration and of his father. As you read, see if you can identify the Thanksgiving lessons Maynard learned that may have contributed to his professional success.*

November 21, 1982—Thanksgiving. To hear the word when we were children was enough to swell the heart with joy. It might be July, and someone would make some vague reference to Thanksgiving, and we would stop and reflect with pleasure.

Thanksgiving was not a holiday to our household. It was a concept. Much planning went into it, the whole family was involved in all the preparatory chores, and we seemed to celebrate it for about a week.

No holiday bore for us the significance of Thanksgiving. We paid very little attention to Christmas because my father's religious doctrine dismissed as fallacy the idea that anyone knew when Christ was born. Easter suffered similar defects, in my father's way of thinking.

July 4 was always a great deal of fun and so was Labor day, both of them occasions for fine family picnics. We celebrated birthdays with great fervor, but with six children, it must have seemed to my parents there was always a birthday celebration going on in our home.

Nothing made us feel the richness of oneness as Thanksgiving did. It must have been the combination of fabulous food and fabulous faith.

Forgive me for talking about the food first. My father and his younger brother migrated to New York toward the end of World War I. Their parents had been able to send them off with a few dollars, but it was assumed they would be earning money soon after they arrived in the big city of dreams.

Instead, it took awhile for them to find work. They lived in a furnished flat and neither of them knew enough about how to cook "to boil an egg," as my father put it so often in telling the tales of his youthful adventures.

Their money ran out quickly because they were eating every meal in restaurants. They nearly starved to death. When my father met my mother and discovered she was a masterly cook, he took it as a sure sign their marriage had been arranged in heaven.

My father was a great believer in the philosophy that no life experience is for naught. Each experience, no matter how painful, held a life lesson for him. So he always taught us. The only problem was that sometimes they were his life experiences but his children were the beneficiaries of the lesson.

That's the way it was with cooking. Even though it was he who almost starved to death, it was we who had to learn to cook. He died not knowing much more about cooking than he knew when he came to New York a half-century before. But he laid down an edict that no son of his would pass his 14th birthday without being able to produce all or most of a major meal. He might have made the same rule for my sisters but he did not. It was assumed they would learn to cook in the natural course of things. But he was taking no chance on any son of his finding himself in a faraway place to fend for himself at a stove.

My mother and sisters were our tutors and tormentors in the kitchen. Each of us boys was oriented to the kitchen first by becoming experts in pot and pan washing. When we displayed due diligence in that department, we moved on to vegetable peeling with a paring knife. Chickens and turkeys came from the butcher shop in those days with their feathers firmly in place and it fell to us boys to master the art of feather removal. (I never mastered that one.) Little by little, you got a chance to cook something under the watchful eye of my mother and my sisters.

The day you presented a dish to the whole family was the day you passed in our house from useless boy to promising young man. That kitchen was its own form of school, and the great annual celebration of the virtures of the institution of the kitchen was Thanksgiving Day.

We scrubbed vegetables, chopped onions and scurried about from early morning in an atmosphere of family euphoria. The aromas told us "the bird" was nearing readiness and that spurred us to bring it all together in a grand finale orchestrated by my mother.

I remember as if it were yesterday the Thanksgiving I was assigned to make the marshmallow sweet potatoes all by myself. I burned the marshmallows the first time and got it almost right the second time. When the dish reached the table, my father tasted it and declared that he was pleased that his last-born might actually learn to cook. No medal could have pleased me more.

My father's faith was simple, but it was the center of his being. He lived to worship God and he lived for his family. He cared for little besides church and home. All this came to fit nicely with Thanksgiving.

In this holiday he found the nexus of his love of God and family. He was a man in constant state of thanksgiving. He felt richly blessed by the simple rewards of health and a home.

So at Thanksgiving, he encouraged us to share with each other those things for which we felt most thankful from the previous year. Usually, we were most grateful for good grades, but he stretched us and pushed us to think deeper and search for the really important reasons to be thankful.

That turned out to be difficult to do without thinking about some of our disappointments, things we had to admit had not turned out as well as we might have hoped. He always wanted to hear about those because he always wanted to know what we planned to do to make our disappointments eventually become triumphs.

Well, we would always say to that question, we will try harder.

Yes, yes, he would always say, but how? How?

At such times, he would often exhort us to have a bold spirit and an inquiring mind. None of us ever asked him exactly what a bold spirit was. We surmised from the tone of his voice when he said those words that he wanted us to think first of what had to be done and think only after that about the obstacles.

I remember one of my sisters at the Thanksgiving table describing some excruciating challenge she faced as a freshman in college. She seemed truly daunted by all she faced. She finished describing the challenge and there was a long silence. Finally, she asked my father what she should do.

"A little more prayer will take care of it," he said.

In truth, although he exhorted us to prayer and faith, he never allowed us to overlook the benefits of preparation and hard work. That to me is what was so fabulous about his faith. He gave God the credit for all his successes and ours, but he was not about to allow any of us to say we would pray instead of study for an exam.

He believed in rigorous study and the applied use of knowledge. Knowlege that was acquired and not shared was no knowledge at all as far as he was concerned. One of his favorite phrases was "educated fool," a term he often used to describe people with impressive degrees and an unimpressive degree of common sense.

I still awaken excited on Thanksgiving morning. I still love to make marshmallow sweet potatoes and dressing with mushrooms and sausage. But I rarely find myself thinking of those objects purely as food. They have become, for me, much as they were intended to be, symbols of Thanksgiving in its truest sense, a thankfulness for blessings that have no name.

Exploring the Reading through Discussion

1. Why was Thanksgiving such a special holiday for the Maynard family? What do you think the author means by the "richness of oneness" the family felt? What are the "blessings that have no name" that he is thankful for?

2. Why does the author's father think it is important his sons learn to "produce all or most of a major meal"? Do you agree?

3. "That kitchen was its own form of school," Maynard writes. What did he learn there?

4. In Maynard's essay about Thanksgiving, he explores two subjects: "fabulous food and fabulous faith." Where does each section of the essay start and stop? How does he unify the two parts?

5. Maynard uses several modes in his essay. How many can you identify?

Developing Vocabulary

List at least three words in this selection that are new to you. Write your understanding of each word from the context. Then look up each word in the dictionary, and write the definition that you think best fits the meaning in this writing.

⌒Discovering Connections through Writing

1. Maynard's essay provides a picture of a special family, but it may not reflect the size, interests, or values of your own family. In an essay, explore the topic of family: Compare or contrast your family with the one presented above, define what you think a successful family is, or describe the traditions and values that are important to your family.

2. "Knowledge that [is] acquired and not shared [is] no knowledge at all." Do you agree? Following the guidelines for writing an effective argument, write an essay to persuade a reader to accept your point of view.

3. Describe a person who has been or is a strong influence on you. As Maynard does, provide plenty of examples to help readers understand how and why that person is important.

Go and Conquer the World

Michaela Otway (student)

Have you ever left your home for an extended period? Or have you had to take an action you didn't want to because it was best for you? As you read this student's essay, try to discover what feelings you both may have in common.

Often I wonder if there is anybody else in this world like me. I ponder many questions of life. Are people always forced to take difficult and terrifying actions? If this is the case, do the people closest to them say, "It's best for you"? I suppose such wonderings stem from that unforgettable day in my life. I speak of the day that I said good-bye to almost everything that I know and value and stepped into the world of the unfamiliar.

I woke up that Monday morning feeling nauseous. I wanted just to crawl back between my cotton sheets and fall asleep again. Maybe if I were to wake up later, I would realize that it was all a dream and that I did not really have to leave my beautiful, tropical island, St. Lucia, to go away to school.

The sound of raindrops hitting the galvanized roof of my little wooden house woke me from my reverie. I got out of bed, fumbled my way to the bathroom, and tripped over a little stuffed animal that had fallen from my bed. This was a familiar morning routine for me, one that I would not do again for a while. The scent of my mother's perfume lingered in the air, and I knew she was awake. I figured that she must have been as nervous as I was about the day's events because she did not usually wake up at seven-thirty in the morning.

"Good morning, hon. Sleep well?" My mother always greeted me like that on a morning. I replied with a grunt and made no attempt to smile. I was not hungry, so Mom suggested that we sit on the balcony to smoke a cigarette. This was a usual thing for us to do, but this time it was awkward. Neither of us knew what to say. However, I was not surprised when my mother broke the silence with an attempt to convince me that leaving the island was the best thing for me.

She reminded me of the reason that I was leaving. This was a conversation that I would never forget. "Not many people get the opportunity to go away to school," she said in the affectionate tone that she always used with me. For the next hour she talked about how good an experience it would be for me and how I would return to the island when I was finished, a much more intelligent and mature person than I was. She went on to tell me that she did not want me to make the same mistakes that she had made. When she was my age, she had left college and had given up all the opportunities that a good education brings to marry my father. And where was he now? He had moved to another island to go into business there so that he could make enough money to send me away to college.

I felt a pang of guilt with the mention of my father's efforts to give me everything. Before my dad left, we were such a close family. We spent a lot of time together and did a lot of family things. My father's dream was for me to go to college and take advantage of the education that neither he nor my mother ever did. He decided, though, that he was not making enough money in his job at the time. He then took it upon himself to leave his homeland of forty-four years to go elsewhere in search of a better job. He did this not for himself, but, in fact, to create a better life for his family and to allow for educational opportunities for me, his "baby girl."

My thoughts were brought to a quick end at the sound of a car's horn in our driveway. It was a few of my closest friends and my boyfriend of a year and two months. I had been expecting them because they were all going to accompany me to the airport. What I did not expect, however, was all the gifts they presented to me. I did not want to open them at that time because I knew that I would probably cry. I quickly added them to my suitcases, which were already full, and proceeded to get dressed.

Then it was time to go. I kissed each of my three dogs and six cats good-bye, took one last look at my room, and closed the door. I felt as if I had just closed the door to my life, which was never to be opened again. I watched as my friends struggled to get my suitcases into my mother's Jeep. Beads of sweat formed on my forehead even though I was not the one doing the work. It was unusually humid that day, and I looked at the sky and thought to myself that it was going to rain again. When all my luggage was neatly packed, everybody piled into the two vehicles, and we set off to the airport.

The ride to the airport seemed longer than usual. I lay in my boyfriend's arms and stared out the window. I noticed buildings and roadway signs that I had never seen before. This was probably because these are the things that are taken for granted every day. All of the usually colorful flowers on the roadside seemed to be dull and without life, and they seemed to agree with the general feeling of the day.

When we arrived at the airport, I checked in quickly, and the group of us sat in the waiting area. Everybody began to tell jokes to lighten the dreary atmosphere. Although I was upset, I could not help but laugh at the humor that was going around. I could always count on my friends to cheer me up, or at least to try. About half an hour later, the boarding calls for my flight were announced. We took some group pictures quickly, and I began to say my good-byes.

As I gave and received hugs and kisses from everybody, the tears rolled down my cheeks and wet my green dress. I had been strong thus far, but I could not hold my emotions back anymore. I did not want to say good-bye to these familiar faces. It was hardest to say good-bye to my mother, my idol and mentor. I held onto her so tightly that it was hard to breathe. We embraced each other for about five minutes before she pushed me away. She held my shoulders and looked me in the eye. She was crying too. "Go and conquer the world, my darling," she said. I stepped away and headed for the boarding area. As I walked through the doorway, I turned around to take one last look at everybody through tear-filled eyes, and I blew a kiss to them all.

It was a ten-minute wait before boarding began. I had not stopped crying yet, and my mother's words rang in my head: "Go and conquer the world, my darling." She had so much confidence in me. I had just said good-bye to everything that meant anything to me, and I was entering a world that I did not know much about. However, there was a degree of certainty in me that I was going to conquer it, and this was the confidence I had as I stepped into the airplane and said hello to my new life.

Exploring the Reading through Discussion

1. Why does the author leave home?
2. What details does she provide to help you understand how she feels as she prepares to leave? What does she "know and value" that she has to leave?
3. Does Otway agree with her mother that leaving the island is the best thing for her?
4. Where in the essay does the author explain why her parents are sending her away? Do you think this is an effective way to organize the essay? Why?
5. Otway ends her essay as she steps onto the plane. Do you think this is a good place to conclude her story? Why?

Developing Vocabulary

List any words in this selection that are new to you. Write your understanding of each word from the context. Then look up each word in the dictionary, and write the definition that you think best fits the meaning in this writing.

Discovering Connections through Writing

1. Have you ever had to leave the familiar, as this author did, and enter "a world that [you] did not know much about"? Write about the causes or effects of that experience.

2. Otway describes her familiar morning routine and writes of "the things that are taken for granted every day" that she notices while driving to the airport. Take one day and carefully observe the familiar routines and places of your everyday world. Write about what you discover as a result.

3. Otway's parents struggle to ensure that their daughter obtains "all the opportunities that a good education brings." Write an essay in which you explain why you think a college education is valuable.

The Importance of Wearing a Safety Belt

Larissa R. Houk (student)

This student's essay challenges readers to explore the reasons for wearing a safety belt and to discover the effects on many lives when one person doesn't. Does this essay change your attitude about safety belts?

Many teenagers today seem to scoff at the idea of wearing a safety belt. Perhaps they do so because wearing a belt is not "cool." Maybe friends they drive with don't bother to wear a belt, and they fear being laughed at. Despite these and many other excuses that can be given for not wearing a safety belt, the concrete reasons for wearing a belt far outweigh these in significance.

Brian Machado's death is one example of a concrete reason.

"Mr. Machado died at Boston Medical Center from injuries received in a car accident. . . ." That's all the obituary had to say. The brief death notice failed to tell its readers the personal things that mattered most about Brian.

"Mr. Machado was a life-long resident of New Bedford," the notice read. The notice didn't mention the different houses in New Bedford where Brian had lived, how he used to tear little swatches of the wallpaper off from his bedroom wall in the house on Stapleton Street, how he and his brother wrestled each other in the living room countless times next to the brown couch their grandmother from Portugal had given them, or how very picky he was about everything that went into his room.

"He was a graduate of Roosevelt Jr. High School." Why didn't the article mention the secret crush he had on that cute girl in his math class when he was in seventh grade, how much he liked Tuesdays going home in the bus with his best friends, or how he was the real cause of that food fight that took place one November?

". . . and finished three years at Greater New Bedford Regional Vocational Technical High School." There was no mention of how much Brian hated going to Voke or how he and his friends rejoiced over the way the Packers had played their last game whenever they got together at Brian's locker on the second floor.

The obituary did say that Mr. Machado was eighteen.

It also said that Brian was employed by Stop & Shop and Burger King, but it failed to mention why he felt it necessary to work two part-time jobs when other kids his age struggled with just one. The article never mentioned Brian's plans.

The notice said that he died because of a car accident on Route 18, but it never said that Brian was on the highway because he was headed toward a Portuguese club with some of his new friends from Stop & Shop who had just ended their shift for the night.

"Mr. Machado was survived by . . ." and then a long list of names. If only those who had written the obituary had attended the funeral home, where Brian's mother sobbed loudly and bitterly, screamed and frantically clung to the still coffin surrounded with gaudy flowers, and cried out to her son in Portuguese. Maybe then they wouldn't have used the word "survived."

Perhaps the most important element of Brian's tragic death was the one thing that was most grueling to accept as fact. Bad enough that Brian was eighteen and just starting to feel more secure about himself. Bad enough that Brian's dreams for the future will never be realized. Bad enough that teenagers witnessed Brian's accident and were in the car with him when he drove. Bad enough that Brian's close friends and family lost a precious son, friend, brother, rival, and buddy that they will never see again. But worst of all, Brian's death could have been so easily prevented.

In the awful words of a state trooper at the scene of the accident, "the accident would not have been fatal if the victim had worn a belt."

If only Brian had taken a moment to click the safety belt into place over his waist, he would be alive today, working at Burger King, bagging at Stop & Shop, talking with friends, making plans for the future. Only one small click would have saved his life.

How many more of these horrible stories will we have to face? How many more times will we have to read the obituary of a teenage brother, student, sportsman, friend?

Brian's could be the last unnecessary death if only teenagers would take a moment from whatever it is they are doing in the car and simply click that safety belt over their waist. One small click. Please let's make Brian's death the last and learn from the tragedy of an eighteen-year-old boy who could have been and done so many things.

Exploring the Reading through Discussion

1. What are "the personal things that mattered most about Brian" according to Houk? Why aren't these details included in his obituary?

2. What do you think is the author's purpose in writing this essay? Does she succeed?

3. When you drive in a car, do you wear a seatbelt or insist that your passengers do? Why?

4. Does Houk use a subject-by-subject or point-by-point organization of her comparison of the obituary and the personal details of her friend's life? Do you think the organization is effective? Why?

5. Several of the paragraphs in the essay are very short. Why do you think the author chose to write them this way?

Developing Vocabulary

List any words in this selection that are new to you. Write your understanding of each word from the context. Then look up each word in the dictionary, and write the definition that you think best fits the meaning in this writing.

Discovering Connections through Writing

1. Should using safety belts or wearing motorcycle helmets be mandated by law? Should the driving age be raised, or should increased restrictions be placed on drivers under age eighteen? Write an argument in which you clearly state and support your point of view on one of these issues. Your instructor may ask you to research your topic and document the information you include.

2. Houk suggests in her introduction that peer pressure may be one reason that keeps teenagers from wearing safety belts. Write an essay in which you explore other examples of peer pressure. How do you define peer pressure? What are its causes? What effects does it have? Is peer pressure limited to people in their teens?

3. Write an essay about "the personal things that mattered most" about a friend or relative you have lost.

Exposed Toes

Diane Riva (student)

Are your old basketball shoes, the ones with the holes, your favorites? Maybe you couldn't spend a day without your floppy slippers? As you read student author Diane Riva's essay about shoes, try to discover the special connection she has to these everyday items.

The shoes scattered throughout the house belong to me. I will find a pair under the dining room table, a pair in the parlor, one or two pairs in the kitchen, and even a few in my bedroom. In my childhood memories, I can still hear my mother asking me to pick up my wayward shoes. Some habits are hard to break, and leaving my shoes wherever my feet release them is one I am still trying to overcome. When I look at my shoes, I see endless memories. They are part of my personality, and if they could talk, what colorful tales they would tell.

I own three pairs of black sneakers; they are my proud work shoes, and we spend the most time together. There are times when my feet melt when I enter them. My work as a bartender has enabled my sneakers to taste Guinness Irish stout, fine Russian vodkas, assorted hot coffee drinks, or whatever else I am rushing around the bar to make. They are the constant recipients of the over-filled glass of alcohol.

My black, tattered sneakers with tiny knots in the shoelaces have heard hours of endless stories from lonely travelers stopping in the hotel lounge, guests pouring out tales of love, heartache, job stress, divorce, battles won, battles lost, and hundreds of irritating jokes. At the end of my shift, if we are fortunate and it has rained, I give the bottoms of my hard-working sneakers a bath in a fresh puddle. It feels good to wash away work. When my feet arrive home, my sneakers are usually slipped off and left in the parlor to slumber. This is where they will quietly remain until I torture them for another eight hours of work.

Along with my sneakers, I own a pair of boat shoes. The tops are a reddish brown, the same color as an Irish Setter, and the soles are made of rubber. I have had these shoes for over six years, and still they do not age as I do. When I occasionally wear my boat shoes, I don't like the way they look on my wide feet, but they feel so good. They know me the least but struggle to be in my world. I will probably have these shoes for the rest of my life. They are like memories of past boyfriends: hard to get rid of.

When I open my closet door, my dress shoes lie dead in dusty boxes. About every four months, I will remove a pair and struggle into them. When I wear these high-heeled shoes, it is usually for a wedding, a Christmas party, or a night on the town. When I add one or two inches to my height, I end up having this pretty feeling, and my legs have a tendency to like the way they look. The sound of a high-heeled shoe on a polished marble floor at a posh restaurant, I will admit, has a certain appeal to me. I gather it is my whole look, from the top of my perfectly set hair to the ends of my smothered toes, that gives me this feeling of attractiveness.

But how I look forward to removing these falsely overstated dress shoes and returning them to their dusty coffins. Funny how these shoes never lounge around the house; they are always returned to their boxes. I would not want to insult the everyday, comfortable shoe with the high society heel.

Among my most treasured shoes is a pair of sandals. They can be worn throughout all the seasons, with or without socks. My huaraches are from Tiajuana, and on a hot day many years ago, I handpicked them myself from among many of their twins. The soles are made from black, recycled tires, and the upper portion consists of thick, tan leather strips that entwine to form an interesting open-toe design. They call my name constantly, but unfortunately, they are the most inappropriate shoe for all occasions. As I picked up my paycheck from work one cold November day, my boss commented on my unusual footwear for this time of year. He could not help but notice my well-worn extra-wide huaraches and my thick woolen socks, so he stated that it seemed an unsuitable time of year for sandals. I tried to explain the comfort zone of these broken-in shoes, but he just looked at me with confusion. I don't think that he could relate to the love–hate affair that women have with their shoes. I have had the pleasure of spoiling my feet with these huaraches for over eight years. Each spring they take a trip to the cobbler for their yearly checkup. I think the cobbler looks forward to this annual visit and admires the workmanship in these weary old sandals.

I must admit my shoes of choice were given to me by my parents, and I wear these constantly. Nothing has to be tied; they have no straps, no buckles, no leather between the toes, no heels. They are never too tight and always fit perfectly—my natural feet. Whenever possible, my feet are out of confinement, barefoot and happy. I love for my feet to touch and feel all the materials of life. They can be tickled, washed, counted, and colored. They hold all of my memories. They were on my honeymoon; they were at my daughter's birth; they feel spring and the ocean first; they have been bitten, cut, and bruised. I never have to look for them, they are always where I left them, and they never have to be put away.

As I search throughout my house and pick up my wayward shoes before my mother arrives for a visit, I look down at the bundle of leather and laces in my arms, and days of my past shout out to me. I know why these shoes are scattered about. They are my memories, and I do not want to put them away.

Exploring the Reading through Discussion

1. What is the main point that the author wants to make about her shoes? On what basis does she categorize them?
2. What details help you picture the author's shoes and understand how she feels about them?
3. What are Riva's "shoes of choice"? Why are these her favorites?
4. How do the introduction and the conclusion contribute to the effectiveness of this essay?
5. In what order does the author arrange the types of shoes? Do you think this order is effective? Why?

Developing Vocabulary

List any words in this selection that are new to you. Write your understanding of each word from the context. Then look up each word in the dictionary, and write the definition that you think best fits the meaning in this writing.

Discovering Connections through Writing

1. Describe a favorite article of clothing that brings back fond memories or makes you feel good when you wear it. Help your reader understand your feelings by describing the clothing and explaining why it is special to you.

2. As Riva does with shoes, classify another type of clothing or accessory that you own, such as hats, T-shirts, or earrings. Be sure to follow a consistent method of classification.

3. The author writes about struggling into pairs of high-heeled dress shoes. Write an essay in which you support the thesis that being fashionable doesn't always mean being comfortable.

A Religion?

Henry Bousquet (student)

For Henry Bousquet, fishing is more than a hobby. As you read, see if the description of fishing this student author presents in his essay changes your attitude about the sport.

Can anyone imagine what a summer would be like if you couldn't go fishing at least once a week? Total hell, if you were to ask me. Not many people go about their "fishing ritual" in quite the way that I and my fishing buddies do.

I must call your attention to the fact that I am not an expert on the art or technique of any kind of fishing, be it salt water or fresh. I can merely illustrate what works for me and a few faithful observers of our ritualistic method.

Sure, there are those who would try to tell me to run out and spend five hundred (absurd) dollars on all the best equipment like fish finders, lures, hip waders, power-bait, a canoe, a "scanoe" (part skiff, part canoe with motor), gloves, hooks, pliers, nets, sun screen, polarized sun glasses, sweat bands, and tons of other useless junk. This stuff usually ends up polluting the waters and killing the fish as opposed to enabling you to catch them.

Instead of following the blind consumer majority, I adhere to my own list of basics and fool-proof techniques. I grab a twenty-dollar rod of any style from my local sporting goods shop, a box of hooks, two bobbers, a packet of sinkers, and a dozen night-crawlers. After spending a total of maybe twenty-nine dollars and change, I throw the worms in the refrigerator and set my alarm clock for 5 A.M., making damn sure to get a good night's rest.

When I have had my night's rest, the pot of joe goes on, and it's time to assemble my gear and wake up my friends. I take a bucket in case I catch the big one. (The big one will earn me a pin from the Massachusetts Wildlife and Fisheries Commission; I have all the "approximate" weights for pin-earning fish memorized, of course.) When I have everything and am ready to go jump in the car and get the guys, I try to remember one thing: Not every one, not every time, can catch the fish; the important thing is to have fun.

Just one quick thing before I continue. The state law requires that you have a fishing license on you when you fish. When I don't have one, I pretend I forgot it: They almost always let you go the first time with a warning.

Once I reach my favorite fishin' hole or my buddy's, we bait up, lean way back, and let it rip for the nearest patch of lily pads. If after a little while I don't get a nibble, I just reel in the line and try another spot. But the larger fish always seem to like the cover of vegetation. They wait, and as soon as a little "food" swims by, they dart out and nab it for supper. I am also told fish love structure; they hang out there waiting for some angler (like me) to come by and fish them out.

As the first fish strikes, a new feeling comes over me. I wait for the bobber to go down and the line to go taut. As soon as it does, I tug in the opposite direction the fish goes and BANG! set the hook. Some fish can put up a struggle—even the small ones. So I don't get too excited. Then, I allow it to run some by letting out a little line. This will tire the fish, I hope. Once I've landed it, no matter the size, it will be mine.

Whether I am the first or only one to catch anything or it is someone else, we all ("ritual worshipers") follow one rule: "He who gloats, floats!" Since I'd rather stay dry in the boat than float in the water, I keep my glee in check.

Exploring the Reading through Discussion

1. Why does Bousquet refer to his fishing expeditions as "a ritual"?

2. What are the main steps in every fishing trip?

3. Even though the author writes that he is not an expert on the subject, what tips do you learn about fishing by reading?

4. How does the author arrange the information in his essay? What transitional expressions does he use to provide coherence?

5. What is the dominant mode of this essay? What do you think is the author's purpose for writing?

Developing Vocabulary

List any words in this selection that are new to you. Write your understanding of each word from the context. Then look up each word in the dictionary, and write the definition that you think best fits the meaning in this writing.

Discovering Connections through Writing

1. What do you do to relax and get away from everyday stress? Write about what you do so that readers can follow the same steps.

2. The author writes about a "blind consumer majority" buying expensive equipment, although he thinks basic, less expensive gear is adequate. Do you think our pursuit of sports and hobbies is becoming too materialistic? Are we more concerned with the toys that we have than with the fun we can have?

3. Do you know how to do something that most people don't know how to do? Do you have a special skill or talent? Explain to others what strategies or steps are involved in applying your skill or talent.

A Bully Who Wore Bobby Pins

Amanda Beaulieu (student)

Why do children think that some toys and games are for boys and some are for girls? How are children who challenge the stereotyped roles treated? As you read this student's story, see if you discover any connections to your own playground memories.

As a little girl, I was never too interested in dolls or patent leather shoes or other girls my age, for that matter. I suppose one might say I was a bit of a tomboy. I played sports, I liked bugs (except spiders, of course), and I wasn't afraid to get hurt or dirty. All my friends were boys because, in some small way, they could respect a girl who'd knock them out if they looked at her the wrong way. I guess they all figured that my "cooties" weren't as bad as the other girls'.

Being the bully with the pigtails was never an easy job, but it was a title I carried proudly. As a member of the boys' crowd, I valued my school playground as my kingdom. I could run the fastest, spit the farthest, and swing the highest. I was shameless and cruel, but I had a good time. If you were on my swing, you'd get a black eye. If you were in my way, you'd get pushed. If you had candy or a toy I liked, I took it, no questions asked. I was sitting on top of the world, and I was only in first grade!

Of course my reign was challenged over my four years on that playground. It was like going to war and having your home at stake. I can remember our playground having a jungle gym like no other I've seen. It was a massive bug with an arching tail, high eyeballs, and a gaping mouth. If the paint hadn't been so chipped and worn, it would have been green and red. Near the end of my second grade year, a myth started circulating. It was being said that only the toughest kids in school could climb to the top of the bug's eyes and jump down. Normally, myths and rumors never scared me, but this was a threat to my reputation. Of course no one had seen someone do it, so I did what anyone would have: I lied like a rug. I swore I'd done it last year. I'd done it dozens of times. Everything was perfect until another girl, with ripped corduroys and dirt-smudged cheeks, called my bluff. She bet me a whole dollar that I couldn't do it. Then she bet me another dollar that she could. Now by this point, I was ready to move to another town, but I couldn't walk away from a challenge. I never had before. I accepted and shook her sticky hand, which was covered in McDonald's Band-Aids. It was agreed that we would meet at recess that day after lunch.

Eleven-thirty came too quickly, and I found myself standing in a ring of people waiting for my challenger. She came out late and with a clean face, as if she had washed it for the occasion. We glared at one another and began climbing. I moved up and up, one Barbie sneaker over the other, chewing my Chinese fortune gum and promising myself that even if I lost, I was going to beat the stuffing out of that girl. Finally I was at the very top. I looked down to see this sloppy girl, this threat, grinning back up at me. I was so angry, I jumped down without thinking. I landed on my feet, regained by balance, and punched her right in the stomach. I left her on her backside in the sand, holding her stomach and gasping for air. As I walked away and waited for the red to leave my cheeks, I realized what I'd done. I had climbed and jumped from the bug!

I had always liked being tough and boyish, but never so much as that day. And of all the boys and a few girls who ever dared challenge me, I was beaten only when the school closed down and they paved my little kingdom.

Exploring the Reading through Discussion

1. Do you like the little girl in this story? Why? Why is she proud to be called "the bully with the pigtails"?
2. What does the author mean when she says she was a tomboy? Do you agree with her description of what girls like to do?
3. Why does the author use the word *kingdom* to describe the playground? What other words does she use to develop this comparison? Do you think this metaphor is effective?
4. What is Beaulieu's tone in this essay? What details in the essay help you understand her attitude about this childhood experience?
5. Find examples of parallelism in this essay.

Developing Vocabulary

List any words in this selection that are new to you. Write your understanding of each word from the context. Then look up each word in the dictionary, and write the definition that you think best fits the meaning in this writing.

⟜Discovering Connections through Writing

1. Describe a challenge that you met or a time you stood up for yourself when you were a child. Provide plenty of concrete details to help your reader understand why that experience was important.

2. What have you done that makes you particularly proud? Write an essay about that accomplishment, and be sure to describe how the achievement made you feel.

3. This story may raise some questions you would like to explore further. What should a child who is confronted by a bully do? What should children learn about resolving conflicts, and who should teach them?

Fear Not

Greg Andree (student)

Before this student author took a long walk across a dance floor, he considered what fear is and how it can affect us. As you read, ask yourself whether you have experienced each of the fears Greg Andree describes.

I looked across the dance floor; one of the most attractive women I had ever seen sat talking with some friends. She glanced toward me, but I turned away. Was she really looking at me? Why not? I'm a handsome guy. In fact, my mom tells me that all the time. I took a quick look back at her; she was still looking in my direction.

Why wouldn't she be looking at me? But she might just be looking at my friend who was sitting near me, or for that matter, she might just be trying to see what time it was (a clock hung just above my head). I could have misinterpreted a look at a clock for a glance in my direction.

What was keeping me from just getting up, walking over to her, and asking her to dance? Well, besides the fear of rejection from her and the dread of humiliation in front of her friends and mine, nothing at all.

I remember that as a kid I often sat alone in my basement doing my homework. It was the only place in the house I could go to be alone—well, besides the bathroom. If you spent too much time in there, though, people began to talk.

As daylight turned to dusk and then to darkness, the basement's shadows seemed to take on a life of their own; sounds that might have been ordinary before now sounded strange and menacing. I decided that this was no longer the ideal place for me to be alone with my thoughts. I got up and started walking slowly towards the steps that led to my family and the safety of their number. I wanted to run but refused to give the monster the satisfaction of knowing that it drove me from my own basement. I had to be brave and fight the panic that was welling up inside me. By the time I reached the stairs, I could feel its hot breath on my neck. I was sure that the creature was about to attack and drag me down into his hidden lair. Before it could, I ran, taking the stairs two at a time. If I could only reach the top, I would be safe.

Looking back now, it seems silly, but to a nine-year-old it was life or death. It's the same as when a thirteen-year-old, afraid of not fitting in, does everything within his power to belong. The worst thing in the world to a young teenager is the "problem" of being unique, having special talents or interests that are outside the margins of acceptability to the "popular" kids in school.

An example of this, from a boy's perspective, is that you're accepted if you excel in sports but are hopelessly doomed to exile if you are talented in music or art. As we get older, we realize these talents are gifts, not curses, and are grateful for our uniqueness, although knowing this now didn't make it easier then.

Now, as a college student, I have other fears. What if I fail in the career I've chosen, if I don't fulfill my dreams? How will I support myself, my family? Someday, if I do prosper in my career, will I look back at my college years and laugh at fears that now seem so enormous? What will my fears be then? Old age, senility, death? I don't really know.

What I do know is that no matter who we are or what our station in life is, we all have fears. Some are reasonable and keep us safe from the dangers that surround us constantly, and others are unreasonable and ridiculous, or seem so to those of us who don't share them. Some make us strive to do better; others keep us from attempting the things we would really like to do. If there's a fear holding you back from accomplishing your dreams, you have two choices: Either find a way to overcome it, or cower in its shadow and learn to live with what could have been.

But enough of all that. I was in the middle of one of my adventures. Now, where was I? Never mind, I remember. . . .

What should I do? Just sit there and not take the chance, or seize the day as Robin Williams would have in the movie *Dead Poets Society*? Which is best, to have loved and lost, or, in this case, tried and failed, or to have never tried at all? Finally, I thought of the advice Kevin Kline had given to a young pirate in Gilbert and Sullivan's *Pirates of Penzance:* "Always follow the dictates of your heart, my boy, and chance the consequences."

With this in mind, I got to my feet and made my way across the room to where she and her friends were sitting. I stood just a few feet from her. Doing my best Christian Slater imitation, I looked into her eyes and said, "Excuse me, Miss, would you care to dance?" She seemed to think it over for a moment, then took my hand and nodded her approval. "You do understand you'll be dancing with me, right?" I said. She laughed and said that she understood that I was included in the bargain.

As we danced, she leaned in close to me, her face inches from mine, and I felt her warm breath caress my cheek. She looked into my eyes and said, "Do you know what time it is? I really couldn't see the clock that well from where I was sitting."

Exploring the Reading through Discussion

1. What types of fear does the writer describe? In what order does he present these? Which fear do you think is the worst?

2. What did the author learn about what he feared as he grew older?

3. Some fears "are reasonable and keep us safe from the dangers that surround us constantly, and others are unreasonable and ridiculous." What examples can you think of to support this statement?

4. What is the thesis of this essay? Why do you think the author placed it where he did?

5. The author's story begins and ends at a dance. Where does the author shift from the chronological order of his narrative? How does he help readers understand that they are reading a flashback?

Developing Vocabulary

List any words in this selection that are new to you. Write your understanding of each word from the context. Then look up each word in the dictionary, and write the definition that you think best fits the meaning in this writing.

Discovering Connections through Writing

1. Write about a time you were afraid. Help readers understand not only what happened but also how the fear affected you. Did it hold you back or make you find a way to overcome it?

2. "If I only had known then what I know now." Have you ever had this thought? Write to explain why.

3. Andree quotes a line he heard in a film version of a Gilbert and Sullivan play: "Always follow the dictates of your heart, my boy, and chance the consequences." Do you agree with this advice? Provide specific examples to help your readers understand why you think the way you do.

To Smoke or Not to Smoke

Charlotte Medeiros (student)

In this reading selection, the student author shares not only her essay but also the outline she used to begin writing and her thoughts about her writing process. As you read, explore what you have learned about your own writing process. What have you discovered about who you are as a writer?

Thesis: In general, smokers, as a group, are much more pleasant to be around than nonsmokers.

1. Smokers never tell you that you smell.
   a. They don't hold their nose and wave their hands when you walk into a room.
   b. They don't break out the air freshener.
   c. They don't open all the windows.

2. Smokers are much more sociable and generous than nonsmokers.
   a. They always gather in a group.
   b. They're willing to share a light.
   c. They let you bum a cigarette if you run out.

3. Smokers are more fun to be with in restaurants.
   a. You don't have to worry about making conversation.
   b. They don't complain about the food and service.
   c. They don't complain about the bill.

I was a smoker throughout my teenage years and continued until I became pregnant at the age of twenty-five. I resumed the habit about a year ago, after not having had a cigarette for over eighteen years. Why would I begin again an addiction that I had so fiercely fought against for such a long time? I had my reasons. After being on both sides of the fence, I must make an observation: In general, smokers are much more pleasant to be around than nonsmokers. Smokers are ostracized, ridiculed, preached at, banned from public places, and pretty much treated as lepers. But, even in the face of all this adversity, we stand our ground and band together like the gladiators did when facing the lion. In spite of the intolerance we face, we are much more tolerant than nonsmokers.

Enter a room filled with smokers, and you'll be welcomed. Walk into the classroom of a smokefree school building, and you're greeted with the teacher wrinkling her nose, waving her hands, and saying, "You smell like a dirty ashtray. This is a smokefree building. You should have to remove your clothing before you're allowed in." A smoker would never tell you that you smell. A smoker would never break out the air freshener or open the windows in the dead of winter, as do your nonsmoking friends if you dare to light a cigarette in their homes.

Smokers are much more sociable and generous than nonsmokers. This is partially due to necessity. Since smoking is taboo in so many buildings, at any given time you are sure to find a group of smokers outside huddled together in the freezing cold or pouring rain. This close proximity to one another makes conversation inevitable, as does someone asking for a light or bumming a cigarette if he or she has run out. A smoker would never refuse these requests for help. If you're hungry, try asking a nonsmoker for a sandwich or a granola bar. I can guarantee that this request would be met with a mumbled excuse and a quick exit.

Have you ever gone to a restaurant with friends or family and been forced to sit with them in the nonsmoking section? This can be a nerve-wracking experience. Nonsmokers find fault with everything from the decor to the service and prices. A typical nonsmoking table's conversation: "It's cold in here." "You think so? I know my food is cold." "These prices are outrageous! Sally ate at this restaurant last week, and I know her meal didn't cost this much." "What about the service? That waitress is so slow, she must be taking naps in the kitchen." "By the time I get my dessert, I won't want it anymore." "Who cares about dessert? I just want my bill so I can leave." "I can't believe I have to pay for this cold, tasteless crap."

Smokers, on the other hand, rarely complain about these things. They are much more fun to be with in restaurants. Bad service? Smokers don't care. They just light up another cigarette while they wait. Lull in the conversation? No problem. A few puffs on the good old Marlboros, and the talk will soon be resumed. Lousy food? Who cares? Smoking pretty much destroys the taste buds, so food is mainly eaten for sustenance. Time to pay the bill? No sweat. Anyone who can afford twenty bucks for a carton of cigarettes isn't worried about a restaurant tab.

Have I convinced you to join the constantly dwindling numbers of the smoking minority? I sincerely hope not. For every single reason to take up smoking, there are ten good reasons not to. But any intelligent person already knows this, and I refuse to become an antismoking crusader; we have too many of these zealots around as it is. Just as an overweight person can't be nagged and belittled into losing weight, a smoker can't be browbeaten into giving up smoking. He or she must make the decision to quit when the time is right.

As for me, I want to give my family a special Christmas gift this year. I've set a personal goal that by Christmas day, I'll once again join the ranks of the non-smoking world. But I won't abandon my smoking friends or preach to them or tell them that they smell. And I'll even sit with them in the smoking sections, and stand with them in the cold and the rain. After all, what's a little second-hand smoke among friends?

Thoughts about Writing

Charlotte Medeiros

As a writer, I am who I am. This course is, after all, Writing from Experience. Each paper is based, somehow, on my personal life and opinions. I've always loved to read, and I enjoy writing, but I've never really learned to follow grammatical rules and regulations. I tend to just sit and write. The constructive criticism I received on my papers was beginning to guide me in the right direction. I wish that this course had a second semester, because I would like to learn more about getting my thoughts and ideas down on paper in the proper way. I find it very difficult to express what I want to say, both in speaking and in writing. Writing these papers gave me some encouragement, but I wish it could have gone further.

I definitely like writing pieces with a humorous theme. I tend to be facetious in my writing, as well as in my interaction with others (sometimes inappropriately so). This is how I deal with uncomfortable or difficult situations.

Freewriting and clustering are the two forms of prewriting that I find the easiest, because I can put down ideas and see how they connect. This is basically how I write. I just put everything up on the monitor of my word processor and then take out what I don't want. To help me decide what to revise, I usually read my writing aloud to another person. I make changes as I'm reading. It's a very undisciplined way of writing, but it's what I'm the most comfortable with.

"To Smoke or Not to Smoke" I found a little difficult to write because I had some trouble deciding on a topic. I also had a hard time with outlining, but once I got moving on it, it was a little easier. I can see the benefits of outlining as a writing aid, but I find the process somewhat restrictive compared to the methods I usually use to develop ideas.

I got the idea for this paper by observing the obstacles that the students who smoke at Bristol Community College have to deal with every day. But what really made me choose this topic was the day my friend and I walked into a class, and the teacher told us that we smelled like dirty ashtrays. My friend was furious, and I thought it was hysterical! I'm long past the stage of letting ignorant remarks bother me. I usually just ignore them or counterattack with a sarcastic answer (my aforementioned inappropriate sense of humor), but this seemed to me to be a great idea for a paper.

Exploring the Reading through Discussion

1. Do you think Medeiros is writing to inform, to entertain, or to persuade her readers? Explain your answer based on evidence in the essay.

2. Is the author writing to convince readers that smoking is good? Point to evidence in the essay to support your answer.

3. "I definitely like writing pieces with a humorous theme," this author writes. Is "To Smoke or Not to Smoke" humorous or serious in tone? Does the essay make you smile, or do you respond to it in a different way?

4. Find and underline or list five examples of concrete language that the author used to amplify her ideas. How is the language of the final essay different from the language of the beginning outline?

5. What modes does the author use to help her fulfill her purpose?

6. Compare the structure of the outline and the essay. What is the thesis and where is it located? What are the main points in the outline? Are they expressed as topic sentences? In what order does the author present her ideas in the outline and the essay? Do you think this order is effective? Why or why not? Does she include all the points in the outline in the essay? What ideas were added as the writer composed her essay?

7. How do you decide on a topic? Is your own writing process similar to or different from Medeiros's? In what ways do you think she could improve her writing process?

Developing Vocabulary

List any words in this selection that are new to you. Write your understanding of each word from the context. Then look up each word in the dictionary, and write the definition that you think best fits the meaning in this writing.

Discovering Connections through Writing

1. Respond to Medeiros by writing an essay to support this thesis: Nonsmokers are more _____ than smokers. (You fill in the blank.)

2. The generalizations of conventional wisdom suggest that it is better to be slim than overweight, better to exercise than to be inactive, better to have ambition than to be satisfied, better to embrace technology than to question it. Choose one of these comparisons—or another that you think of—and, as Medeiros does in her essay, support the viewpoint that goes against conventional wisdom. Be specific, and use concrete details to help readers understand your ideas and build your case.

3. Choose an essay you have completed, and write about your own writing process and the results. Here are some questions to explore. What prewriting technique did you use? What helped you discover your thesis? What was challenging about the assignment? How did you revise your writing? What pleases you about your finished essay? What would you like to improve even more?

Appendix **A**

Writing with a **Computer**

Most experienced college writers will tell you that they could not live without their computers. Before these powerful tools came on the scene, writers had to generate draft after draft by hand or on a typewriter. Now you can create one draft and then easily revise it many times without ever having to start again from scratch. If you know a few easy commands, you can change the order of your words, sentences, and paragraphs or add or delete either a single word or a whole chunk of text with little effort.

If you have not used a computer for word processing before, then this appendix will introduce you to some basic functions. If you will be using your school's computer lab, plan on spending some time with an instructional manual or tutorial. Your lab may also have advisors who can help you learn specific commands for the word-processing software you will be using. Especially important is the **Help** command, which provides answers to questions about the software right on the computer screen.

Because Microsoft® Word is one of the most widely used programs for both IBM and Macintosh computers, we will refer to its commands in our discussion below. However, every program is slightly different, so you may have to adapt some of the instructions you are about to read for the software you are using. Be sure to schedule enough lab time both for learning software and for writing.

If you are an experienced computer user, you will probably be familiar with all of the commands described below, and more. However, you may still discover some new ideas to help you become more efficient at writing and rewriting—so read on.

➤ CREATING YOUR FIRST FILE

Most word-processing software will let you begin entering text as soon as you enter the program. Simply type as if you were using a typewriter, and the words will appear on the screen. The program will automatically put breaks in the lines, so do not use the **Enter** key unless you want to start a new paragraph.

Before you enter a great deal of text, however, you should use the **Save** command. This tells your program to store your work in an electronic file. These files are something like the folders you store in file cabinets, but they are on the computer's hard disk or on a floppy disk that you can carry home with you. If you save your prewriting or draft in a file, then next time you want to work on it, you can retrieve it. If you do not save your words in a file, they will be lost when you switch off the computer.

When you use the **Save** command, the computer will display a prompt, or a request, for you to enter a file name. Some programs limit the number of letters you can use for a name, but try to choose one that describes the contents. For example, if you're doing a freewriting (see Chapter 2, pages 14–15) to generate ideas for a psychology paper, then you might name the file "psycfree."

While you are writing, use the **Save** *command every fifteen minutes or so to update the material stored in your file.* When you are finished working, type the file name at the bottom of the page, and use the **Print** command to print out a hard copy that you can highlight or edit. Then, use either the **Close** command to leave the file or the **Exit** command to leave the word-processing program.

➤ WRITING YOUR FIRST DRAFT

As you discovered in Chapter 2, computers are excellent tools for prewriting activities, such as freewriting, brainstorming, and journal writing. Once you have worked out your ideas through one of these activities, you are ready to begin composing on your computer.

If you are writing a paragraph, you can start by working on a topic sentence. If you are writing an essay, then you can begin by developing your thesis statement. For either task, you can quickly draft sentences and leave them on the screen for reference as you expand and refine your statement.

Expanding and Revising Sentences

You can add words to a sentence by moving the cursor (the small flashing line on the screen) to the place where you want to insert them and then typing them in. Eliminate words by pressing the **Backspace** or **Delete** key. The series of thesis statements on page 517 shows how one writer expanded and revised her first sentence until she achieved the results she wanted.

First draft	This past year was the hottest one on record.
Second draft	After the hottest year on record, scientists wonder whether global warming is the cause.
Final draft	Although global warming may have played a role in this year's record-breaking heat, scientists say other factors were also at play.

Once you have a workable sentence, you may want to distinguish it with boldface type to help focus your attention on the topic as you compose. You can also distinguish the topic sentence of each paragraph in boldface as you write your draft. Most programs require that you select the words you want to boldface and then either press a boldface function key or choose boldface from a font style menu. Check with your lab instructor, use the **Help** function, or consult your manual for directions.

When you are satisfied with your sentence, you can delete your earlier versions. Or use the **Cut** and **Paste** functions in your program menu to place them at the end of your document. The **Cut** command will store a copy of the text you select on your program's *clipboard,* a temporary storage area. The **Paste** command will transfer the text from the clipboard to the screen. Again, your program may have different names or keys for these functions, so consult your lab instructor or manual or use the **Help** command.

When you begin composing your supporting sentences or paragraphs, check your manual or use the **Help** command to find out how to set your format for triple line spacing. As you write, you can continue using the **Cut** and **Paste** sequence to rearrange words, sentences, and paragraphs. You can also use the **Copy** command. This command will leave your words in the same place on the screen and will also store a copy of those words on the clipboard. Then you can **Paste** the copy anywhere else you need it in your paragraph or essay.

Remember, however, that it is best not to fuss too much over your first draft. Try to let your thoughts and words flow freely, and avoid criticizing what you have written. As you will recall from Chapter 4, most writers like to put their first draft aside for a time and give it a fresh look later. Most writers also find it easier to review a hard copy than to reread an entire draft on a screen. So close your file: Type the name of the file at the bottom of your page so that you can easily locate the file later, and save your work. Then use the **Print** command to obtain a copy of your work from the closest printer. Finally, use the **Close** command to close the file.

REVISING AND EDITING YOUR DRAFT

As you review the hard copy of your draft, write notes to yourself in the margin, and mark sentences or passages that seem unclear. (Some software programs allow you to do this on the screen if you prefer.) If you have given your draft to a classmate, ask him or her to do the same. Then retrieve the file for your first draft using the **Open** command. When the file is open, use the **Save as** function to create an exact duplicate of it. Assign the duplicate file another name. For a paper on the thesis statement on page 517, for example, you might name your first revision file "Warmrev1." Then revise your paper, inserting and deleting words as you look at the notes on your hard copy, and rethink your thesis or topic sentence and supporting points. Again, use the **Cut** and **Paste** sequence to move text as needed.

Each time you revise your paper, save each new version to a new file so that you will have a complete record of your work. While you are working on a revision, you may decide that you could use a sentence or paragraph from an earlier draft in your paper. Simply open the file, place the text on your clipboard using the **Copy** command, and close the file. Then open your revision file, and use the **Paste** command to place the text in its new position. If you are working with a system that lets you open more than one file at a time, you can switch back and forth between drafts as you revise.

As you revise, you may want to check for logic and coherence by boldfacing all of the transitional words in your paper to see whether you have given your reader enough help to understand the connections between your thoughts. Or you may want to boldface all of the adjectives that appeal to the five senses to see whether you have described your thoughts in enough detail. When you are satisfied with your revision, eliminate the boldface by selecting the words and repeating your boldface command sequence. The words will then appear in regular type on the screen.

Next, use the spell checker, style checker, or any other tools your program offers to check your work. Do not assume, however, that these tools will do the whole job for you. See the section "Using Computer Tools to Your Advantage" in Chapter 4 (page 79) for an explanation of their limitations. Change your format instructions for double line spacing, and then print out your paper. Finally, save your final version before closing the file and exiting the program.

➤ *B*ECOMING A POWER USER

Once you have learned the basic functions we have described, do not stop there. Keep in mind that many of the commands just discussed offer an array of options and possibilities. Experiment with these and other commands that can help you prepare polished papers in your other courses. Your word-processing software may allow you to insert tables, draw boxes, vary your type size and font, and perform many other formatting operations. Moreover, some functions can save you time by storing and inserting text that you use frequently, such as your name and address.

If a short course is offered on your campus, consider signing up to learn even more applications. In addition, take advantage of the opportunities on your campus to join the global community of writers using networked computers to conduct research and work together on projects. Once you become comfortable working on a computer, you will discover countless ways to use and share your writing skills.

Basic Commands for Writers— A Quick Reference Guide Based on Microsoft® Word Software

Command	Basic Function
Backspace	Moves the cursor back one space; deletes text one letter at a time.
Close	Closes the file in which you are working.
Copy	Copies selected text from a document, leaving the original text in place. Stores the copy on the *clipboard*, a temporary storage area.
Cut	Removes selected text from a document and stores it on the *clipboard*, a temporary storage area.
Delete	Deletes either a single letter or a selected block of text.
Exit	Allows you to leave the word processing program.
Help	Provides access to an on-line manual that displays procedures, defines terms, and explains commands on your computer screen.
Open	Retrieves an electronic file that you have saved and named.
Paste	Transfers text stored on the *clipboard* to a location that you select in your document.
Print	Formats and sends your document to a printer that will produce a hard copy.
Save	Stores your document in an electronic file, using a file name that you assign.
Save as	Saves an exact copy of your document in a separate file, using a file name that you assign.

Appendix B

Tips for ESL Writers

When you write in English, you must think about many different possible problems. A sentence with an unusual word order will confuse your readers, so keep in mind the ways your language and English differ in sentence structure and word order. You must also correct the common problems you have with English grammar so that you communicate clearly. The rules for capitalization, articles, spelling, and punctuation can be very confusing. However, they help to make your writing correct, and correct standard English is more easily understood. Most important of all, you must think about the logic of the paragraphs and essays written in English because they might be very different from the logical forms of composition in your language group and culture. Sometimes even the logic of an argument will be different. If your goal is communication, you must learn to use the patterns that English speakers use to understand each other.

SENTENCE BASICS

> ➤ Make sure each sentence has a subject and a verb. If a group of words does not have both, it does not express a complete idea. *See Chapter 17, "The Sentence," and Chapter 18, "Fragments."*

Faulty

`verb`

Thought of a good idea.   *[Subject missing]*

Revised

`subject` `verb`

You thought of a good idea.   *[A report]*

In writing, the subject can be an implied *you* only if you are making a command. *See the section "Correcting Fragments with Missing Subjects or Verbs" on pages 247–249 in Chapter 18.*

Example

`subject` `verb`

[You] Think of a good idea!   *[A command]*

➤ Make sure that *is* and *are* verbs are linked to a subject. The words *it* and *there* and words describing a location can sometimes substitute in the normal location of a subject at the beginning of a sentence. In such cases, the actual subject is then found after the verb. (Usually, in English, the subject comes before the verb.) *See the section "Avoiding Agreement Errors When the Subject Follows the Verb" on page 293 in Chapter 21 and the section "Working with Forms of* to Be" *on page 327 in Chapter 23.*

Faulty

`verb`

Is a good place to eat near here.   *[Subject unclear]*

Revised

`substitute` `verb` `subject`

There is a good *place* to eat near here.   *[There signals subject after verb]*

or

`location` `verb` `subject`

Near here is a good *place* to eat.

➤ In English sentences, the word *there* with some form of the verb *to be* is commonly followed by a noun or pronoun. The noun or pronoun may have modifiers, or it may be followed by a word or phrase that specifies a place.

Examples

noun **modifier**

There will be a new *student entering class today.*

pronoun **place**

There is *no one here.*

noun **place**

There are three *cars in the lot.*

➤ The word *it* with the verb *to be* is commonly followed by an adjective, an adjective with a modifier, an identification, or an expression of time, weather, or distance.

Examples

adjective

It is *hot.*

adjective **modifier**

It is *hot outside and inside.*

identification

What is this? It is *my English book.*

time

It is *eleven o'clock on Wednesday morning.*

weather

It is *cold and rainy.*

distance

It is *twenty miles from school to home.*

The word *there* is not used in these expressions.

Faulty

There is long. *There* has been a long time.

Revised

It is long. *It* has been a long time.

 **ORD ORDER**

➤ In most English sentences, the subject comes first, followed by the verb.

Faulty

verb	subject

Is good the *idea.*

Revised

subject	verb

The *idea is* good.

➤ Adjectives, even a string of adjectives, usually come *before* nouns. *See Chapter 26, "Adjectives, Adverbs, and Other Modifiers," for more information about adjectives.*

Faulty

noun	adjectives

The *man* is talking—*tall, thin,* and *handsome.*

Revised

adjectives	noun

The *tall, thin, handsome man* is talking.

➤ Groups of words that modify a noun, however, usually come immediately *after* the noun if they begin with a relative pronoun: *who, whom, whose, which, that,* and so forth.

Faulty

noun	modifier

The *man* is talking *who won the award.*

Revised

noun	modifier

The *man who won the award* is talking.

➤ Modifiers with an *-ed* or *-ing* verb form must go after a noun they identify. That is, they follow the noun if they add essential identifying information to the sentence. However, they can go either immediately before or immediately after a noun about which they add extra information. Study the following examples, in which the *-ing* modifier is necessary to tell *which man. See the section "Avoiding Dangling and Misplaced Modifiers" on page 373 in Chapter 26.*

Faulty

`modifier`   `which man?`
Sitting next to you, the *man* is blind.

Revised

`noun` `identifying modifier`
The *man sitting next to you* is blind.

Now compare the revised sentence above with the example below, in which the modifier adds extra information.

Example

`modifier`   `noun`
Forgetting his promise, John is talking instead of listening.

➤ If the modifier is necessary to identify the noun, you don't use commas to separate it from the noun. If the modifier adds information about the noun, but the sentence makes sense without it, then set the modifier off with commas. *See the section "Using Commas to Set Off Elements That Interrupt Sentence Flow" on page 441 in Chapter 30.*

Example

`noun` `modifier`
My *friend Frank* works hard.

The modifier is needed to identify which friend, *my friend Frank,* not *my friend Tom,* so no commas are needed.

Example

`noun`   `modifier`
Frank, who lives next door, works hard.

The modifier provides extra information, so it needs commas.

➤ Adverbs usually are placed after *to be* verbs (*is/are/was/were*) but before other one-word verbs. *See the section "Understanding Adjectives and Adverbs" on page 368 in Chapter 26.*

Example

| verb | adverb |

They *are often* late.

Example

| adverb | verb |

Birds *usually arrive* in the spring.

➤ Adverbs often go between verbs which have two parts (verb phrases).

Example

| helping verb | adverb | verb |

They *have often arrived* late.

➤ Pronouns that rename the subject in the same sentence are unnecessary and confusing—even when a long modifier separates the subject from the verb. The word order makes the idea clear.

Faulty

| subject | modifier | subject | verb |

The *place* where they studied *it was* old.

Revised

| subject | modifier | verb |

The *place* where they studied *was* old.

 **A**GREEMENT

➤ Make the subject and verb agree in number. Be especially careful about collective nouns, such as *family* and *class,* and words that specify uncountable things, such as *sugar* and *water. See the section "Working with Collective Nouns and Cue Words" on page 353 in Chapter 25.*

➤ You can count *fingers, books,* or *students,* so they are called *count* words. You cannot count *freedom, advice,* or *machinery,* so they are called *noncount* words. Noncount words always take a singular verb and a singular pronoun reference.

Faulty

| noncount noun | plural verb | | plural pronoun reference | plural verb |

Sugar make the recipe better. *They are* tasty.

Revised

| noncount noun | singular verb | | singular pronoun reference | singular verb |

Sugar makes the recipe better. *It is* tasty.

➤ Some words are count with one meaning and noncount with another meaning.

Examples

Three *chickens are* in the yard.   *[Countable animals]*

Chicken is good with white wine.   *[Noncountable meat]*

Three pieces of *chicken is* enough.   *[Quantity of noncountable meat]*

➤ As the last example shows, some aspects of noncount words can be measured. You can count the number of *lumps* of sugar, *cups* of milk, *tablespoons* of flour, or *gallons* of water, but you cannot say *ten sugars, three milks, two flours,* and *four waters* as a complete grammatical form. Even though you can number *quantities* like *two pounds, six quarts, three minutes, five dollars,* and *ten gallons,* the "*of* phrase" with the noncount word makes a singular subject, which makes the verb singular (*two pounds of butter is*). You must use a *singular verb* with any quantity of noncount items. *See the sections "Using the Simple Present, Simple Future, and Simple Past Tenses" on pages 311–312 in Chapter 22, "Using Indefinite Pronouns" on page 361 in Chapter 25, and "Maintaining Agreement with Indefinite Pronouns" on page 388 in Chapter 27.*

Examples

| count noun |

Twelve *cups are* necessary because we have twelve guests.   *[12 items]*

Two cups of *water is* enough.   *[A measurement of a noncount noun]*

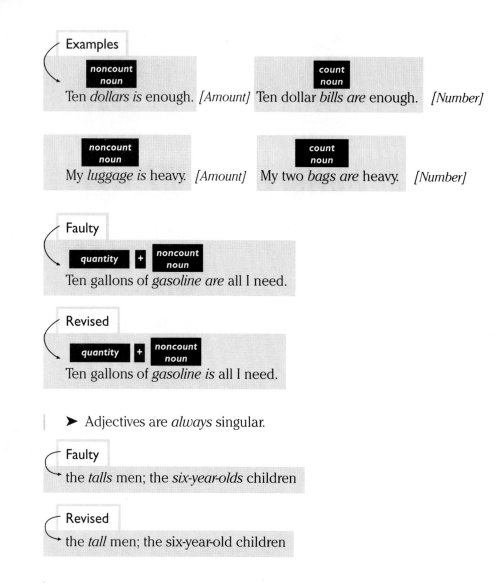

Examples

| noncount noun |
Ten *dollars is* enough. *[Amount]*

| count noun |
Ten dollar *bills are* enough. *[Number]*

| noncount noun |
My *luggage is* heavy. *[Amount]*

| count noun |
My two *bags are* heavy. *[Number]*

Faulty

| quantity | + | noncount noun |
Ten gallons of *gasoline are* all I need.

Revised

| quantity | + | noncount noun |
Ten gallons of *gasoline is* all I need.

➤ Adjectives are *always* singular.

Faulty

the *talls* men; the *six-year-olds* children

Revised

the *tall* men; the six-year-old children

➤ Adjectives that end in *-ing* are active, while adjectives that end in *-ed* are passive. *See the section "Forming the Passive and Active Voice" on page 337 in Chapter 24.*

Example

I am *boring.*

This adjective is formed from the active verb. It shows the effect that I have on others—I make them feel bored.

Example

I am *bored.*

This adjective is derived from the passive verb. It shows the effect some thing has on me—something makes me feel bored.

➤ A single phrase or clause subject takes a singular verb.

Faulty

| phrase as subject | verb | | clause as subject | verb |

Understanding the rules **are** *hard. That they must be followed* **are** *clear.*

Revised

| phrase as subject | verb | | clause as subject | verb |

Understanding the rules **is** *hard. That they must be followed* **is** *clear.*

➤ Verbs connected in a series with commas should agree in tense and form. *See Chapter 28, "Maintaining Parallelism."*

Faulty

The child *was running, jumped,* and *has skipped.*   *[Mixed tense forms]*

Revised

The child *ran, jumped,* and *skipped.*   *[All past tense forms]*

➤ Use the present or present perfect tense, not the future tense, in a subordinate time or if clause, whose main clause is future tense. *See the section "Maintaining Consistency in Tense" on page 342 in Chapter 24 for more on keeping the voice of tense consistent.*

Faulty

| subordinate clause | main clause |

After I will do my homework, I will go out.

Revised

| subordinate clause | main clause |

After I have done my homework, I will go out.

CONFUSING VERB FORMS

➤ Don't omit the *-s* in the third person singular, present tense verb forms. *See the section "Using the Simple Present, Simple Future, and Simple Past Tenses" on page 311 in Chapter 22.*

Faulty

He *come* here every day.

Revised

He *comes* here every day.

➤ Memorize the irregular verbs. *See the section "Identifying Irregular Verbs" on page 321 in Chapter 23.* Some verb pairs such as the following can be confusing, but remembering which takes an object and which does not will help you tell the difference. The verbs *shine/shone, lie, sit,* and *rise* never have an object; the verbs *shine/shined, lay, set,* and *raise* always have an object:

No Object	*Object*
His shoes shone.	He shined *his shoes.*
She lay in the sun.	She laid *her books* on the floor.
She sat in the chair.	She set *the table* for four.
The sun rises every morning.	They raised *the flag.*

➤ Use complete passive verb forms; combine a form of *to be* with the past participle of another verb. *See the section "Forming the Passive and Active Voice" on page 337 in Chapter 24.*

Faulty
His work finished.

Revised
His work *was* finished.   *[Add form of* to be*]*

or

He finished his work.   *[Transform to active voice]*

➤ Use -*'s* to make contractions using *is* and *has,* but shorten *has* only when it is a helping verb. To sound more formal, avoid contractions like *she's.* Write *she is* instead.

Faulty
She's some money.

Revised
She has some money.

Informal
She's ready to help.

Formal

She is ready to help.

➤ Verbs describing a completed mental process (*believe, consider, forget, know, remember, think, understand*), a consistent preference (*drink, swim, eat*), a state of being (*am, appear, have, seem, remember, forget, love*), or a perception (*feel, hear, see, taste*) can never be progressive. If the verb refers to an incomplete process, it can be progressive. *See the section "Using the Progressive and Perfect Progressive Tenses" on page 339 in Chapter 24.*

Examples

I *consider* my choice good.   *[An already completed decision]*

I *am considering* going.   *[A decision-making process not yet complete]*

I *think* he should be president.   *[A completed intellectual position]*

I *am thinking* about what to do this summer.   *[An incomplete thought process]*

I *drink* coffee.   *[A consistent preference]*

I *am drinking* coffee.   *[An incomplete action]*

Faulty

I *am seeing* you. I *am liking* you, but I *am loving* cheeseburgers.

Revised

I *see* you. I *like* you, but I *love* cheeseburgers.

➤ *Do* and *make* do not mean the same thing in English. *Do* often refers to action that is mechanical or specific. *Make* often refers to action that is creative or general: The teacher *makes* up the exercise (creative), but the student *does* the exercise (mechanical). However, there is no clear rule explaining the difference. You will just have to memorize usage.

Mostly Mechanical or Specific	*Mostly Creative or General*
do the dishes	make the bed
do the homework	make an impression
do the laundry	make progress
do your hair	make up your mind

do (brush) your teeth	make (cook) a meal
do (write) a paper	make (build) a house
do the right thing	make mistakes
do someone a favor	make a speech
do good deeds	make a living
do away with	make arrangements

Faulty

I have to *make the homework* before I can *do a speech.*

Revised

I have to *do the homework* before I can *make a speech.*

➤ *Tell* and *say* do not mean the same thing in English:

tell time	say a prayer
tell a story or a joke	say hello
tell me	say that we should go
tell the difference	say, "Let's go!"

Faulty

say me; tell hello; say a joke

Revised

tell me; say hello; tell a joke

ARTICLES

Articles (*a*, *an*, and *the*) are very confusing in English, so you must pay special attention to them.

➤ Use *a* before words that begin with consonants and *an* before words that begin with vowels.

1. *A* and *an* mean the same as *one* or *each*: I want *an* ice cream cone. *[Just one]*
2. *A* and *an* go with an unidentified member of a class: *A* small dog came toward her, *a* bone in its mouth. *[Some unknown dog, some unknown bone]*
3. *A* and *an* go with a representative member of a class: You can tell by the way he talks that he is *a* politician.
4. *A* and *an* go with a noun that places an idea in a larger class: The car is *a* four-wheeled vehicle.

See the section "Working with Collective Nouns and Cue Words" on page 353 in Chapter 25.

➤ *The* serves many functions:

1. *The* modifies known people, objects, or ideas: *the* mother of *the* bride, *the* head of *the* household in which he stayed, *the* Copernican theory
2. *The* goes with superlatives: *the* best, *the* least
3. *The* goes with rank: *the* first book, *the* third child with this problem
4. *The* goes with *of* phrases: the way of *the* world
5. *The* goes with adjective phrases or clauses which limit or identify the noun: *the* topic being discussed
6. *The* refers to a class as a whole: *The* giraffe is an African animal.
7. *The* goes with the names of familiar objects (*the* store) and the names of newspapers (*The Wall Street Journal*), but not the names of most magazines (*Time*).
8. *The* goes with the names of historical periods (*the* French Revolution), legislative acts (*the* Missouri Compromise), political parties (*the* Democratic Party), branches of government (*the* executive branch), official titles (*the* President), government bodies (*the* Navy), and organizations (*the* Girl Scouts).
9. *The* goes with rivers (but not lakes), canals, oceans, channels, gulfs, peninsulas, swamps, groups of islands, mountain ranges, hotels, libraries, museums, and geographic regions: *the* Panama Canal, *the* Mississippi River, Lake Superior, *the* Okefenokee Swamp, *the* Hilton, *the* Smithsonian, *the* South.

Faulty

According to *New York Times*, the Lake Victoria is one of most beautiful lakes in world.

Revised

According to *the New York Times*, Lake Victoria is one of *the* most beautiful lakes in *the* world.

SPELLING

➤ Watch for these common spelling errors:

1. Leaving *h* out of *wh* words: *which*, not *wich*
2. Adding an *e* to words that start with *s*: *stupid*, not *estupid*
3. Confusing words that sound alike in English but have different meanings and different spellings:

his/he's (he is)	which/witch	there/their
whether/weather	here/hear	through/threw
advice/advise (noun/verb)	too/to/two	though/thought

4. Confusing grammatical functions because of familiar sound combinations: *whose* or *who's* (*who is*), not *who his*
5. Confusing words that sound similar using your native language's pronunciation patterns but have different meanings and different sounds in English:

this (singular)/these (plural)	chair/share
read/lead	boat/vote
heat/hit	

See Chapter 29, "Spelling."

OTHER COMMON GRAMMAR PROBLEMS

Double Negatives

➤ Never use a double negative; it is not acceptable in English. As in mathematics, two negatives equal a positive. *See the section "Avoiding Double Negatives" on page 378 in Chapter 26.*

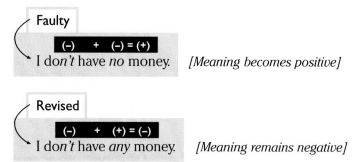

Faulty

(−) + (−) = (+)

I do*n't* have *no* money.   *[Meaning becomes positive]*

Revised

(−) + (+) = (−)

I do*n't* have *any* money.   *[Meaning remains negative]*

Confusing Words

Some key words are confusing:

➤ *Too* does not mean *very*. *Very* is an intensifier; it emphasizes quantity. *Too* is often negative and critical. It is sometimes attached to a word that goes with an infinitive (*to* + verb) to emphasize negative effects.

Examples

It is *very* cold, but we can walk to the restaurant.   *[Very = intensely]*

It is *too* cold to walk, so we should take a taxi.   *[Too = negative]*

Faulty

He is *very* fat to play on the soccer team.

Revised

He is *too* fat to play on the soccer team. *[He cannot play soccer because of so much fat.]*

➤ *Hard* can be an adjective or an adverb, but *hardly* is always an adverb meaning *barely, almost none,* or *almost not at all.*

Examples

`adjective` `noun`
He learned a *hard* lesson. *[A difficult lesson]*

`verb` `adverb`
He worked *hard*. *[With great effort]*

`adverb` `verb`
He *hardly* worked. *[Barely, almost not at all]*

`adverb` `noun`
Hardly anyone watches black-and-white television. *[Almost no one]*

➤ *A few* (count) and *a little* (noncount) mean *some*, while *few* and *little* mean *almost none*. The difference is between a positive attitude and a negative attitude.

Examples

I have *a little* money, so I can lend you some. *[Some, so positive]*

I have *little* money, so I can't lend you any. *[Almost none, so negative]*

A few students came, so we were pleased. *[Some, so positive]*

Few students came, so we were disappointed. *[Almost none, so negative]*

➤ *Some* and *any* both mean an indefinite amount. However, *some* is used in positive statements, while *any* is used in negative statements.

Examples

I have *some* money.   *[Positive]*

I don't have *any* money.   *[Negative]*

➤ Usually, *well* is an adverb, whereas *good* is an adjective. However, *well* can sometimes be an adjective referring to health. *See the section "Working with Confusing Pairs of Adjectives and Adverbs" on page 371 in Chapter 26.*

Examples

noun   adjective
The *boy* is *good*.   *[Well-behaved]*

verb   adverb
He doesn't feel *well*.   *[Poor health]*

noun   adjective
The *boy* is *well*.   *[Healthy, not sick]*

Prepositions

Prepositions can be very confusing. *See the section "Recognizing Subjects" on page 239 in Chapter 17.*

➤ Use *on* when one thing touches the surface of another and *in* when one thing encloses another: *on* the desk (on top), *in* the desk (inside a drawer). Also, use *on* if you must step up to board (get *on* a motorcycle/bus/train/large ship), but use *in* if you must step down (get *in* a small boat/car).

➤ *Since* goes with a specific initial time (*since* 3 P.M.; *since* July 3); *for* goes with duration, a length or period of time (*for* two hours; *for* ten days).

PUNCTUATION AND CAPITALIZATION

English rules for punctuation differ greatly from those in other languages.

➤ All sentences have an ending punctuation mark. Statements end with a period (**.**). Exclamations end with an exclamation mark (**!**). Questions end with a question mark (**?**). Statements, exclamations, and questions end with only one mark. Avoid multiple punctuation marks at the end of sentences. *See the section "Using Periods, Question Marks, and Exclamation Points" on page 451 in Chapter 31.*

➤ Do not use commas to connect complete ideas or statements that can stand alone. Instead, use a period and a capital letter, a semicolon, or a comma and a coordinating conjunction. *See Chapter 20, "Comma Splices and Run-On Sentences."*

Faulty

We finished class, then we got a pizza, later we went to a movie.

[Comma splice]

Revised

We finished class. Then we got a pizza. Later we went to a movie.

[Separate sentences]

or

We finished class; then we got a pizza; later we went to a movie.

[Clauses joined with semicolons]

or

We finished class, then got a pizza, and later went to a movie.

[Simple sentence with compound verb]

➤ Commas go before and after a modifying word, phrase, or clause that adds extra information. This means that the sentence can stand alone without the added information. Modifying words, phrases, or clauses that are necessary for identification take no commas. In other words, if the material is crucial to the meaning of the sentence, then do not use commas. *See the section "Using Commas to Set Off Elements That Interrupt Sentence Flow" on page 441 in Chapter 30.*

Example

`noun`   `modifier`
Never eat pork *that is undercooked.*

Without the modifier, the sentence meaning is changed and incorrect; use no commas.

Example

`noun`   `modifier`
Supermarkets, *which we take for granted,* did not even exist a hundred years ago.

Without the modifier, the sentence retains its basic meaning; use commas.

➤ Semicolons are used to separate independent clauses. They may also be used to separate longer groups of words or lists which already contain commas.

Examples

Cats are lazy; dogs jump around.

Turn in your uniforms on Friday, May 24; Monday, May 27; or Wednesday, May 29.

➤ English rules for capitalization differ greatly from those in other languages. *See the section "Understanding Capitalization" on page 462 in Chapter 31 for the English rules.*

WRITING PARAGRAPHS

Indentation   Don't use a dash (—) to signal the beginning of a new paragraph. Instead, indent the first line of the paragraph to identify your change of subject or focus. *See the section "Recognizing the Structure of a Paragraph" on page 33 in Chapter 3.*

Unity   Every sentence in a paragraph should be connected to the same topic, or main idea. In other words, the material should be unified. *See the section "Maintaining Unity" on page 57 in Chapter 4.* If you change direction in the middle of the paragraph to talk about another idea, even if it is related, your teachers may call it a *digression*. Digressions are allowed in some languages, but not in English. One way to avoid digression is to have a plan for organizing your examples. For example, move from most common to least common, or from the familiar to the unfamiliar, or from the least important to the most important.

Examples

most common traveler's problem in airports

next most common problem

not usual, but still a problem

Examples
an important study habit for final exams

a more important study habit for final exams

the most important study habit for final exams

Finally, avoid digression by keeping sentences short and tightly connected. Don't try to put too many unrelated ideas in one sentence or paragraph. *See Part Two, "Using the Patterns of Paragraph Development."*

Faulty
The writer warned us about the problem, he said it was very dangerous, he gave us convincing statistics.   *[Three separate ideas; comma splice]*

Revised
The writer used convincing statistics to warn about the dangerous problem.   *[Ideas are combined and connected.]*

 RITING ESSAYS

Think about Audience Expectations   Be businesslike: Go directly to your main idea. Don't try to tell your readers everything. Choose and limit your focus as much as possible. This narrowing of the topic may be much more extreme than you are used to in your language or culture.

Strive for Clarity   Most North American readers like everything important to be explained; they don't like to guess. Keep your writing clear. Don't just write in general. These readers like specific information. Give them facts; give them details; give them examples. Choose the best examples to prove your point. Explain, explain, explain!

Keep your writing simple. Don't try to be too formal, but avoid the pronoun *you*. Say *who* you mean: the student, the tourist, the opposition. When you revise your sentences, eliminate extra words and imprecise expressions.

Faulty
the group of people who lead the university and decide on policy

Revised
the board of governors

Reinforce Your Point with a "Close"   Never just stop writing. Always conclude with a few final words about your topic. This conclusion can repeat your main idea, but it should also show the significance of what you have said. Try to say how or why your topic idea is important and worth paying attention to.

Revise to Correct Errors   Proofread before you turn in your paper. When you proofread, watch for the common mistakes discussed above. If possible, have a native speaker in a writing lab look at it before you turn it in. *See Chapter 4, "Refining and Polishing Your Draft," Chapter 14, "Developing an Essay," and Chapter 15, "Examining Types of Essays," for guidelines on how to develop and write an essay.*

Exploring the Dictionary

Several chapters of this textbook have suggested that you refer to the dictionary to find information or to check the accuracy of your spelling. The dictionary is a tool writers use to verify the spelling of a word or to learn the meaning of an unfamiliar word. This reference tool can also provide other valuable information if you know what is available and where it is located. This appendix will help you learn how to explore the dictionary to gather all the information that is available to you.

USING THE DICTIONARY

Good dictionaries are user friendly. They will usually begin with a guide to using the dictionary, sometimes called a usage guide. The guide will probably include a pronunciation key, which uses symbols and phonetic spelling. Phonetic spelling shows the way the word sounds when pronounced correctly. It is necessary because the same letters can be pronounced different ways in English. For example, the double *o* is pronounced differently in *good* and *food*.

The usage guide also lists abbreviations that the dictionary's editors have used, along with the words they stand for. In addition, it may explain what each element of an entry means. Sometimes, you can find a pronunciation key and a list of abbreviations and symbols used in a dictionary on the inside cover.

You can always refer to the usage guide to help you find the information you need when you are using the dictionary.

➤ **A** SAMPLE DICTIONARY ENTRY

To help you discover what information is included in a dictionary, take a look at the entry for the word *knowledge* as it appears in *Webster's New World College Dictionary*.

> **knowl•edge** (näl´ ij) **n.** [ME *knoweleche*, acknowledgement, confession < Late OE *cnawlœc* < *cnawan* (see KNOW) + *-lœc* < *lãcan*, to play, give, move about] **1** the act, fact or state of knowing; specif. *a)* acquaintance or familiarity (with a fact, place, etc) *b)* awareness *c)* understanding **2** acquaintance with facts; range of information, awareness or understanding **3** all that has been perceived or grasped by the mind; learning; enlightenment **4** the body of facts, principles, etc accumulated by mankind **5** [ARCHAIC] carnal knowledge: see CARNAL —***SYN.*** INFORMATION—**to (the best of) one's knowledge** as far as one knows; within the range of one's information

At first glance, this entry might seem confusing, but each dictionary entry follows a pattern. Once you understand what information is listed where, most entries will become clear. For example, here is an explanation of the information about *knowledge* that appears before the definitions of the word:

> ➤ The main entry, the word itself, is written in boldface: **knowl•edge**
> ➤ Each syllable of the word is separated by bold, centered periods: •
> ➤ The phonetic pronunciation follows, with a (´) over the accented, or stressed, syllable(s): (näl´ ij)
> ➤ The word's part of speech, in this case, is a noun: **n.**
> ➤ Finally, the etymology, or origin of the word, is also listed between brackets: [ ].

So before we read the definitions for this word, we know that the word has two syllables, that we should accent the first syllable when we pronounce the word, and that it is a noun. By referring to the usage guide for a list of abbreviations, we can also determine that the word has its roots in Old English (OE) and Middle English (ME). Knowing the etymology of a word helps writers understand its meaning more fully.

Following this information about the word are its definitions. Knowing how to define a word as it is used within a sentence or particular context is important. Some words have more than one meaning or sense, as *knowledge* does. Those multiple meanings are separated here by numbers in boldface. In some dictionaries, the different definitions are separated by a // or a double line. The five meanings of the noun *knowledge* provided in the definition above are as follows:

1. the act, fact or state of knowing; specif. *a)* acquaintance or familiarity (with a fact, place, etc) *b)* awareness *c)* understanding
2. acquaintance with facts; range of information, awareness or understanding
3. all that has been perceived or grasped by the mind; learning; enlightenment
4. the body of facts, principles, etc. accumulated by mankind
5. [ARCHAIC] carnal knowledge: see CARNAL

In addition, this entry provides a **synonym**—the word *information*—and an example and explanation of an idiomatic expression or phrase that includes the word: **to (the best of) one's knowledge.**

Most dictionary entries will follow this basic pattern: the word, its pronunciation, its forms and part(s) of speech, the etymology, and the definition(s). The entry may contain other information, too. For example, you can use the dictionary to check the spelling of plurals *(pl.)*, to find the comparative *(comp.)* and superlative *(superl.)* forms of modifiers, and to learn the various forms of a verb. If the verb will accept a direct or indirect object, that is also indicated by *vt.,* an abbreviation for *transitive verb.* The dictionary will also provide the correct spelling of the word with suffixes. Remember—if you are not sure what an abbreviation means within an entry, check the usage guide or list of abbreviations at the beginning of the dictionary.

Exploration 1a Exploring the Usage Guide

1. Refer to the Usage Guide of your own dictionary and explain what *archaic* means in definition **5** of the word *knowledge.* _____

_____

_____

2. Using the Usage Guide, explain the following terms:

obsolete: _____

colloquial: _____

rare: _____

Exploration 1b Finding Additional Information

1. Look up the word *knowledge* in a dictionary that you use. How does the entry compare with the sample entry on page 542? _____

_____

_____

2. Besides definitions, what additional information does your dictionary con-

tain, such as maps, charts, or other reference information? _____

_____

_____

Challenge 1   Searching the Library

Visit your college or municipal library, and explore the section of the reference
collection that contains dictionaries. What did you discover about the number
and variety of dictionaries that are available? Select one or two specialized dictionaries that you find interesting or unusual. Write a paragraph describing the
content of the dictionary, and explain why you found it intriguing. Share the
results of your exploration with your classmates.

   If you have access to the World Wide Web, your instructor may ask you to
complete this challenge by identifying and exploring on-line dictionaries.

Exploration 2a   Exploring Etymologies

1. Find and write the etymologies of the following words:

   a. education: _____

   _____

   b. college: _____

   _____

   c. student: _____

   _____

   d. write: _____

   _____

2. Does your dictionary include any of the following words?

cyberspace	diskette
World Wide Web	online
digital	hypertext
technology	laser

3. Working with a partner, see what you can discover about the etymologies
   of these words. Be sure to explore the meanings of prefixes, multiple definitions, and references to the root of the word in your search. Share your
   results with the class.

Challenge 2   Playing a Dictionary Game

Play this game with four or five other students. Choose a word from the dictionary that you believe the students in the group do not know. Pronounce and spell the word for the group, distribute an index card or small piece of paper to everybody, and ask each person to write a definition for the word, including its part of speech. At the same time, you should write the correct definition from the dictionary on your own card. Collect the cards and read all the definitions. Ask each student in turn to guess which definition is correct. Students earn points by selecting the correct defintion or by having their definition selected by another student. You earn a point for each incorrect answer. The game continues until every group member has a turn to choose a word.

Here is an example to get you started. Which of the following definitions is correct for the word *dibble*?

1. A dibble is a pointed gardening tool used to make holes for planting seeds and bulbs; it is a noun.
2. Dibble is an adjective that means small and without much worth.
3. Dibble is the technical name for the residue that remains after charcoal briquets are burned. It is a noun.
4. Dibble is a verb that means to do something without much enthusiasm or seriousness.

After you've guessed, use the dictionary to find the right definition.

Rhetorical Index

Writers combine rhetorical modes to communicate their ideas in paragraphs and essays. Often, one mode is dominant, and one or more additional modes are used to provide illustration or support. To help you understand the characteristics of each mode, this index lists the paragraphs and essays in the text both by mode and by chapter. Paragraphs and essays that contain characteristics for more than one mode are listed more than once, under the headings for each of those modes.

PARAGRAPHS AND ESSAYS BY MODES

Narration—Paragraphs

Last summer, I had a great experience, 57
Before I came to the place where I would cross the Rio Grande, 63
I read the character and set description, 70
The most traumatic experience I can remember, 72
For Shirley Vroman, getting caught, 86
And I started to play, 87
One cold Christmas Eve, 88
Ernest first saw the plane from the window of the taxi, 89
The most beautiful sunset I ever witnessed, 93
The boy put the blackberry in his mouth, 94
Last summer, I went into downtown Springfield, 95
When my friend Cerene opened the newspaper, 177

Narration—Essays

Lost and Confused: My First Day in the Hospital Halls, 171
The Fourth of July, My Favorite Day, 198

Bright Lights, Loud Music: Not Your Average Planetarium Show, 200
Fish Cheeks, Amy Tan, 477
Nightwatch, Paul Fletcher, 481
Caesar, Therese C. MacKinnon, 484
How Boys Become Men, Jon Katz, 487
Thanksgiving Is the Greatest Holiday, Robert C. Maynard, 493
Go and Conquer the World, Michaela Otway, 496
A Religion? Henry Bousquet, 504
A Bully Who Wore Bobby Pins, Amanda Beaulieu, 506
Fear Not, Greg Andree, 508

Description—Paragraphs

The worst accident I ever saw, 65
I read the character and set description, 70
The most traumatic experience I can remember, 72
And I started to play, 87

One cold Christmas Eve, 88

Ernest first saw the plane from the window of the taxi, 89

The most beautiful sunset I ever witnessed, 93

The boy put the blackberry in his mouth, 94

Last summer, I went into downtown Springfield, 95

The most unusual restaurant in town, 96

When you have agoraphobia, 103

There were fifteen of them, 186

Description—Essays

Lost and Confused: My First Day in the Hospital Halls, 171

Bright Lights, Loud Music: Not Your Average Planetarium Show, 200

Fish Cheeks, Amy Tan, 477

Nightwatch, Paul Fletcher, 481

Caesar, Therese C. MacKinnon, 484

How Boys Become Men, Jon Katz, 487

Go and Conquer the World, Michaela Otway, 496

Exposed Toes, Diane Riva, 501

A Bully Who Wore Bobby Pins, Amanda Beaulieu, 506

Example—Paragraphs

In the last few years, probably no technological advance, 6

Today, the children's division of our library, 33

My lack of self-confidence is keeping me, 51

Many of the things we use every day, 76

Even the simplest gesture is subject to misunderstanding, 101

When you have agoraphobia, 103

How do expert physicists differ, 104

Among the most popular types of comedy is slapstick, 118

My friend Roscoe is wonderfully frank, 120

In every job I've ever had, I have found that the workers, 146

Television ads for alcoholic beverages, 153

Example—Essays

No Second Chances, Please, 203

Truly Considerate People: A Rarity, 208

The Car Question: To Buy or to Lease? 211

More Than a Promotion, 215

Spine-Chilling Choices, 218

The Beast Is the Beauty Contest, 221

Intimacy and Independence, Deborah Tannen, 479

Thanksgiving Is the Greatest Holiday, Robert C. Maynard, 493

Fear Not, Greg Andree, 508

To Smoke or Not to Smoke, Charlotte Medeiros, 510

Process—Paragraphs

Photosynthesis is the quiet but profound process, 108

Inserting a contact lens, 109

If you follow these steps, water skiing will feel, 111

An important part of regular bicycle maintenance, 111

Process—Essays

The Science of Solving Problems, 205

How Boys Become Men, Jon Katz, 487

"Growing Up" Is Cumulative, Evolutionary and Never-Ending, Brian Dickinson, 490

Thanksgiving Is the Greatest Holiday, Robert C. Maynard, 493

A Religion? Henry Bousquet, 504

Definition—Paragraphs

Thanks to the movie *Jurassic Park,* 117

Among the most popular types of comedy is slapstick, 118

My friend Roscoe is wonderfully frank, 120

Reinforcement is the process of using rewards, 145

Censoring the discussion of certain topics on the Internet, 158

No one is saying that news reporters, 179

Definition—Essays

The Science of Solving Problems, 205

Truly Considerate People: A Rarity, 208

Teaching as an Amusing Activity, Neil Postman, 475

Intimacy and Independence, Deborah Tannen, 479

"Growing Up" Is Cumulative, Evolutionary and Never-Ending, Brian Dickinson, 490

Comparison and Contrast— Paragraphs

In the last few years, probably no technological advance, 6

How do expert physicists differ, 104

Among the most popular types of comedy is slapstick, 118

The big difference between the old Soviet economy and our own, 125

In many ways, breast feeding is much better than bottle feeding, 126

Even though the rules for both games are the same, 128

Venus and the Earth are sister planets, 128

Television ads for alcoholic beverages, 153

Comparison and Contrast—Essays

Bright Lights, Loud Music: Not Your Average Planetarium Show, 200
Truly Considerate People: A Rarity, 208
The Car Question: To Buy or to Lease? 211
The Beast Is the Beauty Contest, 221
Teaching as an Amusing Activity, Neil Postman, 475
Fish Cheeks, Amy Tan, 477
Intimacy and Independence, Deborah Tannen, 479
The Importance of Wearing a Safety Belt, Larissa R. Houk, 499
To Smoke or Not to Smoke, Charlotte Medeiros, 510

Cause and Effect—Paragraphs

Today, the children's division of our library, 33
My lack of self-confidence is keeping me, 51
Computerized listings of holdings, 61
Cigarette smoking should be banned, 67
Many of the things we use every day, 76
For Shirley Vroman, getting caught, 86
Photosynthesis is the quiet but profound process, 108
In many ways, breast feeding is much better than bottle feeding, 126
Although the debate over the causes of the Civil War, 134
When a hot object is placed in contact with a cold object, 135
As the number of farm laborers decreased, 137
Adopted children should be able to read, 151
Television ads for alcoholic beverages, 153
Censoring the discussion of certain topics on the Internet, 158
Condom machines should be installed, 159
When my friend Cerene opened the newspaper, 177

Cause and Effect—Essays

Lost and Confused: My First Day in the Hospital Halls, 171
More Than a Promotion, 215
The Beast Is the Beauty Contest, 221
Teaching as an Amusing Activity, Neil Postman, 475
Caesar, Therese C. MacKinnon, 484
How Boys Become Men, Jon Katz, 487
Go and Conquer the World, Michaela Otway, 496
The Importance of Wearing a Safety Belt, Larissa R. Houk, 499
Fear Not, Greg Andree, 508

Division and Classification—Paragraphs

Cigarette smoking should be banned, 67
How do expert physicists differ, 104
In many ways, breast feeding is much better than bottle feeding, 126
Even though the rules for both games are the same, 128
Venus and the Earth are sister planets, 128
The work of a certified nurse's assistant, 142
The way the federal government spends money, 143
Reinforcement is the process of using rewards, 145
In every job I've ever had, I have found that the workers, 146

Division and Classification—Essays

No Second Chances, Please, 203
Truly Considerate People: A Rarity, 208
Spine-Chilling Choices, 218
The Beast Is the Beauty Contest, 221
Exposed Toes, Diane Riva, 501
Fear Not, Greg Andree, 508

Argument—Paragraphs (developed using various modes)

Cigarette smoking should be banned (Cause and Effect, Division and Classification), 67
Many of the things we use every day (Example), 76
In many ways, breast feeding is much better than bottle feeding (Comparison and Contrast, Cause and Effect), 126
The way the federal government spends money (Division and Classification), 143
Adopted children should be able to read (Cause and Effect), 151
Television ads for alcoholic beverages (Example, Comparison and Contrast, Cause and Effect), 153
Censoring the discussion of certain topics on the Internet (Definition, Cause and Effect), 158
Condom machines should be installed (Cause and Effect), 159
When my friend Cerene opened the newspaper (Narration, Cause and Effect), 177
No one is saying that news reporters (Definition), 179

Argument—Essays (developed using various modes)

The Beast Is the Beauty Contest (Example, Comparison and Contrast, Cause and Effect, Division and Classification), 221
Teaching as an Amusing Activity, Neil Postman (Definition, Comparison and Contrast, Cause and Effect), 475
Caesar, Therese C. MacKinnon (Narration, Description, Cause and Effect), 484
The Importance of Wearing a Safety Belt, Larissa R. Houk (Description, Comparison and Contrast, Cause and Effect), 499

PARAGRAPHS AND ESSAYS BY MODES IN EACH CHAPTER

Part One   STARTING OUT

1   Ensuring Success in Writing

Example
In the last few years, probably no technological
    advance, 6

Comparison and Contrast
In the last few years, probably no technological
    advance, 6

3   Composing: Creating a Draft

Example
Today, the children's division of our library, 33
My lack of self-confidence is keeping me, 51

Cause and Effect
Today, the children's division of our library, 33
My lack of self-confidence is keeping me, 51

4   Refining and Polishing Your Draft

Narration
Last summer, I had a great experience, 57
Before I came to the place where I would cross
    the Rio Grande, 63
I read the character and set description, 70
The most traumatic experience I can remember, 72

Description
The worst accident I ever saw, 65
I read the character and set description, 70
The most traumatic experience I can remember, 72

Example
Many of the things we use every day, 76

Cause and Effect
Computerized listings of holdings, 61
Cigarette smoking should be banned, 67
Many of the things we use every day, 76

Division and Classification
Cigarette smoking should be banned, 67

Argument (developed using various modes)
Cigarette smoking should be banned (Cause and
    Effect, Division and Classification), 67
Many of the things we use every day (Example,
    Cause and Effect), 76

Part Two   USING THE PATTERNS OF PARAGRAPH DEVELOPMENT

5   Narration

Narration
For Shirley Vroman, getting caught, 86
And I started to play, 87

One cold Christmas Eve, 88
Ernest first saw the plane from the window of the
    taxi, 89

Description
And I started to play, 87
One cold Christmas Eve, 88
Ernest first saw the plane from the window of the
    taxi, 89

Cause and Effect
For Shirley Vroman, getting caught, 86

6   Description

Narration
The most beautiful sunset I ever witnessed, 93
The boy put the blackberry in his mouth, 94
Last summer, I went into downtown Springfield,
    95

Description
The most beautiful sunset I ever witnessed, 93
The boy put the blackberry in his mouth, 94
Last summer, I went into downtown
    Springfield, 95
The most unusual restaurant in town, 96

7   Example

Description
When you have agoraphobia, 103

Example
Even the simplest gesture is subject to misunder-
    standing, 101
When you have agoraphobia, 103
How do expert physicists differ, 104

Comparison and Contrast
How do expert physicists differ, 104

Division and Classification
How do expert physicists differ, 104

8   Process

Process
Photosynthesis is the quiet but profound process,
    108
Inserting a contact lens, 109
If you follow these steps, water skiing will feel,
    111
An important part of regular bicycle maintenance,
    111

Cause and Effect
Photosynthesis is the quiet but profound process,
    108

9 Definition

Example
Among the most popular types of comedy is slapstick, 118
My friend Roscoe is wonderfully frank, 120

Definition
Thanks to the movie *Jurassic Park*, 117
Among the most popular types of comedy is slapstick, 118
My friend Roscoe is wonderfully frank, 120

Comparison and Contrast
Among the most popular types of comedy is slapstick, 118

10 Comparison and Contrast

Comparison and Contrast
The big difference between the old Soviet economy and our own, 125
In many ways, breast feeding is much better than bottle feeding, 126
Even though the rules for both games are the same, 128
Venus and the Earth are sister planets, 128

Cause and Effect
In many ways, breast feeding is much better than bottle feeding, 126

Division and Classification
In many ways, breast feeding is much better than bottle feeding, 126
Even though the rules for both games are the same, 128
Venus and the Earth are sister planets, 128

Argument
In many ways, breast feeding is much better than bottle feeding (Comparison and Contrast, Cause and Effect), 126

11 Cause and Effect

Cause and Effect
Although the debate over the causes of the Civil War, 134
When a hot object is placed in contact with a cold object, 135
As the number of farm laborers decreased, 137

12 Division and Classification

Example
In every job I've ever had, I have found that the workers, 146

Definition
Reinforcement is the process of using rewards, 145

Division and Classification
The work of a certified nurse's assistant, 142
The way the federal government spends money, 143
Reinforcement is the process of using rewards, 145
In every job I've ever had, I have found that the workers, 146

13 Argument (developed using various modes)

Example
Television ads for alcoholic beverages, 153

Definition
Censoring the discussion of certain topics on the Internet, 158

Comparison and Contrast
Television ads for alcoholic beverages, 153

Cause and Effect
Adopted children should be able to read, 151
Television ads for alcoholic beverages, 153
Censoring the discussion of certain topics on the Internet, 158
Condom machines should be installed, 159

Part Three MOVING ON TO THE ESSAY

14 Developing an Essay

Narration
Lost and Confused: My First Day in the Hospital Halls, 171
When my friend Cerene opened the newspaper, 177

Description
Lost and Confused: My First Day in the Hospital Halls, 171
There were fifteen of them, 186

Definition
No one is saying that news reporters, 179

Cause and Effect
Lost and Confused: My First Day in the Hospital Halls, 171
When my friend Cerene opened the newspaper, 177

Argument
When my friend Cerene opened the newspaper (Narration, Cause and Effect), 177
No one is saying that news reporters (Definition), 179

15 Examining Types of Essays

Narration
The Fourth of July, My Favorite Day, 198
Bright Lights, Loud Music: Not *Your Average Planetarium Show,* 200

Description
Bright Lights, Loud Music: Not *Your Average Planetarium Show,* 200

Example
No Second Chances, Please, 203
Truly Considerate People: A Rarity, 208
The Car Question: To Buy or to Lease? 211
More Than a Promotion, 215
Spine-Chilling Choices, 218
The Beast Is the Beauty Contest, 221

Process
The Science of Solving Problems, 205

Definition
The Science of Solving Problems, 205
Truly Considerate People: A Rarity, 208

Comparison and Contrast
Bright Lights, Loud Music: Not *Your Average Planetarium Show,* 200
Truly Considerate People: A Rarity, 208
The Car Question: To Buy or to Lease? 211
The Beast Is the Beauty Contest, 221

Cause and Effect
More Than a Promotion, 215
The Beast Is the Beauty Contest, 221

Division and Classification
No Second Chances, Please, 203
Truly Considerate People: A Rarity, 208
Spine-Chilling Choices, 218
The Beast Is the Beauty Contest, 221

Argument (developed using various modes)
The Beast Is the Beauty Contest (Example, Comparison and Contrast, Cause and Effect, Division and Classification), 221

Part Seven CONNECTING: RESPONDING TO READING

Narration
Fish Cheeks, Amy Tan, 477
Nightwatch, Paul Fletcher, 481
Caesar, Therese C. MacKinnon, 484
How Boys Become Men, Jon Katz, 487
Thanksgiving Is the Greatest Holiday, Robert C. Maynard, 493

Go and Conquer the World, Michaela Otway, 496
A Religion? Henry Bousquet, 504
A Bully Who Wore Bobby Pins, Amanda Beaulieu, 506
Fear Not, Greg Andree, 508

Description
Fish Cheeks, Amy Tan, 477
Nightwatch, Paul Fletcher, 481
Caesar, Therese C. MacKinnon, 484
How Boys Become Men, Jon Katz, 487
Go and Conquer the World, Michaela Otway, 496
Exposed Toes, Diane Riva, 501
A Bully Who Wore Bobby Pins, Amanda Beaulieu, 506

Example
Intimacy and Independence, Deborah Tannen, 479
Thanksgiving Is the Greatest Holiday, Robert C. Maynard, 493
Fear Not, Greg Andree, 508
To Smoke or Not to Smoke, Charlotte Medeiros, 510

Process
How Boys Become Men, Jon Katz, 487
"Growing Up" Is Cumulative, Evolutionary and Never-Ending, Brian Dickinson, 490
Thanksgiving Is the Greatest Holiday, Robert C. Maynard, 493
A Religion? Henry Bousquet, 504

Definition
Teaching as an Amusing Activity, Neil Postman, 475
Intimacy and Independence, Deborah Tannen, 479
"Growing Up" Is Cumulative, Evolutionary and Never-Ending, Brian Dickinson, 490

Comparison and Contrast
Teaching as an Amusing Activity, Neil Postman, 475
Fish Cheeks, Amy Tan, 477
Intimacy and Independence, Deborah Tannen, 479
The Importance of Wearing a Safety Belt, Larissa R. Houk, 499
To Smoke or Not to Smoke, Charlotte Medeiros, 510

Cause and Effect
Teaching as an Amusing Activity, Neil Postman, 475
Caesar, Therese C. MacKinnon, 484
How Boys Become Men, Jon Katz, 487
Go and Conquer the World, Michaela Otway, 496
The Importance of Wearing a Safety Belt, Larissa R. Houk, 499
Fear Not, Greg Andree, 508

Division and Classification

Exposed Toes, Diane Riva, 501

Fear Not, Greg Andree, 508

Argument (developed using various modes)

Teaching as an Amusing Activity, Neil Postman (Definition, Comparison and Contrast, Cause and Effect), 475

Caesar, Therese C. MacKinnon (Narration, Description, Cause and Effect), 484

The Importance of Wearing a Safety Belt, Larissa R. Houk (Description, Comparison and Contrast, Cause and Effect), 499

Index

A. See Articles (parts of speech)

Abbreviations
  in dictionaries, 541–542
  forming plurals of, 417–418

Academic subjects, capitalization
  of, 463, 470

Accept, except, 425

Acronyms
  capitalization of, 464, 470
  forming plurals of, 417–418

Action verbs, 237, 244

Active reading
  for answering essay questions,
    226–227
  illustrated, 474–475
  strategies for, 472–473

Active voice
  of adjectives, 528
  of verbs, 337–339, 347

Addition, transitional expressions
  showing, 60

Address (persons), direct, commas
  to set off names in, 444, 449

Addresses (locations)
  capitalization in, 463, 470
  commas in, 444, 445

Adjectives, 367–384
  active and passive, 528
  comparative form of, 369–371,
    383, 384
  confusing, 371–373, 384
  irregular, 370
  number of, 528
  order of, in sentences, 524

positive form of, 368, 383, 384
superlative form of, 369–371, 383,
  384

Adverbs, 367–384, 383
  comparative form of, 369–371,
    383, 384
  confusing, 371–373, 384
  conjunctive. *See* Conjunctive
    adverbs
  irregular, 370
  order of, in sentences, 525–526
  positive form of, 368, 383, 384
  superlative form of, 369–371, 383,
    384
  verbs functioning as, 247

Advice, advise, 425

Affect, effect, 425

Agreement
  ESL writers' tips for, 526–529
  pronoun–antecedent. *See*
    Pronoun–antecedent
    agreement
  subject–verb. *See* Subject–verb
    agreement

Alternating format
  for comparison and contrast
    essays, 211
  for comparison and contrast
    paragraphs, 128, 131

Among, between, 426

An. See Articles (parts of speech)

And
  compound subjects joined by,
    241, 301

compound verbs joined by, 238
phrases connected by,
    parallelism of, 406–408

Andree, Greg, 508–510

Anecdotes, 177–178, 195

Answering essay questions,
  225–233
  anticipation of questions for,
    228–229
  practice questions and, 229–232
  preparation for, 226–228, 233
  rehearsal for, 229–232

Antecedents, 385, 402
  agreement with pronouns. *See*
    Pronoun–antecedent
    agreement
  clarity of relationship between
    pronoun and, 393–396

Anticipation, of essay questions,
  228–229

Any, some, 535–536

Apostrophes, 454–458
  in contractions, 360, 456, 469,
    530–531
  forming plurals with, 418
  to show possession, 360, 455,
    469

Appositive fragments, 255–257,
  259

Argument, as writing purpose, 8–9

Argument *ad hominem*, 157

Argument Essay Checklist, 223

Argument essays, 220–223, 224

Argument Paragraph Checklist, 162

Argument paragraphs, 150–163
    documentation for, 154
    emphatic order for, 159–161
    logical reasoning for, 157–159
    supporting points for, 152–155
    tone for, 156
    topic sentences for, 151–152
    transitional expressions showing,
        160
    writing process for, 163
Articles (parts of speech)
    capitalization in titles, 463
    ESL writers' tips for, 532–533
Articles (publications)
    capitalization in titles, 463, 470
    quotation marks for titles of, 453
Asides, parentheses to enclose,
        460–461
Association names, capitalization
        of, 464, 470
Attacks, on person, 157
Attributions, commas to set off
        quotes from, 445, 452
Audience. *See* Readers

Backspace key, 516, 519
Bad, badly, 370
Bad, good, 370
Badly, well, 370
Balance. *See* Parallelism
Bandwagon approach, 157
Bases for comparison, 125–127,
        131
Be, been. See To be
Beaulieu, Amanda, 506–507
Begging the question, 157
Between, among, 426
Biblical chapters and verses,
        colons to separate, 459
Bibliographies, colons to separate
        city of publication from
        publishing company in, 459
Block format
    for comparison and contrast
        essays, 211
    for comparison and contrast
        paragraphs, 127, 128, 131
Body of essay, 167, 195
Body of paragraph, 34, 42–45. *See
        also* Supporting ideas
    of argument paragraphs, 152–155
    order in, 45–47

Books
    capitalization of titles of, 463,
        470
    quotation marks for chapters in,
        453
Bousquet, Henry, 504–505
Both/and, parallelism with,
        409–411, 414
Brainstorming, 17–19, 30
Brake, break, 426
Branching, 22–24, 31
Brand names, capitalization of, 464,
        470
Break, brake, 426
Breaks, between clauses, commas
        to indicate, 437–438, 449
"Bully Who Wore Bobby Pins, A"
        (Amanda Beaulieu),
        506–507
Business names. *See* Company
        names

"Caesar" (Therese C. MacKinnon),
        484–486
Can, could, 330–332, 335
Can, may, 426
Capitalization, 450, 462–466, 469,
        470
    in addresses, 463, 470
    of direct quotations, 452
    ESL writers' tips for, 538
Case, of pronouns, 455, 456. *See
        also* Possessive case
    personal, 356–359, 366
Cause and effect, transitional
        expressions showing, 60
Cause and Effect Essay Checklist,
        217
Cause and effect essays, 215–217,
        224
Cause and Effect Paragraph
        Checklist, 139
Cause and effect paragraphs,
        133–140
    direct versus related causes and
        effects and, 135–137
    oversimplification in, 137–139
    topic sentences for, 134–135
    transitional expressions
        indicating cause and effect
        for, 135
    writing process for, 140

-cede, -ceed, and *-sede* endings,
        spelling, 423
-ch noun ending, forming plurals
        with, 351, 416
Chapters
    biblical, colons to separate,
        459
    in books, quotation marks for
        titles of, 453
Checklists
    for argument essays, 223
    for argument paragraphs, 162
    for cause and effect essays, 217
    for cause and effect paragraphs,
        139
    for comparison and contrast
        essays, 214
    for comparison and contrast
        paragraphs, 131
    for definition essays, 210–211
    for definition paragraphs,
        122–123
    for descriptive essays, 202
    for descriptive paragraphs, 99
    for division and classification
        essays, 220
    for division and classification
        paragraphs, 149
    for essay answers, 233
    for example essays, 204–205
    for example paragraphs, 106
    for narrative essays, 200
    for narrative paragraphs, 91
    for process essays, 207–208
    for process paragraphs, 114
    for proofreading, 78, 189–190
    for reader assessment, 74, 188
    for reader evaluation, 49–51,
        55
Choose, chose, 426
Chronological order, 63–65, 82
    for narrative essays, 198
    for narrative paragraphs, 87–88
Circular reasoning, 158
Clarity
    in essay writing, 539
    of pronoun–antecedent
        relationship, 393–396
    in topic sentences, 39–42
Classification. *See* Division and
        classification essays; Division
        and classification
        paragraphs

Clauses
    agreement with verbs, 529
    commas to set off, 437–438,
        440–443, 449
    connected by conjunctions,
        commas to set off, 437–438,
        449
    independent. *See* Independent
        clauses
    interrupting sentence flow,
        commas to set off, 441–443,
        449, 525, 537
    introduced by relative pronouns
        agreement with antecedents,
            393–396
        pronoun–antecedent
            agreement with, 396–397
    main. *See* Main clauses
    nonrestrictive, commas to set off,
        440–441
    restrictive, 442
    subordinate. *See* Subordinate
        clauses
Close command, 516, 519
Club names, capitalization of, 464,
    470
Clustering, 19–22, 30
Coherence, 82
    in essays, 184–186
    reassessing for, 59–69
    sentence organization for, 63–69
    transitions for, 59–62
Coincidence, 135, 140
Collective nouns, 353–356, 366
    agreement with verbs, 302, 308,
        526
    cue words for, 354–356
    list of, 353
    pronoun–antecedent agreement
        and, 386–387
Colons, 458–459, 470
Combined nouns, forming plurals
    of, 351, 417
Commands
    computer. *See specific
        commands*
    mood of. *See* Imperative mood
Commas, 436–449
    in addresses, 444, 449
    between clauses connected by
        conjunctions, 437–438, 449
    with coordinating conjunctions,
        278, 289

in dates, 444, 449
with direct address, 444, 449
ESL writers' tips for, 537–538
incorrectly connecting sentences
    with. *See* Comma splices
to indicate pauses between
    clauses, 437–438, 449
to indicate thousands in
    numbers, 444, 449
with quotation marks, 443–444,
    445
to separate items in series,
    438–440, 449
to set off direct quotations,
    443–444, 445, 449
to set off elements that interrupt
    sentence flow, 441–443, 449,
    525, 537
to set off introductory materials,
    440–441, 449
to set off salutation of friendly
    letter, 444, 449
to set quotes off from
    attributions, 445, 452
Comma splices, 274–289
    coordinating conjunctions to
        correct, 277–279, 289
    identifying, 275–277, 289
    periods to correct, 285–287, 289
    semicolons to correct, 281–284,
        289
    subordinating conjunctions to
        correct, 279–281, 289
Commonly confused words,
    425–431
    accept, except, 425
    adjective and adverb pairs,
        371–373, 383, 384
    advice, advise, 425
    affect, effect, 425
    among, between, 426
    any, some, 535–536
    bad
        badly, 372
        good, 370
    badly, well, 370
    between, among, 426
    brake, break, 426
    can, may, 426
    can/could, 330–332, 335
    choose, chose, 426
    conscience, conscious, 426
    could/can, 330–332, 335

council, counsel, 426
desert, dessert, 426
effect, affect, 425
ESL writers' tips for, 533–534
except, accept, 425
few, little, 535
fewer, less, 427
for, since, 536
good
    bad, 370
    well, 372, 427, 536
hard, hardly, 535
have, of, 423
hear, here, 427
in, on, 536
its, it's, 427
knew, new, 427
know, no, now, 427
lay, lie, 427
lead, led, lead, 427
less, fewer, 427
lie, lay, 427
little, few, 535
loose, lose, 427
may, can, 426
new, knew, 427
no, now, know, 427
of, have, 423
of, off, 428
on, in, 536
passed, past, 428
personal, personnel, 428
precede, proceed, 428
principal, principle, 428
quiet, quite, 428
say, tell, 532
since, for, 536
some, any, 535–536
tell, say, 532
than, then, 428
their, there, they're, 428
then, than, 428
there, they're, their, 428
they're, their, there, 428
threw, through, 429
through, threw, 429
to, too, two, 429
too, very, 534–535
two, to, too, 429
verb forms, ESL writers' tips for,
    529–532
very, too, 534–535
weather, whether, 429

Commonly confused words, *(continued)*
well, badly, 370
well, good, 372, 427, 536
were, we're, where, 429
where, were, we're, 429
who, whom, 429
who's, whose, 429
will/would, 330–332, 335
would/will, 330–332, 335
your, you're, 429
Communication triangle, 3–8, 12
Company names
capitalization of, 464, 470
forming possessives of, 455
Comparative form, of adjectives and adverbs, 369–371, 383
Comparison
comparative form of modifiers and, 369–371, 383
superlative form of modifiers and, 369–371, 383
transitional expressions for, 61, 128–129
Comparison and Contrast Essay Checklist, 214
Comparison and contrast essays, 211–214, 223
Comparison and Contrast Paragraph Checklist, 131
Comparison and contrast paragraphs, 124–132
bases for comparison and, 125–127
organization for, 127–130
topic sentences for, 125
writing process for, 132
Complete drafts, 51–53, 55
Complete groupings, for division and classification paragraphs, 146–148, 149
Complete sentences, 236
Complete subjects, 239, 240–242, 245
Complex sentences, 262–264, 271
joining to one another, 265–266
joining to simple sentences, 265–266
simple sentences contrasted with, 262
structure of, 272

Complimentary closes
capitalization of, 464, 470
list of, 464
Composing, 14, 32–55. *See also* Drafts; Paragraph(s); Topic sentences
complete drafts and, 51–53
for essays, 176
focusing topics for, 36–39
process of, 55
reader-centered writing and, 47–51
Compound sentences, 265–267, 272
combining simple sentences to form. *See* Coordination
structure of, 273
Compound subjects, 241, 245
agreement with verbs, 301–305, 308
forming possessives of, 455
Compound verbs, 238, 244
Compound words, possessive, 455
Computers. *See* Word processing
Conciseness, for effective language, 70–74
Conclusions, of essays, 167, 178–179, 195, 540
Confusing words. *See also* Commonly confused words
ESL writers' tips for, 534–536
modifiers, 371–373, 384
Conjunctions, 271. *See also And; Or*
capitalization of, in titles, 463
coordinating. *See* Coordinating conjunctions
correlative, parallelism with, 409–411, 413
subordinating. *See* Subordinating conjunctions
Conjunctive adverbs, 265–267, 272
list of, 267
semicolons with, 281–284, 289, 460
Connotation, 120–122, 123, 208
Conscience, conscious, 426
Consistency in tense, 342–345, 347
Consistent presentation, for division and classification paragraphs, 145–146, 149

Consonants
a before words beginning with, 532
doubling when adding suffixes, 420
suffixes beginning with, 435
verbs ending in, forming past tense of, 312
Context, active reading and, 473
Contractions
apostrophes in, 360, 456, 469, 530–531
with *has,* 530–531
with *is,* 530–531
it's, 360, 427, 456, 458
list of, 456
Contrast. *See also* Comparison and contrast essays; Comparison and contrast paragraphs
transitional expressions showing, 61, 128–129
Coordinating conjunctions, 265–267, 272
commas with, 278, 437–438, 449
to correct comma splices and run-on sentences, 277–279, 289
joining words in series, 405
list of, 265
Coordination, 261, 267–269, 271
conjunctive adverbs for, 267–268
coordinating conjunctions for. *See* Coordinating conjunctions
errors in. *See* Comma splices; Run-on sentences
semicolons for, 267–269
Copy command, 517, 518, 519
Correlative conjunctions
commas to indicate pauses between clauses joined by, 437–438, 449
parallelism with, 409–411, 413
Could, can, 330–332, 335
Council, counsel, 426
Count words, agreement with verb, 526–527
Cue words, 302, 354–356
Cut command, 517, 518, 519

-d verb ending, 312, 315, 319
Dangling modifiers, 375–376, 383

Dashes, 461–462, 470
   omitting with indentation, 538
Dates
   commas in, 444, 449
   parentheses to enclose, 460
Deduction, 157, 162
Definition(s)
   in dictionaries, 542–543
   extended, 208
   working, 208
Definition Essay Checklist, 210–211
Definition essays, 208–211, 223
Definition Paragraph Checklist,
      122–123
Definition paragraphs, 116–123
   effective, pattern of, 118–120
   topic sentences for, 117–118
   types of meanings and, 120–122
   writing process for, 123
Delete key, 516, 519
Demonstrative pronouns, 402
   agreement with antecedents,
      390–391
   list of, 390
   plural, 390–391
   singular, 390–391
Denotation, 120–122, 123, 208
Descriptive Essay Checklist, 202
Descriptive essays, 200–202, 223
Descriptive Paragraph Checklist,
      99
Descriptive paragraphs, 92–99
   objective description and, 95–96,
      99
   sensory details for, 94–95
   spatial order for, 96–98
   subjective description and,
      95–96, 99
   topic sentences for, 93
   writing process for, 99
Desert, dessert, 426
Dialogue, 452, 469
Dickinson, Brian, 490–492
Dictionaries, 541–545
   entries in, 542–543
   personal, for spelling, 431–432
Digressions, 538–539
Direct address, commas in, 444,
      449
Direct causes and effects, 135–137,
      140
Direct questions, punctuating,
      451

Direct quotations, 469
   capitalization of, 452
   punctuating, 443–444, 449,
      452–454
Distinct groupings, for division and
      classification paragraphs,
      146–148, 149
Division and Classification Essay
      Checklist, 220
Division and classification essays,
      217–220, 224
Division and Classification
      Paragraph Checklist, 149
Division and classification
      paragraphs, 141–149
   consistent presentation for,
      145–146
   distinct and complete groupings
      for, 146–148
   logical method of analysis for,
      143–145
   topic sentences for, 142
   transitional expressions for, 143
   writing process for, 149
Do, make, 531–532
Documentation, 162
   for argument paragraphs, 154
Double negatives, 378–381, 383
   ESL writers' tips for, 534
Drafts, 14
   complete, 51–53, 55
   final, of essays, 190–194
   first, of essays, 180–182
   process of composing, 55
   second, 56, 76–77, 82, 189

-e, suffixes for words ending in, 420,
      435
-ed ending
   forming past tense of verbs with,
      312
   suffixes with words ending in,
      420, 435
-ed modifiers, 435
   order in sentences, 524–525
   passive voice of, 528
-ed verb ending, 312, 315, 319
Editing, 56, 82
   of essays, 189–190
   partners for, 78, 189–190
   personal proofreading list for,
      190

   personal proofreading system for,
      78, 190
   Proofreading Checklists for, 78,
      189–190
   using word processors, 517–518
Effect. See Cause and effect essays;
      Cause and effect paragraphs
Effect, affect, 425
Effective language, 69–74, 82
   conciseness for, 70–74
   in essays, 186–187
   specificity for, 70
ei or ie combinations, spelling,
      422–423
Either/or, parallelism with, 409–411,
      414
Either/or reasoning, 158, 159
Emphasis
   dashes for, 461–462, 470
   exclamation points for, 451
   transitional expressions for, 60
Emphatic order, 67–69, 82
   for argument paragraphs,
      159–161
End punctuation, 451–452, 536–537
Enter key, 516
Entertainment, as writing purpose,
      8
-er modifier ending, 369–371
-es noun ending, adding to form
      plurals, 351, 352, 416, 417
-es verb ending, 319
ESL writers' tips, 521–540
   for agreement, 526–529
   for articles, 532–533
   for capitalization, 538
   for confusing words, 534–536
   for double negatives, 534
   for essay writing, 539–540
   for paragraph writing, 538–539
   for prepositions, 536
   for punctuation, 536–538
   for sentences, 521–523
   for spelling, 533–534
   for verb forms, 529–532
   for word order, 524–526
Essay(s), 165–233. See also
      Answering essay questions
   argument, 220–223, 224
   cause and effect, 215–217, 224
   coherence in, 184–186
   comparison and contrast,
      211–214, 223

Essay(s), *(continued)*
definition, 208–211, 223
descriptive, 200–202, 223
division and classification, 217–220, 224
effective, examining, 171–173
ESL writers' tips for writing, 539–540
example, 202–205, 223
final draft of, 190–194
modes in. *See* Modes of essays
narrative, 197–200, 223
paragraphs as building blocks of, 33
paragraphs compared with, 166
process, 205–208, 223
purpose of, 197
structure of, 167–168
thesis of. *See* Thesis
unity in, 183
writing process for. *See* Essay writing process
Essay Answer Checklist, 233
Essay questions
answering. *See* Answering essay questions
practice, 233
Essay writing process, 173–190, 194–195
composing in, 176
conclusions in, 178–179
editing in, 189–190
feedback in, 189–190
for first draft, 180–182
introductions in, 177–178
organizing in, 176–177
prewriting in, 174–176
redrafting in, 189
relationship between topic sentences and thesis and, 180
revising in, 182–188
-*est* modifier ending, 369–371
Etymologies, in dictionaries, 542
Examinations, essay. *See* Answering essay questions
Example Essay Checklist, 204–205
Example essays, 202–205, 223
Example Paragraph Checklist, 106
Example paragraphs, 100–106
relevant examples for, 103–105
specific examples for, 103
topic sentences for, 101–102

transitional expressions for, 101
writing process for, 106
Examples
relevant, 103–105, 106
specific, 103, 106
Except, accept, 425
Exclamation points, 451–452, 469
Exit command, 516, 519
Expectations, of audience, essay writing and, 539
Explanations, parentheses to enclose, 460–461
"Exposed Toes" (Diane Riva), 501–503
Extended definitions, 208

-*f* noun ending, forming plurals with, 351, 417
Facts, 152, 162
Family relationships, capitalization of words designating, 462–463, 470
-*fe* noun ending, forming plurals with, 351, 417
"Fear Not" (Greg Andree), 508–510
Feedback
in essay writing process, 189–190
Reader Assessment Checklists for, 74, 188
for reassessment, 74–76
Feminine pronouns, agreement with antecedents, 397–400
Few, little, 535
Fewer, less, 427
Figures, forming plurals of, 417–418
Files, creating, 516
Final drafts, of essays, 190–194
First drafts
creating using word processors, 516–517
of essays, developing, 180–182
First person point of view, 198
"Fish Cheeks" (Amy Tan), 477–478
Flashbacks, 63, 87, 91
Fletcher, Paul, 481–483
Footnotes, colons to separate city of publication from publishing company in, 459
For, since, 536
Fragments. *See* Sentence fragments
Freewriting, 14–17, 30

Future perfect progressive tense, 340, 348
Future perfect tense, 315, 319
Future progressive tense, 340, 348
Future tense, 311–314, 315, 318, 319
of *to be*, 327

Gender, 397–400, 402
pronoun–antecedent agreement and, 397–400
sexist language, 398–399, 403
Generalization, hasty, 158
General terms, 70
Geographical regions, capitalization of, 463, 470
"Go and Conquer the World" (Michaela Otway), 496–498
Good
bad, 370
well, 370, 427, 536
Grammar
confusing functions of, ESL writers' tips for, 534–536
editing to eliminate errors in. *See* Editing
Groupings, for division and classification paragraphs, 146–148
" 'Growing Up' Is Cumulative, Evolutionary and Never-Ending" (Brian Dickinson), 490–492

Had, past perfect tense and, 315
Hard, hardly, 535
Has
contractions using, 530–531
present perfect tense and, 315
Hasty generalization, 158
Have, of, 423
Have, present perfect tense and, 315
Hear, here, 427
Help command, 515, 517, 519
Helping verbs, 237–238
with *been*, 327–328
forming perfect tenses with, 314–317
list of, 238
subject following, subject–verb agreement and, 294–295, 308

Homonyms, 425–429. *See also*
Commonly confused words
Houk, Larissa R., 499–500
Hours, colons to separate minutes
from, 459
"How Boys Become Men" (Jon
Katz), 487–489
How-to writing, 107. *See also*
Process paragraphs
Hyphenated words, forming plurals
of, 351, 417

I, capitalization of, 462, 470
Idea mapping, 24–26, 31
ie or *ei* combinations, spelling,
422–423
Illustration, examples for. *See*
Example paragraphs
Imperative mood, 114
for process essays, 205
for process paragraphs, 109–110
"Importance of Wearing a Safety
Belt, The" (Larissa R. Houk),
499–500
In, on, 536
Indefinite pronouns, 361–364, 366
affected by words following
them, 362, 366
agreement with antecedents,
388–390, 398
agreement with verbs, 298–300,
308
forming possessives of, 455
lists of, 298, 309, 361–362
plural, 298–300, 308, 309, 362,
366, 388–390
singular, 298–300, 308, 309,
361–362, 366, 388–390, 398
Indentation, of paragraphs, 33, 538
Independent clauses, 265–267, 272
joining with comma plus
coordinating conjunction,
278–279
joining with subordinating
conjunctions, 279–281
semicolons to join, 267–269,
281–284, 459–461, 538
Indirect quotations, 469
punctuating, 453
Induction, 157, 162
Inductive leaps, 157
Information, as writing purpose, 8

-ing modifiers, 373–378, 383
active voice of, 528
order in sentences, 524–525
progressive tenses and, 339, 340,
347
Instruction sets, 107. *See also*
Process paragraphs
Intensive pronouns, 402
agreement with antecedents,
391–392
list of, 391
Interrupters, commas to set off,
441–443, 449, 525, 537
"Intimacy and Independence"
(Deborah Tannen),
479–480
Introductions, of essays, 167,
177–178, 194
Introductory materials, commas to
set off, 440–441, 449
Irregular modifiers, 370
Irregular plurals, 352, 417
Irregular verbs, 320–330, 334–335,
530. *See also specific verbs*
identifying, 321–327
list of, 321–324
past participles of, 321–327, 334
past tense of, 321–327, 334
present tense of, 321–327, 334
Is. See To be
It, with *to be*, 523
Its, it's, 360, 427, 456, 458

Journals, 27–29, 31

Katz, Jon, 487–489
Knew, new, 427
Know, no, now, 427

Language. *See also* Word(s)
for argument paragraphs, 156
effective. *See* Effective language
sexist, 398–399, 403
Languages, capitalization of names
of, 463, 470
Latin endings, forming plurals of
nouns with, 417
Lay, lie, 427
Lead, led, lead, 427
Less, fewer, 427

Letters (of alphabet). *See also*
Consonants; Vowels
capitalization of. *See*
Capitalization
forming plurals of, 417–418
spelling and. *See* Spelling
Letters (correspondence),
salutations and
complimentary closes of.
See Complimentary closes;
Salutations
Lie, lay, 427
Linear order, for process writing,
111–113, 115
Lines of reasoning, 157–159
Linking verbs, 237, 244
list of, 237
Lists, colons to introduce, 458
Little, few, 535
Location, transitional expressions
showing, 97
Logical analysis, for division and
classification paragraphs,
143–145
Logical fallacies, 157–159, 163
Logical reasoning, for argument
paragraphs, 157–159
Look alike words. *See* Commonly
confused words
Loose, lose, 427
-ly ending, 420, 435

MacKinnon, Therese C., 484–486
Magazines
capitalization of titles of, 463, 470
quotation marks for titles of
articles in, 453
Main clauses, 262–263, 272
joining. *See* Coordination
joining subordinate clauses to,
252–255, 256, 259, 261
Main ideas
active reading and, 473
unity and, 538–539
Make, do, 531–532
Masculine pronouns, agreement
with antecedents, 397–400
May, can, 426
Maynard, Robert C., 493–495
Meanings. *See also* Definition(s);
Definition paragraphs
types of, 120–122

Means, in communication triangle, 3, 6, 12

Medeiros, Charlotte, 510–513

Messages, in communication triangle, 3, 6, 12

Minutes, colons to separate hours from, 459

Misplaced modifiers, 375–376, 383

Misspellings. *See* Spelling

Modes of essays, 196–197. *See also specific modes*
  active reading and, 473
  purpose related to, 197, 224
  uses of, 196

Modifiers, 239, 245, 367–384. *See also* Adjectives; Adverbs
  comparative form, 369–371, 383
  confusing pairs of, 371–373
  dangling, 375–376, 383
  -ing words as. *See -ing* modifiers
  irregular, 370
  misplaced, 375–376, 383
  order of, in sentences, 524–526
  positive form, 368, 383, 384
  superlative form, 369–371, 383, 384

More, with modifiers, 369–371

Most, with modifiers, 369–371

Names
  business. *See* Company names
  capitalization of, 462–464, 470
  in direct address, commas to set off, 444, 449

Narrative Essay Checklist, 200

Narrative essays, 197–200, 223

Narrative Paragraph Checklist, 91

Narrative paragraphs, 84–91
  chronological order for, 87–88
  point of view for, 88–90
  for processes, 107
  topic sentences for, 85–87
  transitional expressions for, 88
  writing process for, 91

Negatives, double. *See* Double negatives

Neither/nor, parallelism with, 409–411, 414

-ness ending, 420, 435

New, knew, 427

Newspapers
  capitalization of titles of, 463, 470
  quotation marks for titles of articles in, 453

"Nightwatch" (Paul Fletcher), 481–483

No, now, know, 427

Noncount words, agreement with verb, 526–527

Nonrestrictive elements, commas to set off, 440–441

Non sequiturs, 158

Note-taking
  for answering essay questions, 227–228
  reading and, 472

Not only/but also, parallelism with, 409–411, 414

Nouns, 239, 245, 350–366. *See also* Subject(s) (of sentences)
  appositive fragments, 255–257, 259
  collective. *See* Collective nouns
  count and noncount, agreement with verb, 526–527
  as objects, 240–241
  plural. *See* Plural nouns
  pronouns substituting for. *See* Pronoun(s)
  singular. *See* Singular nouns
  singular and plural cue words and, 354–356
  as subjects. *See* Subject(s) (of sentences)
  verbs functioning as, 247

Number
  of adjectives, 528
  pronoun–antecedent agreement in, 386–387

Numbers
  commas to indicate thousands in, 444, 449
  forming plurals of, 417–418

-o noun ending, forming plurals with, 352, 416

Object(s)
  nouns as, 240–241
  of prepositions, 240–241, 356, 357, 359
  pronouns as, 240, 356–357, 359
  of verbs, 356, 357, 359, 530

Objective case, of personal pronouns, 356, 357, 359, 366

Objective description, 95–96, 99, 200

Of, have, 423

Of, off, 428

On, in, 536

Open command, 518, 519

Opinions, 152, 162
  stance for argument paragraphs and, 152–155, 162

Or
  compound subjects joined by, 241, 301
  compound verbs joined by, 238
  joining masculine and feminine pronouns, 398
  phrases connected by, parallelism of, 406–408

Order. *See also* Organization
  in paragraphs, 45–47
  of supporting ideas, 45–47, 159–161
  of words in sentences, 524–526

Organization. *See also* Order
  active reading and, 473
  for argument paragraphs, 159–161
  for coherence, 63–69
  for comparison and contrast, 127–130
  for description, 96–98
  for descriptive essays, 200
  for essays, 176–177, 185–186, 198, 200
  linear order and, 111–113, 115
  for narration, 87–88
  for narrative essays, 198
  of paragraphs, 45–47
  for process writing, 111–113
  of sentences, 63–69

Otway, Michaela, 496–498

Oversimplification, 137–139, 140, 158

Paragraph(s), 54, 83–163. *See also* Paragraph writing process
  body of. *See* Body of paragraph; Supporting ideas
  as building blocks of essays, 33

comparison and contrast. *See* Comparison and contrast paragraphs
definition. *See* Definition paragraphs
descriptive. *See* Descriptive paragraphs
for dialogue, 452
drafts of. *See* Drafts; Redrafting
ESL writers' tips for writing, 538–539
essays compared with, 166
illustrative. *See* Example paragraphs
indentation of, 33, 538
narrative. *See* Narrative paragraphs
organization of, 45–47
structure of, 33–36
topic sentences of. *See* Topic sentences
Paragraph writing process. *See also* Composing; Prewriting; Revising
for argument paragraphs, 163
for cause and effect paragraphs, 140
for comparison and contrast paragraphs, 132
for definition paragraphs, 123
for descriptive paragraphs, 99
for division or classification paragraphs, 149
for example paragraphs, 106
for narrative paragraphs, 91
for process paragraphs, 115
Parallelism, 404–414
with correlative conjunctions, 409–411
with phrases, 406–408, 413
in series, 405–406
Parentheses, 460–462, 470
Partners, for editing, 78, 189–190
Passed, past, 428
Passive voice, 337–339, 346, 530
of adjectives, 528
Paste command, 517–518, 519
Past participles, 314–315, 319
forming perfect tenses with, 314–317
of irregular verbs, 321–327, 334
Past perfect progressive tense, 340, 348

Past perfect tense, 315, 319
Past progressive tense, 339, 348
Past tense, 311–314, 315, 319
of irregular verbs, 321–327, 334
Patterns, of effective definitions, 118–120, 123
Pauses between clauses, commas to indicate, 437–438, 449
Perfect progressive tenses, 340, 347, 348
Perfect tenses, 314–317, 319
Periodicals
capitalization of titles of, 463, 470
quotation marks for titles of articles in, 453
Periods, 451–452, 469
to correct comma splices and run-on sentences, 285–287, 289
at ends of sentences, 451
Personal, personnel, 428
Personal attacks, 157
Personal pronouns, 366
agreement with antecedents, gender and, 398–399
capitalization of, 462
case of, 356–359, 366
possessive, 455
proper use of, 359–361
Personal proofreading list, 190
Personal spelling dictionary, 431–432
Phonetic spellings, in dictionaries, 541, 542
Phrase(s)
interrupting sentence flow, commas to set off, 441–443, 449, 525, 537
introductory, commas to set off, 440–441, 449
nonrestrictive, commas to set off, 440–441
parallelism with, 406–408, 413
prepositional, 240–241, 245, 455
restrictive, 442
as sentence fragments, 250–252, 259
in series, commas to separate, 438–440, 449
subject–verb agreement and, 529
verb, 237–238, 244, 526
Phrase fragments, 250–252, 259

Place. *See also* Addresses (locations)
transitional expressions showing, 60
Placement. *See* Order; Organization
Plural cue words, 354–356
Plural nouns
agreement with pronouns, 386–387
agreement with verbs. *See* Subject–verb agreement
apostrophes for, 418, 455, 469
forming, 351–353, 418
forming possessives of, 455, 469
irregular, 417
nonword, 417–418
same as singular form, 417
spelling, 351–353, 416–419
words discussed as words, 417–418
Plural pronouns
as antecedents, 386–387
for avoiding sexist language, 398
demonstrative, 390–391
indefinite, 298–300, 308, 309, 362, 366, 388–390
Plural subjects
agreement with verbs. *See* Subject–verb agreement
compound, 301–305, 308
joined as compound subject, 301
Poems
capitalization of titles of, 463
quotation marks for titles of, 453
Point of view, 91
for narrative essays, 198
for narrative paragraphs, 88–90
Positive form, of adjectives and adverbs, 368, 383, 384
Possession, apostrophes to show, 360, 455, 469
Possessive case
of compound words, 456
of personal pronouns, 357, 360, 366, 455
Post hoc, ergo propter hoc, 158
Postman, Neil, 475–476
Practice essay questions, 229–232, 233
Precede, proceed, 428
Prefixes, 419, 435

Preparation, for answering essay questions, 226–228
Prepositional phrases, 240–241, 245, 455
Prepositions, 240–241
    capitalization of, in titles, 463
    ESL writers' tips for, 536
    list of, 240
    objects of, 356, 357, 359
Present participles, 339, 347
    as modifiers. *See -ing* modifiers
    progressive tenses and, 339, 340, 348
Present perfect progressive tense, 340, 348
Present perfect tense, 315, 319
Present progressive tense, 339, 348
Present tense, 311–314, 315, 318, 319
    of irregular verbs, 321–327, 334
Prewriting, 13–31
    brainstorming for, 17–19, 30
    branching for, 22–24, 31
    clustering for, 19–22, 30
    for essays, 174–176
    freewriting for, 14–17, 30
    idea mapping for, 24–26, 31
    journals for, 27–29, 31
Primary reinforcers, 145–146
Principal, principle, 428
Print command, 516, 519
Process analysis, 107
Processes, 107, 114
    incomplete, progressive verbs to refer to, 531
    narrative paragraphs for, 107
Process Essay Checklist, 207–208
Process essays, 205–208, 223
Process Paragraph Checklist, 114
Process paragraphs, 107–115
    dividing process into steps for, 110–111
    imperative mood for, 109–110
    linear order for, 111–113
    topic sentences for, 108–109
    types of, 107
    writing process for, 115
Product titles, capitalization of, 464, 470
Progressive tenses, 339–342, 347, 348, 531

Pronoun(s), 239, 245, 356–365, 366
    antecedents of, 385, 402. *See also* Pronoun–antecedent agreement
    appositive fragments, 255–257, 259
    case of, 356–359, 366, 455, 456
    clarity of relationship to antecedent, 393–396
    demonstrative. *See* Demonstrative pronouns
    indefinite. *See* Indefinite pronouns
    intensive. *See* Intensive pronouns
    as objects, 240, 356, 357, 359
    order of, in sentences, 526
    personal. *See* Personal pronouns
    reflexive (intensive). *See* Reflexive pronouns
    relative. *See* Relative pronouns
    renaming subject, unnecessary, 526
    as subjects. *See* Subject(s) (of sentences)
Pronoun–antecedent agreement, 385–403
    with clauses introduced by relative pronouns, 396–397
    with demonstrative pronouns, 390–391
    eliminating ambiguity and, 393–396
    in gender, 397–400
    with indefinite pronouns, 388–390
    with intensive pronouns, 391–392
    in number, 386–387
    with reflexive pronouns, 391–392
Pronunciation keys, in dictionaries, 542
Proofreading. *See* Editing
Proofreading Checklists
    for essays, 189–190
    for paragraphs, 78
Proper names. *See* Company names; Names
Punctuation, 450–470, 469–470. *See also specific punctuation marks*
    with clauses, 437–438, 441–443, 449
    commas to set off, 525, 537

    of contractions, 360, 456, 469, 530–531
    of direct questions, 451
    of direct quotations, 443–444, 449, 452–454
    editing to eliminate errors in. *See* Editing
    end, 451–452, 536–537
    ESL writers' tips for, 536–538
    of possessive forms, 455
    sentences joined without. *See* Run-on sentences
Purpose
    of essays, modes related to, 197, 224
    of writing, 8–11, 12

Question(s)
    direct, punctuating, 451
    essay. *See* Answering essay questions
    rhetorical, 178, 195
Question marks, 451–452, 469
Quiet, quite, 428
Quotation marks, 443–444, 452–454, 469
    commas with, 445
Quotations
    attributions for, commas to set off, 445, 452
    colons to introduce, 458
    direct. *See* Direct quotations
    indirect. *See* Indirect quotations

Reader(s)
    in communication triangle, 3, 6, 12
    expectations of, essay writing and, 539
    feedback from. *See* Feedback
Reader Assessment Checklists
    for essays, 188
    for paragraphs, 74
Reader-centered writing, 47–51, 55
Reader Evaluation Checklists, 49–51, 55
Reading
    active. *See* Active reading
    note-taking during, 472
Reasoning
    circular, 158

either/or, 158, 159
lines of, 157–159
logical, 157–159
Reassessing, 56, 57–76, 82
for coherence, 59–69
for effective language, 69–74
feedback for, 74–76
timing of, 57
for unity, 57–59
Red herrings, 158
Redrafting, 56, 76–77, 82, 189
Reflexive pronouns, 402
agreement with antecedents,
391–392
list of, 391
Regions of country, capitalization
of, 463, 470
Regular verbs. *See* Verb(s)
Rehearsal, for answering essay
questions, 229–232
Reinforcement, 145–146
Related causes and effects,
135–137, 140
Relative pronouns, 271, 402
agreement with antecedents,
396–397
functions of, 263
list of, 262
Relevant examples, 103–105, 106
"Religion, A?" (Henry Bousquet),
504–505
Repetition, for transition, 59
Restatement, transitional
expressions showing, 60
Restrictive elements, 442
Revising, 14, 56–82, 540. *See also*
Editing; Reassessing;
Redrafting
of essays, 182–188
process of, 82
using word processors, 516–517
Rhetorical questions, 178, 195
Riva, Diane, 501–503
Run-on sentences, 274–289
coordinating conjunctions to
correct, 277–279, 289
identifying, 275–277, 289
periods to correct, 285–287,
289
semicolons to correct, 281–284,
289
subordinating conjunctions to
correct, 279–281, 289

-'s ending. *See also* -s noun
ending
in contractions, 530–531
to form plurals, 418
pronoun, 456
-s noun ending
to form plurals, 351, 352, 416,
417, 469
to show possession, 455
subject–verb agreement and,
302–303, 308
-s verb ending, 302–303, 308, 319,
529
Salutations
capitalization of, 464, 470
in formal letters, colons with,
459
in friendly letters, commas to set
off, 444, 449
list of, 464
Save as command, 518, 519
Save command, 516, 519
Say, tell, 532
School subjects, capitalization of,
463, 470
Second drafts, 76–77, 82
-sede, -ceed, and -cede endings,
spelling, 423
Semicolons, 459–461, 470
with conjunctive adverbs,
281–284, 289
for coordination, 267–269
to correct comma splices and
run-on sentences, 281–284,
289
ESL writers' tips for, 538
to separate independent
clauses, 282–283, 289,
538
Sensory details, 94–95, 99
Sentence(s), 235–289
basic elements of, 244–245
capitalization of first word of,
462, 470
commas to set off elements
interrupting, 441–443, 449,
525, 537
complete, 236
complex. *See* Complex
sentences
complexity of, 261
compound. *See* Compound
sentences

errors in combining. *See* Comma
splices; Run-on sentences
ESL writers' tips for, 521–523
organization of, 63–69
punctuating. *See* Punctuation;
specific punctuation marks
reader-centered, changing writer-
centered sentences into,
47–51
run-on. *See* Run-on sentences
simple. *See* Simple sentences
subjects in. *See* Subject(s) (of
sentences)
supporting, 42–45
topic. *See* Topic sentences
verbs in, 237–239
word order in, 524–526
Sentence fragments, 246–260
appositive, 255–257, 259
correcting, 260
ESL writers' tips for, 522
identifying, 260
with missing subjects or verbs,
247–250
phrase, 250–252, 259
subordinate clause, 252–255,
259
Series
commas to set off items in,
438–440, 449
parallelism in, 405–406
verbs in, agreement with subject,
529
Sexist language, 398–399, 403
-sh ending, forming plurals of
nouns with, 351, 416
Short story titles, quotation marks
for titles of, 453
Simple future tense, 311–314
Simple past tense, 311–314
Simple sentences, 262, 271
complex sentences contrasted
with, 262
joining to form compound
sentences. *See* Coordination
Simple subjects, 239–240, 245
Simple tenses. *See also* Future
tense; Past tense; Present
tense
forming for regular verbs, 312,
319
Since, for, 536
Singular cue words, 354–356

Singular nouns
  agreement with pronouns. *See* Pronoun–antecedent agreement
  agreement with verbs. *See* Subject–verb agreement
  forming plurals of. *See* Plural nouns
  forming possessives of, 455, 469
  same as plural, 417
Singular pronouns
  as antecedents, 386
  demonstrative, 390–391
  indefinite, 298–300, 308, 309, 361–362, 366, 388–390, 398
Singular subjects
  agreement with verbs. *See* Subject–verb agreement
  cue words for, 354–356
  joined as compound subject, 301
Some, any, 535–536
Song titles
  capitalization of, 463
  quotation marks for, 453
Sound-alike words. *See* Commonly confused words
Spatial order, 65–67, 82
  for descriptive essays, 200
  for descriptive paragraphs, 96–98
Specific examples, 103, 106
Specificity
  for effective language, 70
  general terms versus, 70
  in topic sentences, 39–42
Spelling, 415–435
  checking with computers, 79, 190
  of commonly confused words, 425–431
  editing to eliminate errors in. *See* Editing
  ESL writers' tips for, 533–534
  with *ie* or *ei* combinations, 422–423
  importance of, 415
  list of most commonly misspelled words, 431–432
  personal dictionary for, 431–432
  phonetic, in dictionaries, 541, 542
  of plurals, 351–353, 416–419
  of prefixes, 419, 435

  with *-sede, -ceed, -cede,* and other sound-alike endings, 423–425
  of suffixes, 419, 420–422, 435
Stance, for argument paragraphs, 152–155, 162
Subject(s) (of sentences), 239–242, 245
  agreement with verbs. *See* Subject–verb agreement
  complete, 239, 240–242, 245
  compound. *See* Compound subjects
  ESL writers' tips for, 521–523
  following verbs or helping verbs, subject–verb agreement and, 293–295, 308
  indefinite pronouns as, subject–verb agreement and, 298–300, 308
  missing, fragments with, 248–250
  order of, in sentences, 524
  plural. *See* Plural subjects
  simple, 239–240, 245
  singular. *See* Singular subjects
  words coming between verbs and, subject–verb agreement and, 295–298, 308
Subject(s) (topics). *See* Thesis; Topics
Subjective case, of personal pronouns, 356, 359, 366
Subjective description, 95–96, 99, 200
Subject–verb agreement, 240, 292–309, 353–356
  with compound subjects, 241
  ESL writers' tips for, 526–529
  indefinite pronouns and, 361–364
  when subject follows verb or helping verb, 293–295, 308
  when subject is compound, 301–305, 308
  when subject is indefinite pronoun, 298–300, 308
  when words come between subject and verb, 295–298, 308
Subordinate clause fragments, 252–255, 259

Subordinate clauses, 261, 271
  joining to main clauses, 252–255, 256, 259, 261
  as sentence fragments, 252–255, 259
Subordinating conjunctions, 262, 271
  commas to indicate pauses between clauses joined by, 437–438, 449
  to correct comma splices and run-on sentences, 279–281, 289
  functions of, 263
  list of, 262
Subordination, 261, 262–264, 271. *See also* Subordinate clauses; Subordinating conjunctions
Substitutions, for transition, 59
Suffixes, 419, 420–422, 435
Superlative form, of adjectives and adverbs, 369–371, 383, 384
Supporting ideas. *See also* Body of paragraph
  order of, 45–47, 159–161
Supposed to, 423
Syllables, number of
  adding suffixes and, 420–422
  forming comparative and superlative forms of modifiers and, 369–371, 383
Synonyms, 82
  in dictionaries, 543
  as transitions, 59, 184

Tan, Amy, 477–478
Tannen, Deborah, 479–480
"Teaching as an Amusing Activity" (Neil Postman), 475–476
Tell, say, 532
Tenses. *See* Verb tenses
Tests, essay. *See* Answering essay questions
Than, then, 428
"Thanksgiving Is the Greatest Holiday" (Robert C. Maynard), 493–495
That, agreement with antecedents, 390–391, 396–397
The. See Articles (parts of speech)
Their, there, they're, 428

Then, than, 428
There
ESL writers' tips for, 522–523
with *to be*, 522–523
There, they're, their, 428
These, agreement with
antecedents, 390–391
Thesis, 167, 168–171, 195
developing, 175–176
topic sentences related to, 180
They're, their, there, 428
Third person point of view, 198
This, agreement with antecedents,
390–391
Those, agreement with
antecedents, 390–391
"Thoughts about Writing" (Charlotte
Medeiros), 512–513
Thousands, commas to indicate,
444, 449
Threw, through, 429
Through, threw, 429
Time. *See also* Verb tenses
chronological order and, 63–65,
82, 87–88, 198
colons to separate hours and
minutes and, 459
linear order and, 111–113, 155
for proofreading, 78
transitional expressions showing,
60
Time order, 63–65, 87–88
Titles (of books, periodicals, and
productions)
capitalization of, 463, 470
quotation marks for, 453
Titles (of people), capitalization of,
463, 470
To, too, two, 429
To be
adverb position with, 525–526
be used by itself as verb and,
327, 328
contractions using, 530–531
ESL writers' tips for, 522–523
forms of, 327–330, 335
helping verbs with *been* and,
327, 328
with *it*, 523
as linking verbs, 237
in passive verb forms, 530
progressive tenses and, 339, 340
with *there*, 522–523

Tone, 162
for argument paragraphs, 156
Too, very, 534–535
Topics. *See also* Thesis
in communication triangle, 3, 6,
12
focusing, 36–39
Topic sentences, 34, 55
for argument paragraphs,
151–152
for cause and effect paragraphs,
134–135
clear and specific, 39–42
for comparison and contrast, 125
for definition paragraphs,
117–118
for description, 93
for division and classification
paragraphs, 142
for example paragraphs,
101–102
focusing topics and, 36–39
for narration, 85–87
for process writing, 108–109
support for, 42–45
theses related to, 180
"To Smoke or Not to Smoke"
(Charlotte Medeiros),
510–512
Transition(s), 59–62
expressions used for. *See*
Transitional expressions
repetition for, 59
synonyms as, 59
Transitional expressions, 60–61,
82
to add, restate, or emphasize,
60
for argument, 160
to compare or contrast, 61,
128–129
in essays, 184
for examples, 101
indicating cause, 135
indicating effect, 135
for narratives, 88
for process writing, 112
to show cause and effect, 60
showing division or
classification, 143
showing location, 97
to show time or place, 60
Two, to, too, 429

Unity, 82
ESL writers' tips for, 538–539
in essays, 183
reassessing for, 57–59
Usage guides, in dictionaries,
541–542
Used to, 423

Verb(s), 237–239, 244. *See also*
specific verbs
action, 237, 244
adverb position with, 525–526
agreement with subjects. *See*
Subject–verb agreement
compound, 238, 244
ESL writers' tips for, 529–532
frequently confused, 330–332,
335
functioning as adjectives or
adverbs, 247
helping. *See* Helping verbs
irregular. *See* Irregular verbs;
specific verbs
linking, 237, 244
missing, fragments with, 247–248
objects of, 356, 357, 359, 530
in series, agreement with subject,
529
subject following, subject–verb
agreement and, 293–295,
308
tenses for. *See* Verb tenses
voice of, 337–339, 346–347, 530
words coming between subjects
and, subject–verb
agreement and, 295–298,
308
Verbals, 247–248, 259
commas to separate from rest of
sentence, 440–441
Verb phrases, 237–238, 244
adverb position with, 526
Verb tenses, 310–319
consistency in, 342–345, 347
in dictionaries, 543
future. *See* Future tense
past. *See* Past tense
perfect, 314–317, 319
perfect progressive, 340, 347, 348
present. *See* Present tense
progressive, 339–342, 347, 348,
531

Very, too, 534–535
-*ves* noun ending, adding to form plurals, 351, 417
Voice
  of adjectives, 528
  of verbs, 337–339, 346–347, 530
Vowels
  an before words beginning with, 532
  suffixes beginning with, 420, 435

Weather, whether, 429
Well, badly, 370
Well, good, 370, 427, 536
Were, we're, where, 429
Where, were, we're, 429
Whether, weather, 429
Whether/or, parallelism with, 409–411, 414
Which
  agreement with antecedents, 396–397
  pronoun–antecedent agreement with clauses introduced by, 396–397
Who
  agreement with antecedents, 396–397
  pronoun–antecedent agreement with clauses introduced by, 396–397
Who, whom, 429
Who's, whose, 429

Will
  forming future perfect tense with, 315
  forming future tense with, 319
Will, would, 330–332, 335
Word(s). *See also* Language; *specific words*
  commonly confused. *See* Commonly confused words
  count, 526–527
  cue, 302, 354–356
  definitions of, in dictionaries, 542–543
  discussed as words, forming plurals of, 417–418
  etymologies of, 542
  general, 70
  hyphenated, 351, 417
  interrupting sentence flow, commas to set off, 441–443, 449, 525, 537
  meanings of. *See* Definition(s)
  order of, ESL writers' tips for, 524–526
  parallelism with, 405–406, 413
  in series. *See* Series
  transitional. *See* Transitional expressions
Wordiness, eliminating, 70–74
Word processing, 515–519
  creating files for, 516
  effective use of, 518–519
  revising and editing using, 517–518

  spell checking and, 79, 190
  writing first draft using, 51, 516–517
Working definitions, 208
Would, will, 330–332, 335
Writer-centered writing, 47, 55
Writers, in communication triangle, 3, 6, 12
Writing dynamics, 3–5
Writing process
  communication triangle and, 3–8, 12
  computers for. *See* Word processing
  as discovery process, 2
  for essays. *See* Essay writing process
  for paragraphs. *See* Paragraph writing process
  purpose of, 8–11, 12
Writing skills, importance of, 2

-*x* noun ending, forming plurals with, 351, 416

-*y* ending
  forming past tense of verbs with, 312
  forming plurals of nouns with, 351, 416
  suffixes and, 420, 435
Your, you're, 429

Credits

NOTES

1 Singular and _plural_ nouns that don't end on "S" by adding ꞌs.

2 Plural nouns that end on "S" just add apostrophy.

There are many legal drugs in medicine to treat sick people; meanwhile, people, using the illegal drugs, spend millions $ every day.